Making Things Talk

First Edition

Tom Igoe

BEIJING · CAMBRIDGE · FARNHAM · KÖLN · PARIS · SEBASTOPOL · TAIPEI · TOKYO

Making Things Talk

by Tom Igoe

Published by Make:Books, an imprint of Maker Media, a division of O'Reilly Media, Inc.
1005 Gravenstein Highway North, Sebastopol, CA 95472.

O'Reilly books may be purchased for educational, business, or sales promotional use.
For more information, contact our corporate/institutional sales department:
800-998-9938 or *corporate@oreilly.com*.

Print History	**Publisher:** Dale Dougherty
September 2007	**Associate Publisher and Executive Editor:** Dan Woods
First Edition	**Editor:** Brian Jepson
	Copy Editor: Nancy Kotary
	Creative Director: Daniel Carter
	Designer: Katie Wilson
	Production Manager: Terry Bronson
	Indexer: Patti Schiendelman
	Cover Photograph: Tom Igoe

ISBN-10: 0-596-51051-9
ISBN-13: 978-0-596-51051-0

Contents

Preface

A few years ago, Neil Gershenfeld wrote a smart book called *When Things Start to Think*. In it, he discussed a world in which everyday objects and devices are endowed with computational power: in other words, today. He talked about the implications of devices that exchange information about our identities, abilities, and actions. It's a good read, but I think he got the title wrong. I would have called it *When Things Start to Gossip*. Because let's face it, even the most exciting thoughts are worthwhile only once you start to talk to someone else about them. This is a book about learning to make things that have computational power talk to each other, and about giving people the ability to use those things to communicate with each other.

For a couple of decades now, computer scientists have used the term object-oriented programming to refer to a style of software development in which programs and subprograms are thought of as objects. Like physical objects, they have properties and behaviors. They inherit these properties from the prototypes from which they descend. The canonical form of any object in software is the code that describes its type. Software objects make it easy to recombine objects in novel ways. You can reuse a software object, if you know its interface, the collection of properties and methods that its creator allows you access to (and documents, so that you know how to use them). It doesn't matter how a software object does what it does, as long as it does it consistently. Software objects are most effective when they're easy to understand and when they work well with other objects.

In the physical world, we're surrounded by all kinds of electronic objects: clock radios, toasters, mobile phones, music players, children's toys, and more. It can take a lot of work and a significant amount of knowledge to make a useful electronic gadget. It can take almost as much knowledge to make those gadgets talk to each other in useful ways. But that doesn't have to be the case. Electronic devices can be — and often are — built up from modules with simple, easy-to-understand interfaces. As long as you understand the interfaces, you can make anything from them. Think of it as object-oriented hardware. Understanding the ways in which things talk to each other is central to making this work. It doesn't matter whether the object is a toaster, an email program on your laptop, or a networked database. All of these objects can be connected if you can figure out how they communicate. This book is a guide to some of the tools for making those connections.

X

❝ Who This Book Is For

This book is written for people who want to make things talk to other things. Maybe you're a science teacher who wants to show your students how to monitor weather conditions at several locations around your school district simultaneously, or a sculptor who wants to make a whole room of choreographed mechanical sculptures. You might be an industrial designer who needs to be able to build quick mockups of new products, modeling both their forms and their functions. Maybe you're a cat owner, and you'd like to be able to play with your cat while you're away from home. It's a primer for people with little technical training and a lot of interest. It's for people who want to get projects done.

The main tools in this book are personal computers, web servers, and microcontrollers, the tiny computers inside everyday appliances. Over the past decade, microcontrollers and the programming tools for them have gone from being arcane items to common, easy-to-use tools. Elementary school students are using the tools that graduate students were baffled by only a decade ago. During that time, my colleagues and I have taught people from diverse backgrounds (few of them computer programmers) how to use these tools to increase the range of physical actions that computers can sense, interpret, and respond to.

In recent years, there's been a rising interest among people using microcontrollers to make their devices not only sense and control the physical world, but also talk to other things about what they're sensing and controlling. If you've built something with a Basic Stamp or a Lego Mindstorms kit, and wanted to make that thing communicate with other things you or others have built, this book is for you. It is also useful for software programmers familiar with networking and web services who want an introduction to embedded network programming.

If you're the type of person who likes to get down to the very core of a technology, you may not find what you're looking for in this book. There aren't detailed code samples for Bluetooth or TCP/IP stacks, nor are there circuit diagrams for Ethernet controller chips. The components used here strike a balance between simplicity, flexibility, and cost. They use object-oriented hardware, requiring relatively little wiring or code. They're designed to get you to the end goal of making things talk to each other as fast as possible.

X

❝ What You Need to Know

In order to get the most from this book, you should have a basic knowledge of electronics and programming microcontrollers, some familiarity with the Internet, and access to both.

Many people whose experience of programming begins with microcontrollers can do wonderful things with some sensors and a couple of servomotors, but may not have done much in the way of communication between the microcontroller and other programs on a personal computer. Similarly, many experienced network and multimedia programmers have never experimented with hardware of any sort, including microcontrollers. If you're either of these people, this book is for you. Because the audience of this book is diverse, you may find some of the introductory material a bit simple, depending on which background you're coming from. If so, feel free to skip past the stuff you know and get to the meaty parts.

If you've never used a microcontroller, you'll need a little background before starting with this book. My previous book, *Physical Computing: Sensing and Controlling the Physical World with Computers*, co-authored with Dan O'Sullivan, introduces the fundamentals of electronics, microcontrollers, and physical interaction design for beginning readers.

You should also have a basic understanding of computer programming before reading much further. If you've never done any programming, check out the Processing programming environment at www.processing.org. Processing is a simple language designed for nonprogrammers to learn how to program, yet it's powerful enough to do a number of advanced tasks. It will be used throughout this book whenever graphic interface programming is needed.

There are code examples in a few different programming languages in this book. They're all fairly simple examples, however, so if you don't want to work in the languages provided, you can rewrite them in your favorite language using the comments in these examples.

X

❝ Contents of This Book

This book is composed of explanations of the concept that underlie networked objects, followed by recipes to illustrate each set of concepts. Each chapter contains instructions on how to build working projects that make use of the new ideas introduced in that chapter.

In Chapter 1, you'll encounter the major programming tools in the book, and get to "Hello World!" on each of them.

Chapter 2 introduces the most basic concepts needed to make things talk to each other. It covers the characteristics that need to be agreed upon in advance, and how keeping those things separate in your mind helps troubleshooting. You'll build a simple project that features one-to-one serial communication between a microcontroller and a personal computer using Bluetooth radios as an example of modem communication. You'll learn about data protocols, modem devices, and address schemes.

Chapter 3 introduces a more complex network: the Internet. It covers the basic devices that hold it together, and the basic relationships between devices. You'll see the messages that underlie some of the most common tasks you do on the Internet every day, and learn how to send those messages. You'll write your first set of programs to allow you to send data across the Net based on a physical activity in your home.

In Chapter 4, you'll build your first embedded device. You'll get more experience with command-line connections to the Net, and you'll connect a microcontroller to a web server without using a desktop or laptop computer as an intermediary.

Chapter 5 takes the Net connection a step further by explaining socket connections, which allow for longer interaction. In this chapter, you'll learn how to write a server program of your own that you can connect to from an embedded device, a personal computer, or anything else connected to the Net. You'll connect to this server program from the command line and from a microcontroller, in order to understand how devices of different types can connect to each other through the same server.

Chapter 6 introduces wireless communication. You'll learn some of the characteristics of wireless, along with its possibilities and limitations. Several short examples in this chapter enable you to say "Hello World!" over the air in a number of ways.

Chapter 7 offers a contrast to the socket connections of Chapter 5, introducing message-based protocols like UDP on the Internet and ZigBee and 802.15.4 for wireless networks. Instead of using the client-server model used in the earlier chapters, here you'll learn how to design conversations where each object in a network is equal to the others, exchanging information one message at a time.

Chapter 8 is about location. It introduces a few tools to help you locate things in physical space, and some thoughts on the relationship between physical location and network relationships.

Chapter 9 deals with identification in physical space and network space. In that chapter, you'll learn a few techniques for generating unique network identities based on physical characteristics. You'll also learn a bit about how a networked device's characteristics can be determined.

In the appendices, you'll find a few extra pieces that weren't appropriate to the main chapters, but that are very useful nonetheless. You'll also find a list of hardware and software resources for networked projects. In the final appendix, you'll find code listings for all of the programs in the book.
X

❝ On Buying Parts

You'll need a lot of parts for all of the projects in this book. As a result, you'll learn about a lot of vendors. Because there are no large electronics parts retailers in my city, I buy parts online all the time. If you're lucky enough to live in an area where you can buy from a brick-and-mortar store, good for you! If not, get to know some of these vendors.

Some of them, like Jameco (www.jameco.com), Digi-Key (www.digikey.com), and Newark (www.newarkinone.com; their sister company in Europe is Farnell, www.farnell.com), are general electronics parts retailers, and sell many of the same things as each other. A full list of suppliers is listed in Appendix B. If a part is commonly found at many retailers, it is noted. Other parts are specialty parts, available from only one or two vendors. I've noted that too. Feel free to use substitute parts for things you are familiar with.

Because it's easy to order goods online, you might be tempted to communicate with vendors entirely through their websites. Don't be afraid to pick up the phone as well. Particularly when you're new to this type of project, it helps to talk tosomeone about what you're ordering, and to ask questions. You're likely to find helpful people at the end of the phone line for most of the retailers listed here. In Appendix B, I've listed phone numbers wherever possible. Use them.
X

" Using Code Examples

This book is here to help you get your job done. In general, you may use the code in this book in your programs and documentation. You do not need to contact us for permission unless you're reproducing a significant portion of the code.

For example, writing a program that uses several chunks of code from this book does not require permission. Selling or distributing a CD-ROM of examples from O'Reilly books does require permission. Answering a question by citing this book and quoting example code does not require permission. Incorporating a significant amount of example code from this book into your product's documentation does require permission.

We appreciate attribution. An attribution usually includes the title, author, publisher, and ISBN. For example: "*Making Things Talk: Practical Methods for Connecting Physical Objects*, by Tom Igoe. Copyright 2007 O'Reilly Media, 978-0-596-51051-0.*" If you feel that your use of code examples falls outside fair use or the permission given above, feel free to contact us at permissions@oreilly.com.

X

" Using Circuit Examples

In building the projects in this book, you're going to break things and void warranties. If you're averse to this, put this book down and walk away. This is not a book for those who are squeamish about taking things apart without knowing whether they'll go back together again.

Even though we want you to be adventurous, we also want you to be safe. Please don't take any unnecessary risks in building the projects that follow. Every set of instructions is written with safety in mind. Ignore the safety instructions at your own peril. Be sure you have the appropriate level of knowledge and experience to get the job done in a safe manner.

Please keep in mind that the projects and circuits shown in this book are for instructional purposes only. Details like power conditioning, automatic resets, RF shielding, and other things that make an electronic product certifiably ready for market are not included here. If you're designing real products to be used by people other than yourself, please do not rely on this information alone.

⚠ Technology, and the laws and limitations imposed by manufacturers and content owners, are constantly changing. Thus, some of the projects described may not work, may be inconsistent with current laws or user agreements, or may damage or adversely affect some equipment.

Your safety is your own responsibility, including proper use of equipment and safety gear, and determining whether you have adequate skill and experience. Power tools, electricity, and other resources used for these projects are dangerous, unless used properly and with adequate precautions, including safety gear. Some illustrative photos do not depict safety precautions or equipment, in order to show the project steps more clearly. These projects are not intended for use by children.

Use of the instructions and suggestions in this book is at your own risk. O'Reilly Media, Inc., disclaims all responsibility for any resulting damage, injury, or expense. It is your responsibility to make sure that your activities comply with applicable laws, including copyright.

❝ Acknowledgments

This book is the product of many conversations and collaborations. It would not have been possible without the support and encouragement of my own network.

The Interactive Telecommunications Program in the Tisch School of the Arts at New York University has been my home for the past decade or more. It is a lively and warm place to work, crowded with many talented people. This book grew out of a class called Networked Objects that I have taught there for several years. I hope that the ideas herein represent the spirit of the place, and give you a sense of my own enjoyment working there.

Red Burns, the department's chair and founder, has supported me since I first entered this field. She's indulged my many flights of fancy, and brought me firmly down to earth when needed. She has challenged me on every project to make sure that I use technology not for its own sake, but always in the service of empowering people.

Dan O'Sullivan introduced me to physical computing and then generously allowed me to share in teaching it and shaping its role at ITP. He's been a great advisor and collaborator, and offered constant feedback as I worked. Most of the chapters started with a rambling conversation with Dan. His fingerprints are all over this book, and it's a better book for it.

Clay Shirky, Daniel Rozin, and Dan Shiffman have also been close advisors on this project. Clay's watched indulgently as the pile of parts mounted in our office and interrupted his own writing to offer opinions on my ideas as they came up. Daniel Rozin has and offered valuable critical insight as well, and his ideas are heavily influential in this book. Dan Shiffman read many drafts and offered great feedback. He also contributed many great code samples and libraries.

Fellow faculty members Marianne Petit, Nancy Hechinger, and Jean-Marc Gauthier have been supportive throughout the writing, offering encouragement and inspiration, covering departmental duties for me, and offering inspiration through their work.

The rest of the faculty and staff at ITP have also made this possible. George Agudow, Edward Gordon, Midori Yasuda, Megan Demarest, Nancy Lewis, Robert Ryan, John Duane, Marlon Evans, Tony Tseng, and Gloria Sed have tolerated all kinds of insanity in the name of physical computing and networked objects, and made things possible for me and the other faculty and students. Research residents Carlyn Maw, Todd Holoubek, John Schimmel, Doria Fan, David Nolen, Peter Kerlin, and Michael Olson have assisted both faculty and students over the past few years to realize projects that have influenced the ones you see in these chapters, both in their own classes and in general. Faculty members Patrick Dwyer, Michael Schneider, Greg Shakar, Scott Fitzgerald, Jamie Allen, Shawn Van Every, James Tu, and Raffi Krikorian have used the tools from this book in their classes, or have lent techniques of their own to the projects described here.

The students of ITP have pushed the boundaries of possibility in this area, and their work is reflected in many of the projects. I have cited specifics where they come up, but in general I'd like to thank all the students who've taken the Networked Objects class over the years, as they've helped me to understand what this is all about. Those from the 2006 and 2007 classes have been particularly influential, as they've had to learn the stuff from early drafts of this book, and have caught several important mistakes in the manuscript.

A few people have contributed significant amounts of code, ideas, or labor to this book. Geoff Smith gave me the original title for the course, Networked Objects, and introduced me to the idea of object-oriented hardware. John Schimmel showed me how to get a microcontroller to make HTTP calls. Dan O'Sullivan's server code was the root of all of my server code. All of my Processing code is more readable because of Dan Shiffman's coding style advice. Robert Faludi contributed many pieces of code, made the XBee examples in this book simpler to read, and corrected errors in many of them. Max Whitney helped me get Bluetooth exchanges working, and to get the cat bed finished (despite her allergies!). Dennis Crowley made the possibilities and limitations of 2D barcodes clear to me. Chris Heathcote heavily influenced my ideas on location. Durrell Bishop helped me to think about identity. Mike Kuniavsky and the folks at the Sketching in Hardware workshops in 2006 and 2007 helped me to see this work as part of a larger community, and introduced me to a lot of new tools. Noodles the cat put up with all manner of silliness in order to finish the cat bed and its photos. No animals were harmed in the making of this book, though one was bribed with catnip.

Casey Reas and Ben Fry have made the software side of this book possible by creating Processing. Without Processing, the software side of networked objects was much more painful. Without Processing, there would be no simple, elegant programming interface for Arduino and Wiring. The originators of Arduino and Wiring have made the hardware side of this book possible. Massimo Banzi, Gianluca Martino, David Cuartielles, and David Mellis on Arduino, Hernando Barragán on Wiring, and Nicholas Zambetti bridging the two. I have been lucky to work with them.

Though I've tried to use and cite many hardware vendors in this book, special mention must be made of Nathan Seidle at SparkFun. This book would not be what it is without him. While I've been talking about object-oriented hardware for years, Nathan and the folks at SparkFun have been quietly making it a reality.

Thanks also to the support team at Lantronix. Their products are good and their support is excellent. Garry Morris, Gary Marrs, and Jenny Eisenhauer have answered countless emails and phone calls from me helpfully and cheerfully.

I have drawn ideas from many colleagues from around the world in these projects through conversations in workshops and visits. Thanks to the faculty and students I've worked with at the Royal College of Art's Interaction Design program, UCLA's Digital Media | Arts program, the Interaction Design program at the Oslo School of Architecture and Design, Interaction Design Institute Ivrea, and the Copenhagen Institute of Interaction Design.

Many networked object projects have inspired this writing. Thanks to those whose work illustrates the chapters: Tuan Anh T. Nguyen, Joo Youn Paek, Doria Fan, Mauricio Melo, and Jason Kaufman, Tarikh Korula and Josh Rooke-Ley of Uncommon Projects, Jin-Yo Mok, Alex Beim, Andrew Schneider, Gilad Lotan and Angela Pablo, Mouna Andraos and Sonali Sridhar, Frank Lantz and Kevin Slavin of Area/Code, and Sarah Johansson.

Working for MAKE has been a great experience. Dale Dougherty has been encouraging of all of my ideas, patient with my delays, and indulgent when I wanted to try new things. He's never said no without offering an acceptable

alternative (and often a better one). Brian Jepson has gone above and beyond the call of duty as an editor, building all of the projects, suggesting modifications, debugging code, helping with photography and illustrations, and being endlessly encouraging. It's an understatement to say that I couldn't have done this without him. I could not have asked for a better editor. Thanks to Nancy Kotary for her excellent copyedit of the manuscript. Katie Wilson made this book far better looking and readable that I could have hoped for. Thanks also to Tim Lillis for the illustrations. Thanks to all of the MAKE team.

Thanks to my agents: Laura Lewin, who got the ball rolling; Neil Salkind, who picked it up from her; and the whole support team at Studio B. Thanks finally to my family and friends who listened to me rant enthusiastically or complain bitterly as this book progressed. Much love to you all.

We'd Like to Hear from You

Please address comments and questions concerning this book to the publisher:

O'Reilly Media, Inc.
1005 Gravenstein Highway North
Sebastopol, CA 95472
(800) 998-9938 (in the United States or Canada)
(707) 829-0515 (international or local)
(707) 829-0104 (fax)

We have a website for this book, where we list errata, examples, and any additional information. You can access this page at: www.makezine.com/go/MakingThingsTalk

To comment or ask technical questions about this book, send email to: bookquestions@oreilly.com

Maker Media is a division of O'Reilly Media devoted entirely to the growing community of resourceful people who believe that if you can imagine it, you can make it. Consisting of *MAKE Magazine*, *CRAFT Magazine*, Maker Faire, and the Hacks series of books, Maker Media encourages the Do-It-Yourself mentality by providing creative inspiration and instruction.

For more information about Maker Media, visit us online:
MAKE: www.makezine.com
CRAFT: www.craftzine.com
Maker Faire: www.makerfaire.com
Hacks: www.hackszine.com

1

The Tools

This book is a cookbook of sorts, and this chapter covers the staple ingredients. The concepts and tools you'll use in every chapter are introduced here. There's enough information on each tool to get you to the point where you can make the tool say **"Hello World!"** Chances are you've used some of the tools in this chapter before, or other tools just like them. Skip past the things you know and jump into learning the tools that are new to you. You may want to explore some of the less-familiar tools on your own to get a sense of what they can do. The projects in the following chapters only scratch the surface of what's possible for most of these tools. References for further investigation are provided.

◄◄ **Happy Feedback Machine by Tuan Anh T. Nguyen**
The main pleasure of interacting with this piece comes from the feel of flipping the switches and turning the knobs. The lights and sounds produced as a result are secondary, and most people who play with it remember the feel of it rather than its behavior.

❝ It Starts with the Stuff You Touch

All of the objects that you'll encounter in this book, tangible or intangible, will have certain behaviors. Software objects will send and receive messages, store data, or both. Physical objects will move, light up, or make noise. The first question to ask about any of them is: what does it do? The second is: how do I make it do what it's supposed to do? Or, more simply, what is its interface?

An object's interface is made up of three elements. First, there's the physical interface. This is the stuff you touch. The knobs, switches, keys, and other sensors that make up the physical interface react to your actions. The connectors that join objects are also part of the physical interface. Many of the projects in this book will show you how to build physical interfaces. Every network of objects begins and ends with a physical interface. Even though some objects in a network (software objects) have no physical interface, people build their mental models of how a system works based on the physical interface. A computer is much more than the keyboard, mouse, and screen, but that's what we think of it as, because that's what we see and touch. You can build all kinds of wonderful functions into your system, but if those functions aren't apparent in the things people get to see, hear, and touch, your wonderful functions will never get used. Remember the lesson of the VCR clock that constantly blinks 12:00 because no one can be bothered to learn how to set it: if the physical interface isn't good, the rest of the system suffers.

Second, there's the software interface, the commands that you send to the object to make it respond. In some projects, you'll invent your own software interface, and in others, you'll rely on existing interfaces to do the work for you. The best software interfaces have simple, consistent functions that result in predictable outputs. Unfortunately, not all software interfaces are as simple as you'd like them to be, so be prepared to have to experiment a little to get some software objects to do what you think they should do. When you're learning a new software interface, it helps to approach it mentally in the same way you do with a physical interface. Don't try to use all the functions at once. Learn what each function does on its own before you try to use them all together. You don't learn to play the piano by starting with a Bach fugue — you start one note at a time. Likewise, you don't learn a software interface by writing a full application with it — you learn it one function at a time. There are many projects in this book; if you find any of their software functions confusing, write a simple program that demonstrates just that function, then return to the project.

Finally, there's the electrical interface, the pulses of electrical energy sent from one device to another to be interpreted as information. Unless you're designing new objects or the connections between them, you never have to deal with this interface. When you're designing new objects or the networks that connect them, however, you have to know and understand a few things about the electrical interface, so that you know how to match up objects that might have slight differences in their electrical interfaces.
X

❝ It's About Pulses

In order to communicate with each other, objects use communications protocols. A protocol is a series of mutually agreed-upon standards for communication between two or more objects.

Serial protocols like RS-232, USB, and IEEE 1394 (also known as FireWire and i.Link) connect computers to printers, hard drives, keyboards, mice, and other peripheral devices. Network protocols like Ethernet and TCP/IP connect multiple computers to each other through network hubs, routers, and switches. A communications protocol usually defines the rate at which messages are exchanged, the arrangement of data in the messages, and the grammar of the exchange. If it's a protocol for physical objects, it will also specify the electrical characteristics, and sometimes even the physical shape of the connectors. Protocols don't specify what happens between objects, however. The commands to make an object do something rely on protocols in the same way that clear instructions rely on good grammar. You can't give good instructions if you can't form a good sentence.

One thing that all communications protocols share, from the simplest chip-to-chip message to the most complex network architecture, is this: it's all about pulses of energy. Digital devices exchange information by sending timed pulses of energy across a shared connection. The USB connection from your mouse to your computer uses two wires for transmission and reception, sending timed pulses of electrical energy across those wires. Likewise, wired network connections are made up of timed pulses of electrical energy sent down the wires. For longer distances and higher bandwidth, the electrical wires may be replaced with fiber optic cables carrying timed pulses of light. In cases where a physical connection is inconvenient or impossible, the transmission can be sent using pulses of radio energy between radio transceivers (a transceiver is two-way radio, capable of transmitting and receiving). The meaning of data pulses is independent of the medium that's carrying them. You can use the same sequence of pulses whether you're sending them across wires, fiber optic cables, or radios. If you keep in mind that all of the communication you're dealing with starts with a series of pulses, and that somewhere there's a guide explaining the sequence of those pulses, you can work with any communication system you come across.

X

❝ Computers of all Shapes and Sizes

You'll encounter at least four different types of computers in this book, grouped according to their physical interfaces. The most familiar of these is the personal computer. Whether it's a desktop or a laptop machine, it's got a keyboard, a screen, and a mouse, and you probably use it just about every working day. These three elements: the keyboard, the screen, and the mouse — make up its physical interface.

The second type of computer you'll encounter in this book, the microcontroller, has no physical interface that humans can interact with directly. It's just an electronic chip with input and output pins that can send or receive electrical pulses. Using a microcontroller is a three-stage process:

1. You connect sensors to the inputs to convert physical energy like motion, heat, and sound into electrical energy.
2. You attach motors, speakers, and other devices to the outputs to convert electrical energy into physical action.
3. Finally, you write a program to determine how the input changes affect the outputs.

In other words, the microcontroller's physical interface is whatever you make of it.

The third type of computer in this book, the network server, is basically the same as a desktop computer, and may even have a keyboard, screen, and mouse. Even though it can do all the things you expect of a personal computer, its primary function is to send and receive data over a network. Most people using servers don't think of them as physical things, because they only interact with them over a network, using their local computers as physical interfaces to the server. A server's most important interface for most users' purposes is its software interface.

The fourth group of computers is a mixed bag: mobile phones, music synthesizers, and motor controllers, to name a few. Some of them will have fully developed physical interfaces, some of them will have minimal physical interfaces but detailed software interfaces, and most will have a little of both. Even though you don't normally think of these devices as computers, they are. When you think of them as programmable objects, with interfaces that you can manipulate, it's easier to figure out how they can all communicate with each other, regardless of their end function.

X

“ Good Habits

Networking objects is a bit like love. The fundamental problem in both is that when you're sending a message, you never really know whether the receiver understands what you're saying, and there are a thousand ways for your message to get lost or garbled in transmission.

You may know why you feel the way you do, but your partner doesn't. All he or she has to go on are the words you say and the actions you take. Likewise, you may know exactly what message your local computer is sending, how it's sending it, and what all the bits mean, but the remote computer has no idea what they mean unless you program it to understand them. All it has to go on are the bits it receives. If you want reliable, clear communications (in love or networking), there are a few simple things you have to do:

- Listen more than you speak.
- Never assume that what you said is what they heard.
- Agree on how you're going to say things in advance.
- Ask politely for clarification when messages aren't clear.

Listen More Than You Speak

The best way to make a good first impression, and to maintain a good relationship, is to be a good listener. Listening is more difficult than speaking. You can speak anytime you want to, but you never know when the other person is going to say something, so you have to listen all the time. In networking terms, this means that you should write your programs such that they're listening for new messages most of the time, and sending messages only when necessary. It's often easier to send out messages all the time rather than figure out when it's appropriate, but it can lead to all kinds of problems. It usually doesn't take a lot of work to limit your sending, and the benefits far outweigh the costs.

Never Assume

What you say is not always what the other person hears. Sometimes it's a matter of misinterpretation, and other times, you may not have been heard clearly. If you assume that the message got through and continue on obliviously, you're in for a world of hurt. Likewise, you may be tempted to work out all the logic of your system, and all the steps of your messages before you start to connect things together, then build it, then test it all at once. Avoid that temptation.

It's good to plan the whole system out in advance, but build it and test it in baby steps. Most of the errors that occur in building these projects occur in the communication between objects. Always send a quick "Hello World!" message from one object to the others and make sure that the message got there intact before you proceed to the more complex details. Keep that "Hello World!" example on hand for testing when communication fails.

Getting the message wrong isn't the only wrong step you can make. Most of the projects in this book involve building the physical, software, and electrical elements of the interface. One of the most common mistakes people make when developing hybrid projects like these is to assume that the problems are all in one place. Quite often, I've sweated over a bug in the software transmission of a message, only to find out later that the receiving device wasn't even connected, or wasn't ready to receive messages. Don't assume that communication errors are in the element of the system with which you're most familiar.

They're most often in the element with which you're least familiar, and therefore are avoiding. When you can't get a message through, think about every link in the chain from sender to receiver, and check every one. Then check the links you overlooked.

Agree on How You Say Things

In good relationships, you develop a shared language based on shared experience. You learn the best ways to say things so that your partner will be most receptive, and you develop shorthand for expressing things that you repeat all the time. Good data communications also rely on shared ways of saying things, or protocols. Sometimes you make up a protocol yourself for all the objects in your system, and other times you have to rely on existing protocols. If you're working with a previously established protocol, make sure you understand what all the parts are before you start trying to interpret it. If you have the luxury of making up your own protocol, make sure you've considered the needs of both the sender and receiver when you define it. For example, you might decide to use a protocol that's easy to program on your web server, but turns out to be impossible to handle on your microcontroller. A little thought to the strengths and weaknesses on both sides of the transmission and a little compromise before you start to build will make things flow much more smoothly.

Ask Politely for Clarification

Messages get garbled in countless ways. Sometimes you hear one thing; it may not make much sense, but you act on it ... only to find out that your partner said something entirely different from what you thought. It's always best to ask nicely for clarification to avoid making a stupid mistake. Likewise, in network communications, it's wise to check that any messages you receive make sense. When they don't, ask for a repeat transmission. It's also wise to check that a message was sent, rather than assume. Saying nothing can be worse than saying something wrong. Minor problems can become major when no one speaks up to acknowledge that there's a problem. The same thing can occur in network communications. One device may wait forever for a message from the other side, not knowing that the remote device is unplugged, or perhaps it didn't get the initial message. When no response is forthcoming, send another message. Don't resend it too often, and give the other party time to reply before resending. Acknowledging messages may seem like a luxury, but it can save a whole lot of time and energy when you're building a complex system.
X

66 Tools

As you'll be working with the physical, software, and electrical interfaces of objects, the tools you'll need are physical tools, software, and (computer) hardware.

Physical Tools

If you've worked with electronics or microcontrollers before, chances are you have your own hand tools already. Figure 1-1 shows the ones used most frequently in this book. They're common tools, and can be obtained from many vendors. A few are listed in Table 1-1.

In addition to hand tools, there are some common electronic components that you'll use all the time. They're listed as well, with part numbers from the retailers featured most frequently in this book. Not all retailers will carry all parts, so there are many gaps in the table.

NOTE: You'll find a number of component suppliers in this book. I buy from different vendors depending on who's got the best and the least expensive version of each part. Sometimes it's easier to buy from a vendor that you know carries what you need rather than search through the massive catalog of a vendor who might carry it cheaper. Feel free to substitute your favorite vendors. A list of vendors can be found in Appendix B.

Figure 1-1. See list at right for number references.

Table 1-1. Common tools for electronic and microcontroller work.

D Digi-Key (digikey.com) **J** Jameco (jameco.com)
I Images SI (imagesco.com) **S** SparkFun Electronics (sparkfun.com)

RESISTORS
100Ω .... **D** 100QBK-ND, **J** 690620
220Ω .... **D** 220QBK-ND, **J** 690700
470Ω .... **D** 470QBK-ND, **J** 690785
1K .... **D** 1.0KQBK, **J** 29663
10K .... **D** 10KQBK-ND, **J** 29911
22K .... **D** 22KQBK-ND, **J** 30453
100K .... **D** 100KQBK-ND, **J** 29997
1M .... **D** 1.0MQBK-ND, **J** 29698

CAPACITORS
0.1µF ceramic .... **D** 399-4151-ND, **J** 15270
1µF electrolytic .... **D** P10312-ND, **J** 94161
10µF electrolytic ...... **D** P11212-ND, **J** 29891, **S** COM-00523
100µF electrolytic ... **D** P10269-ND, **J** 158394, **S** COM-00096

VOLTAGE REGULATORS
3.3V .... **D** 576-1134-ND, **J** 242115, **S** COM-00526
5V .... **D** LM7805CT-ND, **J** 51262, **S** COM-00107

ANALOG SENSORS
Flex sensors .... **J** 150551, **I** FLX-01
FSRs .... **P** 30056, **I** FSR-400, 402, 406, 408

LED
T1, Green clear .... **D** 160-1144-ND, **J** 34761
T1, Red, clear .... **D** 160-1665-ND, **J** 94511

TRANSISTORS
2N2222A .... **J** 38236
TIP120 .... **J** 32993

DIODES
1N4004-R .... **D** 1N4004-E3 or 23GI-ND, **J** 35992
3.3V zener (1N5226) .... **D** 1N5226B-TPCT-ND, **J** 743488

PUSHBUTTONS
PCB .... **D** SW400-ND, **J** 119011, **S** COM-00097
Panel Mount .... **D** GH1344-ND, **J** 164559PS

SOLDERLESS BREADBOARDS
various .... **D** 438-1045-ND, **J** 20723, 20600, **S** PRT-00137

HOOKUP WIRE
red .... **J** 36856, **S** PRT-08023
black .... **J** 36792, **S** PRT-08022
blue .... **J** 36767
yellow .... **S** PRT-08024

POTENTIOMETER
10K .... **D** 29081

HEADER PINS
straight .... **D** A26509-20-ND, **J** 103377, **S** PRT-00116
right angle .... **D** S1121E-36-ND, **S** PRT-00553

HEADERS
female .... **S** PRT-00115

BATTERY SNAP
9V .... **D** 2238K-ND, **J** 101470PS, **S** PRT-00091

🔊 Handy hand tools for networking objects.

1 Soldering iron Middle-of-the-line is best here. Cheap soldering irons die fast, but a mid-range iron like the Weller WLC-100 work great for small electronic work. Avoid the Cold Solder irons. They solder by creating a spark, and that spark can damage static-sensitive parts like micro-controllers. Jameco (jameco.com): 146595; RadioShack: 640-2802 and 640-2078

2 Solder 21-23 AWG solder is best. Get lead-free solder if you can, it's healthier for you. Jameco: 668271; RadioShack: 640-0013

3 Desoldering pump This helps when you mess up while soldering. Jameco: 305226; SparkFun (sparkfun.com): TOL-00082

4 Wire stripper, Diagonal cutter, Needle-nose pliers Avoid the 3-in-1 versions of these tools. They'll only make you grumpy. These three tools are essential for working with wire, and you don't need expensive ones to have good ones.
Wire stripper: Jameco: 159291; RadioShack: 640-2129A; SparkFun: TOL-00089
Diagonal cutter: Jameco: 161411; Radio–Shack: 640-2043; SparkFun: TOL-00070
Needlenose pliers: Jameco: 35473; Radio–Shack: 640-2033; SparkFun: TOL-00079

5 Mini-screwdriver Get one with both Phillips and slotted heads. You'll use it all the time. Jameco: 127271; RadioShack: 640-1963

6 Helping hands These make soldering much easier. Jameco: 681002

7 9–12V DC power supply You'll use this all the time, and you've probably got a spare from some dead electronic device. Make sure you know the polarity of the plug so you don't reverse polarity on a component and blow it up! Most of the devices shown in this book have a DC power jack that accepts a 2.1mm inner diameter/5.5mm outer diameter plug, so look for an adaptor with the same dimensions. Jameco: 170245 (12V, 1000mA); RadioShack: 273-1667 (3–12V, 800mA); SparkFun: TOL-00298

8 Power connector, 2.1mm inside diameter/5.5mm outside diameter You'll need this to connect your microcontroller module or breadboard to a DC power supply. This size connector is the most common for the power supplies that will work with the circuits you'll be building here. Jameco: 159610; Digi-Key (digikey.com): CP-024A-ND

9 Multimeter You don't need an expensive one. As long as it measures voltage, resistance, amperage, and continuity, it'll do the job. Jameco: 220812; RadioShack: 22-810; SparkFun: TOL-00078

10 USB cables You'll need both USB A-to-B (the most common USB cables) and USB A-to-mini-B (the kind that's common with digital cameras) for the projects in this book. SparkFun: CAB-00512, CAB-00598

11 Serial-to-USB converter This converter lets you speak TTL serial from a USB port. Breadboard serial-to-USB modules like the FT232 modules shown here are cheaper than the consumer models, and easier to use in the projects in this book. SparkFun: BOB-00718 or DEV-08165

12 Alligator clip test leads It's often hard to juggle the five or six things you have to hold when metering a circuit. Clip leads make this much easier. Jameco: 10444; RadioShack: 278-016; SparkFun: CAB-00501

13 Microcontroller module The microcontrollers shown here are the Arduino NG and the Arduino Mini. Available from SparkFun and Make (store.makezine.com) in the U.S., PCB-Europe in Europe (pcb-europe.net/catalog/) and from multiple distributors internationally. See arduino.cc/en/Main/Buy for details in your region.

14 Header pins You'll use these all the time. It's handy to have female ones around as well. Jameco: 103377; Digi-Key: A26509-20-ND; SparkFun: PRT-00116

15 Spare LEDs for tracing signals LEDs are to the hardware developer what print statements are to the software developer. They let you see quickly if there's voltage between two points, or if a signal's going through. Keep spares on hand. Jameco: 3476; RadioShack: 276-0069; Digi-Key: 160-1144-ND, 160-1665-ND

16 Resistors You'll need resistors of various values for your projects. Common values are listed in Table 1-1.

17 Analog sensors (variable resistors) There are countless varieties of variable resistors to measure all kinds of physical properties. They're the simplest of analog sensors, and they're very easy to build into test circuits. Flex sensors and force-sensing resistors are handy for testing a circuit or a program.
Flex sensors: Jameco: 150551; Images SI: FLX-01

Force-sensing resistors: Parallax: 30056; Images SI: FSR-400, 402, 406, 408

18 Capacitors You'll need capacitors of various values for your projects. Common values are listed in Table 1-1.

19 Voltage regulators Voltage regulators take a variable input voltage and output a constant (lower) voltage. The two most common you'll need for these projects are 5V and 3.3V. Be careful when using a regulator that you've never used before. Check the data sheet to make sure you have the pin connections correct.
3.3V: Digkey: 576-1134-ND; Jameco: 242115; SparkFun: COM-00526
5V: Digkey: LM7805CT-ND; Jameco: 51262; SparkFun: COM-00107

20 Pushbuttons There are two types you'll find handy: the PCB-mount type like the ones you find on Wiring and Arduino boards, used here mostly as reset buttons for breadboard projects; and panel-mount types used for interface controls for end users. But you can use just about any type you want.
PCB-mount type: Digi-Key: SW400- ND; Jameco: 119011; SparkFun: COM-00097
Panel-mount type: Digi-Key: GH1344-ND; Jameco: 164559PS

21 Potentiometers You'll need potentiometers to let people adjust settings in your project. Jameco: 29081

22 Solderless breadboard Having a few around can be handy. I like the ones with two long rows on either side, so you can run power and ground on both sides. Jameco: 20723 (2 bus rows per side); Radio-Shack: 276-174 (1 bus row per side); Digi-Key: 438-1045-ND; SparkFun: PRT-00137

23 Ethernet cables A couple of these will come in handy. Jameco: 522781

24 Black, red, blue, yellow wire 22 AWG solid-core hook-up wire is best for making solderless breadboard connections. Get at least three colors, and always use red for voltage and black for ground. A little organization of your wires can go a long way.
Black: Jameco: 36792
Blue: Jameco: 36767
Green: Jameco: 36821
Red: Jameco: 36856; RadioShack: 278-1215
Yellow: Jameco: 36919
Mixed: RadioShack: 276-173

Figure 1-2
The Processing editor window.

Software Tools

Processing

The multimedia programming environment used in this book is called Processing. It's based on Java, and made for designers, artists, and others who don't need to know all the gory details of programming, but want to get something done. It's a useful tool for explaining programming ideas because it takes relatively little Processing code to make big things happen, such as opening a network connection, connecting to an external device through a serial port, or controlling a camera through FireWire. It's a free, open source tool available from www.processing.org. Because it's based on Java, you can include Java classes and methods in your Processing programs. It runs on Mac OS X, Windows, and Linux, so almost anyone can run Processing on their favorite operating system. If you don't like working in Processing, you should be able to use the code samples here and their comments as pseudocode for whatever multimedia environment you prefer. Once you've downloaded and installed Processing on your computer, open the application. You'll get a screen that looks like Figure 1-2.

Here's your first Processing program. Type this into the editor window, and press the Run button on the top left-hand side of the toolbar:

```
println("Hello World!\n");
```

It's not too flashy a program, but it's a classic. It should print Hello World! in the message box at the bottom of the editor window. It's that easy.

Programs in Processing are called sketches, and all the data for a sketch is saved in a folder with the sketch's name. The editor is very basic, without a lot of clutter to get in your way. The toolbar has buttons to run and stop a sketch, create a new file, open an existing sketch, save the current sketch, or export to a Java applet. You can also export your sketch as a standalone application from the File menu. Files are normally stored in a subdirectory of your **Documents** folder called **Processing**, but you can save them wherever you prefer if you don't like them there.

▸▸ Here's a second program that's a bit more exciting. It illustrates some of the main programming structures in Processing:

```
/*
    Triangle drawing program
    Language: Processing

    Draws a triangle whenever the mouse button is not pressed.
    Erases when the mouse button is pressed.

*/

// declare your variables:
float redValue = 0;    // variable to hold the red color
float greenValue = 0;  // variable to hold the green color
float blueValue = 0;   // variable to hold the blue color

// the setup() method runs once at the beginning of the program:

void setup() {
  size(320, 240);     // sets the size of the applet window
  background(0);      // sets the background of the window to black
  fill(0);            // sets the color to fill shapes with (0 = black)
  smooth();           // draw with antialiased edges
}

// the draw() method runs repeatedly, as long as the applet window
// is open.  It refreshes the window, and anything else you program
// it to do:

void draw() {

  // Pick random colors for red, green, and blue:
  redValue = random(255);
  greenValue = random(255);
  blueValue = random(255);

  // set the line color:
  stroke(redValue, greenValue, blueValue);

  // draw when the mouse is up (to hell with conventions):
  if (mousePressed == false) {
    // draw a triangle:
    triangle(mouseX, mouseY, width/2, height/2,pmouseX, pmouseY);
  }
  // erase when the mouse is down:
  else {
    background(0);
    fill(0);
  }
}
```

Every Processing program has two main routines, setup() and draw(). setup() happens once at the beginning of the program. It's where you set all your initial conditions, like the size of the applet window, initial states for variables, and so forth. draw() is the main loop of the program. It repeats continuously until you close the applet window.

In order to use variables in Processing, you have to declare the variable's data type. In the preceding program, the variables redValue, greenValue, and blueValue are all float types, meaning that they're floating decimal-point numbers. Other common variable types you'll use are ints (integers), booleans (true or false values), Strings of text, and bytes.

Like C, Java and many other languages, Processing uses C-style syntax. All functions have a data type, just like variables (and many of them are the void type, meaning that they don't return any values). All lines end with a semicolon, and all blocks of code are wrapped in curly brackets. Conditional statements (if-then statements), for-next loops, and comments all use the C syntax as well. The preceding code illustrates all of these except the for-next loop.

» Here's a typical for-next loop. Try this in a sketch of its own (to start a new sketch, select New from Processing's File menu):

```
for (int myCounter = 0; myCounter <=10; myCounter++) {
    println(myCounter);
}
```

Processing is a fun language to play with, because you can make interactive graphics very quickly. It's also a simple introduction to Java for beginning programmers. If you're a Java programmer already, you can include Java directly in your Processing programs. Processing is expandable through code libraries. You'll be using two of the Processing code libraries frequently in this book: the serial library and the networking library.

For more on the syntax of Processing, see the language reference guide at www.processing.org. To learn more about programming in Processing, check out *Processing: A Programming Handbook for Visual Designers and Artists*, by Casey Reas and Ben Fry (MIT Press, 2007), the creators of Processing.

BASIC users: If you've never used a C-style for-next loop, it can seem a bit forbidding. What this bit of code does is establish a variable called myCounter. **As long as number is less than or equal to ten, it executes the instructions in the curly brackets.** myCounter++ **tells the program to add one to** myCounter **each time through the loop. The equivalent BASIC code is:**

```
for myCounter = 0 to 10
    Print myCounter
next
```

Mac OS X Users: Once you've downloaded and installed Processing, there's an extra step you'll need to take that will make the projects in this book that use Processing possible.

Go to the Processing application directory, then to the libraries/serial/ subdirectory. There's a file there called macosx_setup. command. Double-click this. It will run a script that enables Processing to use serial communication to USB, Bluetooth, and other devices. A terminal window will open and run a script that will ask you a few questions. It will also ask for your administrator password, so don't run it unless you have administrator access to your machine. Say "yes" to anything it asks, and provide your password when needed. When it's done, you'll be able to use the serial ports of your computer through Processing. You'll be making heavy use of this capability later on in this book.

Remote Access Applications

One of the most effective debugging tools you'll use in making the projects in this book is a command-line remote access program, which allows you access to the command-line interface of a remote computer. If you've never used a command-line interface before, you'll find it a bit awkward at first, but you get used to it pretty quickly. This tool is especially important when you need to log into a web server, as you'll need the command line to create PHP scripts that will be used in this book.

Most web hosting providers are based on Linux, BSD, Solaris or some other Unix-like operating system. So, when you need to do some work on your web server, you may need to make a command-line connection to your web server.

> If you already know how to create PHP and HTML documents and upload them to your web server, you can skip ahead to the "PHP" section.

In a command-line interface, everything is done by typing commands at the cursor. The programs you'll be running and the files you'll be writing and reading aren't on your machine. When you're using the PHP programming language described shortly, for example, you'll be using programs and reading files directly on the web host's computer.

Although this is the most direct way to work with PHP, some people prefer to work more indirectly, by writing text files on their local computers and uploading them to the remote computer. Depending on how restrictive your web hosting service is, this may be your only option (however, there are many inexpensive hosting companies that offer full command-line access). Even if you prefer to work this way, there are times in this book when the command line is your only option, so it's worth getting to know a little bit about it now.

On Windows computers, there are a few remote access programs available, but the one that you'll use here is called PuTTY. You can download it from www.puttyssh.org. Download the Windows-style installer and run it. On Mac OS X and Linux, you can use OpenSSH, which is included with both operating systems, and can be run in the Terminal program with the command ssh.

Before you can run OpenSSH, you'll need to launch a terminal emulation program, which gives you access to your Linux or Mac OS X command line. On Mac OS X, the program is called Terminal, and you can find it in the **Utilities** subdirectory of the **Applications** directory. On Linux, look for a program called xterm, rxvt, Terminal, or Konsole.

NOTE: ssh **is a more modern cousin of a longtime Unix remote access program called** telnet. ssh **is more secure, in that it scrambles all data sent from one computer to another before sending it, so it can't be snooped on en route.** telnet **sends all data from one computer to another with no encryption. You should use** ssh **to connect from one machine to another whenever you can. Where** telnet **is used in this book, it's because it's the only tool that will do what's needed for the examples in question. Think of** telnet **as an old friend: maybe not the coolest guy on the block, maybe he's a bit of a gossip, but he's stood by you forever, and you know you can trust him to do the job when everyone else lets you down.**

X

Making the SSH Connection

Mac OS X and Linux
Open your terminal program. These Terminal applications give you a plain text window with a greeting like this:

Last login: Wed Feb 22 07:20:34 on ttyp1
ComputerName:~ username$

Type ssh username@myhost.com at the command line to connect to your web host. Replace username and myhost.com with your username and host address.

Windows
On Windows, you'll need to start up PuTTY (see Figure 1-3). To get started, type myhost.com (your web host's name) in the Host Name field, choose the SSH protocol, and then click Open.

The computer will try to connect to the remote host, and asks for your password when it connects. Type it (you won't see what you type), followed by the Enter key.

⬆ **Figure 1-3**
The main PuTTY window.

Using the Command Line

Once you've connected to the remote web server, you should see something like this:

```
Last login: Wed Feb 22 08:50:04 2006 from 216.157.45.215
[userid@myhost ~]$
```

Now you're at the command prompt of your web host's computer, and any command you give will be executed on that computer. Start off by learning what directory you're in. To do this, type the following:

```
pwd
```

which stands for "print working directory." It asks the computer to list the name and pathname of the directory in which you're currently working. You'll see that many Unix commands are very terse, so you have to type less. The downside of this is that it makes them harder to remember. The server will respond with a directory path, such as:

```
/home/igoe
```

This is the home directory for your account. On many web servers, this directory contains a subdirectory called **public_html** or **www**, which is where your web files belong. Files that you place in your home directory (that is, outside or **www** or **public_html**) can't be seen by web visitors.

NOTE: You should check with your web host to learn how the files and directories in your home directory are set up.

To find out what files are in a given directory, use the list (ls) command, like so:

```
ls -l .
```

NOTE: The dot is shorthand for "the current working directory." Similarly, a double dot is shorthand for the directory (the parent directory) that contains the current directory.

The –l means "list long." You'll get a response like this:

```
total 44
drwxr-xr-x  13 igoe users 4096 Apr 14 11:42 public_html
drwxr-xr-x   3 igoe users 4096 Nov 25  2005 share
```

This is a list of all the files and subdirectories of the current working directories, and their attributes. The first column lists who's got permissions to do what (read, modify, or execute/run a file). The second lists how many links there are to that file elsewhere on the system; it's not something you'll have much need for, most of the time. The third column tells you who owns it, and the fourth tells you the group (a collection of users) the file belongs to. The fifth lists its size, and the sixth lists the date it was last modified. The final column lists the filename.

In a Unix environment, all files whose names begin with a dot are invisible. Some files, like access-control files that you'll see later in the book, need to be invisible. You can get a list of all the files, including the invisible ones, using the –a modifier for ls, this way:

```
ls -la
```

To move around from one directory to another, there's a "change directory" command, cd. To get into the **public_html** directory, for example, type:

```
cd public_html
```

To go back up one level in the directory structure, type:

```
cd ..
```

To return to your home directory, use the ~ symbol, which is shorthand for your home directory:

```
cd ~
```

If you type cd on a line by itself, it also takes you to your home directory.

If you wanted to go into a subdirectory of a directory, for example the **cgi-bin** directory inside the **public_html** directory, you'd type cd public_html/cgi-bin. You can type the absolute path from the main directory of the server (called the root) by placing a / at the beginning of the file's pathname. Any other file pathname is called a relative path.

To make a new directory, type:

```
mkdir directoryname
```

This command will make a new directory in the current working directory. If you then use ls -l to see a list of files in the working directory, you'll see a new line with the new directory. If you then type cd directoryname to switch to the new directory and ls —la to see all of its contents, you'll see only two listings:

```
drwxr-xr-x  2 tqi6023 users 4096 Feb 17 10:19 .
drwxr-xr-x  4 tqi6023 users 4096 Feb 17 10:19 ..
```

The first file, . , is a reference to this directory itself. The second, .. , is a reference to the directory that contains it. Those two references will exist as long as the directory exists. You can't change them.

To remove a directory, type:

```
rmdir directoryname
```

You can remove only empty directories, so make sure that you've deleted all the files in a directory before you remove it. rmdir won't ask you if you're sure before it deletes your directory, though, so be careful. Don't remove any directories or files that you didn't make yourself until you know your way around.

Controlling Access to Files

Type ls -l . to get a list of files in your current directory and take a closer look at the permissions on the files. For example, a file marked drwx------ means that it's a directory, and that it's readable, writable, and executable by the system user that created the directory (also known as the owner of the file). Or take the file marked -rw-rw-rw. The — at the beginning means it's a regular file, not a directory, and that the owner, the group of users that the file belongs to (usually, this is the group that the owner is a member of), and everyone else who accesses the system can read and write to this file. The first rw- refers to the owner, the second refers to the group, and the third refers to the rest of the world. If you're the owner of a file, you can change its permissions using the chmod command:

```
chmod go -w filename
```

The options following chmod refer to which users you want to affect. In the preceding example, you're removing write permission (-w) for the group (g) that the file belongs to, and for all others (o) besides the owner of the file. To restore write permissions for the group and others, and to also give them execute permission, you'd type:

```
chmod go +wx filename
```

A combination of u for user, g for group, and o for others, and a combination of + and − and r for read, w for write, and x for execute gives you the capability to change permissions on your files for anyone on the system. Be careful not to accidentally remove permissions from yourself (the user). Also, get in the habit of not leaving files accessible to the group and others unless you need to: on large hosting providers, it's not unusual for you to be sharing a server with hundreds of other users!

Creating, Viewing, and Deleting Files

Two other command-line programs you'll find useful are nano and less. nano is a text editor. It's very bare-bones, and you may prefer to edit your files using your favorite text editor on your own computer and then upload them to your server. But for quick changes right on the server, nano is great. To make a new file, type:

```
nano filename.txt
```

The nano editor will open up. Figure 1-4 shows what it looked like after I typed in some text.

All the commands to work in nano are keyboard commands you type using the Control key. For example, to exit the program, type Control-X. The editor will then ask you if you want to save, and prompt you for a filename. The most common commands are listed along the bottom of the screen.

While nano is for creating and editing files, less is for reading them. less takes any file and displays it to the screen one screenful at a time. To see the file you just created in nano, for example, type:

```
less filename.txt
```

You'll get a list of the file's contents, with a : prompt at the bottom of the screen. Press the spacebar for the next screenful. When you've read enough, type q to quit. There's not much to less, but it's a handy way to read long files. You can even send other commands through less (or almost any command-line program) using the pipe (|) operator. For example, try this:

```
ls -la . | less
```

Figure 1-4
The nano text editor.

Once you've created a file, you can delete it using the rm command, like this:

```
rm filename
```

Like rmdir, rm won't ask you if you're sure before it deletes your file, so use it carefully.

There are many other commands available in the Unix command shell, but these will suffice to get you started for now. For more information, type help at the command prompt to get a list of commonly used commands. For any command, you can get its user manual by typing man commandname. For more on getting around Unix and Linux systems using the command line, see *Learning the Unix Operating System* by Jerry Peek, John Strang, and Grace Todino-Gonguet. When you're ready to close the connection to your server, type: logout

PHP

The server programs in this book are mostly in PHP. PHP is one of the most common scripting languages for applications that run on the web server (server-side scripts). Server-side scripts are programs that allow you to do more with a web server than just serve fixed pages of text or HTML. They allow you to access databases through a browser, save data from a web session to a text file, send mail from a browser, and more. You'll need a web hosting account with an Internet service provider for most of the projects in this book, and it's likely that your host already provides access to PHP. If not, talk to your system administrator to see whether it can be installed.

To get started with PHP, you'll need to make a remote connection to your web hosting account using ssh as you did in the last section. Some of the more basic web hosts don't allow ssh connections, so check with yours to see whether they do (and if yours doesn't, look around for an inexpensive hosting company that does; it will be well worth it for the flexibility of working from the command line). Once you're connected, type: php -v

You should get a reply like this:

```
PHP 4.3.9 (cgi) (built: Nov  4 2005 11:49:43)
Copyright (c) 1997-2004 The PHP Group
Zend Engine v1.3.0, Copyright (c) 1998-2004 Zend
Technologies
```

This tells what version of PHP is installed on your server. The code in this book was written using PHP4, so as long as you're running that version or later, you'll be fine. PHP makes it easy to write web pages that can display results from databases, send messages to other servers, send email, and more.

Most of the time, you won't be executing your PHP scripts directly from the command line. Instead, you'll be calling the web server application on your server, most likely a program called Apache, and asking it for a file (this is all accomplished simply by opening a web browser, typing in the address of a document on your web server, and pressing Enter — just like visiting any other web page). If the file you ask for is a PHP script, the web server application will look for your file and execute it. It'll then send a message back to you with the results.

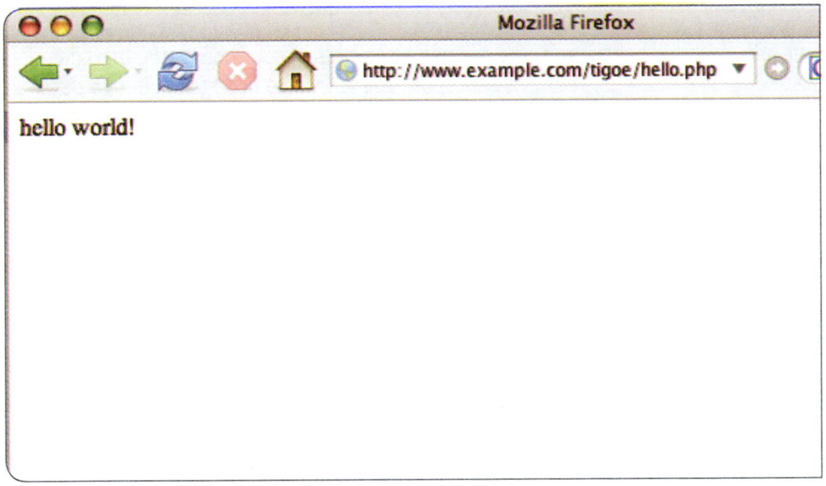

Figure 1-5
The results of your first PHP script, in a browser.

For more on this, see Chapter 3. For now, let's get a simple PHP program or two working. Here's your first PHP program. Open your favorite text editor, type this in, and save it on the server with the name **hello.php** in your **public_html** directory. (Your web pages may be stored in a different directory, such as **www** or **web/public**.)

```
<?php
echo "<html><head></head><body>\n";
echo "hello world!\n";
echo "</body></html>\n";
?>
```

Now, back at the command line, type the following to see the results:

```
php hello.php
```

You should get the following response:

```
<html><head></head><body>
hello world!
</body></html>
```

Now try opening this file in a browser. To see this program in action, open a web browser and navigate to the address of this file on your website. Because you saved it in **public_html,** the address is http://www.example.com/hello.php (replace www.example.com with your web site and any additional path info needed to access your home files, such as http://tigoe.net/~tigoe/hello.php). You should get a web page like the one in Figure 1-5.

> ⚠ **If you see the PHP source code instead of what's shown in Figure 1-5, you may have opened up the PHP script as a local file (make sure your web browser's location bar says** http:// **instead of** file://**).**

If it still doesn't work, your web server may not be configured or PHP. Another possibility is that your web server uses a different extension for php scripts, such as .php4. Consult with your web hosting provider for more information.

You may have noticed that the program is actually printing out HTML text. PHP was made to be combined with HTML. In fact, you can even embed PHP in HTML pages, by using the <? and ?> tags that start and end every PHP script. If you get an error when you try to open your PHP script in a browser, ask your system administrator if there are any requirements as to which directories PHP scripts need to be in on your server, or on the file permissions for your PHP scripts.

Here's a slightly more complex PHP script. Save it to your server in the **public_html** directory as **time.php**:

```php
<?php
/*

   Date printer
   Language: PHP

   Prints the date and time in an HTML page.
*/
//    Get the date, and format it:
$date = date("Y-m-d h:i:s\t");

// print the beginning of an HTML page:
echo "<html><head></head><body>\n";
echo "hello world!<br>\n";
// Include the date:
echo "Today's date: $date<br>\n";
// finish the HTML:
echo "</body></html>\n";
?>
```

To see it in action, type http://www.example.com/time.php into your browser. You should get the date and time. You can see this program uses a variable, $date, and calls a built-in PHP function, date(), to fill the variable. You don't have to declare the types of your variables in PHP. Any simple, or scalar, variable begins with a $ and can contain an integer, a floating point number, or a string. PHP uses the same C-style syntax as Processing, so you'll see that if-then statements, repeat loops, and comments all look familiar.

For more on PHP, check out www.php.net, the main source for PHP, where you'll find some good tutorials on how to use it. You can also check out *Learning PHP 5* by David Sklar (O'Reilly Media, Inc., 2004) for a more in-depth treatment.

Serial Communication Tools

The remote access programs in the earlier section were terminal emulation programs that gave you access to remote computers through the Internet, but that's not all a terminal emulation program can do. Before TCP/IP was ubiquitous as a way for computers to connect to networks, connectivity was handled through modems attached to the serial ports of computers. Back then, many users connected to bulletin boards (BBSes) and used menu-based systems to post messages on discussion boards, download files, and send mail to other users of the same BBS.

Nowadays, serial ports are used mainly to connect to some of peripheral devices of your computer. In microcontroller programming, they're used to exchange data between the computer and the microcontroller. For the projects in this book, you'll find that using a terminal program to connect to your serial ports is indispensable. There are several freeware and shareware terminal programs available, but to keep it simple, stick with the classics: PuTTY (version 0.59 or later) for Windows users, and the GNU screen program running in a terminal window for Mac OS X and Linux users.

Windows Serial Communication

To get started, you'll need to know the serial port name. Click Start→Run (use the Search box on Vista), type devmgmt.msc, and press Enter to launch Device Manager. If you've got a serial device such as a Wiring or Arduino board attached, you'll see a listing for Ports (COM & LPT). Under that listing, you'll see all the available serial ports. Each new Wiring or Arduino board you connect will get a new name, such as COM5, COM6, COM7, and so forth.

Once you know the name of your serial port, open PuTTY. In the Session category, set the Connection Type to Serial, and enter the name of your port in the Serial Line box, as shown in Figure 1-6. Then click the Serial category at the end of the category list, and make sure that the serial line matches your port name. Configure the serial line for 9600 baud, 8 databits, 1 stop bit, no parity, and no flow control. Then click the Open button, and a serial window will open. Anything you type in this window will be sent out the serial port, and any data that comes in the serial port will be displayed here as ASCII text.

NOTE: Unless your Arduino is running a program that communicates over the serial port (and you'll learn all about that shortly), you won't get any response yet.

Mac OS X and Linux Serial Communication

To get started with serial communication in Mac OS X or Linux, open a terminal window and type:

```
ls /dev/tty.*    # Mac OS X
ls /dev/tty*     # Linux
```

This command will give you a list of available serial ports. The names of the serial ports in Mac OS X and Linux are more unique, but more cryptic than the COM1, COM2, and so on that Windows uses. Pick your serial port and type:

```
screen portname datarate.
```

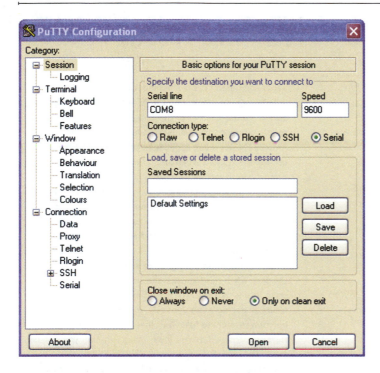

Figure 1-6

Configuring a serial connection in PuTTY.

For example, to open the serial port on an Arduino board (discussed shortly) at 9600 bits per second, you might type screen /dev/tty.usbserial-1B1 9600 on Mac OS X. On Linux, the command might be screen /dev/ttyUSB0 9600. The screen will be cleared, and any characters you type will be sent out the serial port you opened. They won't show up on the screen, however. Any bytes received in the serial port will be displayed in the window as characters. To close the serial port, type Control-A followed by Control-\.

In the next section, you'll use a serial communications program to communicate with a microcontroller.

Hardware

Arduino and Wiring

The main microcontroller used in this book is the Arduino module. Arduino is based on a similar module called Wiring. You should be able to use Arduino or Wiring interchangeably for the examples in this book. Both modules are the children of the Processing programming environment and the Atmel AVR family of microcontrollers. In fact, you'll find that the editors for Processing, Wiring, and Arduino look almost identical. Both programming environments are free and open source, available through hardware.processing.org. You can buy the actual modules from the original developers or from SparkFun at www.sparkfun.com or from Make at store.makezine.com. If you're a hardcore hardware geek and like to make your own printed circuit boards, you can download the plans and make your own. I recommend the former, as it's much quicker (and more reliable, for most people). Figures 1-7 and 1-8 show Wiring and several variants of Arduino.

One of the best things about Wiring and Arduino is that they are cross-platform. This is a rarity in microcontroller development environments. They work well on Mac OS X, Windows, and (with some effort) Linux.

Another good thing about these environments is that, like Processing, they can be extended. Just as you can include Java classes and methods in your Processing programs, you can include C/C++ code, written in AVR-C, in your Wiring and Arduino programs. For more on how to do this, see the Wiring and Arduino websites.

x

Who's Got the Port?

Serial ports aren't easily shared between applications. In fact, only one application can have control of a serial port at a time. If PuTTY or the screen program has the serial port open to an Arduino module, for example, the Arduino programming application can't download new code to the module. When an application tries to open a serial port, it requests exclusive control of it either by writing to a special file called a lock file or by asking the operating system to lock the file on its behalf. When it closes the serial port, it releases the lock on the serial port. Sometimes when an application crashes while it's got a serial port open, it can forget to close the serial port, with the result that no other application can open the port. When this happens, the only thing you can do to fix it is to restart the operating system, which clears all the locks (alternatively, you could wait for the operating system to figure out that the lock should be released). To avoid this problem, make sure that you close the serial port whenever you switch from one application to another. Linux and Mac OS X users should get in the habit of closing down screen with Ctrl-A Ctrl-\ every time, and Windows users should disconnect the connection in PuTTY. Otherwise, you may find yourself restarting your machine a lot.

» opposite page top
▸▸ **Figure 1-7**
Wiring Board, Arduino NG board, Arduino Mini.

» opposite page bottom
▸▸ **Figure 1-8**
The Arduino microcontroller modules.
CLOCKWISE FROM TOP LEFT: the original Arduino serial module; the ArduinoUSB; the Arduino NG; the Arduino Bluetooth; and finally, the Arduino Mini, center.

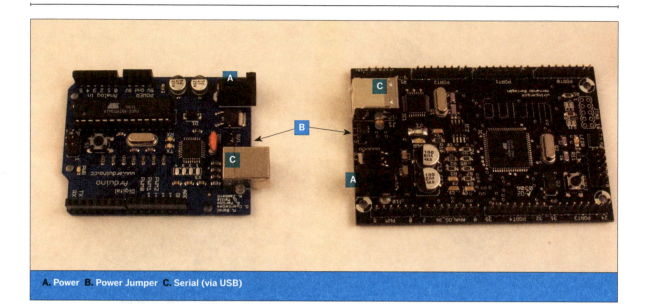

A. Power B. Power Jumper C. Serial (via USB)

Wiring and Arduino Compared

Given the similarities between Wiring and Arduino, you're probably wondering which to choose. The programming language is the same for both, and the programming environments are virtually identical, so the major factors to consider are price, size, and number of inputs and outputs.

Wiring is the larger of the two modules, and the more expensive. It has more input and output connections and some useful features such as hardware interrupt pins and two hardware serial ports. Two serial ports can be handy when you're working on projects in this book, because you can use one serial port to talk to your communications device, and another to talk to the computer on which you're programming the microcontroller. There is a software serial library for both Wiring and Arduino that allows you to use any two I/O pins as a serial port. It's more limited than a hardware serial port, in that it can't send and receive data as quickly as a hardware serial port.

Wiring boards can be ordered online from www.sparkfun. com or directly from www.wiring.org.co.

Arduino is the less expensive of the two modules, and the smaller. It has fewer inputs and outputs than Wiring, and only one hardware serial port. The Arduino developers have made a few different Arduino boards. The original board has an RS-232 serial interface, and all the components are large enough that you can solder them by hand. It was designed for people who want to make their own board from scratch. The Arduino USB board is the default board. It's not as easy to assemble by hand, but most people buy them pre-assembled. It has a USB interface. The Arduino Bluetooth board is a variant on the USB board that has a wireless interface for programming and serial communication. It's the most expensive of the Arduino models to date, but handy if you know you're going to connect to it all the time through Bluetooth. The Arduino Mini is a tiny version of the Arduino, suitable for use on a breadboard. For people familiar with the Parallax BASIC Stamp 2 or the NetMedia BX-24, the Mini is a comfortable alternative. You can also build an Arduino module on a solderless breadboard.

Arduino also features add-on modules called shields, which allow you to add pre-assembled circuits to the main module. At this writing, there are four shields on the market. PCB Europe (pcb-europe.net/catalog) sells a board for controlling DC motors, and a prototyping shield for making your own circuits. SparkFun (www.sparkfun.com) sells a breadboard prototyping shield along with the various Arduino boards. Libelium (www.libelium.com) sells a ZigBee radio shield.

The projects in this book can be built with other micro-controllers as well. Like all microcontrollers, the Arduino and Wiring modules are just small computers. Like every computer, they have inputs, outputs, a power supply, and a communications port to connect to other devices. You can power these modules either through a separate power supply or through the USB connection to your computer. The jumper shown in Figure 1-9 switches power from the external supply to the USB supply. For this introduction, you'll power the module from the USB connection. For many projects, you'll want to disconnect them from the computer once you're finished programming them. To do this, you'll need to switch the power jumper to power the board from the external power supply.

Both Wiring and Arduino have four power pins. On the Wiring board, they're labeled 5V, Gnd, GND and 9-15V. On the Arduino, they're labeled 5V, Gnd, Gnd, and 9V. In both cases, the 5V connection outputs 5V relative to the two ground pins. The 9V or 9-15V pin is connected directly to the voltage input on the external power jack, so the output voltage of that pin is equal to whatever your input voltage is. You can also use this connection to connect these modules directly to 9-15V battery power, if you set the power jumper to external power.

Figure 1-10 shows the inputs and outputs for the Arduino, the Arduino Mini, and the Wiring module. Each module has the same standard features that most microcontrollers have: analog inputs, digital inputs and outputs, and power and ground connections. Some of the I/O pins can also be used for serial communication. The Wiring and Arduino boards also have a USB connector, a programming header to allow you to reprogram the firmware (you'll never do that in this book), and a reset button. The Arduino Mini does not have these features, but they can be added using its companion USB-to-serial board. Figure 1-11 shows a typical breadboard setup for the Mini. You'll see these diagrams repeated frequently, as they are the basis for all of the microcontroller projects in the book.

Getting Started

Because the installation process for Wiring and Arduino is almost identical, I'll detail only the Arduino process here.

Wiring users will find things similar enough to follow along and do the same steps, substituting "Wiring" for "Arduino" in the instructions that follow.

Once you've downloaded the Arduino software, you'll need to do a bit of configuring to get things ready for use. Expand the downloaded file and you'll get a directory called **arduino-0009** (if there is a newer version of the software available, the number will be different). Move this somewhere convenient: on a Mac, you might put it in your **Applications** directory; on Windows, maybe in **C:\Program Files**; on Linux, you might want to keep it in your home directory or drop it into **/usr/local**. Now navigate to the directory **arduino-009/drivers** subdirectory. In that directory, you'll find an installer for the FTDI USB serial driver (not needed under Linux). This is the USB device on the module that allows your computer to communicate with the module via USB. Install it. Macintosh users will also find a file in the **arduino-0009** directory called **macosx_setup. command**. This is the same as the **macosx_setup.command** for Processing that was described earlier, so if you already ran it to configure Processing, you won't need to do it again. If you haven't, double-click the file and follow the instructions that come up.

> ⚠ **Arduino and Wiring are new to the market, and updates to their software occur frequently. The notes in this book refer to Arduino version 0009 and Wiring version 0012. By the time you read this, the specifics may be slightly different, so check the Arduino and Wiring websites for the latest details.**

Now you're ready to launch Arduino. Connect the module to your USB port, and double-click the Arduino icon to launch the software. The editor looks like Figure 1-12.

The environment is based on Processing, and has the same New, Open, Save, and Export buttons on the main toolbar. In Arduino and Wiring, the Run function is called Verify. It compiles your program to check for any errors, and the Export function is called Upload to Module instead. It uploads your code to the microcontroller module. There's an additional button, the Serial Monitor, that you can use to receive serial data from the module while you're debugging.

X

« *opposite page*
Figure 1-9

Arduino and Wiring modules. Note the jumper to switch power from the USB connection to an external power supply.

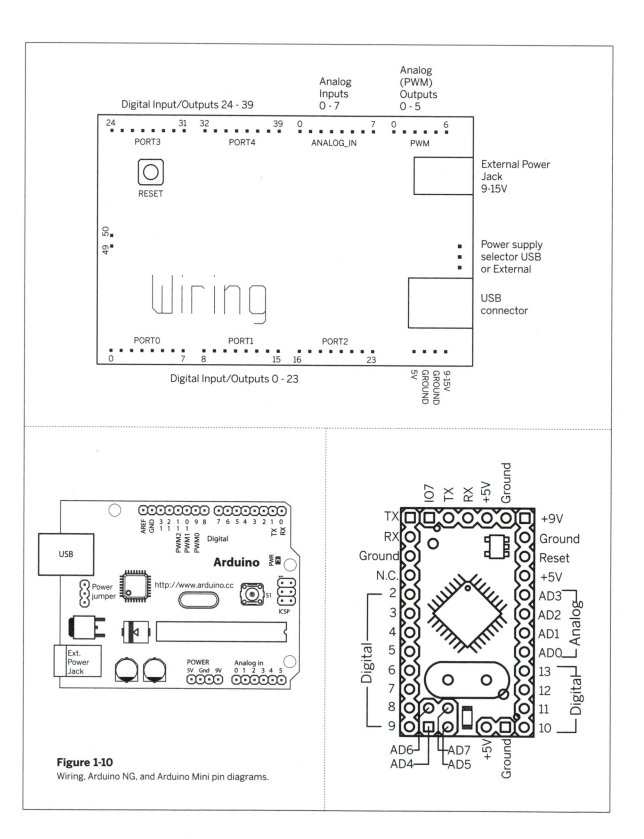

Figure 1-10
Wiring, Arduino NG, and Arduino Mini pin diagrams.

▸▸ Figure 1-12
The Arduino programming environment.
The Wiring environment looks identical.
to this, except for the color.

» bottom left
Figure 1-11
Typical wiring for an Arduino Mini.

» bottom right
Figure 1-13
LED connected to pin 13 of an
Arduino board .

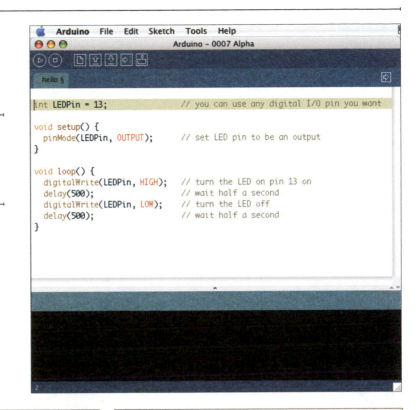

```
int LEDPin = 13;               // you can use any digital I/O pin you want

void setup() {
  pinMode(LEDPin, OUTPUT);     // set LED pin to be an output
}

void loop() {
  digitalWrite(LEDPin, HIGH);  // turn the LED on pin 13 on
  delay(500);                  // wait half a second
  digitalWrite(LEDPin, LOW);   // turn the LED off
  delay(500);                  // wait half a second
}
```

A. Mini TX Mini RX   **B.** Ground   **C.** Reset +5V

Try It

Here's your first program:

```
/*  Blink
    Language: Arduino/Wiring

    Blinks an LED attached to pin 13 every half second.

    Connections:
        Pin 13:  + leg of an LED (- leg goes to ground)
*/

int LEDPin = 13;

void setup() {
  pinMode(LEDPin, OUTPUT);      // set pin 13 to be an output
}

void loop() {
  digitalWrite(LEDPin, HIGH);        // turn the LED on pin 13 on
  delay(500);                        // wait half a second
  digitalWrite(LEDPin, LOW);         // turn the LED off
  delay(500);                        // wait half a second
}
```

" In order to see this run, you'll need to connect an LED from pin 13 of the board to ground (GND) as shown in Figure 1-13. The positive (long) end of the LED should go to 13, and the short end to ground.

Then type the code into the editor. Click on Tools→Serial Port to choose the serial port of the Arduino module. On the Mac or Linux, the serial port will have a name like /dev/tty.usbserial-1B1 (the letters and numbers after the dash will be slightly different each time you connect it). On Windows, it should be COMx, where x is some number (for example, COM5).

Next, select the model of AVR microcontroller on your Arduino or Wiring module (you'll have to inspect the board to determine this). It will be either ATmega8 or ATmega168. Make the appropriate choice from the Tools→Microcontroller (MCU) menu.

NOTE: On Windows, COM1–COM4 are generally reserved for built-in serial ports, whether or not your computer has them.

Once you've selected the port and model, click Verify to compile your code. When it's compiled, you'll get a message at the bottom of the window saying Done compiling. Then press the reset button on the module

to reset it and prepare it to accept a new program. Then click Upload. This will take several seconds. Once it's done, you'll get a message saying Done uploading, and a confirmation message in the serial monitor window that says:

Atmel AVR ATmega168 is found.
Uploading: flash

NOTE: If your Arduino uses an ATmega8, it will report that instead. You must make sure that you have configured the Arduino to use the model of ATmega microcontroller on your board.

Press the reset button on the module again, and after about five seconds, the LED you wired to the output pin will begin to blink. That's the microcontroller equivalent of "Hello World!" (If you're using an Arduino Diecimila or later model, you won't have to press the reset button when you upload.)

NOTE: If it doesn't work, you might want to seek out some external help. The Arduino (www.arduino.cc/cgi-bin/yabb2/YaBB.pl) and Wiring (wiring.org.co/cgi-bin/yabb/YaBB.pl) forums are full of helpful people who love to hack these sort of things.

Serial Communication

One of the most frequent tasks you'll use a microcontroller for in this book is to communicate serially with another device, either to send sensor readings over a network or to receive commands to control motors, lights, or other outputs from the microcontroller. Regardless of what device you're communicating with, the commands you'll use in your microcontroller program will be the same. First you'll configure the serial connection for the right data rate. Then you'll read bytes in, write bytes out, or both, depending on what device you're talking to, and how the conversation is structured.

NOTE: If you've got experience with the Basic Stamp or PicBasic Pro, you will find Arduino serial communications a bit different than what you are used to. In PBasic and PicBasic Pro, the serial pins and the data rate are defined each time you send a message. In Wiring and Arduino, the serial pins are unchangeable, and the data rate is set at the beginning of the program. This way is a bit less flexible than the PBasic way, but there are some advantages, as you'll see shortly.

Where's My Serial Port?

The USB serial port that's associated with the Arduino or Wiring module is actually a software driver that loads every time you plug in the module. When you unplug, the serial driver deactivates and the serial port will disappear from the list of available ports. You might also notice that the port name changes when you unplug and plug in the module. On Windows machines, you may get a new COM number. On Macs, you'll get a different alphanumeric code at the end of the port name.

Never unplug a USB serial device when you've got its serial port open; you must exit the Wiring or Arduino software environment before you unplug anything. Otherwise, you're sure to crash the application, and possibly the whole operating system, depending on how well-behaved the software driver is.

Try It

This next Arduino/Wiring program listens for incoming serial data. It adds one to whatever serial value it receives, and sends the result back out. It also blinks an LED on pin regularly, on the same pin as the last example, to let you know that it's still working:

```
/*
    Simple Serial
    Language: Arduino/Wiring
    Listens for an incoming serial byte, adds one to the byte
    and sends the result back out serially.
    Also blinks an LED on pin 13 every half second.
 */

int LEDPin = 13;            // you can use any digital I/O pin you want
int inByte = 0;             // variable to hold incoming serial data
long blinkTimer = 0;        // keeps track of how long since the LED
                            // was last turned off
int blinkInterval = 1000;   // a full second from on to off to on again

void setup() {
  pinMode(LEDPin, OUTPUT);  // set pin 13 to be an output
  Serial.begin(9600);       // configure the serial port for 9600 bps
                            // data rate.
}

void loop() {
  // if there are any incoming serial bytes available to read:
  if (Serial.available() > 0) {
    // then read the first available byte:
    inByte = Serial.read();
    // and add one to it, then send the result out:
```

»

Continued from previous page.

```
    Serial.print(inByte+1, BYTE);
  }


  // Meanwhile, keep blinking the LED.
  // after a quarter of a second, turn the LED on:
  if (millis() - blinkTimer >= blinkInterval / 2) {
    digitalWrite(LEDPin, HIGH);      // turn the LED on pin 13 on
  }
  // after a half a second, turn the LED off and reset the timer:
  if (millis() - blinkTimer >= blinkInterval) {
    digitalWrite(LEDPin, LOW);       // turn the LED off
    blinkTimer = millis();           // reset the timer
  }
}
```

To send bytes from the computer to the micro-controller module, first compile and upload this program. Then click the Serial Monitor icon (the rightmost icon on the toolbar). The screen will change to look like Figure 1-14. Set the serial rate to 9600 baud.

Type any letter in the text entry box and press Enter or click Send. The module will respond with the next letter in sequence. For every character you type, the module adds one to that character's ASCII value, and sends back the result. Terminal applications represent all bytes they receive as ASCII.

Wiring Components to the Module

The Arduino and Wiring modules don't have many sockets for connections other than the I/O pins, so you'll need to keep a solderless breadboard handy to build subcircuits for your sensors and actuators (output devices). Figure 1-15 shows a standard setup for connections between the two.

Specialty Devices

You'll encounter some specialty devices as well, such as the Lantronix Xport, WiPort, and Cobox Micro. The Lantronix modules are serial-to-Ethernet modules. Their main function is to connect devices with a serial communications interface (such as all microcontrollers) to Ethernet networks. It's possible to program your own serial-to-Ethernet module directly on a microcontroller with a few spare parts, but it's a lot of work. The Lantronix modules cost more, but they're much more convenient. You'll also encounter serial-to-Bluetooth modules, serial-to-ZigBee

modules, RFID modules, and other microcontrollers whose main job is to connect other devices. The details on connecting these will be explained one by one as you encounter them in the projects that follow.

Basic Circuits

There are two basic circuits that you'll use a lot in this book: digital input and analog input. If you're familiar with microcontroller development, you're already familiar with them. Any time you need to read a sensor value, you can start with one of these two. Even if you're using a custom sensor in your final object, you can use these circuits as placeholders, just to see any changing sensor values.

Digital input

A digital input to a microcontroller is nothing more than a switch. The switch is connected to voltage and to a digital input pin of the microcontroller. A high-value resistor (10 kilohms is good) connects the input pin to ground. This is called a pull-down resistor. Other electronics tutorials may connect the switch to ground and the resistor to voltage. In that case, you'd call the resistor a pull-up resistor. Pull-up and pull-down resistors provide a reference to power (pull-up) and ground (pull-down) for digital input pins. When a switch is wired as shown in Figure 1-16, closing the switch sets the input pin high. Wired the other way: closing the switch sets the input pin low.

The circuit in Figure 1-17 is called a voltage divider. The variable resistor and the fixed resistor divide the voltage between them. The ratio of the resistors' values deter-

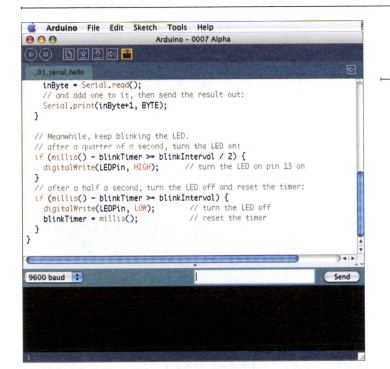

```
  inByte = Serial.read();
  // and add one to it, then send the result out:
  Serial.print(inByte+1, BYTE);
}

// Meanwhile, keep blinking the LED.
// after a quarter of a second, turn the LED on:
if (millis() - blinkTimer >= blinkInterval / 2) {
  digitalWrite(LEDPin, HIGH);      // turn the LED on pin 13 on
}
// after a half a second, turn the LED off and reset the timer:
if (millis() - blinkTimer >= blinkInterval) {
  digitalWrite(LEDPin, LOW);       // turn the LED off
  blinkTimer = millis();           // reset the timer
  }
}
```

◀◀ Figure 1-14
The Serial monitor in Arduino.

⯆ Figure 1-15
Arduino connected to a breadboard. +5V and ground run from the module to the long rows of the board. This way, all sensors and actuators can share the +5V and ground connections of the board. Control or signal connections from each sensor or actuator run to the appropriate I/O pins. In this example, two pushbuttons are attached to digital pins 2 and 3 as digital inputs.

mines the voltage at the connection between them. If you connect the analog-to-digital converter of a microcontroller to this point, you'll see a changing voltage as the variable resistor changes. You can use any kind of variable resistor: photocells, thermistors, force-sensing resistors, flex-sensing resistors, and more.

The potentiometer, shown in Figure 1-18, is a special type of variable resistor. It's a fixed resistor with a wiper that slides along the conductive surface of the resistor. The resistance changes between the wiper and both ends of the resistor as you move the wiper. Basically, a potentiometer (pot for short) is two variable resistors in one package. If you connect the ends to voltage and ground, you can read a changing voltage at the wiper.

Most of the circuits in this book will be shown on a breadboard. By default, the two side rows on each side of the board will be used for power and ground lines, typically +5V for power. On most of the boards, you'll notice wires connecting each of the side rows to two of the top rows. For some projects, the board will be powered from a Wiring or Arduino module or USB power, so there will be no need for a voltage regulator. For others, you will need one. I use separate wires rather than connecting from one side to the other directly, so that when I need a voltage regulator, it can be added easily. Figure 1-19 shows a board with and without a regulator.

There are many other circuits you'll learn in the projects that follow, but these are the staples of all the projects.
X

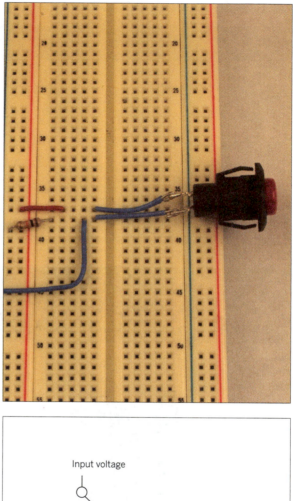

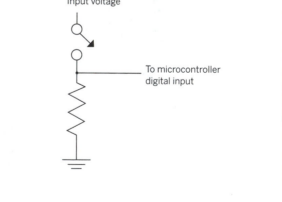

Figure 1-16
Digital input to a microcontroller.

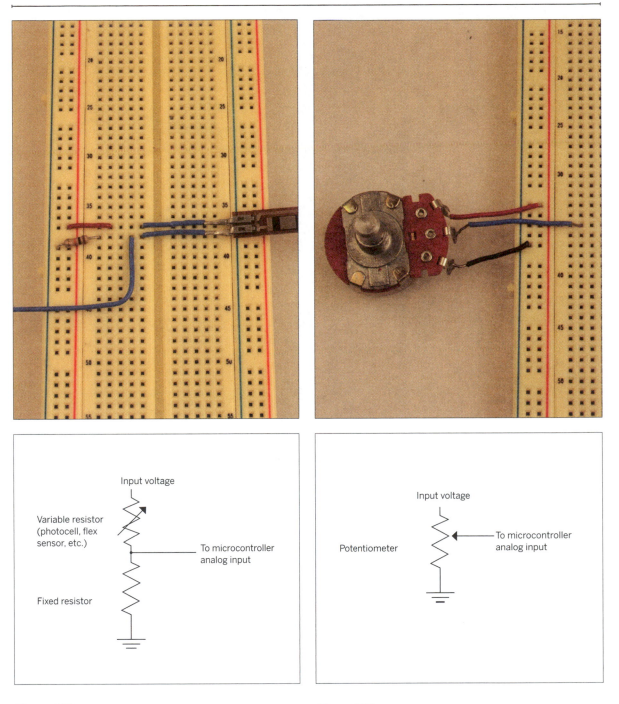

Figure 1-17
Voltage divider used as analog input to a microcontroller.

Figure 1-18
Potentiometer used as analog input to a microcontroller.

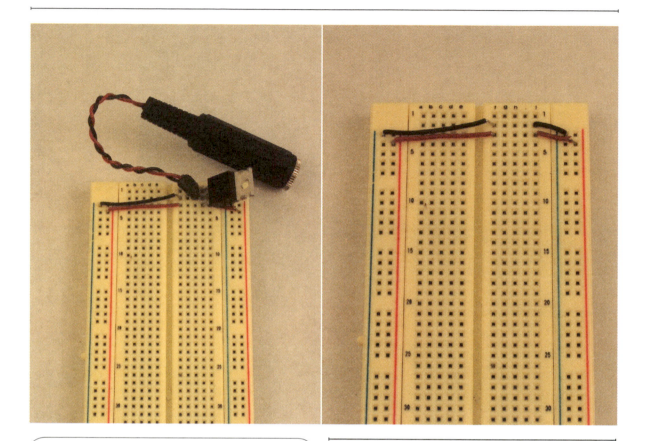

Figure 1-19
Breadboard with a regulator, and without one.

⚠ You will run across different variations on many of the modules and components used in this book. For example, the Arduino module has at least five variations, shown in Figure 1-8. The FTDI USB-to-serial module used in later chapters has at least three variations. Even the voltage regulators used in this book have different variations. Be sure to check the data sheet on whatever component or module you're using, as your version may vary from what is shown here.

❝ It Ends with the Stuff You Touch

Though most of this book is about the fascinating world of making things talk to each other, it's important to remember that you're most likely building your project for the enjoyment of someone who doesn't care about the technical details under the hood.

Even if you're building it only for yourself, you don't want to have to fix it all the time. All that matters to the person using your system are the parts that she can see, hear, and touch. All the inner details are irrelevant if the physical interface doesn't work. So don't spend all of your time focusing on the communication between devices and leave out the communication with people. In fact, it's best to think about the specifics of what the person does and sees first.

There are a number of details that are easy to overlook, but are very important to humans. For example, many network communications can take several seconds or more. In a screen-based operating system, progress bars acknowledge a person's input and keep her informed as to the progress of the task. Physical objects don't have progress bars, but they should incorporate some indicator as to what they're doing — perhaps as simple as an LED that gently pulses while the network transfer's happening, or a tune that plays.

Find your own solution, but make sure you give some physical indication as to the invisible activities of your objects.

Don't forget the basic elements, either. Build in a power switch or a reset button. Don't forget a power indicator. Design the shape of the object so that it's clear which end is up. Make your physical controls clearly visible and easy to operate. Plan the sequence of actions you expect a person to take, and lay out the physical affordances for those actions in a sensible sequence. You can't tell people what to think about your object — you can only show them how to interact with it through its physical form. There may be times when you violate convention in the way you design your controls, perhaps in order to create a challenging game, or to make the object seem more "magical," but make sure you're doing it intentionally. Always think about the participant's expectations first.

By including the person's behavior in your system planning, you solve some problems that are computationally difficult, but easy for human intelligence to solve. Ultimately, the best reason to make things talk to each other is to give people more reasons to talk to each other.
X

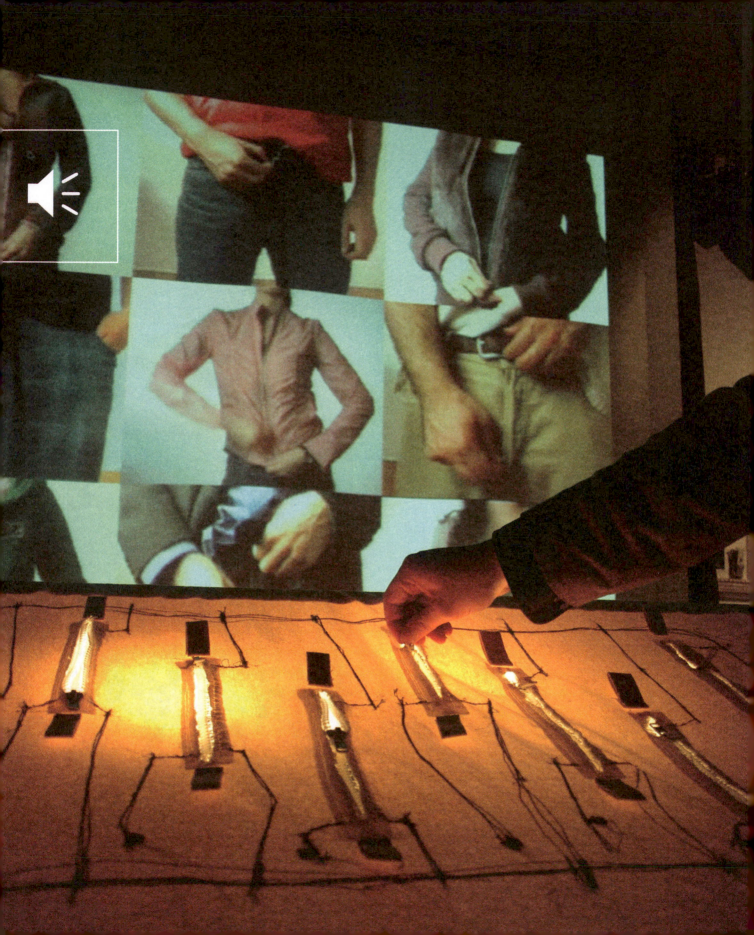

2

The Simplest Network

The most basic network is a one-to-one connection between two objects. This chapter covers the details of two-way communication, beginning with the characteristics that have to be agreed upon in advance. You'll learn about some of the logistical elements of network communications: data protocols, flow control, and addressing. You'll practice all of this by building a simple example: one-to-one serial communication between a microcontroller and a personal computer. Once you've got that working, you'll replace the cable connecting the two with Bluetooth radios and learn about modem communications.

◄◄ **Joo Youn Paek's Zipper Orchestra (2006)** is a musical installation that lets you control video and music using zippers. The zippers are wired to a microcontroller using conductive thread, and the microcontroller communicates serially with a multimedia computer that drives the playback of the zipper movies and sounds as you zip. *Photo courtesy of Joo Youn Paek.*

" Layers of Agreement

Before you can get things to talk to each other, you have to lay some ground rules for the communication between them. These agreements can be broken down into five layers, each of which builds on the previous ones:

• **Physical**
How are the physical inputs and outputs of each device connected to the other? How many connections between the two devices do you need to get messages across?

• **Electrical**
What voltage levels will you send to represent the bits of your data?

• **Logical**
Does an increase in voltage level represent a zero or a one? This is one of the most common sources of problems in the projects that follow.

• **Data**
What's the timing of the bits? Are the bits read in groups of 8, 9, or 10 bits? More? Are there bits at the beginning or end of each group to punctuate the groups?

• **Application**
How are the groups of bits arranged into messages? What is the order in which messages have to be exchanged in order to get something done?

This is a simplified version of a common model for thinking about networking called the Open Systems Interconnect (OSI) model. Networking issues are never really this neatly separated, but if you keep these elements distinct in your mind, troubleshooting any connection will be much easier. Thinking in layers like this gives you somewhere to start looking for the problem, and a way to eliminate parts of the system that are *not* the problem.

No matter how complex the network gets, never forget that the communication between electronic devices is all about pulses of energy. Serial communication involves changing the voltage of an electrical connection between the sender and receiver at a specific rate. Each interval of time represents one bit of information. The sender changes the voltage to send a value of 0 or 1 for the bit in question, and the receiver reads whether the voltage is high or low. There are two methods (see Figure 1-1) that sender and receiver can use to agree on the rate at which bits are sent. In asynchronous serial communication, the rate is agreed upon mutually and clocked independently by sender and receiver. In synchronous serial communication, it's controlled by the sender, who pulses a separate connection high and low at a steady rate. Synchronous serial communication is used mostly for communication between integrated circuits (such as the communication between a computer processor and its memory chips). The rest of this chapter concentrates only on asynchronous serial communication, because that's the form of serial communication underlying the networks in the rest of the book.

X

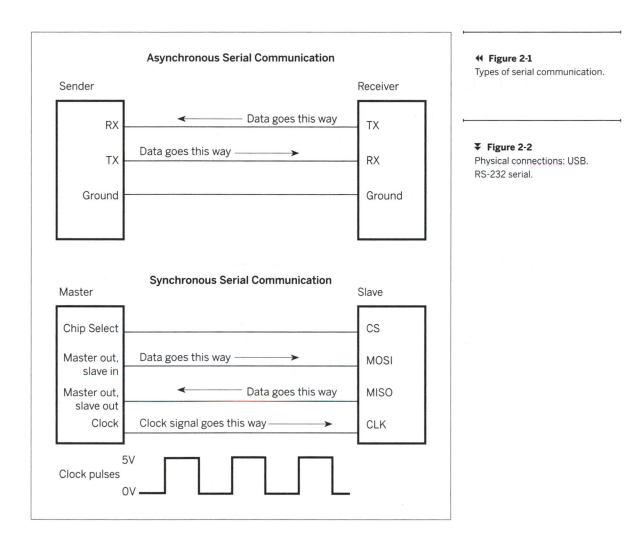

◀◀ **Figure 2-1**
Types of serial communication.

⯯ **Figure 2-2**
Physical connections: USB,
RS-232 serial.

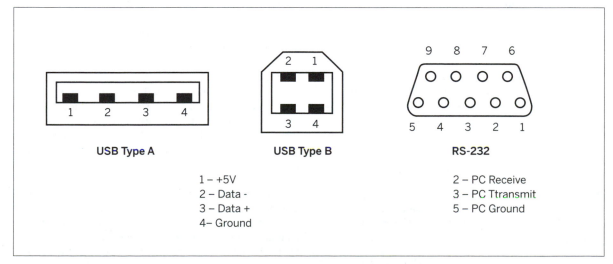

❝ Making the Connection: The Lower Layers

You're already familiar with one example of serial communication, between a microcontroller and a personal computer. In Chapter 1, you connected an Arduino module to a personal computer through the computer's USB port. If you're working with a different microcontroller such as Parallax' Basic Stamp, you probably made the connection using a serial-to-USB converter, or used an older PC that still had a 9-pin serial port. That simple connection involved two serial protocols.

First, there's the protocol that the microcontroller speaks, called TTL serial:

• **Physical layer**
The Arduino module receives data on digital I/O pin 0, and sends it out on pin 1.

• **Electrical layer**
It uses pulses of 5 volts or 0 volts to represent bits.

• **Logical layer**
A 5-volt signal represents the value 1, and a 0-volt signal represents the value 0.

• **Data layer**
Data is sent at 9600 bits per second. Each byte contains 8 bits, preceded by a start bit and followed by a stop bit (which you never have to bother with).

• **Application layer**
At the application layer, you sent one byte from the PC to the Arduino and processed it, and the Arduino sent back one byte to the PC.

But wait, that's not all that's involved. The 5-volt and 0-volt pulses didn't go directly to the PC. First they went to a serial-to-USB chip on the board that communicates using TTL serial on one side, and USB on the other.

Second, there's USB, the Universal Serial Bus protocol. It differs from TTL serial in many ways:

• **Physical layer**
USB sends data on two wires, called Data+ and Data−. Every USB connector also has a 5-volt power supply line and a ground line.

• **Electrical layer**
The signal on Data− is always the polar opposite of what's on Data+, so that the sum of their voltages is always zero. Because of this, a receiver can check for electrical errors by adding the two data voltages together. If the sum isn't zero, the receiver can disregard the signal at that point.

• **Logical layer**
A +5-volt signal (on Data+) or −5-volt signal (on Data−) represents the value 1, and a 0-volt signal represents the value 0.

• **Data Layer**
The data layer of USB is more complex than TTL serial. Data can be sent at up to 480 megabits per second. Each byte contains 8 bits, preceded by a start bit and followed by a stop bit. Many USB devices can share the same pair of wires, sending signals at times dictated by the controlling PC. This arrangement is called a bus (the B in USB). As there can be many devices on the same bus, the operating system gives each one its own unique address, and sees to it that the bytes from each device on the bus go to the applications that need them.

• **Application layer**
At the application layer, the USB-to-serial converter on the Wiring and Arduino boards sends a few bytes to the operating system to identify itself. The operating system then associates the hardware with a library of driver software that other programs can use to access data from the device.

All that control is transparent to you, because the computer's USB controller only passes you the bytes you need. The USB chip on your Arduino board presents itself to the operating system as a serial port, and sends data through the USB connection at the rate you choose (9600 bits per

USB: An Endless Source of Serial Ports

One of the great things about microcontrollers is that because they're cheap, you can use many of them.

For example, in a project with many sensors, you can either write a complex program on the microcontroller to read them all, or you can give each sensor its own microcontroller. If you're trying to get all the information from those sensors into a personal computer, you might think it's easier to use one microcontroller, because you've got a limited number of serial ports. Thanks to USB, however, that's not the case. If your microcontroller speaks USB, or if you've got a USB-to-serial adaptor for it, you can just plug it in and it will show up in the operating system as another serial port.

For example, if you plug three Arduino modules into the same computer through a USB hub, you'll get three new serial ports, named something like this on Mac OS X:

```
/dev/tty.usbserial-5B21
/dev/tty.usbserial-5B22
/dev/tty.usbserial-5B24
```

In Windows, you'd see something like COM8, COM9, COM10.

If you're using a microcontroller that doesn't have its own USB-to-serial converter, you can buy one for about $15 to $40 — Keyspan (www.keyspan.com) and IOGear (www. iogear.com) sell decent models. You can get a USB-to-TTL-serial cable from FTDI for about $20 (part number TTL-232R, also available from Mouser.com), and SparkFun sells a breadboard USB-to-serial module for about $15 (part number BOB-00718). The SparkFun module is shown in a circuit in Figure 2-4. The other converters are self-explanatory.

Like the MAX3323 circuit, this circuit is a handy testing circuit for some of the radio and Ethernet modules you'll see in the chapters that follow that have TTL serial interfaces. In fact, it's the default circuit for interfacing these devices to a computer in this book. If your computer doesn't have USB, you can use the MAX3323 circuit instead. You can also use the MAX3323 circuit in conjunction with the commercially available USB-to-serial adaptors mentioned above.

---

second, in the example in Chapter 1).

One more protocol: if you use a BASIC Stamp or another microcontroller with a non-USB serial interface, you probably have a 9-pin serial connector connecting your microcontroller to your PC, or to a USB-to-serial adaptor. This connector, called a DB-9 or D-sub-9 connector, is a standard connector for another serial protocol, RS-232. RS-232 was the main serial protocol for computer serial connections before USB, and it's still quite common on many computer peripheral devices:

• **Physical layer**
A computer with an RS-232 serial port receives data on pin 2, and sends it out on pin 3. Pin 5 is the ground pin.

• **Electrical layer**
RS-232 sends data at two levels: 5 to 12 volts, and −5 to −12 volts.

• **Logical layer**
A 5 to 12 volt signal represents the value 0, and a −5 to −12 volt signal represents the value 1.

NOTE: Note that this logic is the reverse of TTL serial. It's referred to as inverted logic. Most microcontrollers have the capacity to send serial data using inverted or true logic.

• **Data layer**
This is the same as TTL's, 8 bits per byte with a start and stop bit.

So why is it possible to connect some microcontrollers, like the BASIC Stamp or the BX-24, directly to RS-232 serial ports? It is because the voltage levels of TTL serial, 0 to 5 volts, are just barely enough to register in the higher RS-232 levels, and because you can invert the bits when sending or receiving from the microcontroller. RS-232 doesn't carry any of the addressing overhead of USB, so it's an easier protocol to deal with. Unfortunately, it's becoming obsolete, so USB-to-serial converters are increasingly common tools for microcontroller programmers. Because Wiring and Arduino both have an integrated USB-to-serial converter, you can just plug them into a USB port.

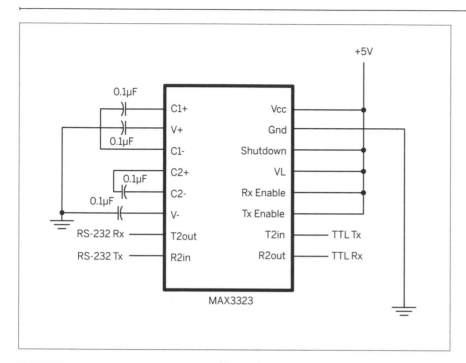

+5V

0.1µF

C1+   Vcc

V+   Gnd

0.1µF

C1-   Shutdown

C2+   VL

0.1µF

C2-   Rx Enable

0.1µF

V-   Tx Enable

RS-232 Rx ——— T2out   T2in ——— TTL Tx

RS-232 Tx ——— R2in   R2out ——— TTL Rx

MAX3323

Figure 2-3
The MAX3323 chip. This circuit is really handy when you need to get any 3.3 to 5-volt TTL device to talk to a personal computer with an RS-232 serial port. This will also work for the MAX232.

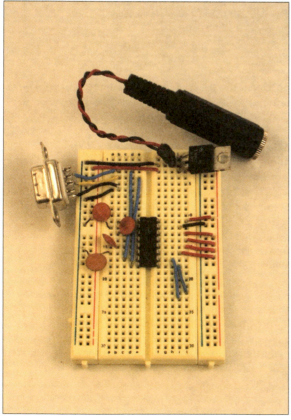

When you're lucky, you never have to think about this kind of protocol mixing, and you can just use converters to do the job for you. You're not always lucky, though, so it's worth knowing a little about what's happening behind the scenes. For example, one of the most common problems in getting a serial device to communicate with a personal computer is converting the device's serial signals to USB or RS-232. A handy chip that does the TTL-to-RS-232 conversion for you is the MAX3323, available from Maxim Technologies (www.maxim-ic.com). It takes in RS-232 serial, and spits out 3.3V to 5-volt TTL serial, and vice versa. If you power it from a 3.3V source, you get 3.3V TTL serial output, and if you power it from 5V, you get 5V TTL serial output. Figure 2-3 shows the typical schematic for a MAX232 and a MAX3323.

If you've done a lot of serial projects, you may know the MAX232, which preceded the MAX3323. In fact, the MAX232 was so common that the name came to be synonymous for all TTL-to-RS-232 converters, whether Maxim made them or not. The MAX232 worked only at 5 volts, but the MAX3323 works at 3.3 to 5 volts. Because 3.3 volts is beginning to replace 5 volts as a standard supply voltage for electronic parts, it's handy to use a chip that can do both.

X

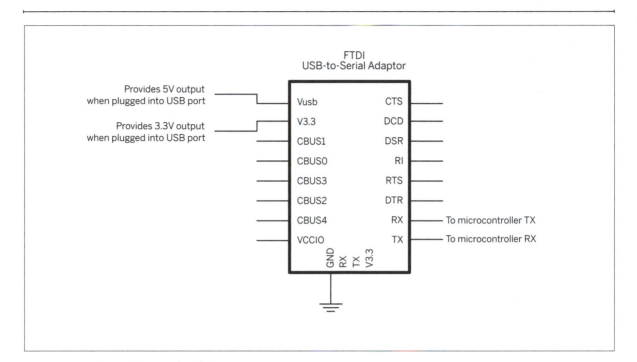

FTDI
USB-to-Serial Adaptor

Provides 5V output when plugged into USB port — Vusb

CTS

Provides 3.3V output when plugged into USB port — V3.3

DCD

CBUS1 — DSR

CBUS0 — RI

CBUS3 — RTS

CBUS2 — DTR

CBUS4 — RX — To microcontroller TX

VCCIO — TX — To microcontroller RX

GND RX TX V3.3

Figure 2-4
SparkFun's FTDI-to-serial module on a breadboard.

❝❝ Saying Something: The Application Layer

Now that you've got a sense of how to make the connections between devices, let's build a couple of projects to understand how to organize the data sent in order to get things done.

🔊 **Project 1**

Monski pong

In this example, you'll make a replacement for a mouse. If you think about the mouse as a data object, it looks like Figure 2-5.

MATERIALS

- » **2 flex sensor resistors** Images SI, Inc, (www. imagesco.com) part number FLX-01, or Jameco (www.jameco.com) part number 150551
- » **2 momentary switches** Available from any electronics retailer. Pick the one that makes you the happiest. Jameco part number 174414 is shown here.
- » **4 10-kilohm resistors** Available at many retailers, for example Digi-Key (www.digikey.com) part number 10K-QBK-ND, and many others.
- » **1 solderless breadboard** For instance, Digi-Key part number 438-1045-ND, Jameco part number 20601
- » **1 Arduino microcontroller module**
- » **1 personal computer**
- » **All necessary converters to communicate serially from microcontroller to computer** For the Arduino and Wiring modules, all you'll need is a USB cable. For other microcontrollers, you'll probably need a USB-to-serial converter and a connector to connect to your breadboard. Whatever you've used in the past for serial communication will work for this project.
- » **1 small pink monkey** aka Monski. You may want a second one for a two-player game.

What the computer does with the mouse's data depends on the application. For this application, you'll make a small pink monkey play pong by waving his arms. He'll also have the capability to reset the game by pressing a button, and to serve the ball by pressing a second button.

Connect long wires to the flex sensors, so that you can sew the sensors into the arms of the monkey without having the microcontroller in his lap. A couple of feet should be fine for testing.

Connect long wires to the buttons as well, and mount them in a piece of scrap foam-core or cardboard until you've decided on a final housing for the electronics. Label the buttons "Reset" and "Serve." Wire the sensors to the microcontroller as shown in Figure 2-6.

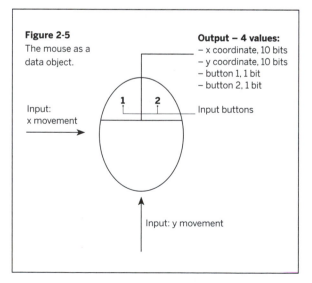

Figure 2-5
The mouse as a data object.

Output – 4 values:
– x coordinate, 10 bits
– y coordinate, 10 bits
– button 1, 1 bit
– button 2, 1 bit

Input buttons

Input: x movement

Input: y movement

Figure 2-6
The Monski pong circuit. Sensors are shown here with short wires so that the image is clear. You should attach longer wires to your sensors, though.

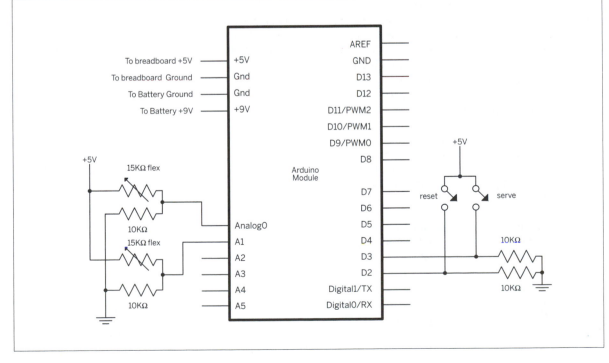

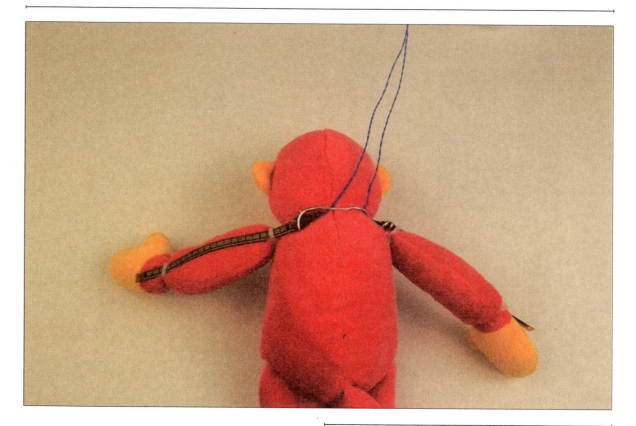

Cut a small slit in each of the monkey's armpits to insert the sensors. If you don't want to damage the monkey, you can use tie-wraps or tape to secure the sensors to the outsides of his arms. The sensors need to be positioned so that their movement is consistent, so you should add some sort of support that keeps them in position relative to each other. A piece of flexible modeling wire will do the job nicely. Make sure that both the sensors are facing the same direction, because flex sensors give different readings when flexed one direction than they do when flexed the other direction. Insulate the connections well, because the foam inside the monkey might generate considerable static electricity when he's moving. Hot glue will do the job nicely.

Make sure that the sensors and electrical connections are stable and secure before you start to work on code. Debugging is much harder if the electrical connections aren't consistent.

X

Figure 2-7
A stable support for the sensors is essential if you want good readings from them. Once you know your support works, move it inside the monkey and test it.

Test It   Now use the following code on the Arduino module to confirm that the sensors are working:

If you open the Serial Monitor in Arduino, or your preferred serial terminal application at 9600 bits per second as you did in Chapter 1, you'll see a stream of results like this:

```
284,284,1,1,
285,283,1,1,
286,284,1,1,
289,283,1,1,
```

⚠️ **Before you go to the next section, where you'll be writing some Processing code to interpret the output of this program, be sure to undo this change.**

```
/*
  Sensor Reader
  Language: Wiring/Arduino

  Reads two analog inputs and two digital inputs and outputs
  their values.

  Connections:
      analog sensors on analog input pins 0 and 1
      switches on digital I/O pins 2 and 3

 */

int leftSensor = 0;     // analog input for the left arm
int rightSensor = 1;    // analog input for the right arm
int resetButton = 2;    // digital input for the reset button
int serveButton = 3;    // digital input for the serve button

int leftValue = 0;      // reading from the left arm
int rightValue = 0;     // reading from the right arm
int reset = 0;          // reading from the reset button
int serve = 0;          // reading from the serve button

void setup() {
  // configure the serial connection:
  Serial.begin(9600);
  // configure the digital inputs:
  pinMode(resetButton, INPUT);
  pinMode(serveButton, INPUT);
}

void loop() {
  // read the analog sensors:
  leftValue = analogRead(leftSensor);
  rightValue = analogRead(rightSensor);

  // read the digital sensors:
  reset = digitalRead(resetButton);
  serve = digitalRead(serveButton);

  // print the results:
  Serial.print(leftValue, DEC);
  Serial.print(",");
  Serial.print(rightValue, DEC);
  Serial.print(",");
  Serial.print(reset, DEC);
  Serial.print(",");
  // print the last sensor value with a println() so that
  // each set of four readings prints on a line by itself:
  Serial.println(serve, DEC);
}
```

▶▶ Just as you programmed it, each value is separated by a comma, and each set of readings is on a line by itself. Try replacing the part of your code that prints the results with this:

When you view the results in the serial monitor or terminal, you'll get something that looks like garbage, like this:

```
// print the results:
Serial.print(leftValue, BYTE);
Serial.print(44, BYTE);
Serial.print(rightValue, BYTE);
Serial.print(44, BYTE);
Serial.print(reset, BYTE);
Serial.print(44, BYTE);
Serial.print(serve, BYTE);
Serial.print(13, BYTE);
Serial.print(10, BYTE);
```

```
.,P,,,
(,F,,,
(,A,,,
),I,,,
```

" What's going on? The original example displays the values of the sensors as their ASCII code numbers, while this modification sends out the raw binary values. The Serial Monitor and the terminal programs assume that every byte they receive is an ASCII character, so they display the ASCII characters corresponding to the raw binary values in the second example. For example, the values 13 and 10 correspond to the ASCII return and newline characters, respectively, and remove the need for the println in the original example. The value 44 corresponds to the ASCII comma character. Those are the bytes you're sending in between the sensor readings in the second example. The sensor variables (leftValue, rightValue, reset, and serve) are the source of the mystery characters. In the third line of the output, when the second sensor's value is 65, you see the character A, because the ASCII character A has the value 65. For a complete list of the ASCII values corresponding to each character, see www.asciitable.com.

Which way should you format your sensor values? As raw binary, or as ASCII? It depends on the capabilities of the system that's receiving the data, and of those that are passing it through. When you're writing software on a personal computer, it's often easier for your software to interpret raw values. However, many of the network protocols you'll use in this book are ASCII-based. In addition, ASCII is readable by humans, so you may find it

What's ASCII?

ASCII is the American Symbolic Code for Information Interchange. It's a scheme that was created in 1967 by the American Standards Association (now ANSI) as a means for all computers, regardless of their operating systems, to be able to exchange text-based messages. In ASCII, each letter, numeral, or punctuation mark in the Roman alphabet is assigned a number. Anything an end user types is then converted to a string of numbers, transmitted, then reconverted on the other end. In addition to letters, numbers, and punctuation marks, certain page-formatting characters, like the linefeed and carriage return (ASCII 10 and 13, respectively) have ASCII values. That way, not only the text of a message, but also the display format of the message, could be transmitted. These are referred to as control characters. They take up first 32 values in the ASCII set (ASCII 0 – 31). All of the numbers, letters, punctuation, and control characters are covered by 128 possible values. ASCII is too limited to display non-English characters, however, and its few control characters don't offer enough control in the age of graphic user interfaces. Unicode, a more comprehensive code that's a superset of ASCII, has replaced ASCII as the standard for text interchange, and markup languages like PostScript and HTML have replaced ASCII's page formatting, but the original code still lingers on.

easier to send the data as ASCII. For Monski pong, use the number-formatted version (the first example), and you'll see why it's the right choice later in the chapter.

So, undo the changes you made to the Sensor Reader program shown earlier, and make sure that it's working as it did originally. Once you've got the microcontroller sending the sensor values consistently to the terminal, it's time to send them to a program where you can use them to display a pong game. This program needs to run on a host computer that's connected to your Wiring or Arduino board. Processing will do this well.

Open the Processing application and enter the following code:

```
/*
Serial String Reader
Language: Processing

reads in a string of characters from a serial port
until it gets a linefeed (ASCII 10).
Then splits the string into sections separated by commas.
Then converts the sections to ints, and prints them out.
*/

import processing.serial.*;     // import the Processing serial library

int linefeed = 10;             // Linefeed in ASCII
Serial myPort;                 // The serial port

void setup() {
  // List all the available serial ports
  println(Serial.list());

  // I know that the first port in the serial list on my mac
  // is always my  Arduino module, so I open Serial.list()[0].
  // Change the 0 to the appropriate number of the serial port
  // that your microcontroller is attached to.
  myPort = new Serial(this, Serial.list()[0], 9600);

  // read bytes into a buffer until you get a linefeed (ASCII 10):
  myPort.bufferUntil(linefeed);
}

void draw() {
  // twiddle your thumbs
}

// serialEvent  method is run automatically by the Processing sketch
// whenever the buffer reaches the byte value set in the bufferUntil()
// method in the setup():

void serialEvent(Serial myPort) {
  // read the serial buffer:
  String myString = myPort.readStringUntil(linefeed);

  // if you got any bytes other than the linefeed:
  if (myString != null) {
```

»

Continued from previous page.

```
myString = trim(myString);

// split the string at the commas
// and convert the sections into integers:
int sensors[] = int(split(myString, ','));
// print out the values you got:
for (int sensorNum = 0; sensorNum < sensors.length; sensorNum++) {
  print("Sensor " + sensorNum + ": " + sensors[sensorNum] + "\t");
}
// add a linefeed after all the sensor values are printed:
println();
  }
}
```

Data Packets, Headers, Payloads, and Tails

Now that you've got data going from one object (the microcontroller attached to the monkey) to another (the computer running Processing), take a closer look at the sequence of bytes you're sending to exchange the data. Generally, it's formatted like this:

Left arm sensor (0–1023)	Right arm sensor (0–1023)	Reset button (0 or 1)	Server button (0 or 1)	Return character, linefeed character
1–4 bytes	1–4 bytes	1 byte	1 byte	2 bytes

Each section of the sequence is separated by a single byte whose value is ASCII 44 (a comma). You've just made your first data protocol. The bytes representing your sensor values and the commas that separate them are the payload, and the return and newline characters are the tail. The commas are the delimiters. This data protocol doesn't have a header, but many do.

A header is a sequence of bytes identifying what's to follow. It might also contain a description of the sequence to follow. On a network, where many possible devices could receive the same message, the header might contain the address of the sender or receiver, or both. That way any device can just read the header to decide whether it needs to read the rest of the message. Sometimes a header is as simple as a single byte of a constant value, identifying the beginning of the message. In this example, the tail performs a similar function, separating one message from the next.

On a network, many messages like this are sent out all the time. Each discrete group of bytes is called a packet, and includes a header, a payload, and usually a tail. Any given network has a maximum packet length. In this example, the packet length is determined by the size of the serial buffer on the personal computer. Processing can handle a buffer of a few thousand bytes, so this 16-byte packet is easy for it to handle. If you had a much longer message, you'd have to divide the message up into several packets, and reassemble them once they all arrived. In that case, the header might contain the packet number, so the receiver knows the order in which the packets should be re-assembled.

▶▶ Make sure that you've shut down the Wiring or Arduino application so that it releases the serial port, then run this Processing application. You should see a list of the sensor values in the message window like this:

```
Sensor 0: 482    Sensor 1: 488    Sensor 2: 1    Sensor 3: 0
Sensor 0: 482    Sensor 1: 488    Sensor 2: 1    Sensor 3: 0
```

▶▶ Next, it's time to use the data to play pong. First, add a few variables at the beginning of the Processing sketch before the setup() method, and change the setup() to set the window size and initialize some of the variables (the new lines are shown in blue):

```
float leftPaddle, rightPaddle;      // variables for the flex sensor values
int resetButton, serveButton;       // variables for the button values
int leftPaddleX, rightPaddleX;      // horizontal positions of the paddles
int paddleHeight = 50;              // vertical dimension of the paddles
int paddleWidth = 10;               // horizontal dimension of the paddles

void setup() {
  // set the window size:
  size(640, 480);

  // List all the available serial ports
  println(Serial.list());

  // Open whatever port you're using.

  myPort = new Serial(this, Serial.list()[0], 9600);

  // read bytes into a buffer until you get a linefeed (ASCII 10):
  myPort.bufferUntil(linefeed);

  // initialize the sensor values:
  leftPaddle = height/2;
  rightPaddle = height/2;
  resetButton = 0;
  serveButton = 0;

  // initialize the horizontal paddle positions:
  leftPaddleX = 50;
  rightPaddleX = width - 50;

  // set no borders on drawn shapes:
  noStroke();
}
```

▶▶ Now replace the serialEvent() method with this version, which puts the serial values into the sensor variables:

```
void serialEvent(Serial myPort) {
  // read the serial buffer:
  String myString = myPort.readStringUntil(linefeed);

  // if you got any bytes other than the linefeed:
  if (myString != null) {
    myString = trim(myString);

    // split the string at the commas
```

»

Continued from previous page.

```
//and convert the sections into integers:
int sensors[] = int(split(myString, ','));

// if you received all the sensor strings, use them:
if (sensors.length == 4) {
  // assign the sensor strings' values to the appropriate variables:
  leftPaddle = sensors[0];
  rightPaddle = sensors[1];
  resetButton = sensors[2];
  serveButton = sensors[3];

  // print out the variables:
  print("left: "+ leftPaddle + "\tright: " + rightPaddle);
  println("\treset: "+ resetButton + "\tserve: " + serveButton);
  }
 }
}
```

▸▸ Finally, put some code into the draw() method to draw the paddles:

```
void draw() {
  background(0);
  // draw the left paddle:
  rect(leftPaddleX, leftPaddle, paddleWidth, paddleHeight);

  // draw the right paddle:
  rect(rightPaddleX, rightPaddle, paddleWidth, paddleHeight);
}
```

“ You may not see the paddles when you first run this code, or until you flex the sensors. You'll need to write a scaling function to scale the range of the sensors to the range of the paddles' vertical motion. For this part, it's important that you have the sensors embedded in the monkey's arms, as you'll be fine-tuning the system, and you want the sensors in the locations where they'll actually get used. Once you're set on the sensors' positions in the monkey, run the Processing program again and watch the left and right sensor numbers as you flex the monkey's arms. Write down of the maximum and minimum values on each arm. To scale the sensors' values to the paddles' movements, use a formula like this:

▸▸
```
paddlePosition = paddleRange * (sensorValue - sensorMinumum) / sensorRange
```

▸▸ Add the maximum and minimum values for your sensors as variables before the setup() method. Change these values to match the actual ones you get when you flex the sensors:

```
float leftMinimum = 250;    // minimum value of the left flex sensor
float rightMinimum = 260;   // minimum value of the right flex sensor
float leftMaximum = 450;    // maximum value of the left flex sensor
float rightMaximum = 460;   // maximum value of the right flex sensor
```

» Then change the serialEvent() method to include the scaling function for the flex sensor variables. You need to modify the if() statement that puts the sensor readings in the paddle variables. Modify the body of the if() statement that appears after the line int sensors[] = int(split(myString, ',')); as shown:

Now the paddles should move from the top of the screen to the bottom as the you wave the monkey's arms.

NOTE: The variables relating to the paddle range in this example are floating-point numbers (floats), because when you divide integers, you get only integer results. 480/400, for example gives 1, not 1.2, when both are integers. Likewise, 400/480 returns 0, not 0.8333. Using integers when you're dividing two numbers that are in the same order of magnitude produces useless results. Beware of this when writing scaling functions.

```
// if you received all the sensor strings, use them:
if (sensors.length == 4) {
  // calculate the flex sensors' ranges:
  float leftRange = leftMaximum - leftMinimum;
  float rightRange = rightMaximum - rightMinimum;

  // scale the flex sensors' results to the paddles' range:
  leftPaddle =  height * (sensors[0] - leftMinimum) / leftRange;
  rightPaddle = height * (sensors[1] - rightMinimum) / rightRange;

  // assign the switches' values to the button variables:
  resetButton = sensors[2];
  serveButton = sensors[3];

  // print the sensor values:
  print("left: "+ leftPaddle + "\tright: " + rightPaddle);
  println("\treset: "+ resetButton + "\tserve: " + serveButton);
}
```

» Finally, it's time to add the ball. The ball will move from left to right diagonally. When it hits the top or bottom of the screen, it will bounce off and change vertical direction. When it reaches the left or right, it will reset to the center. If it touches either of the paddles, it will bounce off and change horizontal direction. To make all that happen, you'll need five new variables at the top of the program, just before the setup() method:

```
int ballSize = 10;      // the size of the ball
int xDirection = 1;     // the ball's horizontal direction.
                        // left is -1, right is 1.
int yDirection = 1;     // the ball's vertical direction.
                        // up is -1, down is 1.
int xPos, yPos;         // the ball's horizontal and vertical positions
```

» In the setup() method, after you set the size of the window (the call to size(640, 480)), you need to give the ball an initial position in the middle of the window:

```
// initialize the ball in the center of the screen:
xPos = width /2;
yPos = height/2;
```

▸▸ Now, add two methods at the end of the program, one called animateBall() and another called resetBall(). You'll call these from the draw() method shortly:

```
void animateBall() {
  // if the ball is moving left:
  if (xDirection < 0) {
    //  if the ball is to the left of the left paddle:
    if  ((xPos <= leftPaddleX)) {
      // if the ball is in between the top and bottom
      // of the left paddle:
      if((leftPaddle - (paddleHeight/2) <= yPos) &&
         (yPos <= leftPaddle + (paddleHeight /2))) {
        // reverse the horizontal direction:
        xDirection =-xDirection;
      }
    }
  }
  // if the ball is moving right:
  else {
    //  if the ball is to the right of the right paddle:
    if  ((xPos >= ( rightPaddleX + ballSize/2))) {
      // if the ball is in between the top and bottom
      // of the right paddle:
      if((rightPaddle - (paddleHeight/2) <=yPos) &&
         (yPos <= rightPaddle + (paddleHeight /2))) {

        // reverse the horizontal direction:
        xDirection =-xDirection;
      }
    }
  }

  // if the ball goes off the screen left:
  if (xPos < 0) {
    resetBall();
  }
  // if the ball goes off the screen right:
  if (xPos > width) {
    resetBall();
  }

  // stop the ball going off the top or the bottom of the screen:
  if ((yPos - ballSize/2 <= 0) || (yPos +ballSize/2 >=height)) {
    // reverse the y direction of the ball:
    yDirection = -yDirection;
  }
    // update the ball position:
    xPos = xPos + xDirection;
    yPos = yPos + yDirection;

  // Draw the ball:
  rect(xPos, yPos, ballSize, ballSize);
}
```

»

Continued from opposite page.

```
void resetBall() {
  // put the ball back in the center
  xPos = width /2;
  yPos = height/2;
}
```

» You're almost ready to set the ball in motion. But first, it's time to do something with the reset and serve buttons. Add another variable at the beginning of the code (just before the setup() method with all the other variable declarations) to keep track of whether the ball is in motion, and two more to keep score:

```
boolean ballInMotion = false;   // whether the ball should be moving
int leftScore = 0;
int rightScore = 0;
```

» Now you're ready to animate the ball. It should move only if it's been served. The following code goes at the end of the draw() method. The first if() statement starts the ball in motion when the serve button is pressed. The second moves it if it's in service, and the third resets the ball to the center and resets the score when the reset button is pressed:

```
// calculate the ball's position and draw it:
if (ballInMotion == true) {
  animateBall();
}

// if the serve button is pressed, start the ball moving:
if (serveButton == 1) {
  ballInMotion = true;
}

// if the reset button is pressed, reset the scores
// and start the ball moving:
if (resetButton == 1) {
  leftScore = 0;
  rightScore = 0;
  ballInMotion = true;
}
```

» Modify the animateBall() method so that when the ball goes off the screen left or right, the appropriate score is incremented (added lines are shown in blue):

```
// if the ball goes off the screen left:
if (xPos < 0) {
  rightScore++;
  resetBall();
}
// if the ball goes off the screen right:
if (xPos > width) {
  leftScore++;
  resetBall();
}
```

Last but not least, add the scoring display. To do this, add two new global variables before the setup() method:

```
PFont myFont;
int fontSize = 36;
```

Then add two lines before the end of the setup() method to initialize the font:

```
// create a font with the third font available to the system:
PFont myFont = createFont(PFont.list()[2], fontSize);
textFont(myFont);
```

Finally, add two lines before the end of the draw() method to display the scores:

```
// print the scores:
text(leftScore, fontSize, fontSize);
text(rightScore, width-fontSize, fontSize);
```

Now you can play Monski pong! For added excitement, get a second pink monkey and put one sensor in each monkey so you can play with a friend.

NOTE: You can find a complete listing for this program in Appendix C.

❝ Flow Control

You may notice that the paddles don't move as smoothly onscreen as Monski's arms move. Sometimes the paddles seem not to move at all for a fraction of a second, and sometimes they seem to lag behind the actions you're taking. This is because the communication between the two devices is asynchronous.

Although they agree on the rate at which data is exchanged, it doesn't mean that the receiving computer's program has to use the bits at the same time as they're sent. Monitoring the incoming bits is actually handled by a dedicated hardware circuit, and the incoming bits are stored in a memory buffer called the serial buffer until the current program is ready to use them. Most personal computers have a buffer that can hold a couple thousand bytes. The program using the bits (Processing, in the previous example) is handling a number of other tasks, like redrawing the screen, handling the math that goes with it, and sharing processor time with other programs through the operating system. It may get bytes from the buffer less than a hundred times a second, even though the bytes are coming in much faster.

There's another way to handle the communication between the two devices that can alleviate this problem. If Processing asks for data only when it needs it, and if the microcontroller only sends one packet of data when it gets a request for data, the two will be in tighter sync.

» To make this happen, first wrap the whole of the loop() method in the **Arduino** program (the Sensor Reader program shown back in the beginning of the "Project #1: Monski pong" section) in an if() statement like this:

Next, add some code to the Monski pong **Processing** program.

```
void loop() {
    // check to see whether there is a byte available
    // to read in the serial buffer:
    if (Serial.available() > 0)   {
        // read the serial buffer;
        // you don't care about the value of
        // the incoming byte, just that one was
        // sent:
        int inByte = Serial.read();
        // the rest of the existing main loop goes here
        // ...
    }
}
```

» First, add a new global variable before the setup() method. This variable will keep track of whether you've received any data from the microcontroller:

```
boolean madeContact = false;      // whether you've made initial contact
                                  // with the microcontroller
```

» At the beginning of the draw() method, add this:

```
// If you haven't gotten any data from the microcontroller yet, send out
// the serial port to ask for data. What value you send doesnt matter,
// since the microcontroller code above isn't doing anything with the
// byte you send. So send a carriage return for debugging purposes:
if (madeContact == false) {
  myPort.write('\r');
}
```

» Finally, change the serialEvent() method. New lines are shown in blue:

```
void serialEvent(Serial myPort) {
    // if serialEvent occurs at all, contact with the microcontroller
    // has been made:
    madeContact = true;
    // read the serial buffer:
    String myString = myPort.readStringUntil(linefeed);

    // if you got any bytes other than the linefeed:
    if (myString != null) {

        myString = trim(myString);
        // split the string at the commas
        // and convert the sections into integers:
        int sensors[] = int(split(myString, ','));
        // if you received all the sensor strings, use them:
        if (sensors.length == 4) {
            // calculate the flex sensors' ranges:
            float leftRange = leftMaximum - leftMinimum;
            float rightRange = rightMaximum - rightMinimum;
```

»

Continued from previous page.

```
    // scale the flex sensors' results to the paddles' range:
    leftPaddle =  height * (sensors[0] - leftMinimum) / leftRange;
    rightPaddle = height * (sensors[1] - rightMinimum) / rightRange;

    // assign the switches' values to the button variables:
    resetButton = sensors[2];
    serveButton = sensors[3];

    // print the sensnor values:
    print("left: "+ leftPaddle + "\tright: " + rightPaddle);
    println("\treset: "+ resetButton + "\tserve: " + serveButton);

    // send out the serial port to ask for data:
    myPort.write('\r');
  }
 }
}
```

"

Now the paddles should move much more smoothly. What's happening now is this: the microcontroller is programmed to check to see whether it's received any bytes serially. If it has, it reads the byte just to clear the buffer, then sends out its data. Whenever it gets no bytes, it sends no bytes. Processing, meanwhile, starts its program by sending a byte out. This triggers the microcontroller to send an initial set of data. Processing reads this data in the serial event() method; then, when it's got all the data, it sends another byte to request more data. The microcontroller, seeing a new byte coming in, sends out another packet of data, and the whole cycle repeats itself. Neither program has more data from the other than it can deal with at any given moment. The slight delay it introduces is not noticeable in the display. In fact, it's less of a delay than the previous program had. Notice that the value of the byte sent is irrelevant. It's used only as a signal from the Processing code to let the microcontroller know when it's ready for new data. This method of handling data flow control is sometimes referred to as a handshake method, or call-and-response. Whenever you're sending packets of data, call-and-response flow control can be a useful way to ensure consistent exchange.
X

Project 2

Wireless Monski pong

Monski pong is fun, but it'd be more fun if Monski didn't have to be tethered to the computer through a USB cable. This project breaks the wired connection between the microcontroller and the personal computer, and introduces a few new networking concepts: the modem and the address.

MATERIALS

» **1 completed Monski pong project** from earlier
» **1 9V battery and battery snap connector** SparkFun (www.sparkfun.com) part number PRT-00091, or Digi-Key (www.digikey.com) part number 2238K-ND
» **1 BlueSMiRF Bluetooth modem module** from SparkFun (part WRL-00582)
» **1 project box** to house the microcontroller, battery, and radio board

---

NOTE: If your personal computer doesn't have a built-in Bluetooth radio, you'll also need a Bluetooth adaptor for it. The Bluetooth v.1.2 USB module that SparkFun carries will work fine, and most computer stores carry USB Bluetooth adaptors.

Bluetooth: A Multilayer Network Protocol

The new piece of hardware in this project is the Bluetooth module. This module has two interfaces: two of its pins, marked RX and TX, are an asynchronous serial port that can communicate with a microcontroller. It also has a radio that communicates using the Bluetooth communications protocol. It acts as a modem, translating between the Bluetooth and regular asynchronous serial protocols.

NOTE: The first digital modems were devices that took data signals and converted them to audio signals to send them across a voice telephone connection. They modulated the data on the audio connection, and demodulated the audio signal back into a data signal. These simple serial-to-audio modems are becoming increasingly rare, but their descendants are everywhere, from the

set-top boxes that modulate and demodulate your Internet connection from the cable television data signal to the sonar modems that convert data into ultrasonic pings to be sent from ships to submarine exploration robots used in marine research.

Bluetooth is a multilayered communications protocol, designed to replace wired connections for a number of applications. As such, it's divided into a group of possible applications protocols called profiles. The simplest Bluetooth devices are serial devices like the module used in this project. These implement the Bluetooth Serial Port Profile (SPP). Other Bluetooth devices implement other protocols. Wireless headsets implement the audio Headset Profile. Wireless mice and keyboards implement the Human Interface Device (HID) Profile. Because there are a number of possible profiles a Bluetooth device might support, there is also a Service Discovery Protocol, via which radios exchange information about what they can do. Because the protocol is standardized, you get to skip over most of the details of making and maintaining the connection so you can concentrate on exchanging data. It's a bit like how RS-232 and USB made it possible for you to ignore most of the electrical details necessary to connect your microcontroller to your personal computer, so you could focus on sending bytes in the last project.

Add the Bluetooth module to the Monski pong breadboard as shown in Figure 2-8. Connect the module's ground to the ground on the Arduino module, and its input pin to the 5-volt output from the module. Move the power jumper on the Arduino module so that it's closest to the DC power jack. Then connect the battery's black wire to the module's ground, and its red wire to the +9V power pin. The module will start up, and the Bluetooth radio's green LED will blink.

Pairing Your Computer with the Bluetooth Module

To make a wireless connection from your computer to the module, you have to pair the two of them. To do this, open your computer's Bluetooth control panel to browse for new devices. In Mac OS X, choose the Apple menu→System Preferences, then click Bluetooth. In the Settings tab, make sure Bluetooth is turned on, and check Discoverable and Show Bluetooth Status in Menu Bar. In the Devices tab, click Set Up New Device to launch the Bluetooth Setup Assistant. When you have to choose a device type,

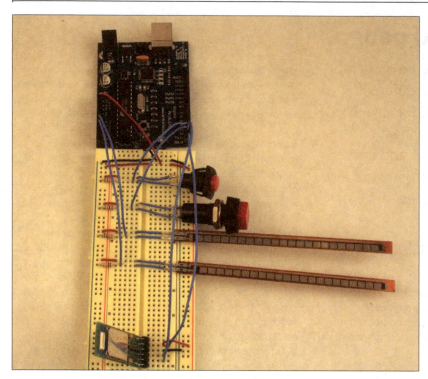

Figure 2-8
Monski pong board, with Bluetooth module added. Be sure to switch the power jumper to the DC power jack side. Once you've built the circuit for this, drill holes in the project box for the buttons and the wires leading to the flex sensors. Mount the breadboard, Arduino module, and battery in the project box.

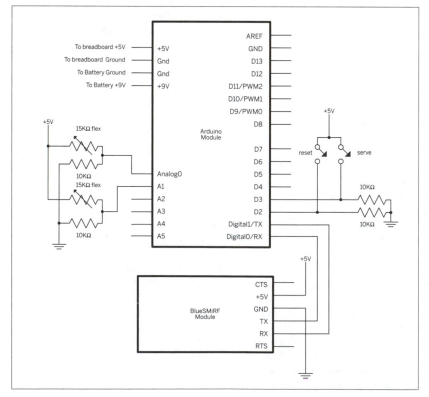

Finishing Touches: Tidy it up, box it up

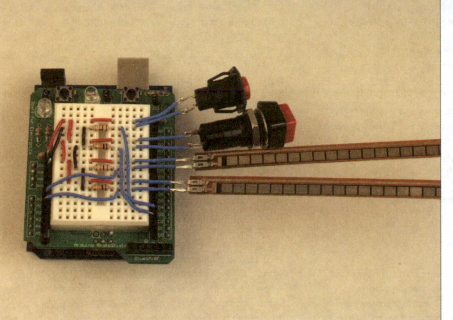

◀◀ **Make it small**
You might want to shrink Monski pong down so it's more compact. This figure shows the Monski pong circuit on a breadboard shield. This is the same circuit as the one in Figure 2-6, just on a different breadboard so it can fit in a project box.

⩢ **All boxed up**
Kitchen storage containers make excellent project boxes. Here's the Monski pong controller with Monski attached.

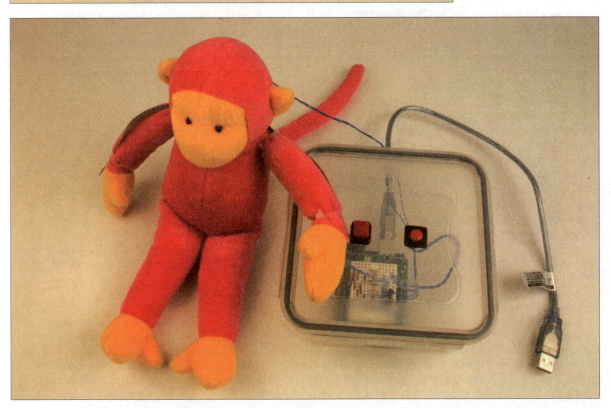

choose Any Device. The computer will search for devices, and will find one called BlueRadios-COM0-1. If you have no other Bluetooth devices nearby, it will be the only one. Choose this device, and when asked for a passkey, enter default. A connection will be established, and you'll be told that there are no selected services on this device. That's okay. Continue until you can quit the Assistant.

> ⚠️ **Mac OS X users: If you're using a version of Mac OS X before version 10.4, you can only enter numeric passkeys. You'll need to change the module's passkey first. To do this, connect the TX and RX pins to a serial port on the computer. See the next project in this chapter for the details on connecting the Bluetooth module to the serial port. Once you're connected, send the following string to the module to change the password:**
>
> ```
>     ATSP,0000,default,\r
> ```
>
> **Replace the 0000 with your own numeric password, and press Enter in place of \r. (In this book, \r denotes a carriage return, or ASCII value 13, and \n denotes a newline character, or ASCII value 10). Then reset the module by unplugging it and plugging it back in. Now you can follow the previous instructions to make a pairing between your computer and the Bluetooth module. Once you've done that, reconnect the Bluetooth module to the Monski pong project as shown above.**

In Windows, the process differs, depending on the Bluetooth radio you have installed. There are several different Bluetooth radios available for Windows machines, and each one has a slightly different user interface. XP Service Pack 2 introduced a unified configuration interface for Bluetooth, but some older radios still use the vendor-specific configuration tools. The user manual for your specific radio will cover the details you need, but the process will be something like this:

Right-click the Bluetooth Icon in the lower righthand corner of the taskbar (this area is called the system tray or notification area) to access the Bluetooth settings. Check the device or security properties to make sure that your computer's Bluetooth device is discoverable, connectable, and pairable. Check the service properties to make sure that Bluetooth COM port service is enabled. Then add a new Bluetooth device. When you get the option to search for new devices, do so, and you should see the BlueSMiRF (with a name such as BlueRadios COM) device show up in

the list of available devices. If you have no other Bluetooth devices nearby, it will be the only one. When prompted for a password, enter default. This step will add a new serial port to your list of serial ports. Make note of the port name (mine is COM40), so you can use it later.

Adjusting the Monski pong Program

Once your computer has made contact with the Bluetooth module, you can connect to it like a serial port. Run the Monski pong Processing sketch and check the list of serial ports. You should see the new port listed along with the others. Take note of which number it is, and change this line in the setup() method:

```
myPort = new Serial(this, Serial.list()[0], 9600);
```

For example, if the Bluetooth port is the ninth port in your list, change the line to open Serial.list[8]. With no other changes in code, you should now be able to connect wirelessly. Monski is free to roam around the room as you play pong When the Processing program makes a connection to the Bluetooth module, the green LED on the module will turn off and the red one will come on.

> ⚠️ **If you plug or unplug any serial devices after you do this, including the Arduino, you'll need to quit and restart the Processing program, as the count of serial ports will have changed.**

If you haven't modified your Arduino and Processing code to match the call-and-response version of the Monski pong program shown in the "Flow Control" section earlier, you might have a problem making a connection to the radio. If so, the green LED will stay on and not flash. What's happening is that the microcontroller module is sending serial data constantly, and the Bluetooth module's serial buffer is filling up. When a wireless connection is made, the Bluetooth module sends a string out on the TX pin with the address of the device that made the connection, like so:

```
CONNECT,000D93039D96
```

Because this line always ends with a carriage return, you can listen for that in your microcontroller code by using the call-and-response method described earlier, so make those modifications before going any further. Now the program will do nothing until it sees an initial carriage return; then it will send data continually.

Project 3

Negotiating in Bluetooth

The steps you went through with the Bluetooth Assistant or Bluetooth Wizard negotiated a series of exchanges between your computer and the BlueSMiRF module that included discovering other radios, learning the services offered by those radios, and pairing to open a connection. It's very convenient to be able to do this from the graphical user interface, but it'd be even better if the devices could negotiate this exchange themselves. In the section that follows, you'll negotiate some parts of that exchange directly, in order to understand how to program devices that can do that negotiation.

MATERIALS

» **1 BlueSMiRF basic module** from SparkFun (part WRL-00582)
» **1 USB-to-serial converter** The SparkFun BOB-00718 is shown next, but you can also use the MAX3323 and USB-to-RS-232 converter version as shown earlier.
» **1 solderless breadboard**

Wire the Bluetooth module to the USB-to-serial converter as shown in Figure 2-9. The USB-to-serial converter converts the TTL serial signals from the BlueSMiRF module to USB. Connect the converter to a USB port on your computer and open your serial terminal program. open a connection to the USB-to-serial converter's serial port at 9600 bits per second.

Modems are designed to open a connection to another modem, negotiate the terms of data exchange, carry on an exchange, then disconnect. To do this, they have to have two operating modes, usually referred to as command mode, in which you talk to the modem, and data mode,

in which you talk *through* the modem. Bluetooth modems are no different in this respect. Most Bluetooth modems use a set of commands based on the original commands designed for telephone modems, known as the Hayes AT command protocol. All commands in the Hayes command protocol (and therefore in Bluetooth command protocols as well) are sent using ASCII characters. There's a common structure to all the AT commands. Each command sent from the controlling device (like a microcontroller or personal computer) to the modem begins with the ASCII string AT followed by a short string of letters and numbers representing the command, followed by any parameters of the command, separated by commas. The command ends with an ASCII carriage return. For example, here's the string to ask the BlueRadios module inside of the BlueSMiRF module for its firmware version:

```
ATVER,ver1\r
```

The \r is a carriage return. Hit the Return key whenever you see it here. Type it into the serial terminal program now. The BlueRadios module should respond with something like this:

```
Ver 3.4.1.2.0
```

Any time you want to just check that the module is working, type AT\r. It will respond with OK. There's a list of all the commands available for this module available from www.sparkfun.com or from www.blueradios.com. A few of them are covered here. Each Bluetooth modem manufacturer has its own set of AT commands, and unfortunately they're all different. But they are all based on the AT command protocol, so they'll all have the same basic format as the one you see here.

Currently, the module is in command mode. One of the first things you'd like it to do is to give you a list of other Bluetooth-enabled devices in the area. If you've got more devices than just your laptop around, take a rough guess of how many, and type this sequence of commands:

```
ATUCL\r
```

This clears any current commands, and puts the module in idle mode. The module will return OK. Then type:

```
ATDI,3,00000000\r
```

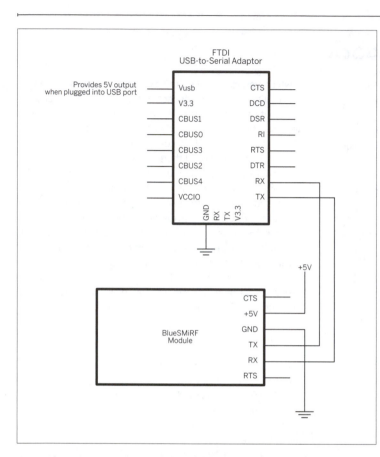

Figure 2-9
BlueSMiRF module connected to a FT232RL
USB-to-serial converter.

ATDI tells it to look for other radios. 3 tells it to look until it finds three others. 00000000 tells it to look for any type of Bluetooth radio (phone, headset, serial device, etc). After several seconds, it will come back with a list like this:

```
00038968505F,00200404
000D93039D96,0010210C
00119FC2AD3C,0050020C
DONE
```

This is a list of all the other Bluetooth devices it found. The first part of every string is the device's unique address. That's the part you need in order to make a connection to it. Manufacturers of Bluetooth devices agree on a standard addressing scheme so no two devices get the same address. The second part is the device class (what type of device it is), and the third, when there is one, the device's name. Names don't have to be unique, but addresses do, which is why you always use the address to connect.

Now that you've got a list of connections, try to connect to the one that represents your computer, like so:

```
ATDM,address,1101\r
```

ATDM tells the module to attempt to connect. The address tells it what device to connect to, and 1101 tells it what profile to use; in this case, the serial port profile. The BlueSMiRF should respond:

```
NO ANSWER
```

Next you need to open the serial port on your computer that's connected to its Bluetooth radio. In **Mac OS X**, it's the Bluetooth PDA-Sync port. Open a second window in your terminal program, and connect to that serial port using GNU Screen, like so:

```
screen /dev/tty.Bluetooth-PDA-Sync 9600
```

For **Windows** users, the COM port varies depending on your Bluetooth device, but if you check the Device Manager's list of serial ports, you'll see several associated with the Bluetooth radio. Use the lowest numbered one that will open in PuTTY (most of them will refuse to open). That should be the port that your radio can connect to.

If you're using the standard Windows Bluetooth interface, right-click the Bluetooth icon in the system tray and choose Device Properties and Security. Make sure your radio is discoverable, connectable, and pairable.

Go back to the window with the serial connection to the BlueSMiRF, and send the following command:

```
ATPAIR,address\r
```

where address is the Bluetooth address of your computer that you discovered earlier using ATDI.

The computer will ask you for a passkey. Enter default. The BlueSMiRF should reply:

```
PAIRED,address
```

Once you're paired, you need to connect, using the following AT command:

```
ATDM,address,1101\r
```

When you get a good connection to the BlueSMiRF, the LED on it will turn red, and you'll get a message like this:

```
CONNECT,000D93039D96
```

You're now out of command mode and into data mode. You should be able to type directly from one window to the other.

NOTE: You can't initiate a connection from the BlueSMiRF to the computer unless you've already paired with the BlueSMiRF from the computer previously. This is so because BlueSMiRF radios can't initiate a serial connection unless they've already made a pairing with the other device. You'll see more on these radios in Chapter 6.

To get out of data mode (to check the modem's status, for example), type:

```
+++\r
```

This will give you an OK prompt again. You can type any of the AT commands you want now, and get replies. To return to data mode, type:

```
ATMD\r
```

Finally, when you're in command mode, you can type ATDH\r to disconnect, and you'll get this reply:

```
NO CARRIER
```

That means you're disconnected. If you want to connect to another device, start by putting the module back in idle mode with `ATUCL\r` and following the same steps as previously.

Because the AT commands are just text strings, you can easily use them in microcontroller programs to control the module, make and break connections, and exchange data.

Because all the commands are in ASCII, it's a good idea to exchange data in ASCII mode, too. So the data string that you set up earlier to send Monski's sensor readings in ASCII would work well over this modem.

X

❝ Conclusion

The projects in this chapter have covered a number of ideas that are central to all networked data communication. First, keep in mind that data communication is based on a layered series of agreements, starting with the physical layer, then the electrical, the logical, the data, and finally the application layer. Keep these layers in mind as you design and troubleshoot your projects and you'll find it easier to isolate problems

Second, remember that serial data can be sent either as ASCII or as raw binary values, and which you choose to use depends both on the capabilities and limitations of the devices you're connecting, and on all the devices in the middle that connect them. It might not be wise to send raw binary data, for example, if the modems or the software environments you program in are optimized for ASCII data transfer.

Third, when you think about your project, think about the messages that need to be exchanged, and come up with a data protocol that adequately describes all the information you need to send. This is your data packet. You might want to add header bytes, separators, or tail bytes to make reading the sequence easier.

Fourth, think about the flow of data, and look for any ways you can ensure a smooth flow with as little overflowing of buffers or waiting for data as possible. A simple call-and-response approach can make data flow much smoother.

Finally, get to know the modems and other devices that link the objects at the end of your connection. Make sure you understand their addressing schemes and any command protocols they use so that you can factor their strengths and limitations into your planning, and eliminate those parts that make your life more difficult. Whether you're connecting two objects or two hundred, these same principles will apply.

X

▸▸ **The JitterBox by Gabriel Barcia-Colombo**

The JitterBox is an interactive video Jukebox created from a vintage 1940's radio restored to working condition. It features a tiny video-projected dancer who shakes and shimmies in time with the music. The viewer can tune the radio and the dancer will move in time with the tunes. The JitterBox uses serial communication from an embedded potentiometer tuner which is connected to an Arduino microcontroller in order to select from a range of vintage 1940's songs. These songs are linked to video clips and played back out of a digital projector. The dancer trapped in the JitterBox is Ryan Myers.

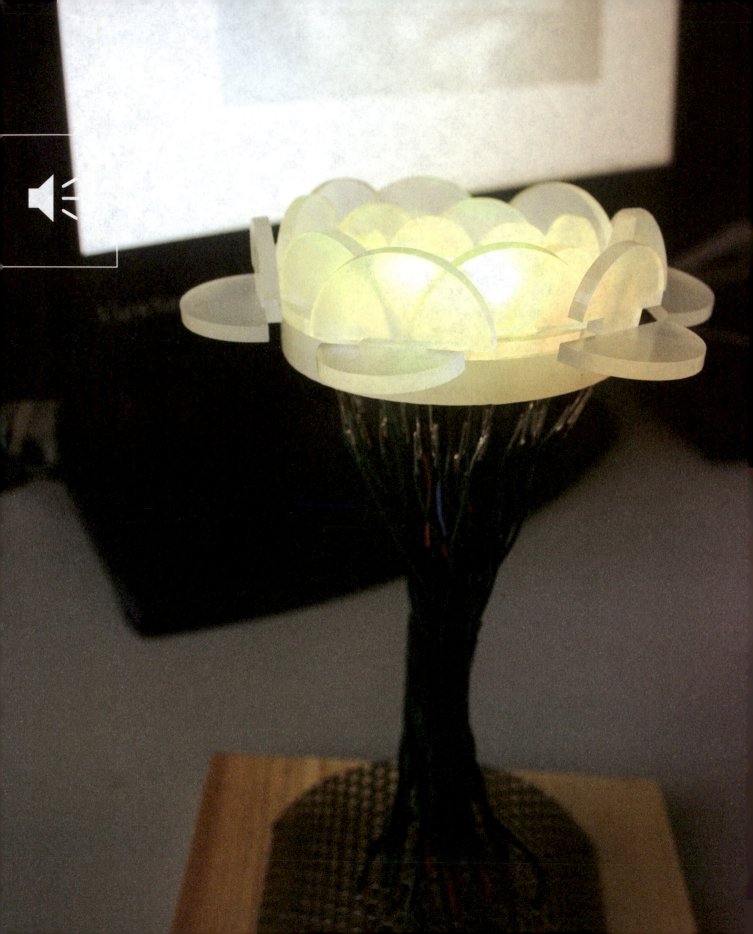

3

A More Complex Network

Now that you've got the basics of network communications, it's time to tackle something more complex. The best place to start is with the most familiar data network: the Internet. It's not actually a single network, but a collection of networks all owned by different network service providers and linked using some common protocols. This chapter describes the structure of the Internet, the devices that hold it together, and the shared protocols that make it possible. You'll get hands-on experience with what's going on behind the scenes when your web browser or email client is doing its job, and you'll use the same messages those tools use to connect your own objects to the Net.

◀◀ **Networked Flowers by Doria Fan, Mauricio Melo, and Jason Kaufman.**
Networked Flowers is a personal communication device for sending someone digital blooms. Each bloom has a different lighting animation. The flower sculpture has a network connection. The flower is controlled from a website that sends commands to the flower when the web visitor chooses a lighting animation.

❝ Network Maps and Addresses

In the last chapter, it was easy to keep track of where messages went, because there were only two points in the network you built: the sender and the receiver. In any network with more than two objects, from three to three billion, you need a map to keep track of which objects are connected to which, and an addressing scheme to know how a message gets to its destination.

Network Maps: How Things Are Connected

The arrangement of physical connections on a network depends on how you want to route the messages on that network. The simplest way is to make a physical connection from each object in the network to every other object. That way, messages can get sent directly from one point to another. The problem with this approach, as you can see from the directly connected network in Figure 3-1, is that the number of connections gets large very fast, and the connections get tangled. A simpler alternative to this is to put a central controller in the middle, and pass all messages through this hub, as seen in the star network. This way works great as long as the hub continues to function, but the more objects you add, the faster the hub has to be to process all the messages. A third alternative is to daisy-chain the objects, connecting them together in a ring. This design makes for a small number of connections, and it means that any message has two possible paths, but it can take a long time for messages to get halfway around the ring to the most distant object.

In practice (such as on the Internet), a multitiered star model like the one shown in Figure 3-2 works best. Each connector (symbolized by a light-colored circle) has a few objects connected to it, and each connector is linked to a more central connector. At the more central tier (the dark-colored circles in Figure 3-2), each connector may be linked to more than one other connector, so that messages can pass from one endpoint to another via several different paths. This system takes advantage of the redundancy of multiple links between central connectors, but avoids the tangle caused by connecting every object to every other object.

If one of the central connectors isn't working, messages are routed around it. The connectors at the edges are the weakest points. If they aren't working, the objects that depend on them have no connection to the network.

⏬ Figure 3-1

Three types of network: direct connections between all elements, a star network, and a ring network.

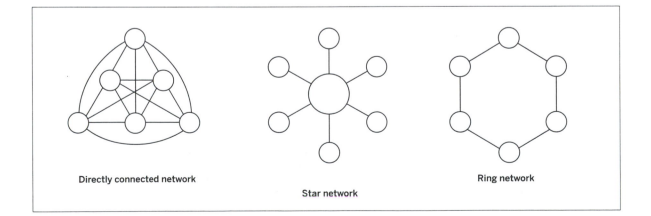

Directly connected network

Star network

Ring network

As long as the number of objects connected to each of these is small, though, the effect on the whole network is minimal. It may not seem minimal when you're using the object whose connector fails, but at least the rest of the network remains stable, so it's easy to reconnect when your connector is working again.

If you're using the Internet as your network, you can take this model for granted. If you're building your own network, however, it's worth comparing all of these models to see which is best for you. In some simpler systems, one of the three networks shown in Figure 3-1 might do the job just fine, and save you some complications. As you get further in the book, you'll see some examples of these, but for the rest of this chapter, you'll work with the multitiered model by relying on the Internet as your infrastructure.

X

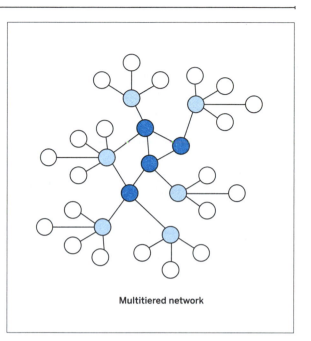

Multitiered network

▸▸ **Figure 3-2**
A complex, multitiered network.

Modems, Hubs, Switches, and Routers

The connectors in Figure 3-2 represent several different types of devices on the Internet. The most common among these are modems, hubs, switches, and routers. Depending on how your network is set up, you may be familiar with one or more of these. There's no need to go into detail as to the differences, but some basic definitions are in order:

A modem is a device that converts one type of signal into another, and connects one object to one other object. Your home cable or DSL modem is an example. It takes the digital data from your home computer or network, converts it to a signal that can be carried across the phone line or cable line, and connects to another modem on the other end of the line. That modem is connected to your Internet service provider's network. By this definition, the Bluetooth radios from Chapter 2 could be considered modems, as they convert electrical signals into radio signals and back.

A hub is a device that multiplexes data signals from several devices and passes them upstream to the rest of the net. It doesn't care about the recipients of the messages it's carrying — it just passes them through in both directions.

All the devices attached to a hub receive all the messages that pass through the hub, and each one is responsible for filtering out any messages that aren't addressed to it. Hubs are cheap and handy, but they don't really manage traffic at all.

A switch is like a hub, but more sophisticated. It keeps track of the addresses of the objects attached to it, and passes on only messages addressed to those objects. Objects attached to a hub don't get to see messages that aren't addressed to them.

Modems, hubs, and switches generally don't actually have their own addresses on the network (though some cable and DSL modems do). A router, on the other hand, is visible to other objects on the network. It has an address of its own, and can mask the objects attached to it from the rest of the net. It can give them private addresses, meaningful only to the other objects attached to the router, and pass on their messages as if they come from the router itself. It can also assign IP addresses to objects that don't have one when they're first connected to the router.

Figure 3-3
Network settings panels for Mac OS X and Windows.

Hardware Addresses and Network Addresses

Whether you're using a simple network model where all the objects are directly connected, a multitiered model, or anything in between, you need an addressing scheme to get messages from one point to another on the network. When you're making your own network from scratch, you have to make up your own addressing scheme. For the projects you're making in this book, however, you're relying on existing network technologies, so you get to use the addressing schemes that come with them. For example, when you used the Bluetooth radios in Chapter 2, you used the Bluetooth protocol addressing scheme. When you connect Internet devices, you use the Internet Protocol (IP) addressing scheme. Because most of the devices you connect to the Internet also rely on a protocol called Ethernet, you also use the Ethernet address protocol. A device's IP address can change when it's moved from one network to another, but its hardware address, or Media Access Control (MAC) address, is burned into the device's memory and doesn't change. It's a unique ID number assigned by the manufacturer that differentiates that device from all the other Ethernet devices on the planet. Wi-fi adapters also have hardware addresses.

You're probably already familiar with your computer's IP address and maybe even its hardware address. In Mac OS X, Click Apple Menu→Location→Network Preferences to open the Network control panel, and you'll get a list of the possible ways your computer can connect to the net. Click on the popup menu labeled Show and you get a list of the network interfaces. It's likely that you have at least a built-in Ethernet interface and an Airport interface. The built-in Ethernet and Airport interfaces both have hardware addresses, and if you choose either interface, you can find out that interface's hardware address. For Airport, it's listed as the Airport ID under the Airport tab, and for the built-in Ethernet, it's called the Ethernet ID under the Ethernet tab. In either interface, click on the TCP/IP tab and you can see the machine's IP address if you're connected to a network.

In Windows, click the Start Menu→Control Panel, then double-click Network Connections. Each network interface has its own icon in this control panel. Click Local Area Connection for your built-in Ethernet connection, or Wireless Network Connection for yourWi-FI connection. Under the Support tab, click Details to see the IP settings and hardware address.

Figure 3-3 shows the network connection settings for Mac OS X and Windows. No matter what platform you're on, the hardware address and the Internet address will take these forms:

The hardware address is made up of six numbers, written in hexadecimal notation, like this: 00:11:24:9b:f3:70

The IP address is made up of four numbers, written in decimal notation, like this: 192.168.1.20

You'll need to know the IP address to send and receive messages, and you'll need to know the hardware address in order to get an IP address on some networks, so make note of both of them for every device you're using whenever you start to work on a new project.

Street, City, State, Country: How IP Addresses Are Structured

Geographic addresses can be broken down into layers of detail, starting with the most specific (the street address) and moving to the most general (the country). Internet addresses are also multilayered. The most specific part is the final number, which tells you the address of the computer itself. The numbers that precede this tell you the subnet that the computer is on. Your router shares the same subnet as your computer, and its number is usually identical except for the last number. The numbers of an IP address are called octets, and each octet is like a section of a geographic address. For example, imagine a machine with this number: 192.168.0.20

The router that this machine is attached to most likely has this address: 192.168.0.1

Each octet can range from 0–255, and some numbers are reserved by convention for special purposes. For example, the router is often the address xxx.xxx.xxx.1. The subnet can be expressed as an address range, 217.123.152.xxx. Sometimes a router manages a larger subnet, or even a group of subnets, each with their own local router. The router that this router is connected to might have the address 192.168.0.1

Each router controls access for a defined number of machines below it. The number of machines it controls is encoded in its subnet mask. You've probably encountered a subnet mask in configuring your personal computer. A typical subnet mask looks like this: 255.255.255.0

You can read the number of machines in the subnet by reading the value of the last octets of the subnet mask. It's easiest if you think of the subnet in terms of bits. Four bytes is 32 bits. Each bit you subtract from the subnet increases the number of machines it can support. Basically, you "subtract" the subnet mask from its maximum value of 255.255.255.255 to get the number of machines. For example, if the subnet were 255.255.255.255, then there could be only one machine in the subnet, the router itself. If the last octet is 0, as it is above, then there can be up to 255 machines in the subnet in addition to the router. A subnet of 255.255.255.192 would support 63 machines and the router (255 – 192 = 64), and so forth. Table 3-1 shows a few other representative values to give you an idea.

Table 3-1. The relationship between subnet mask and maximum number of machines on a network.

Subnet mask	Maximum number of machines on the subnet, including the router
255.255.255.255	1 (just the router)
255.255.255.192	64
255.255.255.0	256
255.255.252.0	1024
255.255.0.0	65,536

Knowing the way IP addresses are constructed helps you to manage the flow of messages you send and receive. Normally, all of this is handled for you by the software you use: browsers, email clients, and so forth. But when you're building your own networked objects, it's necessary to know at least this much about the IP addressing scheme so you can find your router and what's beyond it.

Numbers into Names

By now you're probably thinking that this is ridiculous, because you only know internet addresses by their names, like www.makezine.com, or www.archive.net. You never deal with numerical addresses, nor do you want to. There's a separate protocol, the Domain Name System (DNS), for assigning names to the numbers. Machines on the network called nameservers keep track of which names are assigned to which numbers. In your computer's network configuration, you'll notice a slot where you can enter the DNS address. Most computers are configured to obtain this address from a router using the DHCP protocol (which also provides their IP address), so you don't have

Private and Public IP Addresses

Not every object on the Internet can be addressed by every other object. Sometimes, in order to be able to support more objects, a router hides the addresses of the objects attached to it, and sends all their outgoing messages to the rest of the net as if they came from the router itself. There are special ranges of addresses set aside in the IP addressing scheme for use as private addresses. For example, all addresses in the range 192.168.xxx.xxx are to be used for private addressing only. This address range is in common use in home routers, and if you have one, all the devices on your home network probably show up with addresses in this range. When they send messages to the outside world, though, those messages show up as if they came from your router's public IP address. Here's how it works:

My computer, with the address 192.168.1.45 on my home network, makes a request for a web page on a remote server. That request goes first to my home router. On my home network, the router's address is 192.168.1.1, but to the rest of the Internet, my router presents a public address, 66.187.145.75. The router passes my message on, sending it from its public address, and requesting that any replies come back to its public address. When it gets a reply, it sends the reply to my computer. Thanks to private addressing and subnet masks, multiple devices can share a single public IP address. This ability expands the total number of things that can be attached to the Internet.

to worry about configuring DNS. In some of this chapter's projects, you won't be going out to the Internet at large, so your devices won't have names, just numbers. When that happens, you'll need to know their numerical addresses.

NOTE: And when you go out to the Internet at large from a microcontroller, you first need to use a DNS utility on your computer to look up the numeric address for the hosts you want to talk to, then embed the numeric address in your microcontroller program. This is because there's just enough room in the Lantronix network modules used here to support basic networking functionality, and unfortunately, DNS support is usually not included.

Packet Switching: How Messages Travel the Net

So how does a message get from one machine to another? Imagine the process as akin to mailing a bicycle. The bike's too big to mail in one box, so first you break it into box-sized pieces. On the network, this is initially done at the Ethernet layer, also called the datalink layer, where each message is broken into chunks of more or less the same size, given a header containing the packet number. Next, you'd put the address (and the return address) on the bike's boxes. This step is handled at the IP layer, where the sending address and the receiving address are attached to the message in another header. Finally, you send it. Your courier might want to break the shipment up among several trucks to make sure each truck is used

to its best capacity. On the Internet, this happens at the transport layer. This is the layer of the network responsible for making sure packets get to their destination. There are two protocols used to handle transport of packets on the Internet: Transmission Control Protocol, or TCP, and User Datagram Protocol, or UDP. You'll learn more about these later. The main difference between them is that TCP provides more error checking from origin to destination, but is slower than UDP. UDP trades off error checking for speed.

Each router sends off the packets one at a time to whatever routers it's connected to. If it's attached to more than one other router, it sends the packets to whichever router is least busy. The packets may each take a different route to the receiver, and they may take several hops across several routers to get there. Once they reach their destination, the receiver strips off the headers and reassembles the message. This method of sending messages in chunks across multiple paths is called packet switching. It ensures that every path through the network is used most efficiently, but sometimes packets are dropped or lost. You'll learn more on how that's handled in Chapters 5 and 6. For now, assume that the network is reliable enough that you can forget about dropped packets.

There's a command-line tool that can be useful in determining if your messages are getting through, called *ping*. It sends a message to another object on the net to say "Are you there?" and waits for a reply.

To use it, open up the command-line application on your computer (Terminal on Mac OS X, the Command Prompt on Windows, and xterm or similar on Linux/Unix). On Mac OS X or Linux, type the following:

```
ping -c 10 127.0.0.1
```

On Windows, type this:

```
ping -n 10 127.0.0.1
```

This sends a message to address 127.0.0.1 and waits for a reply. Every time it gets a reply, it tells you how long it took, like this:

```
64 bytes from 127.0.0.1: icmp_seq=0 ttl=64 time=0.166 ms
64 bytes from 127.0.0.1: icmp_seq=1 ttl=64 time=0.157 ms
64 bytes from 127.0.0.1: icmp_seq=2 ttl=64 time=0.182 ms
```

After counting ten packets (that's what the −c 10 on Mac and -n 10 on Windows means), it stops and gives you a summary like this:

```
--- 127.0.0.1 ping statistics ---
10 packets transmitted, 10 packets received, 0% packet loss
round-trip min/avg/max/stddev = 0.143/0.164/0.206/0.015 ms
```

It gives you a good picture not only of how many packets got through, but also how long they took. It's a useful way to learn quickly if a given device on the Internet is reachable or not, and how reliable the network is between you and that device. Later on, you'll be using devices that have no physical interface that you can see activity on, so you'll need *ping* to know whether they're working or not.

NOTE: 127.0.0.1 is a special address called the loopback address or localhost address. Whenever you use it, the computer you're sending it from loops back and sends the message to itself. You can also use the name localhost in its place. You can test many network applications using this address, even when you don't have a network connection, as you'll see in future examples.
X

❝ Clients, Servers, and Message Protocols

Now you know how the Internet is organized, but how do things get done on the Net? For example, how does an email message get from you to your friend? Or how does a web page get to your computer when you type a URL into your browser or click on a link? It's all handled by sending messages back and forth between objects, using the transport scheme just described. When you know that works, you can take it for granted and concentrate on the messages.

How Web Browsing Works

Figure 3-4 is a map of the routes web pages take to reach your computer. Your browser sends out a request for a page to a web server, and the server sends the page back. Which route the request and the reply take is irrelevant, as long as there is a route. The web server itself is just a program running on a computer somewhere else on the Internet. A server is a program that provides a service to other programs on the Net. The computer that a server runs on, also referred to as a server, is expected to be online and available at all times so that the service is not disrupted. In the case of a web server, the server provides access to a number of HTML files, images, sound files, and other elements of a website to clients from all over the net. Clients are programs that take advantage of services. Your browser, a client, makes a connection to the server to request a page. To facilitate that, the computer that your browser is running on makes a connection to the computer that the server is running on, and the exchange is made.

The server computer shares its IP address with every server program running on it by assigning each program a port number. For example, every connection request

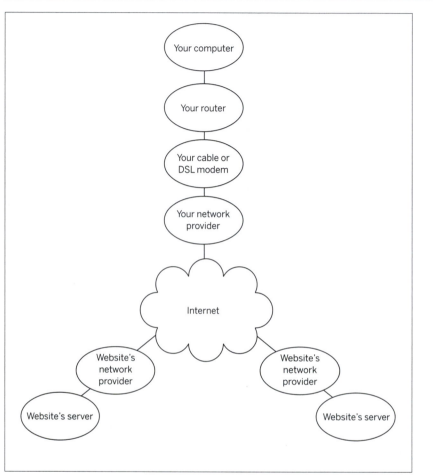

Figure 3-4
The path from a website to your browser. Although the physical computers are in many different locations, that doesn't matter to you, as long as you know the websites' addresses.

for port 80 is passed to the web server program. Every request for port 25 is passed to the email server program. Any program can take control of an unused port, but only one program at a time can control a given port. In this way, network ports work much like serial ports. Many of the lower port numbers are assigned to common applications like mail, file transfer, telnet, and web browsing. Higher port numbers are either disabled or left open for custom applications. (You'll write one of those soon.) A specific request goes like this:

1. You type http://www.makezine.com/index.html into your browser.
2. The browser program contacts www.makezine.com on port 80.
3. The server program accepts the connection.
4. The browser program asks for a specific file name, **index.html**.

5. The server program looks up that file on its local file system, and prints the file out via the connection to the browser. Then it closes the connection.
6. The browser reads the file, looks up any other files it needs (like images, movies, style sheets, and so forth), and repeats the connection request process, getting all the files it needs to display the page. When it has all the files, it strips out any header information and displays the page.

All of the requests from browser to server and all of the responses from server to browser (except the images and movie files) are just strings of text. To see this process in action, you can duplicate the request process in the terminal window. Open up your command program again just as you did for the *ping* example shown earlier. (If you're using Windows Vista, you may need to enable telnet with Control Panel→Programs→Turn Windows features on or off.)

Try It   Type:

`telnet www.google.com 80`

The server will respond as follows (on Windows, you may see only a blank window):

```
Trying 64.233.161.147...
Connected to www.l.google.com.
Escape character is '^]'.
```

> ⚠ **The built-in Windows version of telnet is not especially good. In particular, you won't be able to see what you type without setting the** localecho **option, and the informative "Trying . . . Connected" prompts do not appear. You may want to try a replacement such as Dave's Telnet, aka dtelnet (sourceforge.net/projects/dtelnet).**

▸▸ Type the following:

```
GET /index.html HTTP/1.0
HOST: www.google.com
```

Press the Return key twice after this last line. The server will then respond with:

```
HTTP/1.0 200 OK
Cache-Control: private
Content-Type: text/html; charset=ISO-8859-1
Server: GWS/2.1
Date: Thu, 15 Mar 2007 14:58:20 GMT
Connection: Close
```

> ▸▸ **You'll be using HTTP/1.0 requests in your code to keep things simple. Programs that make HTTP/1.1 requests are required to accept responses in chunks, which would complicate how you handle those responses. You may still see "HTTP/1.1" in the OK response you get from the server.**

NOTE: If telnet doesn't close on its own, you may need to press Control-] to get to the telnet prompt, where you can type q followed by Enter to exit.

After the header, the next thing you'll see is a lot of HTML that looks nowhere near as simple as the normal Google web interface. This is the HTML of the index page of Google. This is how browsers and web servers talk to each other, using a text-based protocol called the hypertext transport protocol (HTTP). The http:// at the beginning of every web address tells the browser to communicate using this protocol. The stuff that precedes the HTML is the HTTP header information. Browsers use it to learn the types of files that follow, how the files are

encoded, and more. The end user never needs this information, but it's very useful in managing the flow of data between client and server.

Remember the PHP time example from Chapter 1? It should still be sitting on your own web server, at www.example.com/time.php (replace www.example.com with the address of your server, which may be 127.0.0.1 if it's running on your local machine). Try getting this file from the command line.

Try It Modify the PHP program slightly, removing all the lines that print any HTML, like so:

Now telnet into the web server on port 80 and request the file from the command line. Don't forget to specify the HOST in your request, as shown earlier in the request to Google.

You should get a much more abbreviated response.

```php
<?php
/* Date page
   Language: PHP
   Prints the date. */

// get the date, and format it:
$date = date("Y-m-d h:i:s\t");
// include the date:
echo "< $date >\n";

?>
```

Even though the results of this approach aren't as pretty in a browser, it's very simple to extract the date from within a Processing program or even a microcontroller program. Just look for the < character in the text received from the server, read everything until you get the > character, and you've got it.

HTTP requests don't just request files. You can add parameters to your request. If the file you're requesting is actually a program (like a CGI script), it can do something with those parameters. To add parameters to a request,

add a question mark at the end of the request, and parameters after that. Here's an example:

http://www.example.com/get-parameters.php?name=tom&age=14

In this case, you're sending two parameters, name and age. Their values are "tom" and "14", respectively. You can add as many parameters as you want, separating them with the ampersand (&).

Test It Here's a PHP script that reads all the values sent in via a request and prints them out:

Save this script to your server as **get-parameters.php** and view it in a browser using the URL shown earlier (you may need to modify the path to the file if you've put it in a subdirectory). You should get a page that says:

name: tom
age: 14

```php
<?php
/*

   Parameter reader
   Language: PHP

   Prints any parameters sent in using an HTTP GET command.
*/
// print the beginning of an HTML page:
echo "<html><head></head><body>\n";

// print out all the variables:
foreach ($_REQUEST as $key => $value)
    {
        echo "$key: $value<br>\n";
    }

// finish the HTML:
echo "</body></html>\n";

?>
```

» You could also request it from the command line like you did earlier (be sure to include the ?name=tom&age=14 at the end of the argument to GET, as in GET /get-parameters.php?name=tom&age=14). You'd get something similar, with the HTTP header:

```
HTTP/1.1 200 OK
Date: Thu, 15 Mar 2007 15:10:51 GMT
Server: Apache
X-Powered-By: PHP/5.1.2
Vary: Accept-Encoding
Connection: close
Content-Type: text/html; charset=UTF-8


<html><head></head><body>
name: tom<br>
age: 14<br>
</body></html>
```

» Of course, because PHP is a programming language, you can do more than just print out the results. Try this script:

Try requesting this script with the same parameter string as the last script, ?name=tom&age=14, and see what happens. Then change the age to something over 21.

NOTE: One great thing about PHP is that it automatically converts ASCII strings of numbers like "14" to their numerical values. Because all HTTP requests are ASCII-based, PHP is optimized for ASCII-based exchanges like this.

```php
<?php
/*
   Age checker
   Language: PHP

   Expects two parameters from the HTTP request:
      name (a text string)
      age (an integer)
   Prints a personalized greeting based on the name and age.
*/
// print the beginning of an HTML page:
echo "<html><head></head><body>\n";

// read all the parameters and assign them to local variables:
foreach ($_REQUEST as $key => $value)
   {
      if ($key == "name") {
         $name = $value;
      }

      if ($key == "age") {
         $age = $value;
      }
   }

if ($age < 21) {
   echo "<p> $name, You're not old enough to drink.</p>\n";
} else {
   echo "<p> Hi $name. You're old enough to have a drink, but do ";
   echo "so responsibly.</p>\n";
}
// finish the HTML:
echo "</body></html>\n";

?>
```

❝❝ How Email Works

Transferring mail also uses a client-server model. It involves four applications: your email program and your friend's, and your email server (also called the mail host) and your friend's. Your email program adds a header to your message to say that this is a mail message, who the message is to and from, and what the subject is. Next, it contacts your mail server, which then sends the mail on to your friend's mail server. When your friend checks her mail, her mail program connects to her mail server and downloads any waiting messages. The mail server is online all the time, waiting for new messages for all of its users.

The transport protocol for mail is called SMTP, the Simple Mail Transport Protocol. Just like HTTP, it's text-based, and you can use it from a command line. When a mail server delivers a message, it has to figure out which servers are responsible for handling incoming mail (for example mail.example.com or smtp.example.com).

If you'd like to find the name of these servers, open a command window/terminal program, and use the *nslookup* command with the -q=mx option (this looks up the mail server for the domain you specify):

```
C:\ >nslookup -q=mx gmail.com
Server:  Unknown
Address:  192.168.254.1:53

Non-authoritative answer:
gmail.com        MX preference = 50,   mail exchanger = gsmtp163.google.com
gmail.com        MX preference = 50,   mail exchanger = gsmtp183.google.com
gmail.com        MX preference = 5,    mail exchanger = gmail-smtp-in.l.google.com
gmail.com        MX preference = 10,   mail exchanger = alt1.gmail-smtp-in.l.google.com
gmail.com        MX preference = 10,   mail exchanger = alt2.gmail-smtp-in.l.google.com
```

❝❝

You could use any of the listed mail exchangers to send email to a gmail.com recipient, but don't. If you accidentally say the wrong thing to someone else's mail server (mistyping one of the SMTP commands, for example), your IP address might get reported to one of the organizations that tracks outbreaks of malicious software, and you could find yourself on a list of banned IP addresses.

Also, if you're connecting to the Internet through a cable or DSL modem, it's very likely that the SMTP port (25) is tightly controlled. Most ISPs allow you to connect only to *their* SMTP servers in order to prevent rogue users (and malicious software) from sending spam messages directly to recipients' SMTP servers. So for this kind of testing, it's best to use the SMTP server that your ISP specifies for outbound email rather than one of the mail exchangers you got from nslookup.

To start with, open a telnet connection to your outgoing SMTP server, like this:

```
telnet smtp.example.com 25
```

The server will respond something like this:

```
Trying 69.49.109.11...
Connected to mail.example.com.
Escape character is '^]'.
220 mail.example.com ESMTP Sendmail 8.13.1/8.13.1; Thu, 16 Mar
2006 16:04:22 -0500
```

Now you have to say hello, or in SMTP syntax, HELO. You must use the domain name of the email address you are sending mail from, for example: HELO example.com

The server will respond:

```
250 example.com  Hello, nice to meet you.
```

The dialogue goes on like this (when you see \r, press Return or Enter instead):

You send: MAIL FROM: <you@example.com>\r

Server responds: `250 Ok`

You: `RCPT TO: <friend@example.com>\r`

NOTE: You might want to send mail to yourself the first time, so you can check whether it works.

Server: `250 Ok`

You: `DATA\r`

Server: `354 enter mail, end with "." on a line by itself`

The server now expects you to send several lines of text, starting with the subject, followed by the body of your email. Different servers expect you to end the message in different ways. Some look for a pair of carriage returns, but most look for a period on a line by itself — in other words: `\r.\r`

```
Subject: test message

Hello,
This is a test.
Goodbye.
```

Press Return twice at the end of your message, or Return followed by a period and then Return again, or whatever else your mail server asked for on the line that started with 354.

The server will respond like this: `250 Ok: queued as 12345`

You respond with: `QUIT\r`

And the server says: `221 Bye`

Finally, it closes the connection. Now check your mail to see whether you got a message from yourself. If you did, do the hokey pokey in celebration. If you didn't get a message, check your spam folder. Mail messages sent in this bare-bones fashion may be misconstrued as spam by eager-to-please email servers.

Because the whole mail transaction is text-based, you can make this happen from any program you want, whether it's on your personal computer or a microcontroller, as long as you've got an Internet connection.
X

⚠ Mail servers are pretty picky about what you type, and if you mistype something, pressing Backspace or Delete might confuse the mail server, even if everything looks OK on your end. If in doubt, close the telnet connection and try again from the beginning.

A Networked Cat

Web browsing and email are all very simple for humans, because we've developed computer interfaces that work well with our bodies. Keyboards work great with our fingers, and mice glide smoothly under our hands. It's not so easy for a cat to send email, though. This project attempts to remedy that, and to show you how to build your first physical interface for the Internet.

If you're a cat lover, you know how cute they can be when they curl up in the sun in their favorite spot for a nap. You might find it useful in stressful times at work to think of your cat, curled up and purring away. Wouldn't it be nice if the cat sent you an email when he lays down for a nap? It'd be even better if you could then check in on the cat's website to see him at his cutest.

The system works like this: The force sensing resistors are mounted under the cat mat and attached to a microcontroller. The microcontroller is attached to a personal computer. There's also a camera attached to the personal computer. When the cat lies down on the mat, its extra weight will cause a change in the sensor readings. The microcontroller then sends a signal to a program on the personal computer, which calls a CGI script on a web server. The CGI script sends an email to the cat owner, notifying him that the cat is being particularly cute. Meanwhile, a separate program is uploading pictures of the cat to the web from a webcam attached to the computer.

Making a Web Page for the CatCam

The new piece of software in this project is a program to take pictures from the webcam and upload them. There are many good shareware and freeware packages available. A quick Google search for "webcam software" and the name of your operating system will turn up several. On Mac OS X, Evocam from Evological (www. evological.com) is a good shareware package. If you use it, please pay your shareware fees. On Windows, Fwink (lundie.ca/fwink) is a good basic freeware package.

All of these applications share some common attributes. There is a configuration menu or panel that lets you choose your camera and control its brightness, contrast, and other settings. There is also one for setting the address of a server to upload to, and for specifying how often to do so.

Any USB camera should work well on Windows. On Mac OS X, you can also use FireWire cameras like Apple's iSight or Unibrain's fire-I. Many of the USB cameras won't work too well on Mac OS X without a driver, but there's a good open-source driver called macam, available on Source-Forge at webcam-osx.sourceforge.net, that works with a number of the USB cameras. To use it with applications

---

MATERIALS

» **Between 2 and 4 force-sensing resistors**
You have options: **Interlink 400 series FSRs** (www.interlinkelec.com). You can get these from Images Co (www.imagesco.com) or Trossen Robotics (www.trossenrobotics.com). The Interlink model 400 is shown in this project, but any of the 400 series will work well. **FlexiForce** from Parallax (www.parallax.com), part number 30056, also works well.

» **Between 2 and 4 10-kilohm resistors**
available at many retailers, including from Digi-Key (www.digikey.com) as part number 10K-QBK-ND, Newark (www.newark.com) as part number 84N2322, and many others.

» **1 solderless breadboard** such as Digi-Key part number 438-1045-ND or Jameco (www.jameco.com) part number 20601.

» **1 Arduino microcontroller module**
(see Chapter 1)

» **1 personal computer**

» **1 web camera** (USB or FireWire)

» **1 webcam program**

» **1 cat mat**

» **1 cat** A dog will do if you have no cat.

» **2 thin pieces of wood or thick cardboard, about the size of the cat mat**

» **1 soft pad, about the size of the cat mat**
A thick hand towel or dish towel will do.

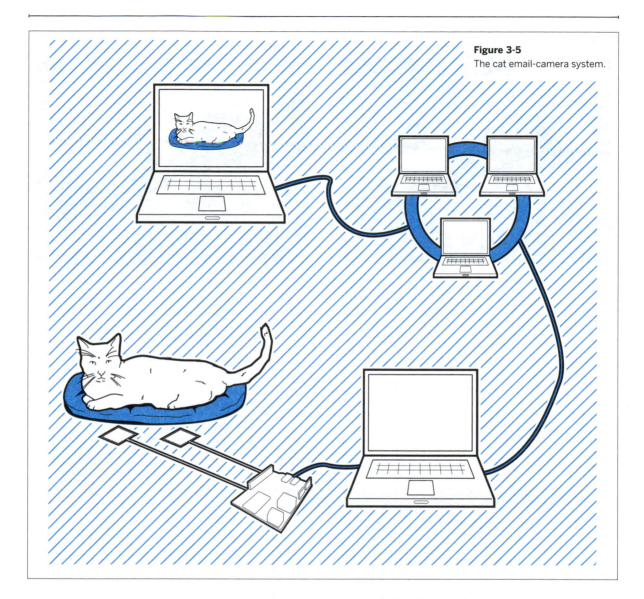

Figure 3-5
The cat email-camera system.

other than the macam program itself, copy the file called **macam.component** to the **/Library/Quicktime** directory of your hard drive. Then open the webcam software you're using and your USB camera should pop up in the list of available cameras.

Once you've got a camera image showing up onscreen, open the FTP settings menu or the configuration panel. Enter the address for your web server, the path to the directory that you want to upload the file to, the filename, and your user name and password. The software will save a picture to a file and then upload it to the server. There is also a setting to control how often a new image

is uploaded. Set it for every 15 seconds or so. Don't set it to update too frequently, or you'll create too heavy a load on the server, and viewers won't even get a full image before you're overwriting it with a new one. Remember the first rule of good networking habits: listen more than you speak. Make sure your software isn't uploading so frequently that users can't access the page.

Make a new directory on your server for this project, call it **catcam**, then have the webcam software upload the image to that directory with a clever filename like **image.jpg**. To make sure it got there, open a web browser and see if you can see the image in the directory you set the camera

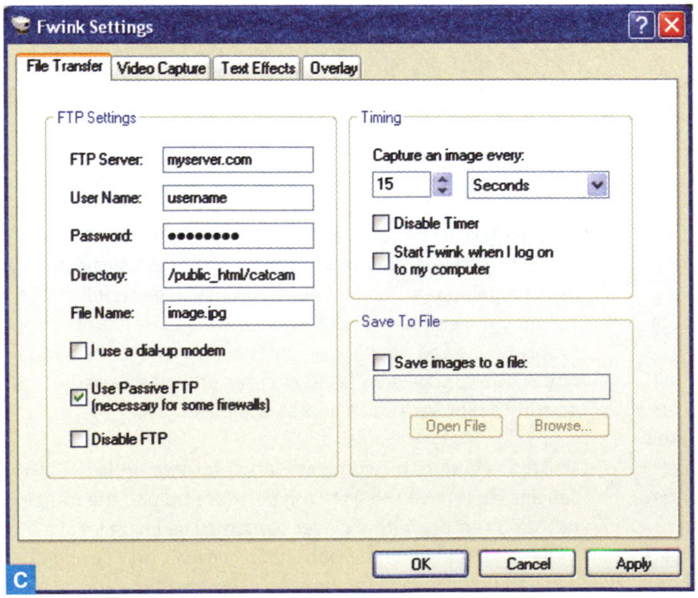

Figure 3-6

Evocam's server panel (A) allows you to set the net address to upload images to. The Refresh panel (2) allows you to set the upload frequency. On Windows, Fwink's Settings panel (C) controls both settings.

to upload to. For example, if your directory is at the root of your website, then the image would be found at www. example.com/catcam/image.jpg.

Once you know the image is there and visible, frame it with a web page in the same directory, called **index.html**. Below

is a bare-bones page that will automatically refresh itself in the user's browser every ten seconds. The meta tag in the head of the document causes the browser to refresh the page every ten seconds. Feel free to make the page as detailed as you want, but keep the meta tag in place.

```
<html>
<head>
    <title>noodles</title>
    <meta http-equiv="refresh" content="10">
</head>
<body>
    <center>
        <h2>Cat Cam</h2>
            <img src="http://www.example.com/catcam/image.jpg">
    </center>
</body>
</html>
```

Putting Sensors in the Cat Mat

Now that the catcam is running, it's time to make the system that notifies you when the cat is there to be viewed. How you do this depends on what kinds of force-sensing resistors you use. Interlink's 400 series FSRs include a long, thin model with adhesive backing that mounts nicely on any firm surface. Because this sensor is very flat and has a relatively large surface area, it gives good readings for this project. Mount the FSRs on strips of firm yet flexible wood or cardboard (Masonite works well), and you've got a great sensor.

If you're using smaller FSRs from another company like CUI or FlexiForce, you'll need to make a larger sensing pad. First, cut two pieces of wood or firm cardboard slightly smaller than the cat's mat. Don't use a really thick or hard piece of wood. You just need something firm enough to provide a relatively inflexible surface for the sensors. Attach the sensors to the corners of one of the pieces of wood or cardboard. Sandwich the sensors between the two boards. Tape the two boards together at the edges loosely, so that the weight of the cat can press down to affect the sensors. If you tape too tightly, the sensors will always be under force; too loose, and

the boards will slide around too much and make the cat uncomfortable. If the sensors don't give enough of a reaction, get some little rubber feet, available at any electronics store, and position them on the panel opposite the sensors so that they press down on the sensors. If the wood or cardboard panels have some flex in them, position an extra rubber foot or two at the center of the panel to reduce the flex. Figures 3-7, 3-8, and 3-9 show a working version of the sensor board.

Next, attach long wires to the force-sensing resistors to reach from the mat to the nearest possible place to put the microcontroller module. Connect the sensors to an analog input of the microcontroller using the voltage divider circuit shown in Figure 3-9. Because you don't care which of the sensors gets triggered, this circuit makes it possible to react to input from any of the four of them.

X

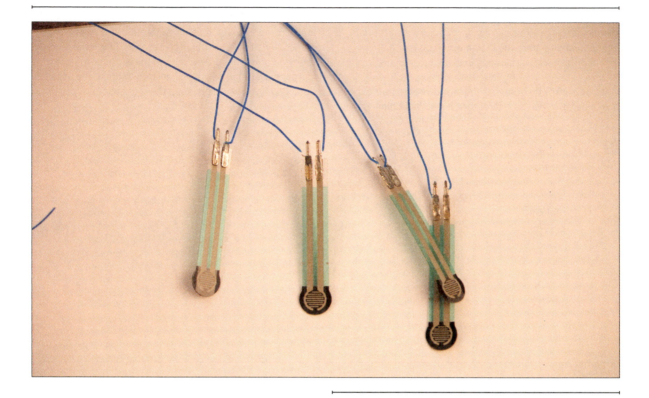

⬆ Figure 3-7
Because the force-sensing resistors melt easily, I used 30AWG wire wrap instead of solder. Wire-wrapping tools are inexpensive and easy to use, but make a secure connection. After wire wrapping, I insulated the connections with heat shrink.

⏭ Figure 3-8
Cat-sensing panel. The four FSRs are wired in parallel. Note the rubber feet that press down more precisely on the sensors. Make sure to insulate the connections before taping the panels together. The connector is just a pair of female wire wrap headers.

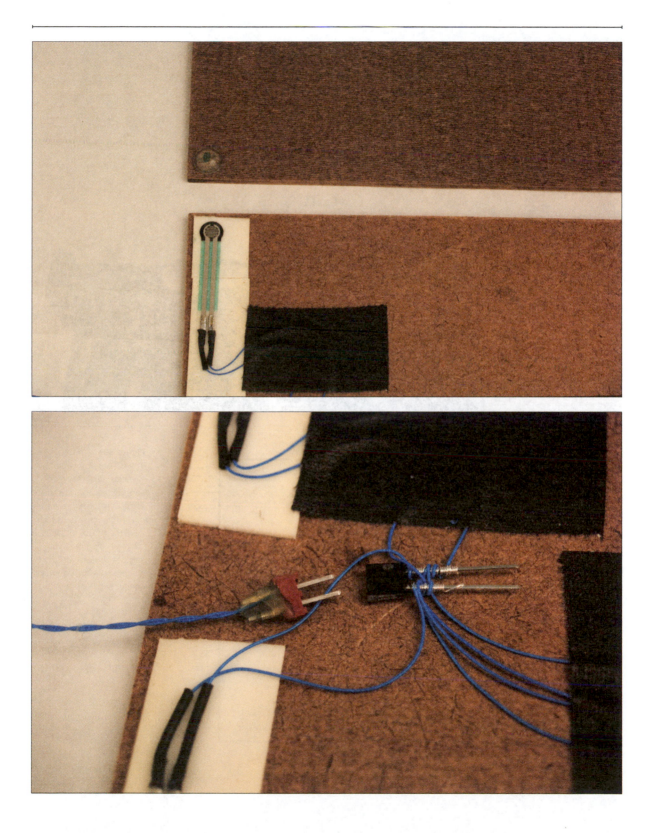

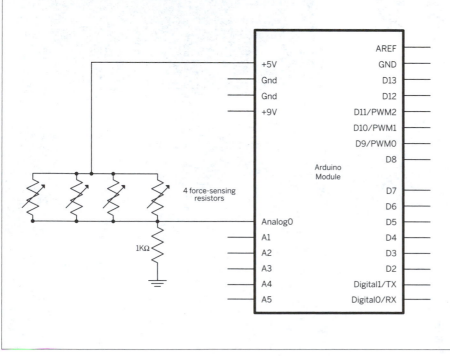

Figure 3-9
The cat-sensing circuit.
Because all of the force-
sensing resistors are all
wired in parallel, there are
only two connections for
all of them. This circuit is
simple enough that you
can just solder a resistor to
a header pin to make the
connection to ground.

Test It   Once you've got the sensor panel together and connected to the microcontroller, run the following on the Arduino or Wiring board to test the sensors:

To see the results, open the Serial Monitor at 9600 bits per second. Now position the cat on the panel and note the number change. This can be tricky, as cats are difficult to command. You may want to put some cat treats or catnip on the pad to encourage the cat to stay there. When you're satisfied that the system works and that you can see a significant change in the value when the cat sits on the panel, you're ready to move on to the next step.

NOTE: Once you've got the serial connection between the microcontroller and the computer working, you might want to add in the Bluetooth radio from the Monski pong project in Chapter 2. It will make your life much easier if your computer doesn't have to be tethered to the cat mat in order to program.

```
/*
    Analog sensor reader
    Language: Arduino/Wiring

    Reads an analog input on Analog in 0, prints the result
    as an ASCII-formatted  decimal value.

    Connections:
      FSR analog sensors on Analog in 0
*/
int sensorValue;              // outgoing ADC value

void setup()
{
  // start serial port at 9600 bps:
  Serial.begin(9600);
}

void loop()
{
  // read analog input:
  sensorValue = analogRead(0);

  // send analog value out in ASCII decimal format:
  Serial.println(sensorValue, DEC);

  // wait 10ms for next reading:
  delay(10);
}
```

Connect It   As the micro-controller can't connect to the Internet on its own, you'll need another computer for that. Your computer and Processing will do the job well. Here's a Processing program similar the Monski pong program from Chapter 2 to read the sensors:

```
/*
  Serial String Reader
  Language: Processing

  Reads in a string of characters until it gets a linefeed (ASCII 10).
  Then converts the string into a number.
  */

import processing.serial.*;

int linefeed = 10;    // linefeed in ASCII
Serial myPort;        // the serial port
int sensorValue = 0;  // the value from the sensor


void setup() {
  size(400,300);
  // list all the available serial ports
  println(Serial.list());
```

»

You don't want Processing sending a message constantly, because you'd get several thousand emails every time the cat sits on the mat. Instead, you want to recognize when the cat's there, send an email, and don't send again until he's left and returned again. If he jumps on and off and on again in a minute or less, you don't want to send again.

What does that look like in sensor terms? To find out, you need to do one of two things: either get the cat to jump on and off the mat on cue (difficult to do without substantial bribery, using treats or a favorite toy) or weigh the cat and use a stand-in of the same weight. The advantage to using the cat is that you can see what happens when he's shifting his weight, preparing the bed by kneading it with his claws, and so forth. The advantage of the stand-in weight is that you don't have to herd cats to finish the project.

Continued from previous page.

```
  // I know that the first port in the serial list on my Mac is always my
  // Arduino, so I open Serial.list()[0]. Open whatever port you're using
  // (the output of Serial.list() can help; the are listed in order
  // starting with the one that corresponds to [0]).
  myPort = new Serial(this, Serial.list()[0], 9600);

  // read bytes into a buffer until you get a linefeed (ASCII 10):
  myPort.bufferUntil(linefeed);
}

void draw() {
  // twiddle your thumbs
}

// serialEvent method is run automatically by the Processing applet
// whenever the buffer reaches the byte value set in the bufferUntil()
// method in the setup():
void serialEvent(Serial myPort) {
  // read the serial buffer:
  String myString = myPort.readStringUntil(linefeed);

  // if you got any bytes other than the linefeed:
  if (myString != null) {
    // trim off the carriage return and convert the string to an integer:
    sensorValue = int(trim(myString));

    // print it:
    println(sensorValue);
  }
}
```

Refine It

If your system is working correctly, you should notice a difference of several points in the sensor readings when the cat gets on the mat. It helps to graph the results so you can see clearly what the difference looks like. To do that, add an extra variable to the variable list at the beginning of your Processing program:

```
int graphPosition = 0;  // the horizontal position of the latest
                        // line to be drawn on the graph
```

» Then add this method at the end of your program:

```
void drawGraph() {
  // adjust this formula so that lineHeight is always less than
  // the height of the window:
  int lineHeight = sensorValue /2;

  // draw the line:
  stroke(0,255,0);
  line(graphPosition, height, graphPosition, height - lineHeight);

  // at the edge of the screen, go back to the beginning:
  if (graphPosition >= width) {
    graphPosition = 0;
    background(0);
  }
  else {
    graphPosition++;
  }
}
```

» Call this method from the serialEvent() method, right after you print the number:

```
  // print it:
  println(sensorValue);
  drawGraph();
}
```

" When you run the program, you'll see a graph of the sensor values. When the cat jumps on the mat, you should see a sudden increase, and when he jumps off, you'll see the graph decrease. You'll also see any small changes, which you might need to filter out. If the changes are small relative to the difference between the two states you're looking for, you can ignore them. You have enough knowledge to start defining the cat's presence on the mat as an event, using the sensor values. To do this, pick a threshold number in between the two states. When the sensor reading goes above the threshold, send a message that he's in place. When the sensor value goes below the threshold, the cat has left the mat, and the event is over. Once you've sent a message, you don't want to send another one right away, even if the cat gets off the mat and back on. Decide on an appropriate interval, wait that long, and start the whole process again.

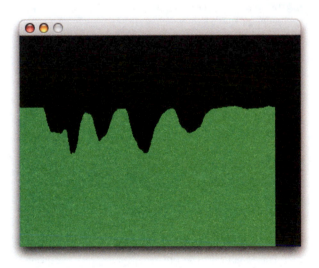

Figure 3-10
Output of the sensor graphing program.

» Add the following new variables to the beginning of your program:

```
int prevSensorValue = 0;      // the previous sensor reading
boolean catOnMat = false;     // whether the cat's on the mat;
int threshold = 320;          // above this number, the cat is on the mat.
```

» Then put this code in your draw() method, which Processing runs in a continuous loop. So far, you haven't put any code in the draw() method, so this is the only code there:

```
if (sensorValue > threshold ) {
  // if the last reading was less than the threshold,
  // then the cat just got on the mat.
  if (prevSensorValue <= threshold) {
    catOnMat = true;
    sendMail();
  }
} else {
  // if the sensor value is less than the threshold,
  // and the previous value was greater, then the cat
  // just left the mat
  if (prevSensorValue >= threshold) {
    catOnMat = false;
  }
}
// save the sensor value as the previous value
// so you can take new readings:
prevSensorValue = sensorValue;
```

» Make the following change at the beginning of the drawGraph() method; change this:

```
// draw the line:
stroke(0,255,0);
```

» to this:

```
// draw the line:
if (catOnMat) {
  // draw green:
  stroke(0,255,0);
}
else {
  // draw red:
  stroke(255,0,0);
}
```

» Finally, add a method that sends mail. For now, it will just print a placeholder to the message window. After the next section, you'll write code to make it send mail for real. Add this method to the end of your program:

```
void sendMail() {
  println("This is where you'd send a mail.");
}
```

▸ When you run the program, the graph should draw in red when the cat's off the mat, and green when it's on. Sometimes, if the cat takes his time getting settled, you can get several mail messages in a second or two. You may notice that the graph switches from red to green several times as it crosses the threshold. This happens because the sensor fluctuates slightly, due to electrical noise. Not all sensors are noisy, and you may be lucky and find out that yours isn't. If it is, you can smooth the transition out slightly by changing your code. Change the first block of the draw() method to read as follows:

When you've got very noisy readings, this method, called debouncing, is very useful. But one hundred milliseconds is a long time in sensor terms, and you're changing the whole system's reaction time by adding this debounce delay. You may even notice the graph pausing slightly at the transitions. Adjust the delay to be as short as possible and still deliver reliable results.

NOTE: Even with the debounce routine in your program, it's possible to get several mail messages a minute, if the cat is fickle. What's needed is a minimum time threshold between mail messages.

```
if (sensorValue > threshold ) {
  // if the last reading was less than the threshold,
  // then the cat just got on the mat.
  if (prevSensorValue <= threshold) {
    // wait a a bit, then check again to see whether the reading
    // is still above the threshold:
    delay(100);
    if (sensorValue > threshold) {
      catOnMat = true;
      sendMail();
    }
  }
} else {
  // if the sensor value is less than the threshold,
  // and the previous value was greater, then the cat
  // just left the mat
  if (prevSensorValue >= threshold) {
    catOnMat = false;
  }
}
```

Tame It   Every time the program sends a mail message, it should take note of the time, and not send a message again no matter what, unless the time threshold has passed. To make this happen, add a couple new variables at the beginning of the program:

```
int timeThreshold = 1;     // minimum number of minutes between emails
int timeLastSent[] = {
  hour(), minute() - 1 };  // time the last message was sent
```

▶▶ Now modify the sendMail() method as follows:

Once you're sure it works, adjust time-Threshold to an appropriate minimum number of minutes between emails.

```
void sendMail() {
  // calculate the current time in minutes:
  int[] presentTime = {hour(), minute()};

  // print the sensor value, the current time,
  // and the last time you sent a message, separated by tabs:
  print(sensorValue + "\t");
  print(presentTime[0] + ":" + presentTime[1] +"\t");
  println(timeLastSent[0] + ":" + timeLastSent[1]);

  // if you're still in the same hour as the last message,
  // then make sure at least the minimum number of minutes has passed:
  if (presentTime[0] == timeLastSent[0]) {
    if (presentTime[1] - timeLastSent[1] >= timeThreshold) {
      println("This is where you'd send a mail.");
      // take note of the time this message was sent:
      timeLastSent[0] = hour();
      timeLastSent[1] = minute();
    }
  }

  // If the hour has changed since the last message,
  // then the difference in minutes is a bit more complex.
  // Use != rather than > to make sure that the shift
  // from 23:59 to 0:00 is covered as well:
  if (presentTime[0] != timeLastSent[0]) {
    // calculate the difference in minutes:
    int minuteDifference = (60 - timeLastSent[1]) + presentTime[1];

    if (minuteDifference >= timeThreshold) {
      println("This is where you'd send a mail.");

      // take note of the time this message was sent:
      timeLastSent[0] = hour();
      timeLastSent[1] = minute();
    }
  }
}
```

❝ Sending Mail from the Cat

Once you've got the Processing program recognizing when the cat lies on the mat, you need to get it to send an email. You could write a program to send an email directly from Processing, using the text strings described in the section on email at the beginning of this chapter, but it's easier to send mail using PHP. The next section shows you how to pass the message on from Processing to PHP to do that. The same technique shown here can be used to call any PHP script from Processing. First, you need to program PHP to send a mail message. The PHP script below takes advantage of PHP's ability to read parameters from the HTTP request:

```php
<?php
/*

    Cat On Mat
    Language: PHP


    Expects a parameter called SensorValue, an integer.
    Prints a custom message depending on the value of SensorValue.
*/

$threshold = 320;     // minimum sensor value to trigger action

// print the beginning of the HTML page:
echo "<html><head></head><body>\n";

// read all the parameters and assign them to local variables:
foreach ($_REQUEST as $key => $value)
    {
        if ($key == "sensorValue") {
            $sensorValue = $value;
        }
    }

// respond depending on the sensor value:
if ($sensorValue > $threshold) {
    echo "<p> The cat is on the mat.</p>\n";
} else {
    echo "<p> the cat is not on the mat.</p>\n";
}
// finish the HTML:
echo "</body></html>\n";
?>
```

▶▶ This value should match the value of the threshold **variable from the Processing sketch.**

▶▶ In order for the PHP scripts to run, you'll need to install them on a web server that supports PHP. There are many web hosting companies with inexpensive (less than $10 a month) web hosting plans that support PHP.

" Save it to your server with the name **cat-script. php**. Test it from a browser with this HTTP request, using different values for sensorValue. Use a URL similar to the one shown here, replacing www.example. com with your server name, and adjusting the path to the script as needed: http://www.example.com/catcam/cat-script.php?sensorValue=12. Any value above 320 should result in a message that the cat is on the mat. When you're satisfied that it works, change your script to make it send an email (change yourname@example.com to your real email address), as shown in the code section below.

Call the script again and then check your mail to see whether the message went through. Some mail servers may require that you send mail only from your proper account name. If that's the case, replace cat@example. com in the send_mail function with your account name on the server that the script is running on.

```php
<?php
/*
   Mail sender
   Language: PHP

   Expects a parameter called SensorValue, an integer
   Sends an email if sensorValue is above a threshold value.
*/

$threshold = 320;     // minimum sensor value to trigger action.
                      // change this value to whatever your sensor threshold is.

// print the beginning of an HTML page:
echo "<html><head></head><body>\n";

// read all the parameters and assign them to local variables:
foreach ($_REQUEST as $key => $value)
   {
      if ($key == "sensorValue") {
          $sensorValue = $value;
      }
   }

if ($sensorValue > $threshold) {
    $messageString = "The cat is on the mat at http://www.example.com/catcam.";
    echo $messageString;
    send_mail("yourname@example.com", "the cat", $messageString);
} else {
    echo "<p> the cat is not on the mat.</p>\n";
}
// finish the HTML:
echo "</body></html>\n";

end;

// End of the main script. Anything after here won't get run
// unless it's called in the code above this line.

///////////////////////////////////////////////////

function send_mail($to, $subject, $message) {
    $from = "cat@example.com";
    mail($to, $subject, $message, "From: $from");
}
?>
```

▶▶ You'll need to change this number.

▶▶ You'll need to change this URL.

▶▶ You'll need to change these email addresses.

⚠ Now that you're sending emails from a program, you need to be very careful about how often it happens. You really don't want 10,000 messages in your inbox because you accidentally called the mail command in a repeating loop.

Putting It All Together

Finally, it's time to get Processing to call the PHP script and complete the connection from the cat to your inbox. To do this, you're going to use the net library in Processing. Like the serial library, it adds some functions to the core of Processing. The serial library allowed you to access the serial ports, and the net library allows you to make network connections. Here's an example that uses the net library to make an HTTP call to the PHP script you just wrote. Use it to confirm that Processing can contact your server:

```
/*
    HTTP sender
    Language: Processing

    Uses the Processing net library to make an HTTP request.
*/

import processing.net.*;        // gives you access to the net library

Client client;                  // a new net client
boolean requestInProgress;      // whether a net request is in progress
String responseString = "";     // string of text received by client
void setup()
{
  // open a connection to the host:
  client = new Client(this, "example.com", 80);

  // send the HTTP GET request:
  client.write("GET /catcam/cat-script.php?sensorValue=321 HTTP/1.0\r\n");
  client.write("HOST: example.com\r\n\r\n");
  // note that you've got a request in progress:
  requestInProgress = true;
}


void draw()
{
  // available() returns how many bytes have been received by the client:
  if (client.available() > 0) {
    // read a byte, convert it to a character, and add it to the string:
    responseString +=char(client.read());

    // add to a line of |'s on the screen (crude progress bar):
    print("|");
  }
  // if there's no bytes available, either the response hasn't started yet,
  // or it's done:
  else {
  // if responseString is longer than 0 bytes, the response has started:
    if(responseString.length() > 0 )  {
      // you've got some bytes, but now there's no more to read. Stop:
      if(requestInProgress == true) {
        // print the response:
        println(responseString);
```

> ▶▶ You'll need to change the hostnames and the path.

Continued from previous page.

```
        // note that the request is over:
        requestInProgress = false;
        // reset the string  for future requests:
        responseString = "";
      }
    }
  }
}
```

» If you check your mail, you should have a message from the PHP script indicating that the cat is on the mat. Once that's working, it's time to combine this sketch with the cat-sensing sketch shown earlier. First, add the net library import right after the serial library import:

```
import processing.net.*;  // gives you access to the net library
```

» Then add the global variables from the HTTP client script to the variable list at the beginning of the sensing script:

```
// HTTP client variables:
Client client;                          // a new net client
boolean requestInProgress  = false;  // whether a net request is in progress
String responseString = "";          // string of text received by client
```

» To send the mail and check the response from the server, add two new methods at the end of the sketch, makeHTTPCall() and checkNetClient() (be sure to change the references to example. com and the path of the requestString):

```
void makeHTTPCall() {
  // do this only if you're not already in the middle of an HTTP request:
  if (requestInProgress == false) {
    // Open a connection to the host:
    client = new Client(this, "example.com", 80);

    // form the request string:
    String requestString = "/catcam/cat-script.php?sensorValue=" + sensorValue;

    // send the HTTP GET request:
    client.write("GET  " + requestString + " HTTP/1.0\n");
    client.write("HOST: example.com\n\n");
    // note that you've got a request in progress:
    requestInProgress = true;
  }
}

void checkNetClient() {
  // available() returns how many bytes have been received by the client:
  if (client.available() > 0) {
    // read a byte, convert it to a character, and add it to the string:
    responseString +=char(client.read());
```

» You'll need to change the hostnames and the path.

»

Continued from opposite page.

```
      // add to a line of |'s on the screen (crude progress bar):
      print("|");
    }
    // if there are no bytes available, either the response hasn't started yet,
    // or it's done:
    else {
      // if responseString is longer than 0 bytes, the response has started:
      if(responseString.length() > 0 ) {
        // you've got some bytes, but now there's no more to read. Stop:
        if(requestInProgress == true) {
          // print the response:
          println(responseString);
          // note that the request is over:
          requestInProgress = false;
          // reset the string  for future requests:
          responseString = "";
        }
      }
    }
  }
}
```

» Call makeHTTPCall() in the sendMail() method, in the two places where you're currently printing out "This is where you'd send a mail," like so:

```
println("This is where you'd send a mail.");
makeHTTPCall();
```

» Call checkNetClient() at the end of the draw() method like so:

```
if (requestInProgress == true) {
  checkNetClient();
}
```

Now run the sketch. When the sensor reading goes above the threshold, if an appropriate number of minutes has passed, you should see a mail message go out. Now the cat can send you email when he's curled up in his bed.

Figure 3-11
The finished cat bed (at right) and a detail of the sensor pad, which sits under the cat bed itself. A bamboo jewelry box from a nearby gift store houses the electronics, and matches the furniture. The USB cable runs to the computer. Make sure to secure the wires throroughly, or the cat may try to chew on them.

❝ Conclusion

Now you've got an understanding of the structure of the Internet, and how networked applications do their business.

The Internet is actually a network of networks, built up in multiple layers. Successful network transactions rely on there being at least one reliable route through the Net from client to server. Client and server applications exchange strings of text messages about the files they want to exchange, transferring their files and messages over network ports. To communicate with any given server, you need to know its message protocols. When you do, it's often possible to test the exchange between client and server using a telnet session and typing in the appropriate messages. Likewise, it's possible to write programs for a personal computer or microcontroller to send those same messages, as you saw in the cat bed project. Now that you understand how simple those messages can be, you'll get the chance to do it without a personal computer in the next chapter, connecting a microcontroller to the Internet through a serial-to-Ethernet converter that's not much bigger than the microcontroller itself.

X

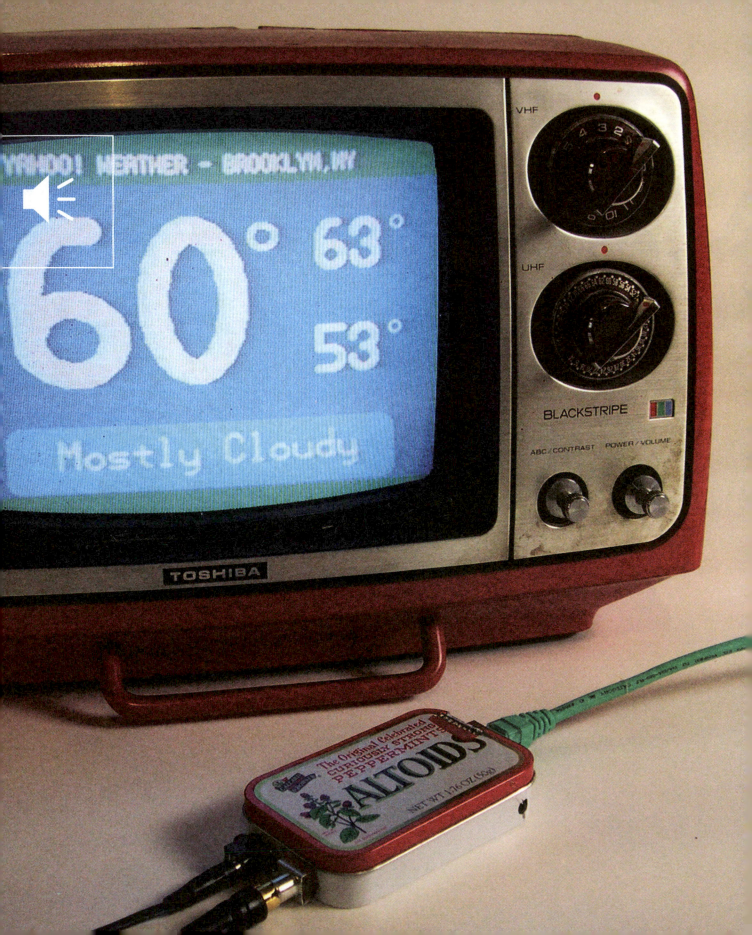

4

Look, Ma, No Computer! Microcontrollers on the Internet

The first response that comes to many people's minds after building a project like the networked cat bed in Chapter 3 is: "Great, but how can I do this without needing to connect to my computer?" It's cumbersome to have to attach the microcontroller to a laptop or desktop computer just to enable it to connect to the Internet. After all, as you saw in Chapter 3, Internet message protocols are just text strings, and microcontrollers are good at sending short text strings. So in this chapter, you'll learn how to connect a microcontroller to the internet through a device that's not much more complex than the Bluetooth radio modem you used in Chapter 2.

◄◄ **Uncommon Projects' YBox** (http://ybox.tv) puts RSS feeds on your TV using an Xport serial-to-ethernet module and a Propeller microchip. *Image courtesy of Uncommon Projects.*

In the past few years, a wide array of commercial appliances has come on the market that can connect directly to the Internet without the aid of a personal computer. Companies like D-Link, Sony, Axis, and others make security cameras with network interfaces, both Ethernet and Wi-Fi. Ceiva, eStarling, and others make picture frames with Wi-Fi connections to which you can upload images from the Net. Ambient Devices makes lamps and displays of various sorts that connect to the Net and change their appearance based on changes in information like stock market data, weather, and other scalar quantities. Cable television set top boxes are computers in a small box, capable of routing streams of audio, video, and data all at the same time. In fact, the operating system in your set-top box might even be a variation of the same Linux operating system that's running on your network provider's web hosting machine. Home alarm systems are made up of networks of microcontrollers that talk among themselves, with one that can communicate with a central server, usually over phone lines using a modem.

All of these appliances engage in networked communication. The simplest ones handle only one transaction at a time, requesting information from a server and then waiting for a response, or sending a single message in response to some physical event. Others manage multiple streams of communication at once, allowing you to surf the Web while watching television. The more processing power a given device has, the more it can handle. For many applications, however, you don't need a lot of processing power, because the device you're making has only one or two functions.
X

Introducing Network Modules

It's possible to write a program for a microcontroller that can manage all the steps of network communication, from the physical and data connections to the network address management to the negotiation of protocols like SMTP and HTTP. A code library that encompasses all the layers needed for network connections is called a network stack, or TCP/IP stack. However, it's much easier to use a network interface module to do the job.

There are many such modules on the market, with varying prices and features. Just as you can choose how technical you want to get when you pick a microcontroller platform, you can also choose your technical level when you pick a network controller. Some modules, like Rabbit Semiconductor's RabbitCore processors, come with all the source code for a TCP/IP stack, and expect you to modify it for your needs and program the device yourself. This module is powerful, but has a steep learning curve. Others have a stack programmed into their firmware, and present you with a serial, telnet, or web-based interface. These are much simpler to use. The web interface gives you access from the browser of your personal computer; the telnet interface gives you access from a server or your personal computer; and the serial interface gives you access from a microcontroller.

The projects in this chapter, and some of the others later in the book, use a family of network modules from Lantronix: the Micro, the XPort, the WiMicro, and the WiPort. These are serial-to-Ethernet modems; as you'll see shortly, they work much like the Bluetooth modems you used in Chapter 2 but have a different serial protocol. The Micro and the XPort require a wired connection on both the serial side and the Ethernet side. The WiMicro and WiPort are wireless counterparts of the Micro and XPort, respectively. Of the four, the XPort is the least expensive and the smallest, about the size of a normal Ethernet jack that you'd find in a computer. It's not designed to be used with a solderless breadboard, though, so you have to make your own printed circuit board for it, or buy one. The WiPort also requires you to make your own board. The Micro and the WiMicro are in the middle of the price range, and both have a more convenient physical interface that can be connected to a breadboard with relative ease.
X

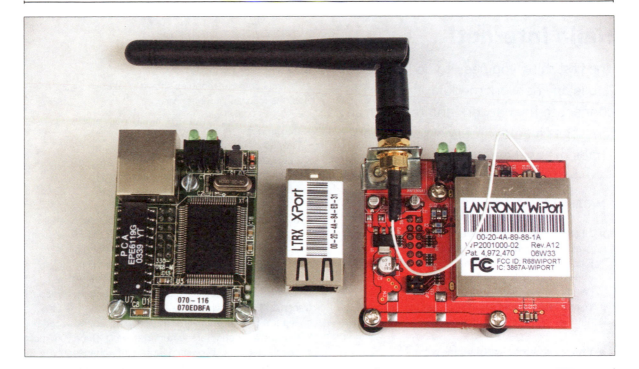

⬆ **Figure 4-1**
The Lantronix Micro (left), XPort (center), and WiMicro (left) serial-to-Ethernet modules. The WiPort is the square silver part of the WiMicro.

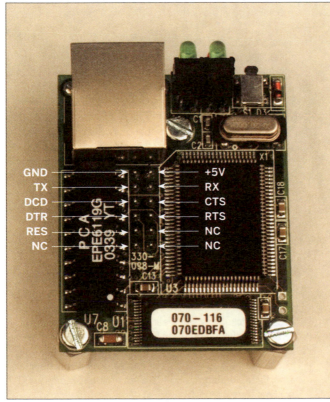

◀◀ **Figure 4-2**
Pin configurations for the Micro. The configuration for the WiMicro is identical.

Project 5

Hello Internet!

The first thing you need to do in order to use any network module is to get it to connect to the network and to return any messages it gets through its serial port. That's the goal of this project.

MATERIALS

» **1 Lantronix embedded device server**
Available from many vendors, including Symmetry Electronics (www.semiconductorstore.com) as part number CO-E1-11AA (Micro) or WM11A0002-01 (WiMicro), or XP1001001-03R (XPort)

» **1 solderless breadboard** such as Digi-Key part number 438-1045-ND, Jameco (www.jameco.com) part number 20601

» **1 micro-to-breadboard connector**

» **1 USB-to-serial circuit** such as the FT232RL or RS-232-to-serial circuit such as the MAX3323, as shown in Chapter 2. Use the second of these if you don't have a spare USB port and plan to use an RS-232 serial port. Otherwise, use the first one.

» **1 7805 5V voltage regulator**

» **1 10μF capacitor**

» **1 1μF capacitor**

For micro-to-breadboard connector:
Option 1 A quick-and-dirty adapter:
» **2 rows of right-angle male headers**
(such as Samtec TSW series, TSW-112-08-T-S). Most retailers carry some version of these. Jameco's equivalent is part number 103351.

» **2 rows of straight female headers**
(such as Samtec SSA series, SSA-106-S-T). Most retailers carry some version of these. Jameco's equivalent is part no. 308567. I prefer the Samtec ones, because they're easier to break off.

Option 2 A DIY ribbon cable adapter:
» **14-pin IDC DIP plug** Jameco part number 42658

» **IDC 14-pin socket** Jameco part number 153948

» **14-conductor rainbow-colored ribbon cable**
Jameco part number 105672

Making the Circuit

All of the Lantronix modules shown in Figure 4-1 have at least the following connections:

- Power
- Ground
- Serial receive (RX)
- Serial transmit (TX)
- Reset

These are the connections you'll use to connect to your microcontroller. The additional pins are for things like a second serial port (Micro, WiPort, and WiMicro) or user-configurable I/O pins (XPort), which you won't need for the projects in this book. As you might expect by now, serial receive (RX) connects to the microcontroller's serial transmit (TX), and vice versa. Figure 4-2 shows the pin configurations for the Micro. This chapter features the Micro, and later chapters feature the XPort. Once you know the circuit for each, they can be used interchangeably for most of the projects in this book. All of the Lantronix modules use virtually the same firmware interface settings.

Before connecting the Lantronix module to a micro-controller, you should configure it and confirm that the module is communicating properly through its serial port. The easiest way to do this is to connect it to a personal computer serially. You can use the FT232RL USB-to-serial module, or the MAX3323 RS-232-to-TTL serial circuit from Chapter 2. Figure 4-3 shows these circuits connected to the Micro module. The Micro module is shown with its own power supply, because it draws more current than the USB connection can supply.

To connect the Micro to the breadboard, you have two choices: you can make a ribbon cable, or you can make a connector out of header pins. You can use a ribbon cable with a connector to match the Micro's two rows of pins. This type of connector is called an IDC connector. In a pinch, you can pull a two-row ribbon connector out of an old PC, chop off one end, solder headers onto the other end, and use that. You can also buy IDC connectors and IDC DIP sockets, as listed earlier. Assembling these connectors is tricky without an IDC crimp tool, however. As an alternative, you can solder two rows of straight female header sockets to two rows of right-angle male header pins. Figure 4-4 shows how to align the header pins and sockets for soldering.

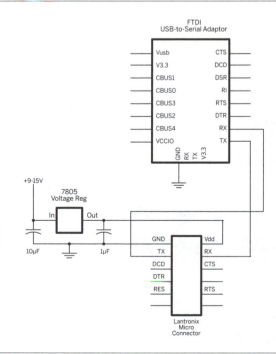

Figure 4-3
The Lantronix Micro connected to an FTDI USB-to-serial
module. The circuit is shown with and without the micro
attached, to show the wiring underneath. This same circuit
can be used for the Micro or WiMicro modules. Note that the
FTDI chip doesn't connect to +5V. It takes its power from
the USB connection. Only a common ground is needed.

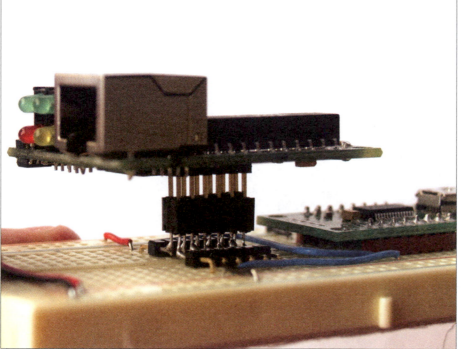

Figure 4-4
Soldering straight female headers to right-angle male headers. Slip the female sockets onto your module. The male header pins should now slip into a breadboard nicely, as shown in the second image, where the finished header assembly is used to mount the Micro module on a breadboard.

Configuring the Micro

Once you've got the circuit assembled, connect it to your PC, connect it to power, and open the serial port using your serial terminal program: GNU screen in Terminal on Mac OS X or Linux/Unix, PuTTY on Windows (see Chapter 2 for instructions on finding your serial ports). Press the reset button of the Micro module, hold down the x key, and release the reset button. This step forces the Lantronix module to go into setup mode. The module should return a configuration menu, like the following:

```
*** Lantronix Universal Device Server ***
Serial Number 6643485  MAC address 00204A66B9DD
Software version 05.2 (030423) LTX
Press Enter to go into Setup Mode
```

▶▶ Press Enter, and you'll get the menu shown at the right:

This menu allows you to configure all the settings of the module. The first menu choice controls the network settings. The second controls the serial settings. The others configure advanced settings, which you can leave at the default. Start by configuring the network settings. Type 0, then press Enter. Then respond as shown below, entering an available IP address on your network.

NOTE: The Lantronix module can find its own address using DHCP, but if you don't know its address, you have no way of contacting it from other devices on the same network. That's why you're entering a fixed address for the module. Pick an address that you know is available on your network. If you're using it on a home network, or any private network, use an address appropriate to the local network.

```
Web Server is          enabled
ECHO is                disabled
Enhanced Password is disabled

*** Channel 1
Baudrate 9600, I/F Mode 4C, Flow 00
Port 10001
Remote IP Adr: --- none ---, Port 00000
Connect Mode : D4
Disconn Mode : 00
Flush  Mode : 00

*** Expert
TCP Keepalive   : 45s
ARP cache timeout: 600s

Change Setup:
 0 Server configuration
 1 Channel 1 configuration
 5 Expert settings
 6 Security
 7 Factory defaults
 8 Exit without save
 9 Save and exit          Your choice ?
```

▶▶ This is the address that the module will have on the network.

NOTE: Sample responses are shown in blue here. Change the numbers as needed for your network.

```
IP Address : (0) 192.(0) 168.(0) 1.(0) 20
```

▶▶ Next you'll set the address of the router through which your module contacts the rest of the Net. Fill in the router's IP address:

```
Set Gateway IP Address (Y) Y
Gateway IP addr (0) 192.(0) 168.(0) 1.(0)1
```

When a router assigns addresses to devices connected to it, it masks part of the address space so that those devices can use only addresses in the same subnet as the router itself. For example, if the router is going to assign only addresses in the range 192.168.1.2 through 192.168.1.254, it masks out the top three numbers (octets). This is called the netmask, or subnet mask. In your PC's network settings, you'll see it written as a full network address, like so: 255.255.255.0. In the Lantronix modules, tell the module the number of bits for the netmask.

» To set a mask equivalent to 255.255.255.0, use the value 8:

```
Netmask: Number of Bits for Host Part (0=default) (0)8
```

For now, don't worry about the telnet config password. You can set it later if you want to.

```
Change telnet config password (N) N
```

» Once you've entered the previous settings, choose option 1 from the menu. This configures the serial settings, as follows. You'll use the default 9600 bits per second, for now:

```
Baudrate (9600) ?
```

» The I/F (interface) mode sets the additional parameters of the serial communication: 8 bits per byte, no parity, one stop bit. These settings are covered by the default value, 4C:

```
I/F Mode (4C) ?
```

» You're not going to use hardware flow control, so the default, 00, turns it off:

```
Flow (00) ?
```

» Following is the number the network port number that will be connected to the device's serial port. Unless you need a specific port, use the default port 10001:

```
Port No (10001) ?
```

» Next comes the ConnectMode. This parameter controls how the module reacts when it gets network connections. Setting D4 tells it to allow all incoming connections, and when it gets an incoming connection, it should send a response out the serial port. You'll see this in action shortly.

```
ConnectMode (C0) ?D4
```

▶▶ With every new outgoing connection, the Lantronix modules can be configured to choose a new outgoing port. You don't need this, so when your module asks, reply with a no:

```
Auto-increment source port (N) ? N
```

▶▶ The Lantronix modules can be configured to connect automatically to a remote address and a remote port number on startup. In this chapter, you won't use this feature, so enter the default values (0 or 000) for all of these:

```
Remote IP Address : (000) .(000) .(000) .(000)
Remote Port  (0) ?
```

▶▶ The Disconnect mode determines how the module handles disconnection from remote addresses. The default value, 00, will meet your needs:

```
DisConnMode (00) ?
```

▶▶ The FlushMode controls how the module flushes its serial port buffers. The default value, 00, tells it to clear both transmit and receive buffers whenever it disconnects from a remote address:

```
FlushMode   (00) ?
```

▶▶ The Disconnect Time sets how long a remote device can be connected to the module with no activity. 00:00 sets the time to infinite:

```
DisConnTime (00:00) ?:
```

▶▶ The SendChar settings allow you to set a string of characters that can be sent to the module either from a remote device or from the local serial port to force it to disconnect. For now, you won't need this feature:

```
SendChar 1  (00) ?
SendChar 2  (00) ?
```

▶▶ Finally, choose option 9 to save your settings and exit setup.

NOTE: For full details on all the settings of the Lantronix modules, check out each module's user guide, found online at www.lantronix.com/support/documentation.html. I'll cover only the settings needed for the projects detailed here. Once you're comfortable using the modules, it's worth exploring some of the other features.

```
Change Setup:
   0 Server configuration
   1 Channel 1 configuration
   5 Expert settings
   6 Security
   7 Factory defaults
   8 Exit without save
   9 Save and exit           Your choice ? 9

Parameters stored ...
```

Now you're ready to connect to the module from the network. Connect the module to your network with an Ethernet cable. Leaving your serial terminal connection open, reset the module by pressing its reset button. After a few seconds, it should return the letter D in the serial window, indicating that it's disconnected from any other device.

Now open your terminal program (xterm on Linux/Unix or Terminal on Mac OS X) and attempt to make a telnet connection to the module's IP address on port number 10001. On Windows, you can run the telnet program from the command prompt or use PuTTY to connect.

```
telnet 192.168.1.20 10001
```

You'll get a response like this:

```
Trying 192.168.1.20...
Connected to 192.168.1.20.
Escape character is '^]'.
```

Back in your serial terminal program, the module will return C for "connected", I for "incoming connection," and the address of the machine that connected to it:

```
CI192.168.1.45
```

Now type messages back and forth. Whatever you type in the telnet session should show up in the serial window, and vice versa. Hello Internet! You've made your first connection. To disconnect, close the telnet session. The Micro module should respond with a D for "disconnected."

Once a Lantronix module is on the network, you can also configure it via telnet. Telnet to the device's IP address on port 9999 and you'll get the same configuration menu that you got in the serial terminal when you reset the module and held down the x button. You can also configure it via a web browser. Open a browser and enter the module's IP address. You'll get a Java-based configuration screen. Sometimes it can be useful to reconfigure your module via the Web or telnet. For initial configuration, however, it's easiest to configure via the serial port, because you don't need to know whether it's successfully obtained an IP address in order to do so.

Connecting Through the Network Module

Now that you've confirmed that your Micro works and that you can connect to it, it's time to make connections to the

---

Modem Responses

The module's responses parallel those of the Bluetooth modem in Chapter 2. When in command mode, it sends messages reporting on its status: the Micro module's D response corresponds to the NO CARRIER response from the Bluetooth module's AT command set. The C address response corresponds to the Bluetooth modem's CONNECT, address response, and so forth. In fact, it's possible to make the Lantronix modules operate using an AT-style command set by changing the ConnectMode to D6. For the programs in this book, however, it's easier to use the less-verbose protocol afforded by setting the ConnectMode to D4.

---

rest of the Net from it. With the serial terminal connection open, press the reset button on the module. It should respond with a D for "disconnected." To force a Lantronix device to connect to a remote address, type C followed by the remote address (numeric only), followed by a slash (/) followed by the port number. For example, to connect to O'Reilly's web server, you'd type:

```
C208.201.239.37/80
```

Once you're connected, you'd request a page just like you did from the command line in Chapter 3. Type:

```
GET /index.html HTTP/1.0
HOST: www.oreillynet.com
```

Then hit the Return key twice.

You won't see what you type, because the Lantronix modules don't echo your characters back to you, but you will see everything the server sends in response. In this case, you'll get the header and full HTML text of O'Reilly's web page, something like this:

```
HTTP/1.1 302 Found
Date: Thu, 15 Mar 2007 21:51:02 GMT
Server: Apache
Location: http://www.oreillynet.com/index.csp
Content-Length: 287
Connection: close
Content-Type: text/html; charset=iso-8859-1
```

Finding a Host's IP Address

The Lantronix modules' connect command takes only numerical IP addresses, so you can't give them host names. For example, typing Cwww.google.com/80 won't work. If you need to find a host's IP address, use the ping command mentioned in Chapter 3. For example, if you open a command prompt and type ping –c 1 www.oreillynet.com, you will get the following response:

```
PING www.oreillynet.com (208.201.239.37): 56 data bytes
64 bytes from 208.201.239.37: icmp_seq=0 ttl=45 time=97.832 ms
```

And there, in the first line, is the numerical IP address you need. Remember, ping is your friend.

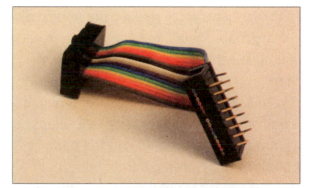

⍗ A DIY ribbon cable adaptor for the Micro. Shown below that is the Micro-to-USV-adaptor circuit using an adaptor made from an IDC DIP plug and an IDC socket. The circuit is the same as in Figure 4-3.

... and so forth. The web server will close the connection when it's sent you the whole page.

You've made two connections now. In the first, the Lantronix module acted as a server. You telnetted into it and saw what you typed come out the serial port. In the second, the module acted as a client, connecting to a remote host, making an HTTP request, and delivering the results through the serial port. Now it's time to write a program to make HTTP requests directly from a microcontroller.

X

⚠ If this doesn't work, your serial program might not be sending a carriage return followed by a line feed at the end of each line. You can either reconfigure your serial program to do this, or type Control-M (shown as ^M next) followed by Control-J (^J) instead of pressing Return (once at the end of each line, and twice at the end of the last line):

```
C208.201.239.37/80<Return>
GET /index.html HTTP/1.0^M^J
HOST: www.oreillynet.com^M^J^M^^J
```

You will probably also find this easier to work with if you copy the contents of each line into a text file so that you can cut and paste them (without the end-of-line characters, because you're typing them yourself) into the serial program.

❝ An Embedded Network Client Application

By now, you should be pretty good at making connections through your module. It's time to build a full application. This project is an embedded web scraper. It takes data from an existing website and uses it to affect a physical output. It's conceptually similar to devices made by Ambient Devices, Nabaztag, and others.

🔊 **Project 6**

Networked Air Quality Meter

In this project, you'll make a networked air quality meter. You'll need an analog panel meter, like the kind you find in speedometers and audio VU meters. I got mine at a yard sale, but you can often find them in electronics surplus stores or junk shops. The model recommended in the parts list here is less picturesque than mine, but it will do for a placeholder until you find one you love.

On the following page, Figure 4-5 shows how it works: the microcontroller makes a network connection to a PHP script through the Lantronix module. The PHP script connects to another web page, reads a number from that page, and sends the number back to the microcontroller. The microcontroller uses that number to set the level of the meter. The web page in question is AIRNow, www.airnow.gov, the U.S. Environmental Protection Agency's site for reporting air quality. It reports hourly air quality status for many U.S. cities, listed by ZIP code. When you're done, you'll have a meter you can set anywhere in your home or office to see the state of the air quality in your city at a glance (assuming you live in the U.S.).

MATERIALS

» **1 Lantronix embedded device server** Available from many vendors, including Symmetry Electronics (www.semiconductorstore.com) as part number CO-E1-11AA (Micro), or WM11A0002-01 (WiMicro), or XP1001001-03R (XPort).

» **1 solderless breadboard** such as Digi-Key part number 438-1045-ND, or Jameco part number 20601.

» **1 USB-to-serial circuit** such as the FT232RL, or RS-232-to-serial circuit such as the MAX3323, as shown in Chapter 2. Use the second of these if you don't have a USB port and have to use an RS-232 serial port. Otherwise use the first.

» **The micro-to-breadboard connector** from the previous project (or make another one if needed).

» **Arduino module** or other microcontroller.

» **1 voltmeter** Get a nice-looking antique one if you can. For a placeholder, you can use part number 48J6151 from Newark (www.newarkinone.com). Ideally, you want a meter that reads a range from 0–5V, or 0–10V at most.

» **5 LEDs**

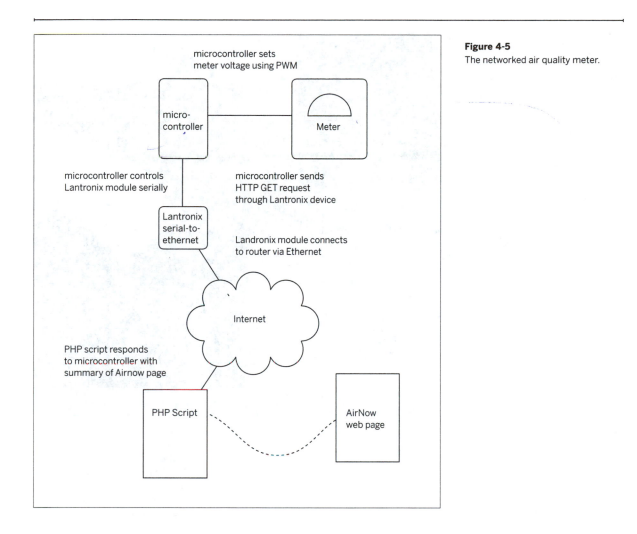

Figure 4-5
The networked air quality meter.

Control the Meter Using the Microcontroller

First, you need to generate a changing voltage from the microcontroller to control the meter. Microcontrollers can't output analog voltages, but they can generate a series of very rapid on-and-off pulses that can be filtered to give an average voltage. The higher the ratio of on-time to off-time in each pulse, the higher the average voltage. This technique is called pulse width modulation (PWM). In order for a PWM signal to appear as an analog voltage, the circuit receiving the pulses has to react much more slowly than the rate of the pulses. For example, if you pulse width modulate an LED, it will seem to be dimming, because your eye can't detect the on-off transitions when they come faster than about 30 times a second. Analog voltmeters are very slow to react to changing voltages, so PWM works well as a way to control these meters. By connecting the positive terminal of the meter to an output pin of the microcontroller and the negative pin to ground and pulse width modulating the output pin, you can easily control the position of the meter.

Figure 4-6 shows the whole circuit for the project. The Lantronix module is connected to the microcontroller's serial pins. You'll use it and the LEDs in the steps that follow.

> ⚠ **If you've hooked this circuit up, you probably won't be able to program the microcontroller, because the Lantronix is using the same serial pins that are used by the USB interface. To program the board, you'll need to disconnect the RX pin (pin 0 on the Arduino).**

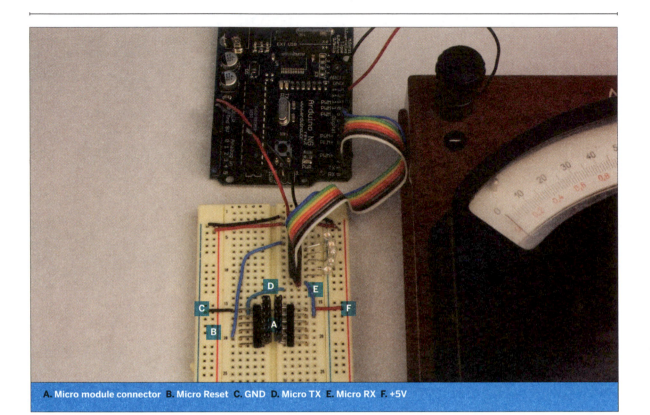

A. Micro module connector **B.** Micro Reset **C.** GND **D.** Micro TX **E.** Micro RX **F.** +5V

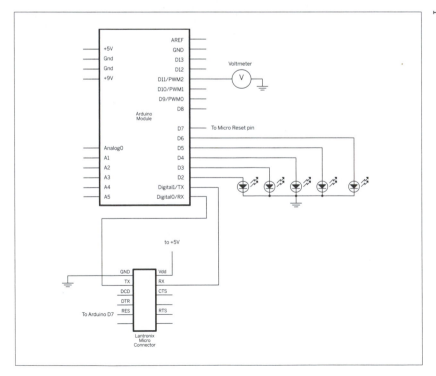

Figure 4-6
The circuit for a networked meter.
The Micro itself has been removed to
show the wiring beneath it. It plugs
into the connector.

Test It

Here's a program to test whether you can control the meter:

You will need to adjust the range of pwmValue depending on the sensitivity of your meter. The meters used to design this project had different ranges. The meter from Newark in the parts list responds to a 0 to 5 volt range, so the preceding program moves it from its bottom to its top. The antique meter, on the other hand, responds to 0 to 3 volts, so it was necessary to limit the range of pwmValue to 0 – 165. When it was at 165, the meter reached its maximum. You'll see in the code that appears later how to limit the range using a maximum value.

```
/*
    Voltmeter Tester
    Uses analogWrite() to control a voltmeter.
    Language: Wiring/Arduino
*/
// the output pin that the meter is attached to:
#define meterPin 11

int pwmValue = 0;  // the value used to set the meter

void setup() {
  // nothing here
}

void loop() {
  // move the meter from lowest to highest values:
  for (pwmValue = 0; pwmValue < 255; pwmValue ++) {
    analogWrite(meterPin, pwmValue);
    delay(10);
  }
  delay(1000);
  // reset the meter to zero and pause:
  analogWrite(meterPin, 0);
  delay(1000);
}
```

" Write a PHP Script to Read the Web Page

Next, you need to get the data from AIRNow's site in a form the microcontroller can read. The microcontroller can read in short strings serially, and converting those ASCII strings to a binary number is fairly simple. Parsing through all of the text of a web page using a microcontroller is difficult, but it's the kind of task that PHP was made for. The program that follows reads the AIRNow page, extracts the current AQI reading, and passes that value on to the microcontroller. The Lantronix module is the microcontroller's gateway to the Net, allowing it to open a TCP connection to your web host, where you need to install this PHP script.

NOTE: You could also run this script on one of the computers on your local network. As long as the microcontroller is connected to the same network, you'll be able to connect to it and request the PHP page. For information on installing PHP or finding a web hosting provider that supports PHP, see www.php.net/manual/en/tutorial.php#tutorial.requirements.

Figure 4-7 shows AIRNow's page for New York City (airnow.gov/index.cfm?action=airnow.showlocal&cityid=164). AIRNow's page is formatted well for extracting the data. The AQI index number is clearly shown in text, and if you remove all of the HTML tags, it appears on a line by itself, always following the line AQI observed at hh:mm AM/PM:.

NOTE: One of the most difficult things about maintaining applications like this, which scrape data from an existing website, is the probability that the designers of the website could change the format of their page. If that happens, your application could stop working, and you'll need to rewrite your code. This is a case where it's useful to have the PHP script do the scraping of the remote site. It's more convenient to rewrite the PHP than it is to reprogram the microcontroller once it's in place.
X

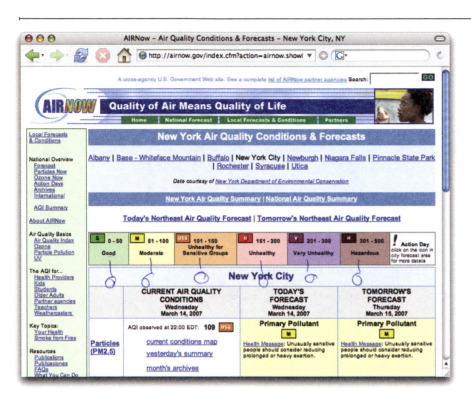

Figure 4-7
AIRNow's page is nicely laid out for scraping. The PHP program used in this project ignores the ozone level.

Fetch It   The PHP script shown here opens the URL of the AIRNow web page and, as long as there are more lines to read, it prints the latest line. The fgetss() command reads a line of text and removes any HTML tags.

When you save this file on your web server and open it in a browser, you should get the text of the AIRNow page without any HTML markup or images. It's not very readable in the browser window, but if you view the source code (click the View→Source menu item in your web browser), you'll see that the text is nicely separated into lines. Scroll down and you'll find some lines like this:

```
AQI observed at 12:00 EDT:
28
```

These are the only two lines you care about.

```php
<?php
/*
    AIRNow Web Page Scraper
    Language: PHP
*/
    // Define variables:
    // url of the page with the air quality index data for New York City:
    $url =
      'http://airnow.gov/index.cfm?action=airnow.showlocal&cityid=164';

    // open the file at the URL for reading:
    $filePath = fopen ($url, "r");

    // as long as you haven't reached the end of the file:
    while (!feof($filePath))
    {
        // read one line at a time, and strip all HTML and
        // PHP tags from the line:
        $line = fgetss($filePath, 4096);
        echo $line;
    }
    // close the file at the URL, you're done:
    fclose($filePath);
?>
```

Scrape It   To extract the data you need from those lines, you'll need a couple more variables. Add these lines at the top of the program (but after the line starting with <?php):

```
$readParticles = 0;    // flag telling you the next line
                       // is the particle value
$particles = -1;       // the particles value
```

▶▶ Then replace the command echo $line; in the program with this block of code:

This block uses the preg_match() command to look for a string of text matching a pattern you give it. In this case, it looks for the pattern AQI observed at. You know that when you see that line, the next line is the number you want. When the PHP script finds the "observed at" line, it sets the variable $readParticles to 1.

```
// if the current line contains the substring "AQI observed at"
// then the line following it is either the particle reading
// or the ozone reading:
if (preg_match('/AQI observed at /', $line)) {
    // if $particles == -1, you haven't gotten
    // a value for it yet:
    if ($particles == -1) {
        $readParticles = 1;
    }
}
```

▶▶ Now, add the following block of code *before* the one you just added (just before the comment that begins with "if the current line"):

This code checks to see if $readParticles is equal to 1. If it does, it reads the current line of text, trims off any excess characters, and prints it out. The result in your web browser should look like this:

```
// if the previous line was the "observed at line" preceding
// the particle matter reading, then $readParticles = 1 and
// you should get this line, trim everything but the number,
// and save the result in $particles:
if ($readParticles == 1) {
    $particles = trim($line);
    echo "< AQI: $particles>";
    $readParticles = 0;
}
```

```
< AQI: 43>
```

Now you've got a short string of text that your microcontroller can read. The next step program your microcontroller to read your PHP script over the Net (be sure to reconnect the Lantronix after you program it). To see the PHP script in its entirety, see Appendix C.

Read the PHP Script Using the Microcontroller

The microcontroller can communicate through the Lantronix module, just like you did from the serial terminal window. First, you send a connect string telling it the numerical address of the server and the port number. When a connection is made, the Lantronix device returns a "C" to let you know it's connected. After that, you send an HTTP GET request for the PHP script. Then the script returns the Air Quality Index string.

Before you start programming, plan the sequence of messages. Using the Lantronix module as a network client is very similar to using Processing as a network client. In both cases, you have to know the correct sequence of messages to send and how the responses will be formatted. You have to write a program to manage the exchange of messages. Whether you're writing that program in Processing or whether you're writing it in Arduino or in another language on another microcontroller, the steps are still the same:

1. Open a connection to the web server
2. Send an HTTP GET request
3. Wait for a response
4. Process the response
5. Wait an appropriate interval and do it all again

Each of these steps involves sending a message and then waiting for a response, so it's worthwhile to keep track of the state that the program is in. Figure 4-8 is a flowchart of what happens in the microcontroller program. The states of the program — disconnected, connecting, connected, requesting, reading, and complete — are laid out on the left of the chart. The actions taken to move from one state to the next follow from the states. You can see that in each state, there's a loop where you take action, then wait. Based on the outcome of the action, you either keep looping, or go to the next state. Laying out the whole program in a flowchart like this will help you keep track of what's going on at any given point.

Because you need to use the serial port to send and receive messages to and from the server, you can't use Serial. print() statements to check what's going on in the program. Instead, you can use LEDs to keep track of the part of the program that you're in. LEDs attached to I/O pins will indicate which state your program is in.

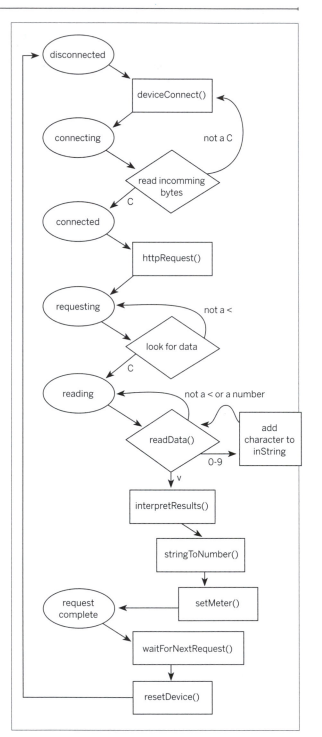

Figure 4-8
A flowchart of the Arduino program for making and processing an HTTP GET request.

Connect It The program starts out by defining each of the states as numerical values, so that you can refer to them later on in a case statement. Then it defines the pin numbers for the various inputs and outputs:

```
// Defines for the program's status (used for status variable):
#define disconnected 0
#define connecting 1
#define connected 2
#define requesting 3
#define reading 4
#define requestComplete 5


// Defines for I/O pins:

#define connectedLED 2          // indicates when there's a TCP connection
#define requestingLED 3         // indicates a HTTP request has been made
#define readingLED 4            // indicates device is reading HTTP results
#define requestCompleteLED 5    // indicates a successful read
#define programResetLED 6       // indicates reset of Arduino
#define deviceResetPin 7        // resets Lantronix Device
#define meterPin 11             // controls VU meter; has to be one of
                                // the PWM pins (9 - 11)
```

▸▸ A couple of constants are defined for converting the AQI reading to a meter level:

```
// defines for voltmeter:
#define meterMax 130            // max value on the meter
#define meterScale 150          // my meter reads 0 - 150
```

▸▸ Next, the global variables are declared and initialized:

```
// variables:
int inByte= -1;                 // incoming byte from serial RX
char inString[32];              // string for incoming serial data
int stringPos = 0;              // string index counter

int status = 0;                 // Lantronix device's connection status
long lastCompletionTime = 0;    // counter for delay after last completion
```

▸▸ In the setup() method, set the state of all the I/O pins, initialize the serial port, call a custom method to reset the Lantronix device, then blink the program reset LED to signal that the main loop is about to begin:

```
void setup() {
  // set all status LED pins and Lantronix device reset pin:
  pinMode(connectedLED, OUTPUT);
  pinMode(requestingLED, OUTPUT);
  pinMode(requestCompleteLED, OUTPUT);
  pinMode(programResetLED, OUTPUT);
  pinMode(deviceResetPin, OUTPUT);
  pinMode(meterPin, OUTPUT);

  // start serial port, 9600 8-N-1:
  Serial.begin(9600);
  //reset Lantronix device:
  resetDevice();
  // blink reset LED:
  blink(3);
}
```

>> You can see from the schematic back in Figure 4-6 that digital pin 7 is connected to the Lantronix module's reset pin. Here's the routine that resets the module:

```
// Take the Lantronix device's reset pin low to reset it:
void resetDevice() {
  digitalWrite(deviceResetPin, LOW);
  delay(50);
  digitalWrite(deviceResetPin, HIGH);
  // pause to let Lantronix device boot up:
  delay(2000);
}
```

>> The blink() method called in the setup is a method to blink the LED on pin 6, so you know the microcontroller's main loop is about to begin:

```
// Blink the reset LED:
void blink(int howManyTimes) {
  int i;
  for (i=0; i< howManyTimes; i++) {
    digitalWrite(programResetLED, HIGH);
    delay(200);
    digitalWrite(programResetLED, LOW);
    delay(200);
  }
}
```

>> The loop() just calls two routines, one to check the state of the program and take appropriate action, and another to set the LEDs depending on the state of the program. Here it is:

```
void loop() {
  stateCheck();
  setLEDs();
}
```

>> The stateCheck() method is a switch-case statement that checks the value of the status variable. In each case, it takes whatever action is appropriate to its current value:

```
void stateCheck() {
  switch (status) {
  case disconnected:
    // attempt to connect to the server:
    deviceConnect();
    break;
  case connecting:
    // until you get a C, keep trying to connect:
    // read the serial port:
    if (Serial.available()) {
      inByte = Serial.read();
      if (inByte == 'C') {  // 'C' in ASCII
        status = connected;
      }
      else {
        // if you got anything other than a C, try again:
        deviceConnect();
      }
    }
    break;
  case connected:
    // send HTTP GET request for CGI script:
    httpRequest();
```

»

Continued from opposite page.

```
      break;
    case requesting:
      lookForData();
      break;
    case reading:
      readData();
      break;
    case requestComplete:
      waitForNextRequest();
    }
}
```

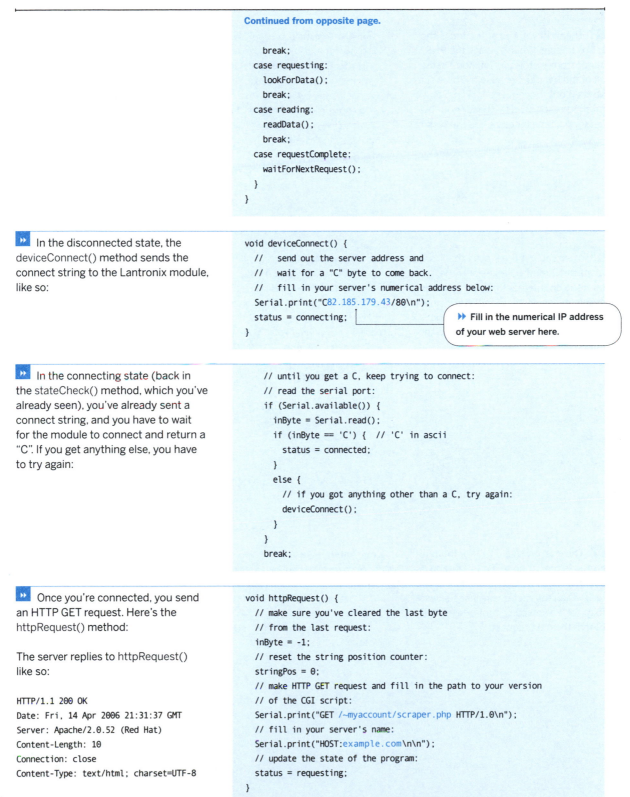

In the disconnected state, the deviceConnect() method sends the connect string to the Lantronix module, like so:

```
void deviceConnect() {
  //   send out the server address and
  //   wait for a "C" byte to come back.
  //   fill in your server's numerical address below:
  Serial.print("C82.185.179.43/80\n");
  status = connecting;
}
```

▶▶ **Fill in the numerical IP address of your web server here.**

In the connecting state (back in the stateCheck() method, which you've already seen), you've already sent a connect string, and you have to wait for the module to connect and return a "C". If you get anything else, you have to try again:

```
  // until you get a C, keep trying to connect:
  // read the serial port:
  if (Serial.available()) {
    inByte = Serial.read();
    if (inByte == 'C') {  // 'C' in ascii
      status = connected;
    }
    else {
      // if you got anything other than a C, try again:
      deviceConnect();
    }
  }
  break;
```

Once you're connected, you send an HTTP GET request. Here's the httpRequest() method:

The server replies to httpRequest() like so:

HTTP/1.1 200 OK
Date: Fri, 14 Apr 2006 21:31:37 GMT
Server: Apache/2.0.52 (Red Hat)
Content-Length: 10
Connection: close
Content-Type: text/html; charset=UTF-8

< AQI: 65>

```
void httpRequest() {
  // make sure you've cleared the last byte
  // from the last request:
  inByte = -1;
  // reset the string position counter:
  stringPos = 0;
  // make HTTP GET request and fill in the path to your version
  // of the CGI script:
  Serial.print("GET /~myaccount/scraper.php HTTP/1.0\n");
  // fill in your server's name:
  Serial.print("HOST:example.com\n\n");
  // update the state of the program:
  status = requesting;
}
```

The stuff you see at the top is the HTTP header. When you call the PHP script from a browser, you don't see all of the header, because the browser strips it out for you. The lookForData() method reads strip the header out by ignoring all the bytes before the < sign:

```
void lookForData() {
  // wait for bytes from server:
  if (Serial.available()) {
    inByte = Serial.read();
    // If you get a "<", what follows is the air quality index.
    // You need to read what follows the <.
    if (inByte == '<') {
      stringPos = 0;
      status = reading;
    }
  }
}
```

After you get the < sign, the readData() method takes only the numeric characters from the remaining string and saves them to the inString[] array. When it gets the > symbol indicating the end of the string, it calls the interpretResults() method:

```
void readData() {
  if (Serial.available()) {
    inByte = Serial.read();
    // Keep reading until you get a ">":
    if (inByte != '>') {
      // save only ASCII numeric characters (ASCII 0 - 9):
      if ((inByte >= '0') && (inByte <= '9')){
        inString[stringPos] = inByte;
        stringPos++;
      }
    }
    // if you get a ">", you've reached the end of the AQI reading:
    else {
      interpretResults();
    }
  }
}
```

The interpretResults() method converts the string to a number and sets the meter. It also takes note of the time when the meter was last successfully set, so you can count one minute before the next request:

```
void interpretResults() {
  // convert the string to a numeric value:
  int airQuality = atoi(inString);
  // set the meter appropriately:
  setMeter(airQuality);
  lastCompletionTime = millis();
  status = requestComplete;
}
```

» The setMeter() method takes the number and scales it to set the meter appropriately. You will need to adjust the formula if your meter is different from the ones shown here.

You will need to adjust meterMax and meterScale to values that work for your meter. You can determine these by using the meter testing program in the last section.

```
void setMeter(int desiredValue) {
  int airQualityValue = 0;
  // if the value won't peg the meter, convert it
  // to the meter scale and send it out:
  if (desiredValue <= meterScale) {
    airQualityValue = (desiredValue * meterMax /meterScale);
    analogWrite(meterPin, airQualityValue);
  }
}
```

» When the request is complete, waitForNextRequest() counts time for two minutes, then sets the status to disconnected to initiate a new request:

You can see that you're waiting two full minutes in between successful reads of the web page. In fact, you could wait even longer, as the page is updated only about once an hour. There's no need to check constantly. It creates undue demand on the server, and wastes energy. Remember, one of the cardinal rules of love and networking is to listen more than you speak.

```
void waitForNextRequest() {
  if (millis() - lastCompletionTime >= 120000) {
    // reset Lantronix device before next request:
    resetDevice();
    status = disconnected;
  }
}
```

» The last thing you need to do in the main loop is to set the indicator LEDs so that you know where you are in the program. Because you gave each of the status settings a numeric value up at the top of the program, you can use those numbers to set the LEDs. The setLEDs() methods does this:

That's the whole program. Once you've got this program working on the microcontroller, the controller will make the HTTP GET request once a minute, and set the meter accordingly.

```
void setLEDs() {
  /* Except for the disconnected and connecting states,
  all the states of the program have corresponding LEDS.
  so you can use a for-next loop to set them by
  turning them all off except for the one that has
  the same number as the current program state:
  */

  for (int thisLED = 2; thisLED <= 5; thisLED++) {
    if (thisLED == status) {
      digitalWrite(thisLED, HIGH);
    }
    else {
      digitalWrite(thisLED, LOW);
    }
  }
}
```

The Finished Project

Figure 4-9

The completed networked air quality meter.

⚠ Before you run the final program for this project, you must change at least three lines of code (emphasized in the code listing), which are in various places in the example:

```
Serial.print("C82.165.199.35/80\n");
Serial.print("GET /netobj/code/php/scraper.php HTTP/1.1\n");
Serial.print("HOST:example.com\n\n");
```

You may also need to change meterScale and meterMax, depending on the sensitivity of your meter.

Servi

CYPRESS

COLLEGE

ED GIARDINA
Assistant Professor
Art Department

9200 Valley View Street
Cypress, CA 90630-5897
(714) 484-7208 • fax (714) 952-9602
email: egiardina@cypresscollege.edu

" Serial-to-Ethernet Modules: Programming and Troubleshooting Tools

You probably hit a number of problems in making the connections in the last section. Perhaps you wired the transmit and receive connections backwards, or perhaps you got the IP configuration wrong. Probably the most challenging thing about troubleshooting your problems was that there was no clear indication from the Micro module that anything had happened at all. This is the norm when you're working with these modules, or with just about any embedded modem-style module that you build yourself. This section covers a few things you should always check, and a few tools that will help you solve problems. These principles apply whether you're using the Lantronix modules or some other embedded network module.

The Three Most Common Mistakes

Power and Ground
Always check whether you have made the power and ground connections correctly. If you're lucky, the module you're using will have indicator LEDs that light up when it's working properly. Whether it does or not, check the voltage between power and ground with a meter to make sure you've got it powered correctly.

Transmit and Receive
Confirm that you've got the module's transmit pin wired to the receive pin of your serial port or microcontroller, and vice versa. If you don't, you'll get nothing either way.

Configuration
If you're sure about the hardware connections, check the device's configuration to make sure it's all correct. In the case of the Lantronix modules, is the IP address you entered one that's on your subnet? Is the router address correct? Is the netmask?

The Lantronix devices, like many modems, can be configured from either end. So far you've seen how to configure them through the serial port, by holding down the x key in the serial terminal while you reset the module. Remember, you can also telnet into port 9999 to change the configuration settings. If you have problems with the serial connection, try checking the configuration via the network connection.

Diagnostic Tools and Methods

Once you know the modem's working, you have to program the sequence of messages that constitutes your application. Depending on the application's needs, this sequence can get complex, so it's useful to have a few simple programs around to make sure things work the way you want them to.

Use a Second Serial Output for Debugging Messages

One of the most difficult aspects of debugging a microcontroller speaking to a Lantronix device is that you can't send serial debugging messages to the Arduino or Wiring Serial Monitor over the serial port, because it's attached to the Lantronix device. Any serial messages you send will interfere with the communication with the server! This is a common problem in networked microcontroller projects. You can use the Wiring and Arduino SoftwareSerial library to send serial debugging messages on another set of pins. SoftwareSerial can send and receive data only at speeds up to 9600 baud, but it's useful for debugging.

NOTE: On a Wiring module, you can use the second serial port instead of using SoftwareSerial.

To use SoftwareSerial, you'll need two spare digital I/O pins and either a USB-to-serial module or an RS-232-to-TTL module to which you can connect them. In the previous project you never used pins 8 and 9, so this example uses those pins. Figure 4-10 shows a modified version of the meter schematic with the FT232RL USB-to-serial module added to pins 8 and 9 for use with SoftwareSerial.

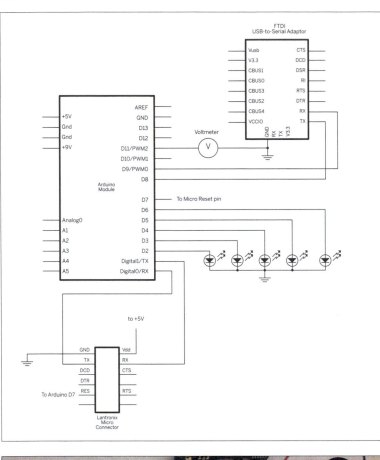

Figure 4-10
Modified network meter circuit, with
serial adaptor added.

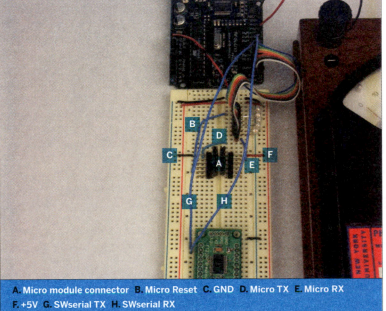

A. Micro module connector **B.** Micro Reset **C.** GND **D.** Micro TX **E.** Micro RX
F. +5V **G.** SWserial TX **H.** SWserial RX

Debug It Wherever you want have a debugging message printed out, use SoftwareSerial instead of Serial. Open your serial terminal program (GNU screen or PuTTY) to see the messages. Here's a simple program that shows how to use the SoftwareSerial library:

```
/*
  SoftwareSerial example
  language: Wiring/Arduino

  This program uses the SoftwareSerial library to send serial messages
  on pins 8 and 9.
*/

// include the SoftwareSerial library so you can use its functions:
#include <SoftwareSerial.h>

#define rxPin 8
#define txPin 9

// set up a new serial port
SoftwareSerial mySerial = SoftwareSerial(rxPin, txPin);

void setup() {
  // define pin modes for tx, rx, led pins:
  pinMode(rxPin, INPUT);
  pinMode(txPin, OUTPUT);
  // set the data rate for the SoftwareSerial port
  mySerial.begin(9600);
}

void loop() {
  // print out a debugging message:
  mySerial.println("Hello from SoftwareSerial");
  delay(100);
}
```

» Here's an abbreviated version of the meter program, showing where you might insert SoftwareSerial debugging messages. Most of the code has been removed here, to show you debugging messages at the beginning or end of each function. New code is shown in blue:

```
// include the SoftwareSerial library so you can use its functions:
#include <SoftwareSerial.h>

#define rxPin 8
#define txPin 9

// Defines go here


// variables go here

// set up a new serial port
SoftwareSerial mySerial = SoftwareSerial(rxPin, txPin);


void setup() {
  // the rest of the setup() code goes here

  // define pin modes for SoftwareSerial tx, rx pins:
```

»

Continued from previous page.

```
  pinMode(rxPin, INPUT);
  pinMode(txPin, OUTPUT);
  // set the data rate for the SoftwareSerial port
  mySerial.begin(9600);

  // print out a debugging message:
  mySerial.println("All set up");

}

void loop() {
  stateCheck();
  setLEDs();
}

void stateCheck() {

  // the rest of stateCheck() code goes here
}

void setLEDs() {
  // setLEDs() code goes here
}

void deviceConnect() {
  // print out a debugging message:
  mySerial.println("connect");

  //   the rest of deviceConnect() code goes here
}


void httpRequest() {
  // print out a debugging message:
  mySerial.println("request");

  // the rest of httpRequest() code goes here
}


void lookForData() {

  // wait for bytes from server:
  if (Serial.available()) {
    inByte = Serial.read();
    mySerial.print(inByte, BYTE);

    // the rest of lookForData() code goes here
}
```

```
void readData() {
  if (Serial.available()) {
    inByte = Serial.read();
    mySerial.print(inByte, BYTE);

    // the rest of readData() code goes here
}


void interpretResults() {
  // print out a debugging message:
  mySerial.println("interpret");

  // the rest of interpretResults() code goes here

  // print out a debugging message:
  mySerial.println("wait");
}


void setMeter(int desiredValue) {
  // print out a debugging message:
  mySerial.println("set");

  // the rest of setMeter() code goes here
}


void resetDevice() {
  // print out a debugging message:
  mySerial.println("reset");

  // the rest of resetDevice() code goes here
}
/*
  Blink the reset LED.
 */
void blink(int howManyTimes) {
  int i;
  for (i=0; i< howManyTimes; i++) {
    digitalWrite(programResetLED, HIGH);
    delay(200);
    digitalWrite(programResetLED, LOW);
    delay(200);
  }
}
```

Write a Test Client Program in Processing

It's easiest to work through the steps of the program if you can step through the sequence of events. More expensive development environments allow you to step through a program one line at a time, but you can make your own version of a step-by-step program in Processing (you'll need to hook the Lantronix device to your computer as shown back in Figure 4-3). The following code goes through each of the steps needed to command a Lantronix module to connect to a remote server. Every time you press any key on the keyboard, it takes the next step. The serialEvent() method waits for data to be returned from each step and prints it out, so you can decide when to take the next step. It's an excellent tool for diagnosing whether you're getting the responses you want from the remote server.

Test It The handy thing about this program is that you can test the exchange of messages without having a microcontroller. Once you know you have the sequence right, you can translate it into code for the Arduino module:

```
/*
Lantronix serial-to-ethernet HTTP request tester
Language: Processing

This program sends serial messages to a Lantronix serial-to-ethernet
device to get it to connect to a remote webserver and make an HTTP
request. To use this program, connect your PC to the Lantronix modules
serial port as you did when you were configuring the Lantronix module
earlier.

*/

// include the serial library
import processing.serial.*;

Serial myPort;         // Serial object
int step = 0;          // which step in the process you're on
char linefeed = 10;    // ASCII linefeed character
void setup()
{
  // get the list of serial ports:
  println(Serial.list());
  // open the serial port apprropriate to your computer:
  myPort = new Serial(this, Serial.list()[2], 9600);
  // configure the serial object to buffer text until it receives a
  // linefeed character:
  myPort.bufferUntil(linefeed);
}

void draw()
{
  //no action in the draw loop
}

void serialEvent(Serial myPort) {
  // print any string that comes in serially to the monitor pane
  print(myPort.readString());
}
```

»

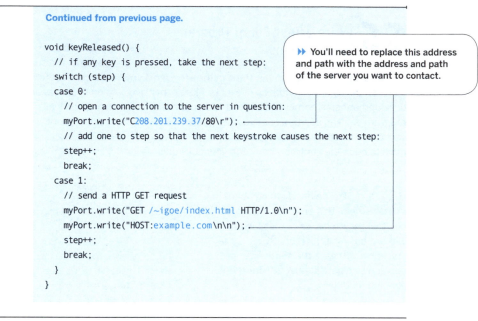

Continued from previous page.

```
void keyReleased() {
  // if any key is pressed, take the next step:
  switch (step) {
  case 0:
    // open a connection to the server in question:
    myPort.write("C208.201.239.37/80\r");
    // add one to step so that the next keystroke causes the next step:
    step++;
    break;
  case 1:
    // send a HTTP GET request
    myPort.write("GET /~igoe/index.html HTTP/1.0\n");
    myPort.write("HOST:example.com\n\n");
    step++;
    break;
  }
}
```

▶▶ You'll need to replace this address and path with the address and path of the server you want to contact.

Write a Test Server Program

The previous program allowed you to connect to a remote server and test the exchange of messages. The remote server was beyond your control, however, so you can't say for sure that the server ever received your messages. If you never made a connection, you have no way of knowing whether the module can connect to any server. To test this, you can write your own server program for it to connect to.

▶▶ Here is a short Processing program that you can run on your PC. It listens for incoming connections, and prints out any messages sent over those connections. It sends any keystrokes typed out over the open connection.

To use this, first make sure your Lantronix module and your PC are on the same network. Then run this program, and connect to it from the module by connecting to your PC's IP address, port 8080. For example, if your PC has the IP address 192.168.1.45, the connect string would be:

```
C192.168.1.45/8080
```

```
/*
 server_test
 Language: Processing

 Creates a server that listens for clients and prints what they say.
 It also sends the last client anything that's  typed on the keyboard.
*/


// include the net library:
import processing.net.*;

int port = 8080;        // the port the server listens on
Server myServer;        // the server object
Client  thisClient;     // incoming client object

void setup()
{
  myServer = new Server(this, port); // Start the server
}

void draw()
{
  // get the next client that sends a message:
```

▶▶

Continued from opposite page.

```
Client speakingClient = myServer.available();

// if the message is not null, display what it sent:
if (speakingClient !=null) {
  String whatClientSaid = speakingClient.readString();
  // print who sent the message, and what they sent:
  println(speakingClient.ip() + "\t" + whatClientSaid);
}
}


// ServerEvent message is generated when a new client
// connects to the server.
void serverEvent(Server myServer, Client someClient) {
  println("We have a new client: " + someClient.ip());
  thisClient = someClient;
}


void keyReleased() {
  // only send if there's a client to send to:
  if (thisClient != null) {
    // if return is pressed, send newline and carriage feed:
    if (key == '\n') {
      thisClient.write("\r\n");
    }
    // send any other key as is:
    else {
      thisClient.write(key);
    }
  }
}
```

! This program uses port 8080, which is a common alternative port for many web servers. If you're running a web server on your PC, you might have to change the port number in this program.

Whether you're connecting from a serial terminal program or have programmed a microcontroller to make the connection, you can use this program to test whether the Lantronix module is making a successful connection. Once you've seen messages coming through to this program in the right sequence, just change the connect string in your microcontroller code to the address of the web server you want to connect to, and everything should work fine. If it doesn't, the problem is most likely with your web server. Contact your service provider for details on how to access any server diagnostic tools they provide, especially any error logs for your server.
X

❝❝ Conclusion

The activities in this chapter show a model for networked objects that's very flexible and useful. The object is basically a browser, requesting information from the Web and extracting the information it needs. You can use this model in many different projects.

The advantage of this model is that it doesn't require a lot of work to repurpose existing web applications. At most, you need to write a variation of the PHP web scraper from this chapter to summarize the relevant information from an existing website. This flexibility makes it easier for microcontroller enthusiasts who aren't experienced in web development to collaborate with web programmers, and vice versa. It also makes it easy to reuse others' work if you can't find a willing collaborator.

The model has its limits, though, and in the next chapter you'll see some ways to get around those limits with a different model. Even if you're not using this model, don't forget the troubleshooting tools mentioned here. Making simple mock-ups of the programs on either end of a transaction can make your life much easier, because they let you see what should happen, and modify what actually is happening to match that.
X

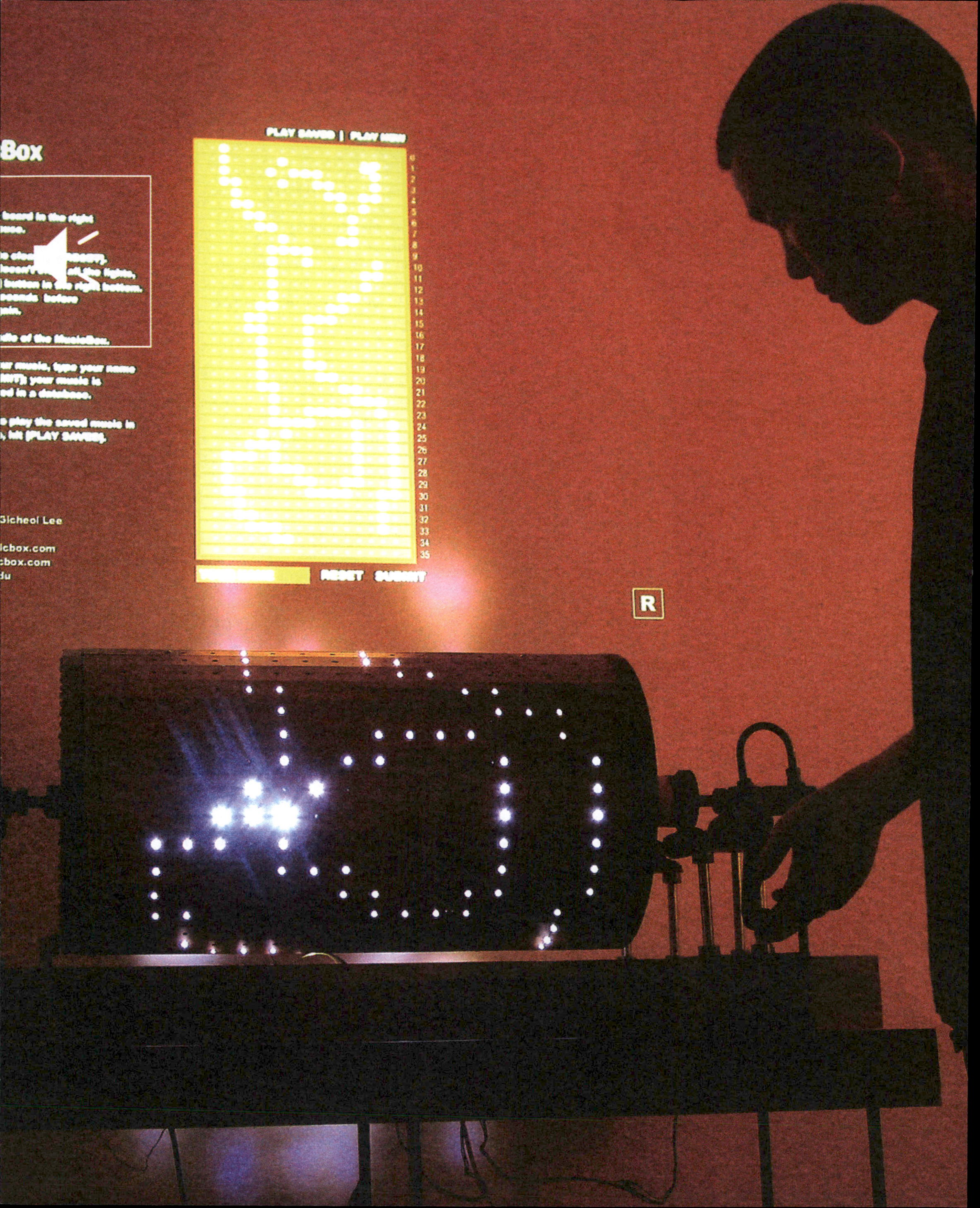
PLAY SAVED | PLAY NEW
RESET
SUBMIT
R

5

Communicating in (Near) Real Time

So far, all of the networked communications you've seen worked like a Web browser. Your object made a request to a remote server, the server ran a program and then sent a response. This transaction worked by making a connection to the web server, exchanging some information, then breaking the connection. In this chapter, you'll learn more about that connection, and you'll write a server program that allows you to maintain the connection in order to facilitate a faster and more consistent exchange between the server and client.

◀◀ **Musicbox by Jin-Yo Mok (2004)**

The music box is connected to a composition program over the Internet using a serial-to-ethernet module. The composition program changes the lights on the music box and the sounds it will play. Real time communication between the two in order to give the player feedback on what he is playing. *Photo courtesy of Jin-Yo Mok.*

" Interactive Systems and Feedback Loops

In every interactive system, there's a feedback loop: you take action, the system responds, you see the response, or a notification of it, and you take another action. In some systems, the timing of that loop can be very loose. In other applications, the timing must be tight.

For example, in the cat bed application in Chapter 3, there's no need for the system to respond in more than a few seconds, because your reaction is not very time-sensitive. As long as you get to see the cat while he's on the bed (which may be true for several minutes or hours), you're happy. Monski pong in Chapter 2 relies on a reasonably tight feedback loop in order to be fun. If it took a half second or more for the paddles to move when you move Monski's arms, it'd be no fun. The timing of the feedback loop depends on the shortest time that matters to the participant.

Any system that requires coordination between action and reaction needs a tight feedback loop. Consider remote control systems, for example. Perhaps you're building a robot that's operated over a network. In that case, you'd need not only a fast network for the control system, but also a fast response from the camera or sensors on the robot (or in its environment) that are giving you information about what's happening. You need to be able to both control it quickly and see the results quickly. Networked action games also need a fast network. It's no fun if your game console reacts slowly, allowing other players with a faster network connection to get the jump on you. For applications like this, an exchange protocol that's constantly opening and closing connections (like HTTP does) wouldn't be very effective.

When there's a one-to-one connection between two objects, it's easy to establish a tight feedback loop. When there are multiple objects involved, though, it gets harder. To begin with, you have to consider how the network of connections between all the objects will be configured. Will it be a star network, with all the participants connected through a central server? Will it be a ring network? Will it be a many-to-many network, where every object has a direct connection to every other object? Each of these configurations has different effects on the feedback loop timing. In a star network, the objects on the edge of the network aren't very busy, but the central one is. In a ring

network, every object shares the load more or less equally, but it can take a long time for a message to reach objects on opposite sides of the ring. In a direct many-to-many network, the load is equally distributed, but each object needs to maintain a lot of connections.

In most cases where you have a limited number of objects in conversation, it's easiest to manage the exchange using a central server. The most common program example of this is a text-based chat server like IRC (Internet Relay Chat), or AOL's instant messenger servers (AIM). Server programs that accept incoming clients and manage text messages between them in real time are often referred to as chat servers. The Processing program you'll write in this chapter is a variation on a chat server. The server will listen for new connections and exchange messages with all of the clients that connect to it. Because there's no guarantee how long messages take to pass through the Internet, the exchange of messages can't be instantaneous. But as long as you've got a fast network connection for both clients and server, the feedback loop will be faster than human reaction time.

X

" Transmission Control Protocol: Sockets & Sessions

Each time a client connects to a web server, the connection that's opened uses a protocol called Transmission Control Protocol, or TCP. TCP is a protocol that specifies how objects on the Internet open, maintain, and close a connection that will involve multiple exchanges of messages. The connection made between any two objects using TCP is called a socket. A socket is like a pipe joining the two objects. It allows data to flow back and forth between them as long as the connection is maintained. Both sides need to keep the connection open in order for it to work.

For example, think about the exchanges between a web client and server that you saw in the last two chapters. The pipe is opened when the server acknowledges the client's contact, and remains open until the server has finished sending the data.

There's a lot going on behind the scenes of a socket connection. The exchange of data over a TCP connection can range in size anywhere from a few bytes to a few terabytes or more. All that data is sent in discrete packets, and the packets are sent by the best route from one end to the other.

NOTE: "Best" is a deliberately vague term: the optimal route is calculated differently by different network hardware, and involves a variety of metrics (such as the number of hops between two points as well as the available bandwidth and reliability of a given path).

The period between the opening of a socket and the successful close of the socket is called a session. During the session, the program that maintains the socket tracks the status of the connection (open or closed) and the port number; counts the number of packets sent and received; notes the order of the packets and sees to it that packets are presented in the right order, even if the later packets arrive first; and accounts for any missing packets by requesting that they be re-sent. All of that is taken care of for you when you use a TCP/IP stack like the Net library in Processing or the firmware on the Lantronix devices you first saw in Chapter 4.

The complexity of TCP is worthwhile when you're exchanging critical data. For example, in an email, every byte is a character in the message. If you drop a couple of bytes, you could lose crucial information. The error checking of

TCP does slow things down a little, though, and if you want to send messages to multiple receivers, you have to open a separate socket connection to each one.

There's a simpler type of transmission protocol that's also common on the net called the User Datagram Protocol, or UDP. Where TCP communication is based on sockets and sessions, UDP is based only on the exchange of packets. You'll learn more about it in Chapter 7.

X

◀€ **Project 7**

A Networked Game

Networked games are a great way to learn about real time connections. This project is a networked variation on pong. In honor of everyone's favorite network status command, let's call it call it *ping* pong. The server will be a Processing program, and the clients will be physical interfaces that connect through Lantronix serial-to-Ethernet (or Wi-Fi) modules. The clients and the server's screen have to be physically near each other so that everyone can see the screen. In this case, you're using a network for its flexibility in handling multiple connections, not for its ability to connect remote places.

From the Monski pong project in Chapter 2, you're already familiar with the methods needed to move the paddles and the ball, so some of the code will be familiar to you. As this is a more complex variation, it's important to start with a good description of the whole system. The system will work like this:

- The game has two teams of multiple players.
- Each player can move a paddle back and forth. The paddles are at the top and bottom of the screen, and the ball moves from top to bottom.
- Players connect to the game server through a TCP connection. Every time a player connects, another paddle is added to the screen. New connections alternate between the top and bottom teams. When a player connects, the server replies with the following string: hi, followed by a carriage return and a line feed (shown as \r\n).
- The client can send the following commands:
  - l (ASCII value 108): move left
  - r (ASCII value 114): move right
  - x (ASCII value 120): disconnect
- When the client sends x, the server replies with the following string, and then ends the socket connection:

    bye\r\n

And that's the communications protocol for the whole game. Keep in mind that it doesn't define anything about the physical form of the client object. As long as the client can make a TCP connection to the server and can send and receive the appropriate ASCII messages, it can work with the server. You can attach any type of physical inputs to the client, or you can write a client that sends all these messages automatically, with no physical input from the world at all (though that would be boring). Later in this chapter, you'll see a few different clients, each of which can connect to the server and play the game.

A Test Server

You need a server to get started. There's a lot of code to control the pong display that you don't need right now (you just want to confirm that the clients can connect). You can start out by using the test server from Chapter 4. It will let you listen for new clients, and send them messages by typing in the applet window that appears when you run the program. Run the server and open a telnet connection to it. Remember, it's listening on port 8080, so if your computer's IP address is, say, 192.168.1.45, then you'd connect like so: telnet 192.168.1.45 8080

If you're telnetting in from the same machine, you can use: telnet localhost 8080, or telnet 127.0.0.1 8080.

Whatever you type in the telnet window will show up in the server's debugger pane, and whatever you type in the server's applet window will show up at the client's command line. This result is useful, as it lets you use telnet as a test client later on. Next, you'll build a client and test it by getting it to connect to this server.

NOTE: If you want to get away with building only one client, you can telnet from a computer to connect to the server (telnet ip-address 8080). However, you'll have to press Return after each command (r, l, or x), unless you make a change after you connect. On Mac OS X or Linux, press the telnet escape key combination (Control-]), type the following, and then press Return:

    mode character

On Windows telnet should not require any special configuration, but if you find otherwise, press Control-], type the following, and press Return twice:

    set mode stream

NOTE: You'll now find that the server will accept commands immediately without requiring you to press Return after each one.

The Clients

Like the air quality meter client in Chapter 4, the pong client has a few states that you care about:

Program State	What to do
Disconnected from the server	Try to connect
Connecting to the server	Read bytes in, wait for a Connect message
Connected to the server	Play the game by sending l, r, or x

The client needs a few basic inputs in order to reach any of these states:

- An input for sending a connect message. The same input can be used to send a disconnect message.
- An input for sending a left message.
- An input for sending a right message.

To let the user know what the client device is doing, add some outputs to indicate its state:

- An output to indicate whether the client is connected to the server.
- An output to indicate when the connect/disconnect button is pressed.
- An output to indicate when it's sending a left message.
- An output to indicate when it's sending a right message.

It's always a good idea to put outputs on the client that indicate when it receives input from the user. For example, pressing the connect/disconnect button doesn't guarantee a connection, so it's important to separate the output that acknowledges a button push from the one that indicates successful connection. If there's a problem, this helps the user to determine whether the problem is with the connection to the server, or with the client object itself. In this application, the person using the client can look at the server's screen to see the state of the client. She can see a new paddle appear when her client connects, and she can see her paddle moving back and forth. In many cases, however, there's no way to get confirmation from the server except through the client, so local feedback is essential.

It's also good to indicate the client's status using outputs. You can see in the code that follows that in addition to indicating when the sensors are triggered, you'll also indicate whether the client is connected or disconnected. If this client had a more complex set of potential states, you'd need better indication.

For this project, I built two different clients. They have different methods of physical interaction and different input sensors, but they both behave the same way to the server. You can build either, or both, or use the principles from them to build your own. Building both and comparing the two will give you an idea of how the same protocol can result in very different behavior. One of these clients is much more responsive than the other, but the responsiveness has nothing to do with the communications protocol. It's all in the sensing and in the player's action.

X

❝❝ Client #1: A Seesaw Client

This client is basically a seesaw, as shown in Figure 5-1. The basic structure is a plank mounted on a piece of pipe. The electronics sit in a case at the center of the plank. The user puts her feet on either end of the plank and balances her weight on the plank. As she tilts to the left, the client sends a left message. As she tilts right, it sends a right message. The pushbutton in the center allows her to connect to the server or disconnect by stomping on it. Use a sturdy button for this, and make sure that the LEDs are out of foot-stomping range.

In Chapter 4, you saw the Lantronix Micro in action. In this chapter and the following ones, you'll see the Lantronix XPort. The XPort is smaller than the Micro module, and operates on 3.3 volts instead of 5 volts. Its input pins can tolerate 5 volts, though, so it's easy to interface to a 5-volt microcontroller. There are no other significant differences, so you can use the Micro if you prefer. For the purposes of these projects, the two are functionally identical — use whichever you please.

The circuit for the seesaw client uses an accelerometer to read the tilt of the seesaw. The one shown in Figure 5-2 is a three-axis accelerometer, but you'll only use one axis. You can use a different accelerometer if you choose, as long as it outputs an analog voltage for tilt along one axis.

Because the XPort's pins don't fit nicely in a breadboard, you need the RJ45 breakout board. Figure 5-3 shows the XPort mounted on the breakout board.

A pencil box from your friendly neighborhood stationery store works well as a case for this project. Drill holes in the lid for the switch and the LED, cut holes in the side for the XPort and Arduino jacks, and you're all set. Figure 5-4 shows the outside of the pencil box case, and Figure 5-5 shows the inside and a detail of the wiring to the switches and LEDs. The configuration for the XPort is identical to the one for the Micro in Chapter 4:

```
*** Channel 1
Baudrate 9600, I/F Mode 4C, Flow 00
Port 10001
Remote IP Adr: --- none ---, Port 00000
Connect Mode : D4
Disconn Mode : 00
Flush   Mode : 00
```

As you're using a Lantronix device again, the code for the client has some elements in common with the code for the air quality meter in Chapter 4. You'll reuse the device Connnect() method, the resetDevice() method, and the blink() method from that application.

MATERIALS FOR CLIENT 1

» **1 Lantronix embedded device server** available from many vendors, including Symmetry Electronics (www.semiconductorstore.com), part number CO-E1-11AA (Micro) or WM11A0002-01 (WiMicro), or XP1001001-03R (XPort)

» **1 RJ45 breakout board** SparkFun (sparkfun.com) part number BOB-00716 (needed only if you're using an XPort)

» **1 3.3V regulator** The LM7833 from SparkFun, part number COM-00526, or the MIC2940A-3.3WT from Digi-Key, part number 576-1134-ND, will each work well.

» **1 solderless breadboard** such as Digi-Key (digikey.com) part number 438-1045-ND, or Jameco (www.jameco.com) part number 20601

» **1 Arduino** module or other microcontroller

» **4 LEDs** It's best to use at least two colors with established semantics: a big red one, a big green one, and two others of whatever color suits your fancy.

» **1 accelerometer** The circuit shown uses an ADXL330 accelerometer, available in a module from SparkFun (part number SEN-00692), but most any analog accelerometer should do the job.

» **1 push button** Use one that's robust and can stand a good stomping.

» **1 pencil box**

» **1 pipe, 2- to 3-inches in diameter, approximately 6–8 inches long** Wood, sturdy cardboard, or sturdy plastic will work.

» **1 plank of scrap wood**

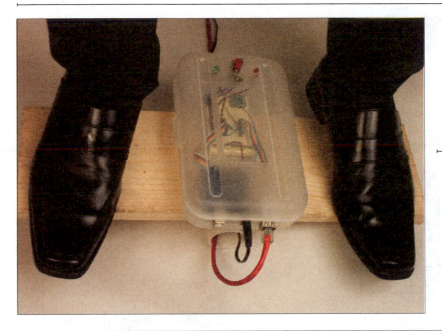

◀◀ Figure 5-1

The seesaw client. Note the red and green LEDs to indicate left and right tilt. This client follows nautical tradition port (left) is red, and starboard (right) is green. Feel free to be less jaunty in your own choices, as long as they're clear.

⯆ Figure 5-2

The seesaw client schematic. The detail photos on the following page show the wiring on the breadboard.

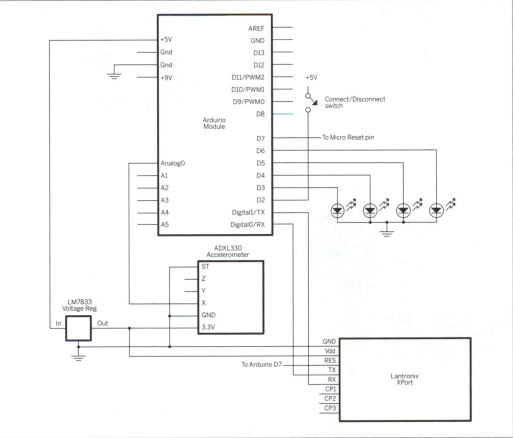

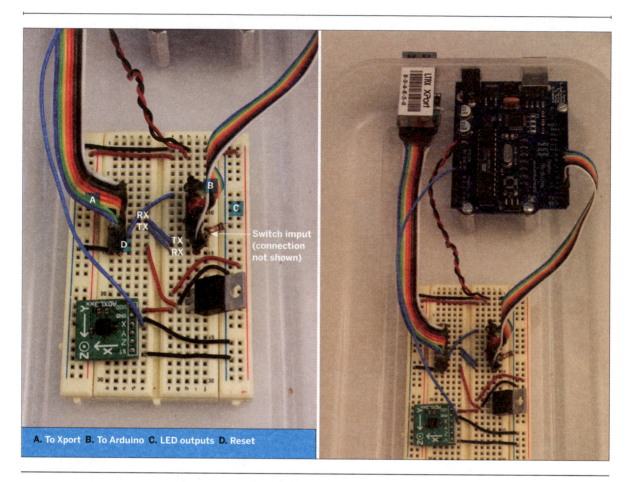

A. To Xport B. To Arduino C. LED outputs D. Reset

RX
TX

TX
RX

Switch imput
(connection
not shown)

⬆ **Figure 5-2**
» continued from previous page
The seesaw client detail photos. The schematic is
shown on the previous page.

◀◀ **Figure 5-3**
The XPort mounted on an RJ45 breakout board. A
couple of dabs of hot glue on the breakout board serve
as spacers to keep the metal of the XPort's case from
contacting the outside pins on the breakout board.

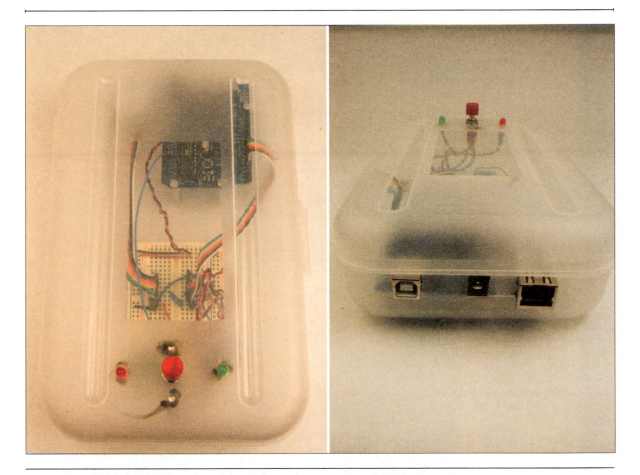

▲ Figure 5-4
The outside of the seesaw control box, and the connectors.

◀◀ Figure 5-5
Inside the box, showing the wiring to the LEDs and the switch in the box cover.

Try It   First, start with the variable declarations and definitions. From the preceding explanation of the program's states and the inputs and outputs earlier, this is all straightforward:

```
/*
  pong client
  Language:  Wiring/Arduino

  This program enables an Arduino to control one paddle in a
  networked pong game.

*/


// defines for the Lantronix device's status (used for staus variable):
#define disconnected 0
#define connected 1
#define connecting 2

// defines for I/O pins:
#define connectButtonPin 2
#define rightLED 3
#define leftLED 4
#define connectionLED 5
#define connectButtonLED 6
#define deviceResetPin 7
```

You need global variables to handle the serial communication, track the sensors, and keep track of the state of the client:

```
// variables:
int inByte= -1;                    // incoming byte from serial RX
int status = disconnected;         // Lantronix device's connection status

// variables for the sensors:
byte connectButton = 0;            // state of the exit button
byte lastConnectButton = 0;        // previous state of the exit button
/*
When the connect button is pressed, or the accelerometer passes
the left or right threshold, the client should send a message to the
server. The next two variables get filled with a value when either
of those conditions is met. Otherwise, they are set to 0.
*/
byte paddleMessage = 0;            // message sent to make a paddle move
byte connectMessage = 0;           // message sent to connect or disconnect
```

The setup() method just sets all the I/O modes, starts the serial port, and resets the Lantronix device:

```
void setup() {
  // set the modes of the various I/O pins:
  pinMode(connectButtonPin, INPUT);
  pinMode(rightLED, OUTPUT);
  pinMode(leftLED, OUTPUT);
  pinMode(connectionLED, OUTPUT);
  pinMode(connectButtonLED, OUTPUT);
  pinMode(deviceResetPin, OUTPUT);

  // start serial port, 9600 8-N-1:
```

»

Continued from opposite page.

```
  Serial.begin(9600);

  // reset the Lantronix device:
  resetDevice();
  // blink the exit button LED to signal that we're ready for action:
  blink(3);
}
```

▶▶ In the main loop, you read the sensors, set the indicator LEDs, and take an action that depends on the state that the client's in:

```
void loop() {
  // read the inputs:
  readSensors();
  // set the indicator LEDS:
  setLeds();
  // check the state of the client and take appropriate action:
  stateCheck();
}
```

▶▶ Read the sensors (both the accelerometer and the connect/disconnect switch) using a method called readSensors(). It determines the state of the sensors and indicates the results by setting the values of the connectMessage and paddleMessage variables.

Send a message only when the accelerometer tilts far enough to the left or right. To discover the thresholds for left and right, write a simple program that just reads the analog input that the accelerometer is attached to and print it out. Then get on the seesaw and rock back and forth while watching the values.

The one I used for this example gave a reading of approximately 450 when it was level, and tilted to above 500 to the left, and below 420 to the right. Your results may vary. Based on those values, here's the readSensors() method:

```
void readSensors() {
  // thresholds for the accelerometer values:
  int leftThreshold = 500;
  int rightThreshold = 420;

  // read the X axis of the accelerometer:
  int x = analogRead(0);
  // let the analog/digital converter settle:
  delay(10);

  // if the accelerometer has passed either threshold,
  // set paddleMessage to the appropriate message, so it can
  // be sent by the main loop:
  if (x > leftThreshold) {
    paddleMessage = 'l';
  } else if (x < rightThreshold) {
    paddleMessage = 'r';
  } else {
    paddleMessage = 0;
  }
}
```

▶▶ Change these values to match the values for your own accelerometer.

▶▶ You can't just send a message every time the connect button is high. You want to send a message only when the button changes from low to high, indicating that the player just pressed it. This code block checks for a low-to-high transition by comparing the state of the button with its previous state:

```
// read the connectButton, look for a low-to-high change:
connectButton = digitalRead(connectButtonPin);
connectMessage = 0;
if (connectButton == HIGH ) {
  if (connectButton != lastConnectButton) {
    // turn on the exit button LED to let the user
    // know that he or she hit the button:
    digitalWrite(connectButtonLED, HIGH);
    connectMessage = 'x';
  }
}
// save the state of the exit button for next time you check:
lastConnectButton = connectButton;
}
```

▶▶ Once you've checked the sensors, you can set the LED indicators:

```
void setLeds() {
  // This should happen no matter what state the client is in,
  // to give local feedback every time a sensor senses a change.

  // set the L and R LEDs if the sensor passes the appropriate threshold:
  switch (paddleMessage) {
    case 'l':
      digitalWrite(leftLED, HIGH);
      digitalWrite(rightLED, LOW);
      break;
    case 'r':
      digitalWrite(rightLED, HIGH);
      digitalWrite(leftLED, LOW);
      break;
    case 0:
      digitalWrite(rightLED, LOW);
      digitalWrite(leftLED, LOW);
  }

  // set the connect button LED based on the connectMessage:
  if (connectMessage !=0) {
    digitalWrite(connectButtonLED, HIGH);
  }
  else {
    digitalWrite(connectButtonLED, LOW);
  }

  // set the connection LED based on the client's status:
  if (status == connected) {
    // turn on the connection LED:
    digitalWrite(connectionLED, HIGH);
  }
  else {
    // turn off the connection LED:
    digitalWrite(connectionLED, LOW);
  }
}
```

▶▶ Next, take action depending on the state of the client and the messages to be sent:

```
void stateCheck() {
  // Everything in this method depends on the client's status:
  switch (status) {
  case connected:
    // if you're connected, listen for serial in:
    while (Serial.available() > 0) {
      // if you get a 'D', it's from the Lantronix device,
      // telling you that it lost the connection:
      if (Serial.read() == 'D') {
        status = disconnected;
      }
    }

    // if there's a paddle message to send, send it:
    if (paddleMessage != 0) {
      Serial.print(paddleMessage);
      // reset paddleMessage to 0 once you've sent the message:
      paddleMessage = 0;
    }
    // if there's a connect message to send, send it:
    if (connectMessage != 0) {
      // if you're connected, disconnect:
      Serial.print(connectMessage);
      // reset connectMessage to 0 once you've sent the message:
      connectMessage = 0;
    }
    break;

  case disconnected:
    // if there's a connect message, try to connect:
    if (connectMessage !=0 ) {
      deviceConnect();
      // reset connectMessage to 0 once you've tried to connect:
      connectMessage = 0;
    }
    break;
    // if you sent a connect message but haven't connected, keep trying:
  case connecting:
    // read the serial port:
    if (Serial.available()) {
      inByte = Serial.read();
      // if you get a 'C' from the Lantronix device, then you're connected:
      if (inByte == 'C') {
        status = connected;
      }
      else {  // if you got anything other than a C, try again:
        deviceConnect();
      }
    }
    break;
  }
}
```

▶▶ Finally, here are the device Connect(), resetDevice(), and blink() methods mentioned earlier. Be sure to replace 192.168.1.20 with the IP address of the computer running the Processing server and 8080 with the port number that the server is listening on:

That's the whole client. Once you've assembled the client, compile and run this code on it, and attempt to connect to the test server. You should see it make connections and send messages based on the state of the client and the values from the sensors. If you don't, use the troubleshooting methods at the end of Chapter 4 to determine what's wrong. For the full code, see Appendix C.

```
void deviceConnect() {
  /*
     send out the server address and
   wait for a "C" byte to come back.
   fill in your personal computer's numerical address below:
   */
  Serial.print("C192.168.1.20/8080\n\r");
  status = connecting;
}

// Take the Lantronix device's reset pin low to reset it:
void resetDevice() {
  digitalWrite(deviceResetPin, LOW);
  delay(50);
  digitalWrite(deviceResetPin, HIGH);
  // pause to let Lantronix device boot up:
  delay(2000);
}

// Blink the connect button LED:
void blink(int howManyTimes) {
  for (int i=0; i< howManyTimes; i++) {
    digitalWrite(connectButtonLED, HIGH);
    delay(200);
    digitalWrite(connectButtonLED, LOW);
    delay(200);
  }
}
```

> ▶▶ You will need to change this to the IP address and port that your Processing server is running on.

" Client #2: A Stepper Client

For Client #2, I wanted to see whether there's a big difference between a foot-based input device that requires you to balance and one that you can stand on easily. I found an exercise stepper in the trash that had a missing screen, but the steps still worked. So I attached force-sensing resistors to the foot pads and made a second client. The rest of the client's functionality is the same as the seesaw client.

The stepper client, shown in Figure 5-6, is very similar to the seesaw client. The only difference is that the accelerometer has been replaced by two force-sensing resistors. You can see the FSRs at the back of the foot pads. After much experimenting, I found that I got the most reliable results when the sensors were under the heels. They lift off the pads when you step, giving a nice range of contrast to the readings.

The physical construction for the stepper client is almost identical to the seesaw client, You can use the same pencil box case with the same LED setup. Just drill two holes for the leads to the FSRs and you're all set.

The code for the stepper client is also very similar to the seesaw client. All you have to change is the readSensors() method. Everything else stays the same. That's the beauty of using a clear, simple protocol: it doesn't matter what the physical input is, as long you can map changes recorded by the sensors to a left-right movement, and program the microcontroller to send the appropriate messages. It's worthwhile to try building both these clients, or one of your own, to look at how different physical affordances can affect the performance of different clients, even though it "appears" the same to the server.

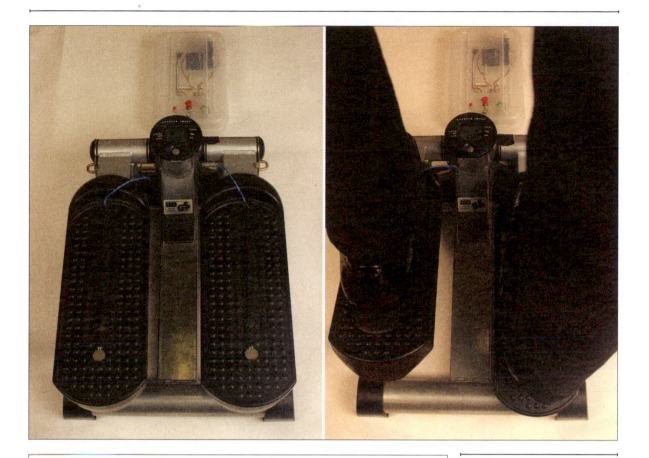

Figure 5-6
The stepper client.

MATERIALS FOR CLIENT 2

» **1 Lantronix embedded device server** Available from many vendors, including Symmetry Electronics (www.semiconductorstore.com) as part number CO-E1-11AA (Micro), WM11A0002-01 (WiMicro), or XP1001001-03R (XPort)

» **1 RJ45 breakout board** SparkFun part number BOB-00716 (needed only if you're using an XPort)

» **1 3.3V regulator** The LM7833 (SparkFun part number COM-00526) or the MIC2940A-3.3WT (Digi-Key part number 576-1134-ND) will work well.

» **1 solderless breadboard** such as Digi-Key part number 438-1045-ND or Jameco (www.jameco.com) part number 20601

» **1 Arduino module** or other microcontroller

» **4 LEDs** For semantic reasons, it's best to use a big red one, a big green one, and two others of whatever color suits your fancy.

» **2 force-sensing resistors (FSRs)**

» **1 pushbutton** Use one that's robust and can stand a good stomping.

» **1 pencil box**

» **1 exercise stepper** The one I found in the trash was a Sharper Image model, but you could also fake it with two foot-size wooden blocks mounted on foam rubber, with the FSRs mounted on the top of the blocks.

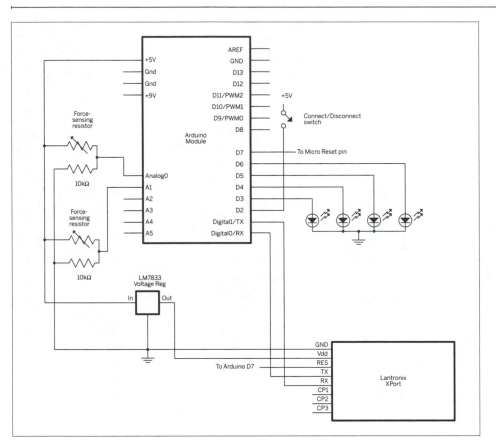

Figure 5-7
The stepper client circuit.

A. To FSRs B. To analog input

▶▶ The next listing is the readSensors() method for the stepper client. All the rest of the code for this client is identical to the previous client. Just as with the seesaw client, you have to discover experimentally what the thresholds for your sensors are, so you may need to write a short program to do that. In this case, the left and right sensors are electrically identical, so they should produce similar values when subjected to similar forces (for example, your left foot and your right foot). So one threshold value will do the job for both.

You can test this client the same way you did the last one, using the test server program shown earlier. Once you're sure it's sending messages correctly, it's time to write the *ping pong* server.

```
void readSensors() {
  int threshold = 500;
  int  left = analogRead(0);
  delay(10);
  int right = analogRead(1);
  delay(10);
  if (left >= right + threshold) {
    paddleMessage = 'l';
  } else if (right >=left + threshold) {
    paddleMessage = 'r';
  } else {
    paddleMessage = 0;
  }

  // read the connectButton, look for a low-to-high change:
  connectButton = digitalRead(connectButtonPin);
  connectMessage = 0;
  if (connectButton == HIGH ) {
    if (connectButton != lastConnectButton) {
      digitalWrite(connectButtonLED, HIGH);
      connectMessage = 'x';
    }
  }
  lastConnectButton = connectButton;
}
```

▶▶ **Change this value to match the value for your own sensors.**

❝❝ The Server

The tasks to be handled by the server can be divided into two groups: tasks related to the game play, like animating the paddles and the ball and scoring, and tasks related to tracking new clients. To manage it all most effectively, you're going to use an object-oriented programming approach. If you've never done this before, there are a few basics you need to know in advance.

Anatomy of a Player Object

The most important thing to know is that all objects have properties and behaviors. You can think about an object's properties in much the same way as you think about physical properties. For example, a pong paddle has width and height, and it has a location, which you can express in terms of its horizontal and its vertical position. In your game, the paddles will have another important property: each paddle will be associated with a client. Of course, clients have properties as well, so each paddle will inherit from its client an IP address. You'll see all of these in the code that defines a paddle as an object.

A paddle also has a characteristic behavior: it moves left or right. That behavior will be encoded into the paddle as a method called movePaddle(). This behavior will update the properties of the paddle that define its location. A second behavior called showPaddle() will actually draw the paddle in its current location. You'll see later why these are kept separate.

Code It   To define an object in Processing (and in Java), create a code block called a class. Here's the beginning of the class that defines a player in the pong server:

```
public class Player {
  // declare variables that belong to the object:
  float paddleH, paddleV;
  Client  client;
```

The variables declared at the beginning of the class as shown in the example are called instance variables. Every new instance of the class created makes its own copies of these variables. Every class has a constructor method. This method gets called to call the object into existence.

You've already used constructors. When you made a new Serial port in Processing, you called the constructor method for the Serial class with something like myPort = new Serial(this, portNum, portSpeed).

▶▶ Here's the constructor for the Player class. It comes right after the instance variables in your code. As you can see, it just takes the values you give it when you call for a new Player and assigns them to variables that belong to an instance (an individual player) of the class:

```
public Player (int hpos, int vpos, Client someClient) {
    // initialize the local instance variables:
    paddleH = hpos;
    paddleV = vpos;
    client = someClient;
}
```

▶▶ Next come the two other methods mentioned earlier, movePaddle() and showPaddle(). As you can see, they use the instance variables (paddleH, paddleV, and client) that belong to the object to store the location of the paddle, and to draw it:

```
public void movePaddle(float howMuch) {
    float newPosition = paddleH + howMuch;
    // constrain the paddle's position to the width of the window:
    paddleH = constrain(newPosition, 0, width);
}

public void showPaddle() {
    rect(paddleH, paddleV, paddleWidth, paddleHeight);
    // display the address of this player near its paddle
    textSize(12);
    text(client.ip(), paddleH, paddleV - paddleWidth/8 );
}
}
```

▶▶ **This bracket closes the class**

❝ That's all the code to define a Player. Put this code at the end of your program (shown next), just as if it were another method. To make a new Player object, write something like Player newPlayer = new Player(h, v, thisClient).

When you do this, the new Player, and all its instance variables and methods, are accessible through the variable called newPlayer (the new Player is not actually stored in this variable; it's stuffed away in a portion of memory somewhere that you can get at through the newPlayer variable). Keep an eye out for this in the program.

The Main pong Server Program

Before you write the code for the server as a whole, it's useful to make a map of what happens. Figure 5-8 shows the main tasks and functions. A few details are left out for clarity's sake, but what's clear are the main relationships between the methods that run the program (setup(), draw(), and serverEvent()) and the Player objects. As with any program, the setup() method kicks things off, then the draw() method takes over. The latter sees to it that the screen is updated and listens to any existing clients. If a new client connects, a serverEvent() message is generated, which causes the method of that name to run. That method creates new Player objects. The draw() method takes advantage of the behaviors inside the Player objects to move and draw their paddles.

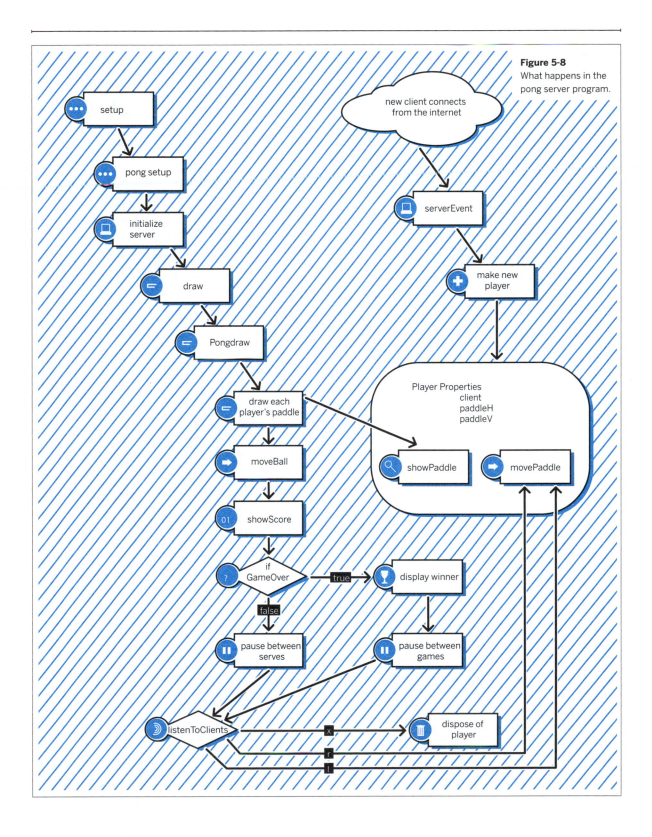

Figure 5-8
What happens in the
pong server program.

The first thing to do in the server program itself is to define the variables. They're grouped here by those needed for keeping track of clients versus those needed for managing the graphics of the game play:

```
// include the net library:
import processing.net.*;

// variables for keeping track of clients:
int port = 8080;                         // the port the server listens on
Server myServer;                         // the server object
ArrayList playerList = new ArrayList(); // list of clients
```

▶▶ This program uses a Java class, ArrayList, that's not explained in the Processing reference guide. Think of it as a super-duper array. ArrayLists don't have a fixed number of elements to begin with, so you can add new elements as the program continues. It's useful when you don't know how many elements you'll have. In this case, you don't know how many clients you'll have, so you'll store them in an ArrayList, and add each new client to the list as it connects. ArrayLists include some other useful methods. For more on ArrayList and other Java classes, check out Head First Java (O'Reilly, 2005) or the online documentation at java.sun.com.

```
// variables for keeping track of the game play and graphics:

int ballSize = 10;              // the size of the ball
int ballDirectionV = 2;         // the ball's horizontal direction
                                // left is negative, right is positive
int ballDirectionH = 2;         // the ball's vertical direction
                                // up is negative, down is positive
int ballPosV, ballPosH;         // the ball's vertical/horizontal and vertical
positions
boolean ballInMotion = false;   // whether or not the ball should be moving

int topScore, bottomScore;      // scores for the top team and the bottom teams
int paddleHeight = 10;          // vertical dimension of the paddles
int paddleWidth = 80;           // horizontal dimension of the paddles
int nextTopPaddleV;             // paddle positions for the next player
                                // to be created
int nextBottomPaddleV;

boolean gameOver = false;       // whether or not a game is in progress
float delayCounter = millis();  // a counter for the delay after
                                // a game is over
long gameOverDelay = 4000;      // pause after each game
long pointDelay = 2000;         // pause after each point
```

▸▸ The setup() method starts the server and calls pongSetup(), which sets all the initial conditions for the game:

```
void setup() {
  // set up all the pong details:
  pongSetup();
  // start the server:
  myServer = new Server(this, port);
}
```

▸▸ Here's the pongSetup() method :

```
void pongSetup() {
  // set the window size:
  size(480, 640);
  // set the frame rate:
  frameRate(90);

  // create a font with the third font available to the system:
  PFont myFont = createFont(PFont.list()[2], 18);
  textFont(myFont);

  // set the default font settings:
  textFont(myFont, 18);
  textAlign(CENTER);

  // initalize paddle positions for the first player.
  // these will be incremented with each new player:
  nextTopPaddleV = 50;
  nextBottomPaddleV = height - 50;

  // initialize the ball in the center of the screen:
  ballPosV = height / 2;
  ballPosH = width / 2;

  // set no borders on drawn shapes:
  noStroke();
  // set the rectMode so that all rectangle dimensions
  // are from the center of the rectangle (see Processing reference):
  rectMode(CENTER);
}
```

▸▸ The draw() method updates the screen using a method called pongDraw(), and listens for any messages from existing clients using a method called listenToClients().

```
void draw() {
  pongDraw();
  listenToClients();
}
```

» When new clients connect to the server, the net library's serverEvent() method is called automatically; your Processing sketch must implement this method in order to respond to the event. It uses the new client to create a new Player object using a method called makeNewPlayer(). Here's the serverEvent() method:

```
// The ServerEvent message is generated when a new client
// connects to the server.
void serverEvent(Server someServer, Client someClient) {
  boolean isPlayer = false;

  if (someClient != null) {
    // iterate over the playerList:
    for (int p = 0; p < playerList.size(); p++) {
      // get the next object in the ArrayList and convert it
      // to a Player:
      Player thisPlayer = (Player)playerList.get(p);

      // if thisPlayer's client matches the one that
      // generated the serverEvent,
      // then this client is already a player:
      if (thisPlayer.client == someClient) {
        // we already have this client
        isPlayer = true;
      }
    }

    // if the client isn't already a Player, then make a new Player
    // and add it to the playerList:
    if (!isPlayer) {
      makeNewPlayer(someClient);
    }
  }
}
```

» Now that you've seen the draw() and the serverEvent() methods, it's time to look at the methods they call. It's best to start with the creation of a new Player, so here's the make NewPlayer() method. It checks the number of players so far created by counting the number of Players in the ArrayList called playerList. If there's an even number of Players, the new Player is added to the top team, and is positioned below the last top player. If there's an odd number of Players, the new one goes on the bottom team. The variables nextTopPaddleV and nextBottomPaddleV keep track of the positions for the next players on each team.

Here's the makeNewPlayer() method:

```
void makeNewPlayer(Client thisClient) {
  // paddle position for the new Player:
  int h = width/2;
  int v = 0;

  /*
   Get the paddle position of the last player on the list.
   If it's on top, add the new player on the bottom, and vice versa.
   If there are no other players, add the new player on the top.
   */
  // get the size of the list:
  int listSize = playerList.size() - 1;
  // if there are any other players:
  if (listSize >= 0) {
    // get the last player on the list:
    Player lastPlayerAdded = (Player)playerList.get(listSize);
    // if the last player's on the top, add to the bottom:
    if (lastPlayerAdded.paddleV == nextTopPaddleV) {
      nextBottomPaddleV = nextBottomPaddleV - paddleHeight * 2;
      v = nextBottomPaddleV;
```

»

Continued from opposite page.

```
  // if the last player's on the bottom, add to the top:
  else if (lastPlayerAdded.paddleV == nextBottomPaddleV) {
    nextTopPaddleV = nextTopPaddleV + paddleHeight * 2;
    v = nextTopPaddleV;
  }
} else {  // if there are no players, add to the top:
  v = nextTopPaddleV;
}

// make a new Player object with the position you just calculated
// and using the Client that generated the serverEvent:
Player newPlayer = new Player(h, v, thisClient);

// add the new Player to the playerList:
playerList.add(newPlayer);

// Announce the new Player:
print("We have a new player: ");
println(newPlayer.client.ip());
newPlayer.client.write("hi\r\n");
}
```

» Once a new Player has been created, you need to listen continuously for that Player's client to send any messages. The more often you check for messages, the tighter the interactive loop between sensor and action.

The listenToClients() method, called continuously from the draw() method, listens for messages from clients. If there's data available from any client, this method takes action. First it iterates over the list of Players to see whether each one's client is speaking. Then it checks to see whether the client sent any of the game messages (that is, l for left, r for right, or x for exit). If any of those messages was received, the program acts on the message appropriately.

```
void listenToClients() {
  // get the next client that sends a message:
  Client speakingClient = myServer.available();
  Player speakingPlayer = null;

  // iterate over the playerList to figure out whose
  // client sent the message:
  for (int p = 0; p < playerList.size(); p++) {
    // get the next object in the ArrayList, convert it to a Player:
    Player thisPlayer = (Player)playerList.get(p);
    // compare the client of thisPlayer to the client that sent a message;
    // if they're the same, then this is the Player we want:
    if (thisPlayer.client == speakingClient) {
      speakingPlayer = thisPlayer;
    }
  }

  // read what the client sent:
  if (speakingPlayer != null) {
    int whatClientSaid = speakingPlayer.client.read();
    /* There a number of things it might have said that we care about:
        x = exit
        l = move left
        r = move right
     */
    switch (whatClientSaid) {
    case 'x':  // If the client says "exit", disconnect it
```

»

Continued from previous page.

```
        // say goodbye to the client:
        speakingPlayer.client.write("bye\r\n");
        // disconnect the client from the server:
        println(speakingPlayer.client.ip() + "\t left");
        myServer.disconnect(speakingPlayer.client);
        // remove the client's Player from the playerList:
        playerList.remove(speakingPlayer);
        break;
      case 'l':  // if the client sends an "l", move the paddle left
        speakingPlayer.movePaddle(-10);
        break;
      case'r':  // if the client sends a "r", move the paddle right
        speakingPlayer.movePaddle(10);
        break;
      }
    }
  }
}
```

So far you've seen how the server receives new connections (using serverEvent()), creates new Players from the new clients (using makeNewPlayer()), and listens for messages (using listenToClients()). That covers the interaction between the server and the clients. In addition, you've seen how the Player class defines all the properties and methods that are associated with each new player. Finally, it's time to look at the methods for controlling the drawing of the game. pongDraw(), called from the draw() method, is the main method for this. This method has four tasks:

- Iterate over the playerList and draw all the paddles at their most current positions.
- Draw the ball and the score.
- If the game is over, show a "Game Over" message and pause.
- Pause after each volley, then serve the ball again.

Show It   Here is the pongDraw() method:

You saw earlier that the listenToClients() method actually updates the positions of the paddles using the movePaddle() method from the Player object.

```
void pongDraw() {
  background(0);
  // draw all the paddles
  for (int p = 0; p < playerList.size(); p++) {
    Player thisPlayer = (Player)playerList.get(p);
    // show the paddle for this player:
    thisPlayer.showPaddle();
  }
```

That method doesn't actually draw the paddles, but this one does, using ach Player's showPaddle() method. This is why the two methods are separated in the object. Likewise, the moveBall() method, called here, checks to see if the ball hit a paddle or a wall, and calculates its new position from there, but doesn't draw the ball itself, as the ball needs to be drawn even if it's not in motion:

```
  // calculate ball's position:
  if (ballInMotion) {
    moveBall();
  }
  // draw the ball:
  rect(ballPosH, ballPosV, ballSize, ballSize);

  // show the score:
  showScore();
```

▶▶ If the game is over, the program stops the serving and displays the winner for four seconds:

```
// if the game is over, show the winner:
if (gameOver) {
  textSize(24);
  gameOver = true;
  text("Game Over", width/2, height/2 - 30);
  if (topScore > bottomScore) {
    text("Top Team Wins!", width/2, height/2);
  }
  else {
    text("Bottom Team Wins!", width/2, height/2);
  }
}
// pause after each game:
if (gameOver && (millis() > delayCounter + gameOverDelay)) {
  gameOver = false;
  newGame();
}
```

▶▶ After each point is scored, the program takes a two-second pause. If there aren't at least two players after that pause, it doesn't serve another ball. This is to keep the game from running when there's no one to play:

That closes out the pongDraw() method itself. It calls a few other methods: moveBall(), which calculates the ball's trajectory; showScore(), which shows the score; and newGame(), which resets the game.

```
// pause after each point:
if (!gameOver && !ballInMotion && (millis() > delayCounter + pointDelay))
{
  // make sure there are at least two players:
  if (playerList.size() >=2) {
    ballInMotion = true;
  }
  else {
    ballInMotion = false;
    textSize(24);
    text("Waiting for two players", width/2, height/2 - 30);
  }
}
}
```

▶▶ The first thing moveBall() does is to check if the position of the ball intersects any of the Players' paddles. To do this, it has to iterate over playerList, pull out each Player, and check to see if the ball position is contained within the rectangle of the paddle. If the ball does intersect a paddle, then its vertical direction is reversed:

```
void moveBall() {
  // check to see if the ball contacts any paddles:
  for (int p = 0; p < playerList.size(); p++) {
    // get the player to check:
    Player thisPlayer = (Player)playerList.get(p);

    // calculate the horizontal edges of the paddle:
    float paddleRight = thisPlayer.paddleH + paddleWidth/2;
    float paddleLeft = thisPlayer.paddleH - paddleWidth/2;
    // check to see if the ball is in the horizontal range of the paddle:
    if ((ballPosH >= paddleLeft) && (ballPosH <= paddleRight)) {

      // calculate the vertical edges of the paddle:
      float paddleTop = thisPlayer.paddleV - paddleHeight/2;
      float paddleBottom = thisPlayer.paddleV + paddleHeight/2;
```

»

Continued from previous page.

```
    // check to see if the ball is in the horizontal range of the paddle:
    if ((ballPosV >= paddleTop) && (ballPosV <= paddleBottom)) {
      // reverse the ball vertical direction:
      ballDirectionV = -ballDirectionV;
    }
  }
}
```

If the ball goes above the top of the screen or below the bottom, then one team or the other has scored:

```
// if the ball goes off the screen top:
if (ballPosV < 0) {
  bottomScore++;
  ballDirectionV = int(random(2) + 1) * -1;
  resetBall();
}
// if the ball goes off the screen bottom:
if (ballPosV > height) {
  topScore++;
  ballDirectionV = int(random(2) + 1);
  resetBall();
}

// if any team goes over 5 points, the other team loses:
if ((topScore > 5) || (bottomScore > 5)) {
  delayCounter = millis();
  gameOver = true;
}
```

Finally, moveBall() checks to see whether the ball hits one of the sides of the screen. If so, the horizontal direction is reversed:

```
// stop the ball going off the left or right of the screen:
if ((ballPosH - ballSize/2 <= 0) || (ballPosH +ballSize/2 >=width)) {
  // reverse the y direction of the ball:
  ballDirectionH = -ballDirectionH;
}
// update the ball position:
ballPosV = ballPosV + ballDirectionV;
ballPosH = ballPosH + ballDirectionH;
}
```

The newGame() method just stops the game play and resets the scores:

```
void newGame() {
  gameOver = false;
  topScore = 0;
  bottomScore = 0;
}
```

▶▶ The showScore() method prints the scores on the screen:

```
public void showScore() {
    textSize(24);
    text(topScore, 20, 40);
    text(bottomScore, 20, height - 20);
}
```

▶▶ Finally, moveBall() calls a method called resetBall(), that resets the ball at the end of each point. Here it is:

For the final code, see Appendix C.

```
void resetBall() {
    // put the ball back in the center
    ballPosV = height/2;
    ballPosH = width/2;
    ballInMotion = false;
    delayCounter = millis();
}
```

> **"** The beauty of this server is that it doesn't really care how many clients log into it; everyone gets to play *ping* pong. There's nothing in the server program that limits the response time for any client, either. The server attempts to satisfy everyone a soon as possible. This is a good habit to get in. If there's a need to limit the response time in any way, don't rely on the server of the network to do that. Whenever possible, let the network and the server remain dumb, fast, and reliable, and let the clients decide how fast they want to send data across. Figure 5-9 shows a screenshot of the server with two clients.

Once you've got the clients speaking with the server, try designing a new client of your own. See if you can make the ultimate *ping* pong paddle.

X

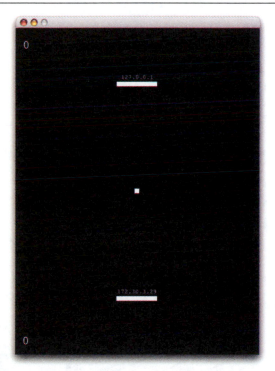

Figure 5-9
The output of the ping pong server sketch.

❝ Conclusion

The basic structure of the clients and server in this chapter can be used any time that you want to make a system that manages synchronous connections between several objects on the network. The server's main jobs are to listen for new clients, to keep track of the existing clients, and to make sure that the right messages reach the right clients. It must place a priority on listening at all times.

The client should also place a priority on listening, but it has to juggle listening to the server with listening to the physical inputs. It should always give a clear and immediate response to local input, and it should indicate the state of the network connection at all times.

The protocol that the objects in this system speak to each other should be as simple and as flexible as possible. Leave room to add commands, because you never know when you might decide to add something. Make sure to build in responses where appropriate, like the "hi" and "bye" responses from the server. Keep the messages unambiguous, and if possible, keep them short as well.

Finally, make sure you've got a reliable way to test the system. Simple tools like the telnet client and the test server will save you much time in building every multi-player server, and help you get to the fun sooner.

Now you've seen examples of both asynchronous client-server exchanges (the HTTP system in Chapter 4) and synchronous exchanges (the chat server here). With those two tools, you can build almost any application in which there's a central server and a number of clients. For the next chapter, you'll step away from the Internet and take a look at various forms of wireless communication.
X

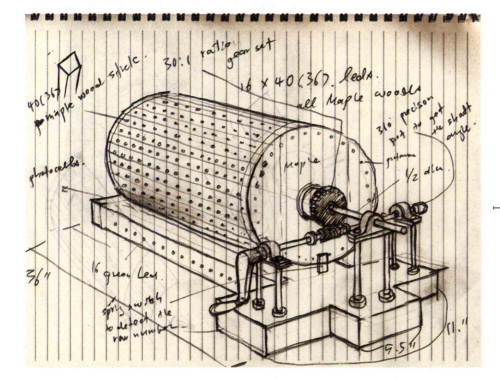

« At right
◀◀ Jin-Yo Mok's original sketches of the music box.

» At left
▶▶ The music box composition interface.

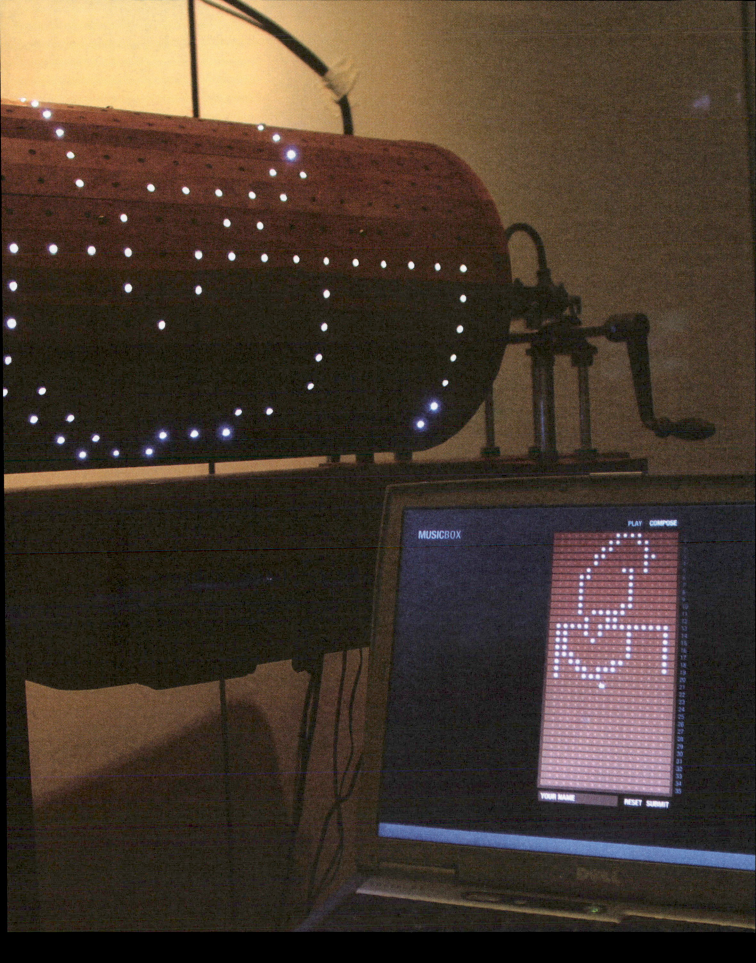

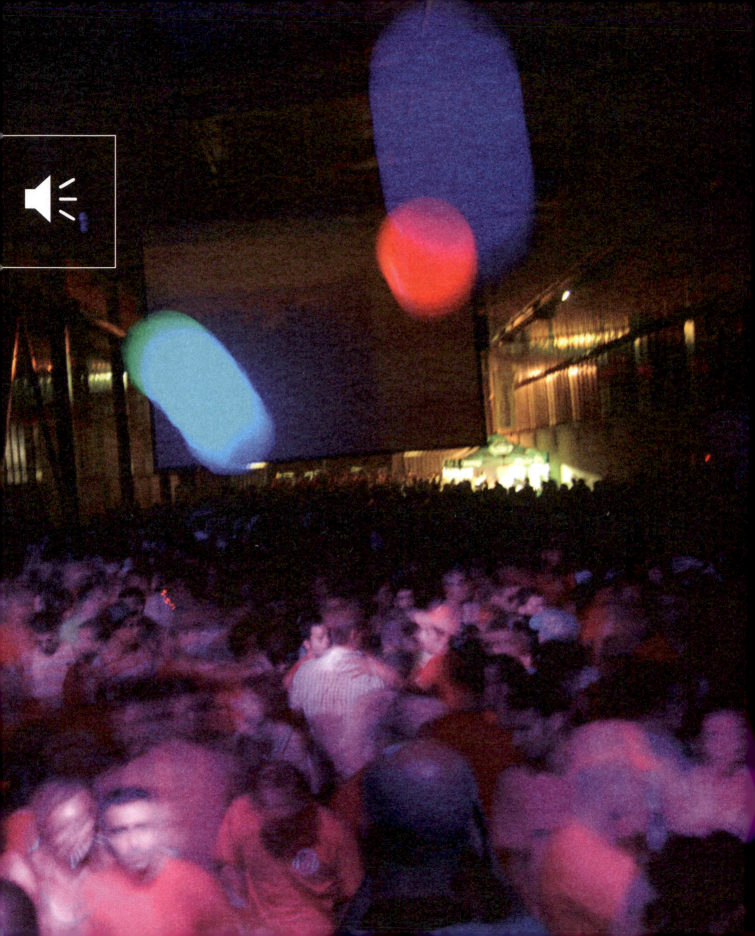

6

Wireless Communication

If you're like most people interested in this area, you've been reading through the early chapters thinking, "but what about wireless?" Perhaps you're so eager that you just skipped straight to this chapter. If you did, go back and read the rest of the book! In particular, if you're not familiar with serial communication between computers and microcontrollers, you'll want to read Chapter 2 before you read this chapter. This chapter explains the basics of wireless communication between objects. In it, you'll learn about two types of wireless communication, and build some working examples.

◄◄ **Alex Beim's Zygotes** (www.tangibleinteraction.com) are lightweight inflatable rubber balls lit from within by LED lights. The balls change color in reaction to pressure on their surface, and communicate with a central computer using ZigBee radios. A network of zygotes at a concert allows the audience to have a direct effect not only on the balls themselves, but also on the music and video projections to which they are networked. *Photo courtesy of Alex Beim.*

The early part of this chapter covers how wireless works, and what makes it stop working, giving you some background and starting places for troubleshooting. The second half of the chapter contains examples. The topic is so broad, even a survey of several different devices only begins to cover the tip of the iceberg. For that reason, the exercises in this chapter will be less fully developed applications than the previous ones. Instead, you'll just get the basic "Hello World!" example for several different forms of wireless device.

x

❝ Why Isn't Everything Wireless?

The advantage of wireless communication seems obvious at first: no wires! This makes physical design much simpler for any project where the devices have to move and talk to each other. Wearable sensor systems, digital musical instruments, and remote control vehicles are all simplified physically by wireless communication. However, there are some limits to wireless communication that you should consider before going wireless.

Wireless communication is never as reliable as wired communication

You have less control over the sources of interference. You can insulate and shield a wire carrying data communications, but you can never totally isolate a radio or infrared wireless link. There will always be some form of interference, so you must make sure that all the devices in your system know what to do if they get a garbled message, or no message at all, from their counterparts.

Wireless communication is never just one-to-one communication

The radio and infrared devices mentioned here broadcast their signals for all to hear. Sometimes that means they interfere with the communication between other devices. For example, Bluetooth, most Wi-Fi radios (802.11b, g, and n) and ZigBee (802.15.4) radios all work in the same frequency range, 2.4 gigahertz. They're designed to not cause each other undue interference, but if you have a large number of ZigBee radios working in the same space as a busy Wi-Fi network, for example, you'll get interference.

Wireless communication does not mean wireless power

You still have to provide power to your devices, and if they're moving, this means using battery power. Batteries add weight, and they don't last forever. The failure of a battery when you're testing a project can cause all kinds of errors that you might attribute to other causes. A classic example of this is the Mystery Radio Error. Many

radios consume extra power when they're transmitting. This causes a slight dip in the voltage of the power source. If the radio isn't properly decoupled with a capacitor across its power and ground leads, the voltage can dip low enough to make the radio reset itself. The radio may appear to function normally when you're sending it serial messages, but it will never transmit, and you won't know why. When you start to develop wireless projects, it's good practice to make sure that you have the communication working first using a regulated, plugged-in power supply, and then create a stable battery supply.

Wireless communication generates electromagnetic radiation

This is easy to forget about, but every radio you use emits electromagnetic energy. The same energy that cooks your food in a microwave sends your mp3 files across the Internet. And while there are many studies indicating that it's safe at the low operating levels of the radios used here, why add to the general noise if you don't have to?

Make the wired version first

The radio and IR transceivers discussed here are replacements for the communications wires used in previous chapters. Before you decide to add wireless to any application, it's important to make sure you've got the basic exchange of messages between devices working over wires first.

x

❝ Two Flavors of Wireless: Infrared and Radio

There are two common types of wireless communication in most people's lives: infrared light communication and radio communication. The main difference between them from a user's or developer's position is their directionality.

Television remote controls typically use infrared (IR) communication. Unlike radio, it's dependent on the orientation between transmitter and receiver. There must be a clear line of sight between the two. Sometimes IR can work by bouncing the beam off another surface, but it's not as reliable. Ultimately, the receiver is an optical device, so it has to "see" the signal. Car door openers, mobile phones, garage door remote controls, and many other devices use radio. All of these work whether the transmitter and receiver are facing each other or not. They can even operate through walls, in some cases. In other words, their transmission is omnidirectional. Generally, IR is used for short-range line-of sight applications, and radio is used for everything else.

Transmitters, Receivers, and Transceivers

There are three types of devices common to both IR and RF systems: transmitters, which send a signal, but can't receive one; receivers, which can receive a signal, but can't send one; and transceivers, which can do both. You may wonder why everything isn't a transceiver, as it's the most flexible device. The answer is that it's more complex and more expensive to make a transceiver than it is to make either of the other two. In a transceiver, you have to make sure the receiver is not receiving its transmitter's transmission, or they'll interfere with each other and not listen to any other device. When you buy a transceiver that does this for you, you pay for the convenience. For many applications, it's cheaper to just use a transmitter-receiver pair, and handle any errors by just transmitting the message many times until the receiver gets the message. That's how TV remote controls work, for example. It makes the components much cheaper.

It's increasingly common, especially in radio, to just make everything a transceiver, and incorporate a microcontroller to manage the transmitter-receiver juggling. All Bluetooth, ZigBee, and Wi-Fi radios work this way. However, it's still possible to get transmitter-receiver pair radios, and they

are still considerably cheaper than their transceiver counterparts. The first two projects in this chapter use transmitter-receiver pairs.

Keep in mind the distinction between transmitter-receiver pairs and transceivers when you plan your projects, and when you shop. Start by asking yourself whether the communication in your project has to be two-way, or whether it can be one-way only. If it's one-way, ask yourself what happens if the communication fails. Can the receiver operate without asking for clarification? Can the problem be solved by transmitting repeatedly until the message is received? If the answer is yes, then you might be able to use a transmitter-receiver pair and save some money.

How Infrared Works

IR communication works by pulsing an IR LED at a set data rate and receiving the pulses using an IR photodiode. It's simply serial communication transmitted using infrared light. Since there are many everyday sources of IR light (the sun, incandescent light bulbs, any heat source), it's necessary to differentiate the IR data signal from other IR energy. To do this, the serial output is sent to an oscillator before it's sent to the output LED. The wave created by the oscillator, called a carrier wave, is a regular pulse that's modulated by the pulses of the data signal. The receiver picks up all IR light, but filters out anything that's not vibrating at the carrier frequency. Then it filters out the carrier frequency so that all that's left is the data signal. This method allows you to transmit data using infrared light without getting interference from other IR light sources, unless they happen to be oscillating at the same frequency as your carrier wave.

The directional nature of infrared makes it more limited than radio, but cheaper than radio, and requires less power. As radios get cheaper, more power-efficient, and more robust, it's less common to see an IR port on a computer or PDA, but it's still both cost-effective and power-efficient for line-of-sight remote control applications.

Data protocols for the IR remote controls of most home electronics vary from manufacturer to manufacturer. To decode them, you need to know both the carrier frequency and the message structure. Most commercial IR remote control devices operate using a carrier wave between 38 and 40 kHz. The frequency of the carrier wave limits the rate at which you can send data on that wave, so IR transmission is usually done at a low data rate, typically between 500 and 2000 bits per second. It's not great for high-bandwidth data transmission, but if you're only sending the values of a few pushbuttons on a remote, it's acceptable. Unlike the serial protocols you've seen so far in this book, IR protocols do not all use an 8-bit data format. For example, Sony's Control-S protocol has three formats: a 12-bit, a 15-bit, and a 20-bit format. Philips' RC5 format, common to many remotes, uses a 14-bit format.

If you have to send or receive remote control signals, you'll save a lot of time by looking for a specialty IR modulator chip to do the job, rather than trying to recreate the protocol yourself. Fortunately, there are many helpful sites on the web to explain the various protocols. Reynolds Electronics (www.rentron.com) has many helpful tutorials, and sells a number of useful IR modulators and demodulators. EPanorama has a number of useful links describing many of the more common IR protocols at www.epanorama. net/links/irremote.html.

If you're building both the transmitter and receiver, your job is fairly straightforward. You just need an oscillator through which you can pass your serial data to an infrared LED, and a receiver that listens for the carrier wave and demodulates the data signal. It's possible to build your own IR modulator using a 555 timer IC, but there are a number of inexpensive modules you can buy to modulate or demodulate an IR signal, as shown in this next project. X

Making Infrared Visible

Even though you can't see infrared light, cameras can. If you're not sure whether your IR LED is working, one quick way to check is to point the LED at a camera and look at the resulting image. You'll see the LED light up. Here's a look at the IR LED in a home remote control, viewed through a webcam attached to a personal computer. You can even see this in the LCD viewfinder of a digital camera. If you try this with your IR LED, you may need to turn the lights down to see this effect.

⊻ Having a camera at hand is useful when troubleshooting IR projects.

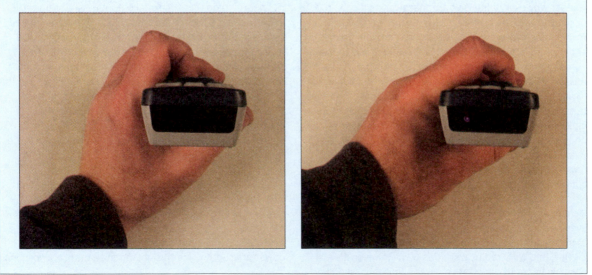

Infrared Transmitter-Receiver Pair

This example uses custom IR transmitter and receiver ICs (integrated circuits) from Reynolds Electronics to establish a one-way link between transmitter and receiver. This transmitter-receiver pair can operate up to 19200 bits per second, much faster than normal household remote controls.

In this example, you'll connect the IR transmitter and a potentiometer to your microcontroller. The receiver will connect to your personal computer through a USB-to-serial adaptor. The microcontroller will continually send the potentiometer's value to the receiving computer.

You could also build this project with two microcontrollers, of course, but it's good practice to test the modules on a PC first so that can you troubleshoot the circuit and test the range of your IR transmitter and receiver. In testing, I got about 12 feet (nearly 4 meters) of range with this system.

There are two circuits for this project: the transmitter, which is connected to a microcontroller, and the receiver, which is connected to your computer via a USB-to-serial adaptor.

The transmitter's connections:
1. Voltage: to 5V
2. Oscillator 1: to ceramic resonator pin 1
3. Oscillator 2: to ceramic resonator pin 3
4. Duty cycle select: to ground. This sets the duty cycle of the carrier wave.
5. Data inversion select: to ground. This setting specifies whether the transmitter sends data as true (logic 0 = 0V, logic 1 = 5V), or inverted (logic 0 = 5V, logic 1 = 0V).
6. Data out: sends data out to IR LED
7. Data in: to microcontroller TX
8. Ground: to ground

The receiver's connections:
1. Data out: to the USB-to-serial adaptor's receive (RX) line
2. Ground: to ground
3. Voltage: to 5V power through a 100-ohm resistor

Figures 6-1 and 6-2 show the transmitter and receiver.

MATERIALS

» **1 solderless breadboard** such as Digi-Key (www.digikey.com) part number 438-1045-ND, or Jameco (www.jameco.com) part number 20601
» **1 Arduino module** or other microcontroller
» **1 USB-to-TTL serial adaptor** SparkFun's BOB-00718 from Chapter 2 will do the job (www.sparkfun.com). If you use a USB-to-RS-232 adaptor such as a Keyspan or Iogear dongle, refer to Chapter 2 for the schematics to convert RS-232 to TTL serial.
» **1 IR transmitter IC** Reynolds (www.rentron.com) part number TX-IRHS
» **1 20MHz ceramic resonator with internal caps** for use with the IR transmitter IC, from Reynolds
» **1 infrared LED** Reynolds part number TSAL7200, or any other IR LED will do the job.
» **1 high-speed IR detector module** Reynolds (www.rentron.com) part number TSOP7000
» **1 100-ohm resistor**
» **1 220-ohm resistor**
» **1 potentiometer**

A. TSOP7000 receiver   B. 20MHz resonator   C. TX-IRHS transmitter   D. IR LED

Figure 6-1

At left, a TSOP7000 IR receiver connected to a USB-to-serial adaptor. At right, a TX-IRHS infrared transmitter connected to a microcontroller. A potentiometer is attached to an analog input of the microcontroller. The microcontroller sends the value of the pot to the serial adaptor via IR communication. You can see the wiring diagrams for this on the opposite page.

Try It   Once you've got the circuit connected, transmission is very straightforward. Here's a program that transmits the value of a potentiometer:

Once you've got this code running on your microcontroller, connect the IR receiver circuit to your computer. Then open your serial terminal program and connect to the circuit at 19200 bits per second. You should see the value of the potentiometer printed in the serial terminal window like so:

```
127
128
128
129
130
129
```

```
/*
   IR transmit example
   Language: Wiring/Arduino
*/
void setup(){
  // open the serial port at 19200 bps:
  Serial.begin(19200);
}
void loop(){
  // read the analog input:
  int analogValue = analogRead(0);
  // send the value out via the transmitter:
  Serial.println(analogValue, DEC);
  // delay 10ms to allow the analog-to-digital receiver to settle:
  delay(10);
}
```

▶▶ As you can see, serial communication over infrared isn't that different than serial communication over a wire. You can send data in only one direction, so you can't use a handshaking protocol, and you're limited to the data rate of your transmitter-receiver pair. Otherwise, you won't have to make any major code changes to use IR.

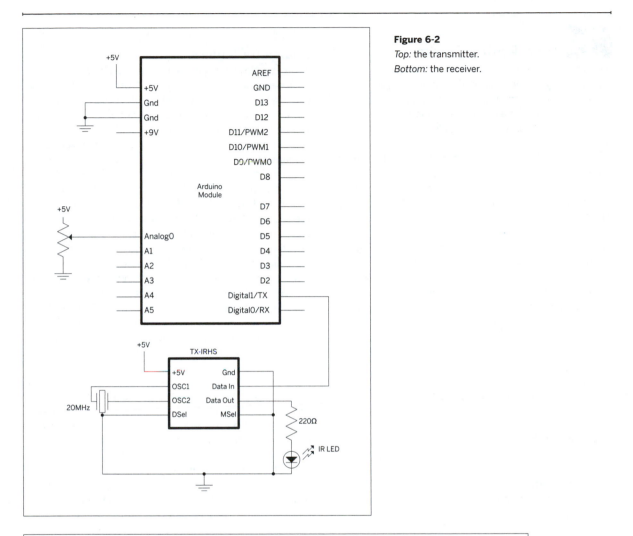

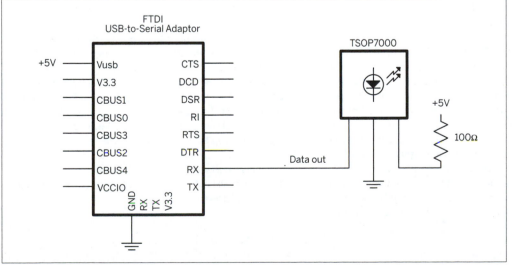

Figure 6-2

Top: the transmitter.

Bottom: the receiver.

❝ How Radio Works

Radio relies on the electrical property called induction. Any time you vary the electrical current in a wire, you generate a corresponding magnetic field that emanates from the wire. This changing magnetic field induces an electrical current in any other wires in the field. The frequency of the magnetic field is the same as the frequency of the current in the original wire. This means that if you want to send a signal without a wire, you can generate a changing current in one wire at a given frequency and attach a circuit to the second wire to detect current changes at that frequency. That's how radio works.

The distance that you can transmit a radio signal depends on the signal strength, the sensitivity of the receiver, the nature of the antennas, and any obstacles that block the signal. The stronger the original current and the more sensitive the receiver, the farther apart the sender and receiver can be. The two wires act as antennas. Any conductor can be an antenna, but some work better than others. The length and shape of the antenna and the frequency of the signal all affect transmission. Antenna design is a whole field of study on its own, so I can't do it justice here, but a rough rule of thumb for a straight wire antenna is as follows:

Antenna length
  5,616 in. / frequency in MHz

Antenna length
  14,266.06 cm. / frequency MHz

For more information, consult the technical specifications for the specific radios you're using. Instructions on making a good antenna are common in a radio's documentation.

Radio Transmission: Digital and Analog

As with everything else in the microcontroller world, it's important to distinguish between digital and analog radio transmission. Analog radios simply take an analog electrical signal such as an audio signal, and superimpose it on the radio frequency in order to transmit it. The radio frequency acts as a carrier wave, carrying the audio signal. Digital radios superimpose digital signals on the carrier wave, so there must be a digital device on either end to encode or decode those signals. In other words, digital radios are basically modems, converting digital data to radio signals, and radio signals back into digital data.

Radio Interference

Though radio is omnidirectional, it can be blocked by obstacles, particularly metal ones. A large metal sheet, for example, will reflect a radio signal rather than allowing it to pass through. This principle is used not only in designing antennas, but also in designing shields. If you've ever cut open a computer cable and encountered a thin piece of foil wrapped around the inside wires, you've encountered a shield. Shields are used to prevent random radio signals from interfering with the data being transmitted down a wire. A shield doesn't have to be a solid sheet of metal, though. A mesh of conductive metal will block a radio signal as well, if the grid of the mesh is small enough. The effectiveness of a given mesh depends on the frequency it's designed to block. In fact, it's possible to block radio signals from a whole space by surrounding the space with an appropriate shield and grounding the shield. You'll hear this referred to as making a Faraday cage. A Faraday cage is just an enclosure that's shielded to be radio-free. The effect is named after the physicist Michael Faraday, who first demonstrated and documented it.

Sometimes radio transmission is blocked by unintentional shields. If you're having trouble getting radio signals through, look for metal that might be shielding the signal. Transmitting from inside a car can sometimes be tricky because the car body acts as a Faraday cage. Putting the antenna on the outside of the car improves reception. This is true for just about every radio housing.

All kinds of electrical devices emit radio waves as side effects of their operation. Any alternating current can generate a radio signal, even the AC that powers your home or office. This is why you get a hum when you lay speaker wires in parallel with a power cord. The AC signal is inducing a current in the speaker wires, and the speakers are reproducing the changes in current as sound. Likewise, it's why you may have trouble operating a wireless data network near a microwave oven. Wi-Fi operates at frequencies in the gigahertz range. That range is commonly called the microwave range, because the wavelength of those signals is only a few micrometers long. Microwave ovens use those same frequencies, transmitted at very high power, to cook food. Some of that energy leaks from the oven at low power, which is why you get all kinds of radio noise in the gigahertz range around a microwave.

Motors and generators are especially insidious sources of radio noise. A motor also operates by induction; specifically, by spinning a pair of magnets around a shaft in the center of a coil of wire. By putting a current in the wire, you generate a magnetic field, and that attracts or repulses the magnets, causing them to spin. Likewise, by using mechanical force to spin the magnets, you generate a current in the wire. So a motor or a generator is essentially a little radio, generating noise at whatever frequency it's rotating.

Because there are so many sources of radio noise due to the ubiquitous use of alternating currents, there are many ways for a radio signal to be interfered with. It's important to keep these possible sources of noise in mind when you begin to work with radio devices. Knowledge of common interference sources, and knowing how to shield against them, is a valuable tool in radio troubleshooting.

Multiplexing and Protocols

When you're transmitting data via radio, anyone with a compatible receiver can receive your signal. There's no wire to contain the signal, so if two transmitters are sending at the same time, they will interfere with each other. This is the biggest weakness of radio: a given receiver has no way to know who sent the signal it's receiving. In contrast, consider a wired serial connection: you can be reasonably sure when you receive an electrical pulse on a serial cable that it came from the device on the other end of the wire. You have no such guarantee with radio. It's as if you were blindfolded at a cocktail party and everyone else there had the same voice. The only way you'd have of knowing who was saying what is if everyone were polite about not interrupting each other, clear about beginning and ending their sentences, and identifying themselves when they speak. In other words, it's all about protocols.

The first thing everyone at that cocktail party would have to do is to agree on who speaks when. That way they could all share your attention by dividing up the time they get. Sharing in radio communication is called multiplexing, and this form of sharing is called time division multiplexing. Each transmitter gets a given time slot in which to transmit.

Of course, it depends on all the transmitters being in synch. When they're not, time division multiplexing can still work reasonably well if all the transmitters speak

much less than they listen (remember the first rule of love and networking from Chapter 1: listen more than you speak). If a given transmitter is transmitting for only a few milliseconds in each second, and if there's a limited number of transmitters, the chance that any two messages will overlap, or collide, is relatively low. This guideline, combined with a request for clarification from the receiver (rule number three), can ensure reasonably good RF communication.

Back to the cocktail party. If every speaker spoke in a different tone, you could distinguish them by their tones. In radio terms, this is called frequency division multiplexing. It means that the receiver has to be able to receive on several frequencies simultaneously. But if there's a coordinator handing out frequencies to each pair of transmitters and receivers, it's reasonably effective.

Various combinations of time and frequency division multiplexing are used in every digital radio transmission system. The good news is that most of the time you never have to think about it, because it's handled for you by many of the radios on the market today, including the ones you'll see shortly.

Multiplexing helps transmission by arranging for transmitters to take turns and to distinguish themselves based on frequency, but it doesn't concern itself with the content of what's being said. This is where data protocols come in. Just as you saw how data protocols made wired networking possible, you'll see them come into play here as well. It's common to use a data protocol on top of using multiplexing methods, to make sure that the message is clear. For example, Bluetooth, ZigBee, and Wi-Fi are nothing more than data networking protocols layered on top of a radio signal. All three of them could just as easily be implemented on a wired network (and in a sense, Wi-Fi is: it uses the same TCP/IP layer that Ethernet uses). The principles of these protocols are no different than those of wired networks, which makes it possible to understand wireless data transmission even if you're not a radio engineer. Remember the principles and troubleshooting methods you used when dealing with wired networks, because you'll use them again in wireless projects. The methods mentioned here are just new tools in your troubleshooting toolkit. You'll need them in the projects that follow.

x

◀┋ Project 9

Radio Transmitter-Receiver Pair

When your project is simple enough to work with one-way communication, but you need the omnidirectionality that radio affords, RF transmitter-receiver pairs are the way to go. There are several models on the market, from companies like Abacom (www.abacomdirect.com), Reynolds (www.rentron.com), Glolab (www.glolab.com), and others. Most of them are very simple to interface with a microcontroller, requiring nothing more than power, ground, and a connection to the serial I/O lines of the controller. Many of them even come with built-in antennas. This example uses a TX/RX pair made by Laipac, sold by SparkFun. The transmitter and receiver both connect directly to a microcontroller's serial lines as described above, and can operate at voltages in the 3.3V to 5V range.

In this example, you'll connect the RF transmitter and a potentiometer to your microcontroller. The receiver will connect to your personal computer through a USB-to-serial adaptor. The microcontroller will continually send the potentiometer's value to the receiving computer.

There are two circuits for this project: the transmitter, which is connected to a microcontroller, and the receiver, which is connected to your computer via a USB-to-serial adaptor. The connections are as follows:

Transmitter
1. Ground
2. Data in: to microcontroller transmit pin
3. Voltage: to 5V
4. Antenna: to a 30cm piece of wire, acting as an antenna

Receiver
1. Ground
2. Data out: to USB-to-serial RX pin
3. Linear out: not connected
4. Voltage: to +5V
5. Voltage: to +5V. Be sure to put a 0.1µF capacitor across voltage and ground to decouple the radio's power supply.
6. Ground
7. Ground
8. Antenna: to a 30cm piece of wire, which acts as an antenna.

Figure 6-3 shows the transmitter, and Figure 6-4 shows the receiver.

MATERIALS

» **1 solderless breadboard** such as Digi-Key part number 438-1045-ND or Jameco part number 20601
» **1 Arduino module** or other microcontroller
» **1 USB-to-TTL serial adaptor** SparkFun's BOB-00718 from Chapter 2 will do the job. If you use a USB-to-RS-232 adaptor such as a Keyspan or logear dongle, refer to Chapter 2 for the schematics to convert RS-232 to 5V TTL serial.
» **1 RF transmitter-receiver pair** Available from SparkFun as part number WRL-07813, but similar models from the other retailers will work as well.
» **1 10KΩ potentiometer**
» **2 0.1µF capacitors**

A. RF transmitter B. 0.1 μF capacitor C. Antenna (30cm wire)

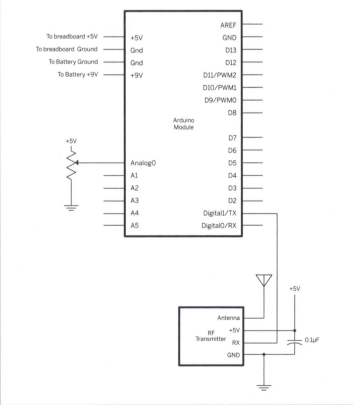

Figure 6-3

RF transmitter connected to a microcontroller. A potentiometer is connected to the micro-controller's analog input. The coil of wire is the antenna.

A. RF receiver B. 0.1 μF capactior C. Antenna (30cm wire)

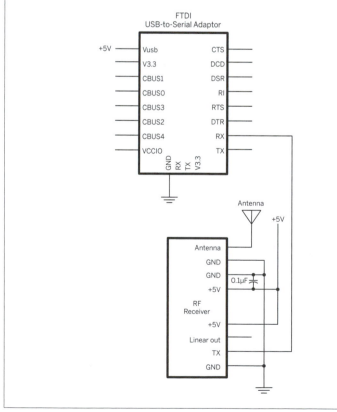

Figure 6-4
RF receiver connected to a personal computer via a USB-to-serial adaptor. The coil of wire is the antenna.

Try It Once you've got the circuit connected, program the microcontroller with the following code, which reads the analog input and sends its value out as an ASCII-encoded string:

```
/*
RF Transmitter
Language: Wiring/Arduino

This program reads an analog input on pin 0
and sends the result out as an ASCII-encoded string.
The TX line of the microcontroller is connected to
an RF transmitter that is capable of reading at 2400 bps.

*/

void setup(){
  // open the serial port at 2400 bps:
  Serial.begin(2400);
}
void loop(){
  // read the analog input:
  int analogValue = analogRead(0);
  // send the value out via the transmitter:
  Serial.println(analogValue, DEC);
  // delay 10ms to allow the analog-to-digital receiver to settle:
  delay(10);
}
```

> When you've got the microcontroller programmed, open the serial port that the receiver is connected to using your serial terminal program, at 2400 bits per second (thus far you've operated at 9600 or 19200 bps. For this example, just set your serial terminal program to communicate at 2400 bps instead of 9600). You might see a string of garbage characters. That's because the transmitter started sending before the receiver was activated. Reset the microcontroller while the serial port is open. After a few seconds, it should start sending again, and you should see a string of numbers representing the potentiometer's value, like this:

```
127
128
128
129
130
129
```

You may also get garbage characters on the screen, even when the transmitter is turned off. This is because the receiver's picking up random noise in its frequency range. This can be generated by a wide range of sources. All electrical devices emit some RF waves, so if your receiver is sitting beside an LCD or CRT display, for example, it could be picking up noise from that. In the absence of a signal from the transmitter, the receiver will display anything it gets. This is one of the downsides of working with simple transmitter-receiver pairs like this: you need to filter out the garbage in your program. More advanced transceivers like the ones in the next example will do some or all of that filtering for you.

One simple way to filter out the noise is to limit your transmission to a definite range of values. If you transmit only in ASCII-encoded strings separated by commas, linefeeds, or return characters, you can ignore any bytes received that don't fit within those values. Furthermore, if you send the data in a particular format every time, your receiving program can ignore any strings it receives that don't match the pattern. The bytes you're receiving from the example program are always in the ASCII numeral range ("0" through "9", or ASCII values 48 through 57), or a linefeed and carriage return (ASCII 10 and 13). In addition, the strings are never more than four digits long, because the analog input value never exceeds 1023. So you can test whether the bytes match the accepted values, and whether the string is of the appropriate length.

Tune In   Here's a Processing program that does this. Close your serial terminal and try this Processing program instead. Make sure to change the serial port number in this program to what-ever port you're using. All the interesting work is done in the serialEvent() method:

Although the program is written in Processing, the same algorithm can work in other programming environments.

```
/*
  RF Receive
  Language: Processing

  This program listens for data coming in through a serial port.
  It reads a string and throws out any strings that contain values
  other than ASCII numerals, linefeed, or carriage return, or that
  are longer than four digits.

  This program is designed to work with a Laipac RF serial receiver
  connected to the serial port, operating at 2400 bps.

*/

import processing.serial.*;

Serial myPort;              // the serial port
int incomingValue = 0;      // the value received in the serial port

void setup() {
  // list all the available serial ports:
  println(Serial.list());

  // Open the appropriate serial port. On my computer, the RF
  // receiver is connected to a USB-to-serial adaptor connected to
  // the first port in the list. It may be on a different port on
  // your machine:

  myPort = new Serial(this, Serial.list()[0], 2400);
  // tell the serial port not to generate a serialEvent
  //until a linefeed is received:
  myPort.bufferUntil('\n');
}

void draw() {
  // set the background color according to the incoming value:
  background(incomingValue/4);
}

// serialEvent method is run automatically by the Processing applet
// whenever the buffer reaches the byte value set in the bufferUntil()
// method in the setup():

void serialEvent(Serial myPort) {
  boolean validString = true;  // whether the string you got is valid
  String errorReason = "";     // a string that will tell what went wrong

  // read the serial buffer:
  String myString = myPort.readStringUntil('\n');

  // make sure you have a valid string:
```

»

Continued from opposite page.

```
if (myString != null) {
  // trim off the whitespace (linefeed, carriage return) characters:
  myString = trim(myString);

  // check for garbage characters:
  for (int charNum = 0; charNum < myString.length(); charNum++) {
    if (myString.charAt(charNum) < '0' ||
        myString.charAt(charNum) > '9') {
      // you got a garbage byte; throw the whole string out
      validString = false;
      errorReason = "Received a byte that's not a valid ASCII numeral.";
    }
  }
  // check to see that the string length is appropriate:
  if (myString.length() > 4) {
    validString = false;
    errorReason = "Received more than 4 bytes.";
  }

  // if all's good, convert the string to an int:
  if (validString == true) {
    incomingValue = int(trim(myString));
    println("Good value: " + incomingValue);
  }
  else {
    // if the data is bad, say so:
    println("Error: Data is corrupted. " + errorReason);
  }
}
}
```

Now that you've seen the basics of sending serial data in one direction over a radio link, the next example will demonstrate how to send it in two directions, using a pair of RF transceivers. Even though the transceivers in the next example incorporate their own error checking, you might want to keep this checking method in mind, in case you need it.

❝ Radio Transceivers

In many cases, one-way communication isn't enough. For example, you might have noticed in the previous example that sometimes the message doesn't get through, even when you've got the circuitry and the code fully working. In that case, you might want the PC to be able to query the microcontroller occasionally to see the state of the inputs. Or perhaps you're making an application in which there's input and output on both sides. In that case, transceivers are essential.

There are many different kinds of data transceivers on the market. Some connect directly to the serial I/O of the microcontroller and send the data as is. Some, like the Bluetooth module you saw in Chapter 2, add an additional protocol layer on top of the data communication, so you have to be able to implement that protocol on both sender and receiver. The cost of transceivers varies widely.

Until recently, most digital radio transceivers on the market implemented only the most basic serial communications protocol. For example, the RTF-DATA-SAW transceivers from Abacom do a good job of sending and receiving serial information. They connect directly to the serial transmit and receive pins of your microcontroller. Any serial data that you send out the transmit line goes directly out as a radio signal. Any pulses received by the transceiver are sent into your microcontroller's receive line. The benefit is that you don't have to learn any serial protocol — you can send data in any form you want. The cost is that you have to manage the whole conversation yourself. If the receiving transceiver misses a bit of data, you'll get a garbled message, just like you did with the transmitter-receiver pair in the preceding project. Furthermore, any radio device in the same frequency range can affect the quality of your reception. As long as you're working with just two radios and no interference, transceivers like the RTF-DATA-SAW do a fine job. There are other companies on the market who sell similar transceivers, including Linx Technologies (www.linxtechnologies.com) and Low Power Radio Solutions (www.lprs.co.uk).

There are an increasing number of cheap transceivers on the market that implement networking protocols, handling the conversation management for you. The Bluetooth modem in Chapter 2 ignored signals from other radios that it wasn't associated with, and took care of error checking for you. The XBee radios you'll use in the next project will do the same, and much more, as you'll see in Chapter 7. These particular transceivers are in the same general price range as the plain serial transceivers mentioned earlier. They require you to learn a bit more in terms of networking protocols, but the benefits you gain make them well worth that minor cost.

There's one other difference between the serial transceivers and the networked ones: the networked modules tend to operate at much higher speeds, both in terms of transmission frequency and serial data rate. For example, the Abacom modules mentioned previously operate at 315 MHz and a maximum serial data rate of 9600 bits per second. The XBee modules in the following project operate at 2.4Ghz and up to 115,200 bits per second. Hence, the XBee radios can send a message at nearly 100 times the speed. Even if you're sending only a few bytes per second, this means that your transceiver can spend more time listening and less time speaking, thus reducing the chance that it'll miss a given message from another transceiver. X

Project 10

Duplex Radio Transmission

In this example, you'll connect an RF transceiver and a potentiometer to the microcontroller. Each microcontroller will send a signal to the other when its potentiometer changes by more than ten points. When either one receives a message, it will light up an LED to indicate that it got a message. Each device also has an LED for local feedback as well.

The RF transceivers used in this project implement the 802.15.4 wireless networking protocol on which ZigBee is based. In this example, you won't actually use any of the benefits of ZigBee, and few of the 802.15.4 benefits. 802.15.4 and ZigBee are designed to allow many different objects to communicate in a flexible networking scheme. Each radio has an address, and every time it sends a message, it has to specify the address to send to. It can also send a broadcast message, addressed to every other radio in range. You'll see more of that in Chapter 7. For now, you'll give each of your two radios the other's address, so that they can pass messages back and forth.

As you may have discovered with the previous project, there are many things that can go wrong with wireless transmission, and as radio transmissions are not detectable without a working radio, it can be difficult to troubleshoot. Because of that, you're going to build this project up in stages. First you'll communicate with the radio module itself serially, in order to set its local address and destination address. Then you'll write a program for the microcontroller to make it send messages when the potentiometer changes, and listen for the message to come through on a second radio attached to your personal computer. Finally, you'll make two microcontrollers talk to each other using the radios.

→ Step 1: Configuring the XBee Modules Serially

The RF transceivers used in this project implement the 802.15.4 wireless networking protocol on which ZigBee is based. In this example, you won't actually use any of

MATERIALS

» **2 solderless breadboards** such Digi-Key part number 438-1045-ND or Jameco part number 20601
» **1 USB-to-TTL serial adaptor** SparkFun's PCB-BOB-00718 from Chapter 2 will do the job. If you use a USB-to-RS-232 adaptor such as a Keyspan or Iogear dongle, refer to Chapter 2 for the schematics to convert RS-232 to 5V TTL serial.
» **2 Arduino modules** or other microcontrollers
» **2 Maxstream XBee OEM RF modules** available from www.maxstream.net or www.gridconnect.com, part number GC-WLM-XB24-A
» **2 XBee breakout boards** or 2 XBee Arduino shields

For the breakout boards:
» **2 2mm breakout boards** The XBee modules listed here have pins spaced 2mm apart. To use them on a breadboard, you'll need a breakout board that shifts the spacing to 0.1 inches. You could solder wires on to every pin, or you could make or purchase a printed circuit board that shifts the pins. SparkFun's Breakout Board for XBee Module (part number BOB-08276) will do the trick.
» **4 rows of 0.1 inch header pins** available from most electronics retailers
» **4 2mm female header rows,** Samtec (www.samtec.com) part number MMS-110-01-L-SV. Samtec, like many part makers, supplies free samples of this part in small quantities. SparkFun also offers header rows for the XBee (part number PRT-08272).
» **2 potentiometers**
» **2 1µF capacitors**
» **2 10µF capacitors**
» **6 LEDs**

the benefits of ZigBee, and few of the 802.15.4 benefits. 802.15.4 and ZigBee are designed to allow many different objects to communicate in a flexible networking scheme. Each radio has an address, and every time it sends a message, it has to specify the address to send to. It can also send a broadcast message, addressed to every other radio in range. You'll see more of that in Chapter 7. For now, you'll give each of your two radios the other's address, so

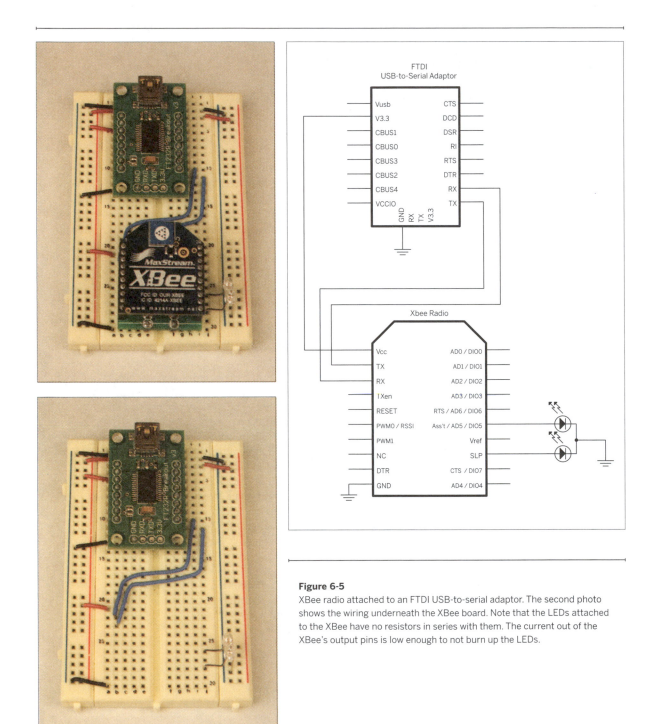

Figure 6-5
XBee radio attached to an FTDI USB-to-serial adaptor. The second photo
shows the wiring underneath the XBee board. Note that the LEDs attached
to the XBee have no resistors in series with them. The current out of the
XBee's output pins is low enough to not burn up the LEDs.

Figure 6-6
XBee printed circuit board, in various stages. *Bottom left:* bare board shown from the bottom. *Bottom right:* board with headers soldered to inner rows. *Top right:* finished board with no female sockets (radio is soldered directly to the board). *Top left:* finished board with female sockets.

Mounting the XBee Radios on a Breakout Board

The XBee radios have pins spaced 2mm apart, which is too narrow to fit on a breadboard. You can either solder wires to each pin to extend the legs, or you can mount the module on a breakout board. SparkFun has such a board: the Breakout Board for XBee Module (part number BOB-08276). The breakout board in Figure 6-6 is a custom-designed board developed before there was a commercially available solution. It's functionally identical to the SparkFun board. You'll need two breakout boards for this project, one for each radio.

Once you've got the breakout board, solder headers to the inner rows. These will plug into your breadboard. Next, attach the radio to the breakout board. You can either solder it directly or use 2mm female headers to mount it on. If you solder the radio directly to the board, make sure that you leave space between the radio and the inner header pins, so they're not touching. If they are, you will short the radio out.

that they can pass messages back and forth.

As you may have discovered with the previous project, there are many things that can go wrong with wireless transmission, and as radio transmissions are not detectable without a working radio, it can be difficult to troubleshoot. Because of that, you're going to build this project up in stages. First you'll communicate with the radio module itself serially, in order to set its local address and destination address. Then you'll write a program for the microcontroller to make it send messages when the potentiometer

changes, and listen for the message to come through on a second radio attached to your personal computer. Finally, you'll make two microcontrollers talk to each other using the radios.

Figure 6-5 shows an XBee module connected to a USB-to-serial adaptor. The USB adaptor draws power from the USB bus, and the radio draws power from the adaptor via its 3.3V voltage output.

Once you've got the XBee module's circuit built and

Arduino XBee Shield

There is an alternative to the breadboard circuit shown in Figure 6-5 for Arduino users. Libelium (www.libelium.com) and PCB Europe (pcb-europe.com) have teamed up to make an XBee shield for the Arduino module. The shield comes with an XBee radio, and connects to the Arduino's TX and RX pins. To connect the radio to the Arduino, set the XBEE/USB jumpers to the left, as shown in Figure 6-7. When you're programming the Arduino, you might want to remove the jumpers, so that the radio's serial communications don't interfere with the program upload.

You can also use your Arduino board as a USB-to-serial converter to configure the XBee radio on the shield. To do this, unplug your Arduino from its power source, then remove the microcontroller chip, as shown in Figure 6-8. Be careful not to bend the pins, so that you can put it back

when you are done. Pay attention to the orientation of the microcontroller as well, as you have to put it back the same way. Once you've removed the chip, set the shield's XBEE/USB jumpers to the right, as shown in Figure 6-9, and put the shield on the board. Open a serial terminal connection to the Arduino board's serial port, and send commands as shown in "Step 1: Configuring the XBee Modules Serially." Once you've configured the radio, unplug the Arduino board, replace the microcontroller chip, set the XBEE/USB jumpers to the left, put the shield back on, and you're all set to program the Arduino to talk to the XBee radio.

These shields may change their form by the time this book is published, but even in their initial form, they are a convenient way to combine Arduinos and XBees.

---

powered, the LED on pin 13 should stay on steadily, and the LED on pin 15 will blink. The former is lit when the module is active (LED on), and the latter blinks whether the radio is associated with another radio (LED blinking) or not (LED on steadily). Make sure that your circuit is connected to your computer (USB port or serial port) and open the port in your favorite serial terminal program:

+++

Don't type the return key or any other key for at least one second afterward. It should respond like so:

OK

This step should look familiar to you from the Bluetooth modem you saw in Chapter 2. The XBee is using an AT-style command set like the Bluetooth modem did, and the +++ puts it into command mode. The one-second pause after this string is called the guard time. If you do nothing, the module will drop out of command mode after ten seconds, so if you're reading this while typing, you may need to enter another +++ string before the next stage.

Once you get the OK response, set the XBee's address. The 802.15.4 protocol uses either 16-bit or 64-bit long addresses, so there are two parts to the address, the high word and the low word (two or more bytes in computer

memory used for a single value are sometimes referred to as a word). For this project, you'll use 16-bit addressing and therefore get to choose your own address. You'll need only the low word of the address do to this. Type:

ATMY1234\r

To confirm that you set it, type:

ATMY\r

The module should respond:

1234

You'll see that the responses from the XBee overwrite each other, because the XBee sends only a carriage return at the end of every message, not a linefeed.
X

A. XBEE/USB jumpers set to left

» at left, above

◀◀ **Figure 6-7**
Arduino XBee shield. The XBEE/USB jumpers are set to the left to connect the radio's TX to the Arduino's RX, and vice versa.

» above

⬆ **Figure 6-8**
Arduino module with the microcontroller removed. In this configuration, the Arduino can act as a USB-to-serial converter.

» at left, below

◀◀ **Figure 6-9**
Arduino XBee shield. The XBEE/USB jumpers are set to the right so that the XBee's TX connects directly to the FTDI chip's RX, and vice versa. There is no microcontroller chip on the board underneath the shield.

A. XBEE/USB jumpers set to right

❝ An XBee Serial Terminal

Because the GNU screen program in Mac OS X, Unix, and Linux doesn't print newlines when the XBees send only a return character, it can be difficult to read the results.

▸ Here's a Processing program that substitutes newlines for return characters when it prints the results onscreen. GNU screen users may find it useful in place of screen for communicating with XBee radios.

Figure 6-10 shows a screenshot of the XBee terminal program.

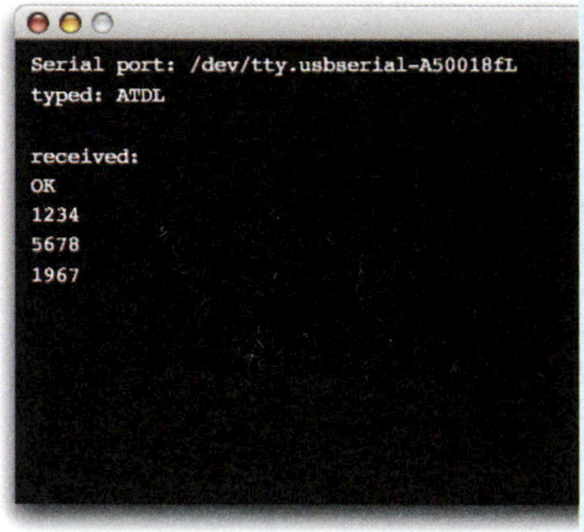

Figure 6-10
The XBee terminal sketch in action.

```
/*
  XBee terminal
  language: processing

  This program is a basic serial terminal program.
  It replaces newline characters from the keyboard
  with return characters. It's designed for use with
  Linux, Unix, and Mac OS X in combination with XBee radios,
  because the XBees don't send newline characters back.
*/

import processing.serial.*;

Serial myPort;            // the serial port you're using
String portnum;           // name of the serial port
String outString = "";    // the string being sent out the serial port
String inString = "";     // the string coming in from the serial port
int receivedLines = 0;    // how many lines have been received
int bufferedLines = 10;   // number of incoming lines to keep

void setup() {
  size(400, 300);         // window size

  // create a font with the third font available to the system:
  PFont myFont = createFont(PFont.list()[2], 14);
  textFont(myFont);

  // list all the serial ports:
  println(Serial.list());

  // based on the list of serial ports printed from the
  // previous command, change the 0 to your port's number:
  portnum = Serial.list()[0];
  // initialize the serial port:
  myPort = new Serial(this, portnum, 9600);

}

void draw() {
  // clear the screen:
  background(0);
  // print the name of the serial port:
  text("Serial port: " + portnum, 10, 20);
```

»

Continued from opposite page.

```
  // Print out what you get:
  text("typed: " + outString, 10, 40);
  text("received:\n" + inString, 10, 80);
}

// this method responds to key presses when the
// program window is active:
void keyPressed() {
  switch (key) {
    // In OS X, if the user types return, a linefeed is returned. But
    // to communicate with the XBee, you want a carriage return:

  case '\n':
    myPort.write(outString + "\r");
    outString = "";
    break;
  case 8:    // backspace
    // delete the last character in the string:
    outString = outString.substring(0, outString.length() -1);
    break;
  case '+':  // we have to send the + signs even without a return:
    myPort.write(key);
    // add the key to the end of the string:
    outString += key;
    break;
  case 65535:  // if the user types the shift key, don't type anything:
    break;
    // if any other key is typed, add it to outString:
  default:
    // add the key to the end of the string:
    outString += key;
    break;
  }
}

// this method runs when bytes show up in the serial port:
void serialEvent(Serial myPort) {
  // read the next byte from the serial port:
  int inByte = myPort.read();
  // add it to  inString:
  inString += char(inByte);
  if (inByte == '\r') {
    // if the byte is a carriage return, print
    // a newline and carriage return:
    inString += '\n';
    // count the number of newlines:
    receivedLines++;
    // if there are more than 10 lines, delete the first one:
    if (receivedLines >  bufferedLines) {
      deleteFirstLine();
```

»

Continued from previous page.

```
      }
    }
  }
// deletes the top line of inString so that it all fits on the screen:
void deleteFirstLine() {
  // find the first newline:
  int firstChar = inString.indexOf('\n');
  // delete it:
  inString= inString.substring(firstChar+1);
}
```

Once you have the sketch working, you're ready to set the XBee's destination address. Make sure you're in command mode (+++), then type: `ATDL\r`

You'll likely get this: `0`

The default destination address on these modules is 0. The destination address is two words long, so to see the high word, type:

`ATDH\r`

This pair of commands can also be used to set the destination address, like so:

`ATDL5678\r`
`ATDH0\r`

These radios also have a group, or Personal Area Network (PAN) ID. All radios with the same PAN ID can talk to each other, and ignore radios with a different PAN ID. Set the PAN ID for your radio like so:

`ATID1111\r`

The XBee will respond to this command, like all commands, with:

`OK`

Make sure to add the parameter WR after your last command, to write the parameters to the radio's memory. That way they'll remain the way you want them even after the radio is powered off. For example:

`ATID1111,WR\r`

Once you've configured one of your radios, quit the Processing sketch (or disconnect your serial terminal program) and unplug the board from your computer. Next, remove the XBee from the circuit, insert the second one, and configure it using the same procedure. Don't set a radio's destination address to the same value of its source address, or it will only talk to itself! You can use any 16-bit address for your radios. Here's a typical configuration for two radios that will talk to each other (don't forget to add the ,WR to the last command):

	ATMY	ATDL	ATDH	ATID
Radio 1	1234	5678	0	1111
Radio 2	5678	1234	0	1111

You can combine commands on the same line by separating them with commas. For example, to get both words of a module's source address, type this:

`ATDL, DH\r`

The module will respond with both words at once. Likewise, to set both destination words and then make the module write them to its memory so that it saves the address when it's turned off, type:

`ATDL5678, DH0, WR\r`

The module will respond to all three commands at once:

`OK OK OK`
X

Step 2: Programming a Microcontroller to use the XBee Module

Okay! Now you're ready to get two modules to talk to each other. If you happen to have two serial ports, or two USB adaptors, you could duplicate the circuit shown previously and wire the second radio to the second serial port, then open a second serial terminal window to the second port and communicate between the two radios that way. But it's clearer to see what's going on if one of the radios is attached to another device, like a microcontroller. Figure 6-11 shows a diagram of what's connected to what in this step.

Figure 6-12 shows an XBee module attached to a regular Arduino using the XBee shield. Figure 6-13 shows an XBee attached to an Arduino mini along with the circuit diagram. Note the 3.3V regulator. The XBee's serial I/O connections are 5V tolerant, meaning that they can accept 5V data signals, even though the module operates at 3.3V, just like the XPort in Chapter 5. You need to power the module from 3.3 volts, however.

Once your module is connected, it's time to program the microcontroller to configure the XBee, then to send data through it. In this program, the microcontroller will configure the XBee's destination address on startup. Once that's done, it will watch for a switch to change from low to high, and send data across when the switch changes.

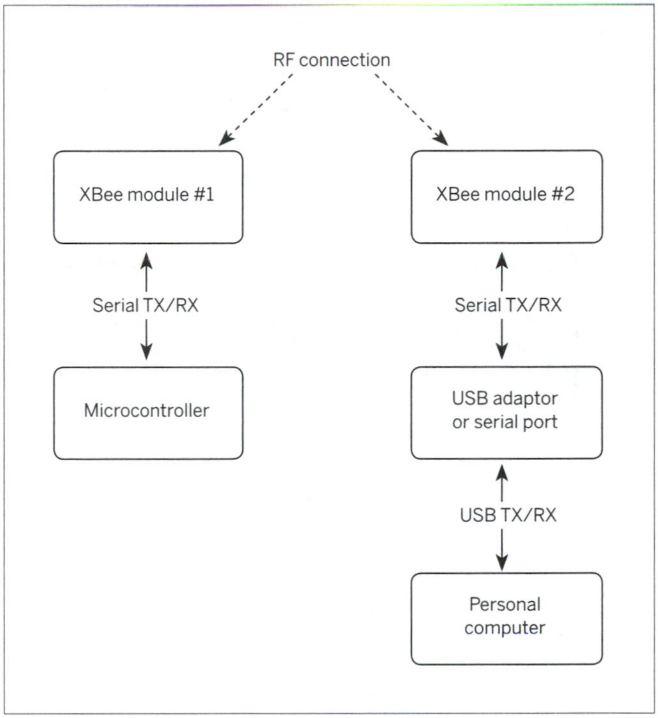

» at right, above

Figure 6-11

XBee #1 is connected to the microcontroller. XBee #2 is connected via USB or serial to the PC. This enables a wireless link between the PC and the microcontroller.

» at right, below

Figure 6-12

Arduino and XBee shield with potentiometer attached to analog pin 0, and LED attached to digital pin 9. This circuit is the same as the one shown in Figure 6-13, but without the TX and RX LEDs on digital pins 2 and 3.

RF connection

XBee module #1 → Serial TX/RX → Microcontroller

XBee module #2 → Serial TX/RX → USB adaptor or serial port → USB TX/RX → Personal computer

Figure 6-13
Top: XBee connected to an Arduino
Mini. This Mini is using a SparkFun
version of the USB-to-serial adaptor
rather than the Arduino model.
The two adaptors are functionally
identical. *Bottom:* Circuit diagram for
Arduino-Xbee connection.

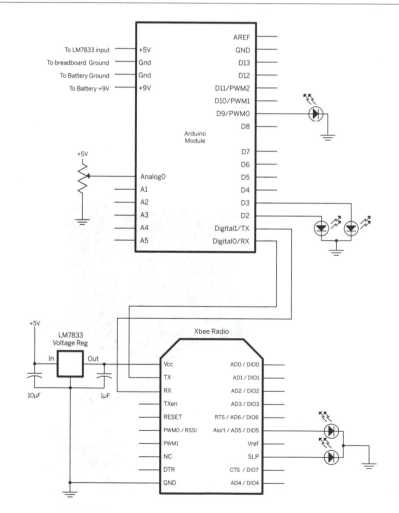

Make It   First, give the I/O pins names and set up some variables for tracking the change in the switch:

```
#define sensorPin 0      // input sensor
#define txLed 2          // LED to indicate outgoing data
#define rxLed 3          // LED to indicate incoming data
#define analogLed 9      // LED that changes brightness with incoming value
#define threshold 10     // how much change you need to see on
                         // the sensor before sending

int lastSensorReading = 0;  // previous state of the switch

int inByte= -1;             // incoming byte from serial RX
char inString[6];           // string for incoming serial data
int stringPos = 0;          // string index counter
```

▸▸ Next, in the setup() method, configure serial transmission, set the modes on the I/O pins, and configure the XBee's destination address:

```
void setup() {
  // configure serial communications:
  Serial.begin(9600);

  // configure output pins:
  pinMode(txLed, OUTPUT);
  pinMode(rxLed, OUTPUT);
  pinMode (analogLed, OUTPUT);

  // set XBee's destination address:
  setDestination();
  // blink the TX LED indicating that the main program's about to start:
  blink(3);
}
```

▸▸ The XBee configuration, handled by the setDestination() method, looks just like what you did earlier, only now you're instructing the microcontroller to do it:

```
void setDestination() {
  // put the radio in command mode:
  Serial.print("+++");
  // wait for the radio to respond with "OK\r"
  char thisByte = 0;
  while (thisByte != '\r') {
    if (Serial.available() > 0) {
      thisByte = Serial.read();
    }
  }

  // set the destination address with 16-bit addressing. This radio's
  // destination should be the other radio's MY address and vice versa:
  Serial.print("ATDH0, DL1234\r");
  Serial.print("ATMY5678\r");   // set my address (16-bit addressing)

  // set the PAN ID. If you're in a place where many people
  // are using XBees, choose a unique PAN ID
  Serial.print("ATID1111\r");
  Serial.print("ATCN\r"); // go into data mode:
}
```

> ▸▸ Change the destination address to the destination address of the radio you're attaching to your personal computer, not the one that's attached to your microcontroller.

» The blink() method is just like ones you've seen previously in the book. It blinks an LED to indicate that setup is over:

```
// Blink the tx LED:
void blink(int howManyTimes) {
  for (int i=0; i< howManyTimes; i++) {
    digitalWrite(txLed, HIGH);
    delay(200);
    digitalWrite(txLed, LOW);
    delay(200);
  }
}
```

» The main loop handles incoming serial data, reads the potentiometer, and sends data out if there's a sufficient change in the potentiometer's reading:

```
void loop() {
  // listen for incoming serial data:
  if (Serial.available() > 0) {
    // turn on the RX LED whenever you're reading data:
    digitalWrite(rxLed, HIGH);
    handleSerial();
  }
  else {
    // turn off the receive LED when there's no incoming data:
    digitalWrite(rxLed, LOW);
  }

  // listen to the potentiometer:
  char sensorValue = readSensor();

  // if there's something to send, send it:
  if (sensorValue > 0) {
    //light the tx LED to say you're sending:
    digitalWrite(txLed, HIGH);
    Serial.print(sensorValue, DEC );
    Serial.print("\r");

    // turn off the tx LED:
    digitalWrite(txLed, LOW);
  }
}
```

» There are two other methods called from the loop, handleSerial(), which listens for strings of ASCII numerals and converts them to bytes in order to set the brightness of the led on the PWM output, and readSensor(), which reads the potentiometer and checks to see whether the change on it is high enough to send the new value out via radio. Here are those methods:

```
void handleSerial() {
  inByte = Serial.read();
  // save only ASCII numeric characters (ASCII 0 - 9):
  if ((inByte >= '0') && (inByte <= '9')){
    inString[stringPos] = inByte;
    stringPos++;
  }
  // if you get an ASCII carriage return:
  if (inByte == '\r') {
    // convert the string to a number:
    int brightness = atoi(inString);
```

»

Continued from opposite page.

NOTE: You might need to disconnect the XBee's receive and transmit connections to the microcontroller while programming, if your microcontroller is programmed serially like the Arduino and Wiring modules are. The serial communications with the XBee can interfere with the serial communications with the programming computer Once the microcontroller's programmed, you can re-connect the transmit and receive lines.

```
  // set the analog output LED:
  analogWrite(analogLed, brightness);

  // put zeroes in the array
  for (int c = 0; c < stringPos; c++) {
    inString[c] = 0;
  }
  // reset the string pointer:
  stringPos = 0;
  }
}

char readSensor() {
  char message = 0;
  // read the sensor:
  int sensorReading = analogRead(sensorPin);

  // look for a change from the last reading
  // that's greater than the threshold:
  if (abs(sensorReading - lastSensorReading) > threshold) {
    message = sensorReading/4;
    lastSensorReading = sensorReading;
  }
  return message;
}
```

Notice that in the main loop, you're not using any AT commands. That's because the XBee goes back into data mode (called idle mode in the XBee user's guide) automatically when you issue the ATCN command in the setDestination() method.

Remember, in data mode, any bytes sent to an AT-style modem go through as is. The only exception to this rule is that if the string +++ is received, the modem switches to command mode. This behavior is the same as that of the Bluetooth module from Chapter 2, and as almost any device that implements an AT-style protocol. It's great, because it means that once you're in data mode, you can send data with no extra commands, letting the radio itself handle all the error corrections for you.

Once you've programmed the microcontroller, set the destination address on the computer's XBee to the address of the microcontroller's radio. (If you did this in the earlier step, you shouldn't need to do it again.) Then turn the potentiometer on the microcontroller. You should get a message like this in your serial terminal window:

120

The actual number will change as you turn the potentiometer. It will overwrite itself in the serial window, because you're not sending a newline character (unless you are using the serial terminal Processing sketch shown earlier). Congratulations! You've made your first wireless transceiver link. Keep turning the potentiometer until you're bored, then move on to step 3.

X

➲ Step 3: Two-Way Wireless Communication Between Microcontrollers

This step is simple. All you have to do is to replace the computer in the previous step with a second microcontroller (connect it to your second XBee module as shown in Figure 6-12 or Figure 6-13). The program for both microcontrollers will be almost identical to each other; only the destination address of the XBee radio will be different. This program will both send and receive data over the modules. Turning the potentiometer causes it to send a number to the other microcontroller. When the microcontroller receives a number in the serial port, it uses it to set the brightness of an LED on pin 9.

First, connect the second XBee module to the second microcontroller using the circuit in Figure 6-13. It's same

circuit you created in the previous step. Then program both microcontrollers with the previous program, making sure to set the destination addresses as noted in the program. Look in Appendix C for the program in its entirety.

When you've programmed both modules, power them both on and turn the potentiometer several times. As you turn the potentiometer, the LED on pin 9 of the other module should fade up and down. Now you've got the capability for duplex wireless communication between two microcontrollers. This opens up all kinds of possibilities for interaction.

X

🔌 Wireless and Mobile

Now that you're able to communicate wirelessly, you might want to make your microcontroller mobile as well. To do this, all you have to do is to power it from a 9-volt battery. If you're using an Arduino module or a Wiring module, you can do this by connecting a 9-volt battery to the power input terminals as shown in Figure 6-14 (and in the schematic shown earlier). If you're working with a different microcontroller and it's powered by a 5-volt voltage regulator, just connect the battery to the input terminals of the voltage regulator. It's a good idea to keep your microcontroller module connected to a power adaptor or USB power while programming and debugging, however. When a battery starts to weaken, your module will operate inconsistently, and that can make debugging impossible.

Figure 6-14
Left: Arduino module powered by a 9V battery. *Right:* Wiring module powered by 9V battery.

🔊 **Project 11**

Bluetooth Transceivers

In Chapter 2, you learned how to connect a microcontroller to your personal computer using a Bluetooth radio. This example shows you how to connect two microcontrollers using Bluetooth in a similar manner.

As mentioned in Chapter 2, Bluetooth was originally intended as a protocol for replacing the wire between two devices. As a result, it requires a tighter connection between devices than you saw in the preceding XBee project. In that project, a radio sent a signal out with no awareness of whether the receiver got the message, and could send to a different receiver just by changing the destination address. In contrast, Bluetooth radios must establish a connection with each other before sending data over a given channel, and must break that connection before starting a conversation with a different radio over that channel. The advantage of Bluetooth is that it's built into many commercial devices today, so it's a convenient way to connect microcontroller projects to personal computers, phones, and more. For all its complications, it offers reliable data transmission.

The modules used here, the BlueSMiRF radios from Sparkfun, use a radio from BlueRadios. The AT command set used here was defined by BlueRadios. Other Bluetooth modules from other manufacturers also use AT-style command sets, and they may execute similar functions, but their syntax is not the same. Unfortunately, Bluetooth radio manufacturers haven't set a standard AT syntax for their devices.

➡ Step 1: Getting to Know the Commands

Because the Bluetooth connection process involves many steps, it's easiest to learn and understand it using a serial terminal program. Figure 6-15 shows the wiring to connect a BlueSMiRF radio to an FTDI USB-to-serial connector. If you're not using the FTDI connector, you can use the MAX3323 circuit from Chapter 2 (Figure 2-3). Build this circuit, then connect it to your computer and open a serial connection to it at 9600 bits per second using your serial terminal program.

MATERIALS

» **2 solderless breadboards** such as Digi-Key part number 438-1045-ND, or Jameco part number 20601
» **1 USB-to-TTL serial adaptor** SparkFun's BOB-00718 from Chapter 2 will do the job. If you use a USB-to-RS-232 adaptor such as a Keyspan or logear dongle, refer to Chapter 2 for the schematics to convert RS-232 to 5V TTL serial.
» **2 Arduino modules** or other microcontrollers
» **2 BlueSMiRF Bluetooth modem modules** from SparkFun
» **2 potentiometers**
» **6 LEDs**

Figure 6-16 shows the connection you're about to make. First, you'll open a serial terminal window to connect to the radio's serial interface, then you'll open a second serial terminal window to connect via your computer's Bluetooth radio to the BlueSMiRF's radio. Your computer's Bluetooth radio will show up as a second serial port on your computer, as it did after you established a pairing with it in Chapter 2 in Project #2, Wireless Monski Pong. If you didn't make that pairing, this would be a good time to go back and do it.

The BlueSMiRF radios use an AT-style command set for command and configuration, and have two modes — command mode and data mode — just like the XBee radios. When you first power up a BlueSMiRF and connect to its serial interface, it's in command mode. To see that it's alive, type: AT\r. It will respond:

\r\nOK\r\n

All of the radio's responses will be preceded and followed by a linefeed and carriage return as shown here. All of your input commands should be followed by a carriage return (press Enter or Return).

In order for one radio to connect to another, the second radio must be discoverable. In the BlueRadios syntax, a radio is discoverable when it's in Slave mode. The radio connecting to it is said to be in Master mode. In this step,

Figure 6-15
BlueSMiRF radio
attached to a USB-to-
serial adaptor.

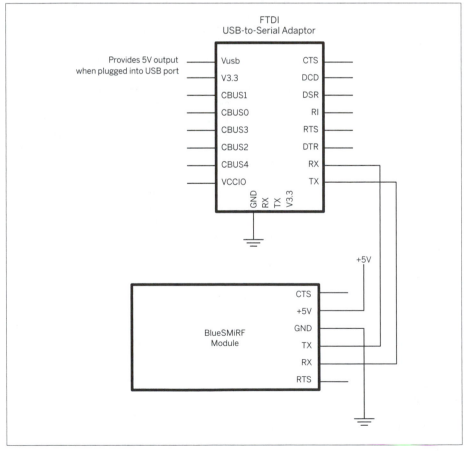

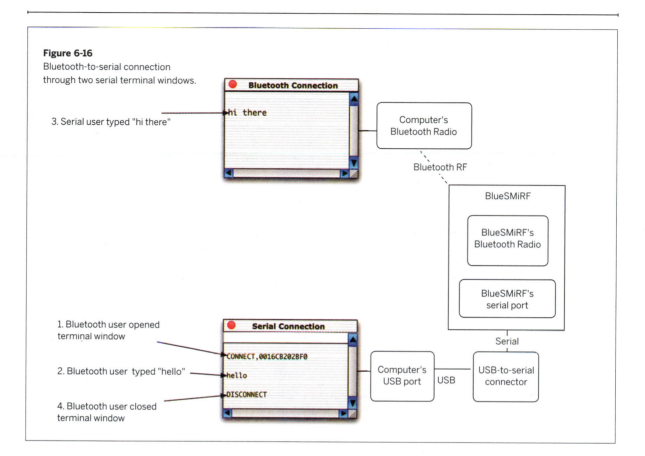

Figure 6-16
Bluetooth-to-serial connection through two serial terminal windows.

3. Serial user typed "hi there"

Bluetooth Connection

hi there

Computer's Bluetooth Radio

Bluetooth RF

BlueSMiRF

BlueSMiRF's Bluetooth Radio

BlueSMiRF's serial port

1. Bluetooth user opened terminal window

2. Bluetooth user typed "hello"

4. Bluetooth user closed terminal window

Serial Connection

CONNECT,0016CB202BF0

hello

DISCONNECT

Computer's USB port

USB

Serial

USB-to-serial connector

you'll learn a radio's Bluetooth address and check its connection status.

A series of status commands tell you about the radio's configuration. To learn the radio's Bluetooth address, type:

    ATSI,1\r

It will respond with an address in hexadecimal notation, like this:

    OK
    1122334455AA

Write down this address, or copy it to a text document. You'll need it in a moment. Next, check its connection status by typing ATSI,3\r. It will respond like so:

    OK
    0,0

The first digit is telling you that the radio is in slave mode,

and the second, that it's not connected. Now you can open a second serial terminal window, open the serial port that corresponds to the radio's Bluetooth connection (you established this number when you paired the radio with your computer in the Wireless Monski Pong project), and you'll be speaking via your computer's Bluetooth radio to the BlueSMiRF's radio. You'll get a message like this back in the serial terminal:

    CONNECT, 1122334455AA

Following that, anything you type in the Bluetooth connection window shows up in the serial connection window, and vice versa. When you close the Bluetooth serial window, you'll get the following message in the serial window:

    DISCONNECT

There are other status commands as well, but these ones are the ones that are most important to you at first.
X

➡ Step 2: Connecting Two Bluetooth Radios

Now that you've got basics of connecting and disconnecting, it's time to connect to a microcontroller using Bluetooth. For this step, you'll connect via the same USB-to-serial connection, but instead of speaking to your computer's own radio, you'll connect to a radio attached to a microcontroller.

First, get the Bluetooth addresses for both of your radios. You already wrote down one. Replace it with the second radio in your serial-to-USB circuit and follow the same steps to get that radio's address as well.

Next, build the microcontroller circuit shown in Figure 6-17. Just like the XBee example, it's got a potentiometer attached to the analog pin so that you can send its values. There's also a connection to the BlueSMiRF's Clear-to-Send (CTS) pin. When the BlueSMiRF reads 5V on this pin, it stops sending data until the pin goes low again. You'll use it to stop the BlueSMiRF sending serial data to the microcontroller when you don't want it to.

NOTE: You'll probably have to remove your BlueSMiRF while programming the Arduino or Wiring boards, just as you've had to for all other serial devices.

The program that follows connects to another BlueSMiRF with a set address, and when it connects, it sends its potentiometer value as an ASCII string, terminated by an asterisk, like this: 123*

Because there are so many newline characters and carriage returns in the AT command responses, it's simplest just to use a terminator that isn't used in the command set. That's why you're using an asterisk in this case.

Just like the XBee example, this program also looks for incoming ASCII strings (terminated by an asterisk this time) and converts them to use as a PWM value to dim an LED on pin 9.

➤➤ First, the constants and variables for this program are as follows:

```
/*
  BlueRadios master connection
  Language: Wiring/Arduino

*/

#define sensorPin 0          // input sensor
#define txLed 2              // LED to indicate outgoing data
#define rxLed 3              // LED to indicate incoming data
#define CTSpin 4             // clear-to-send pin
#define analogLed 9          // LED that will change brightness with
                             // incoming value
#define threshold 10         // how much change you need to see on the
                             // sensor before sending


byte lastSensorReading = 0;  // previous state of the pot
long lastConnectTry;         // milliseconds elapsed since the last
                             // connection attempt
long connectTimeout = 5000;  // milliseconds to wait between
                             // connection attempts
int inByte= -1;              // incoming byte from serial RX
char inString[6];            // string for incoming serial data
int stringPos = 0;           // string index counter

// address of the remote BT radio --
// replace with the address of your remote radio:
char remoteAddress[13] = "112233445566";

byte connected = false;      // whether you're connected
```

Figure 6-17
BlueSMiRF radio attached to a
microcontroller. This circuit is almost
identical to the XBee microcontroller
circuit discussed earlier; only the
radio is different.

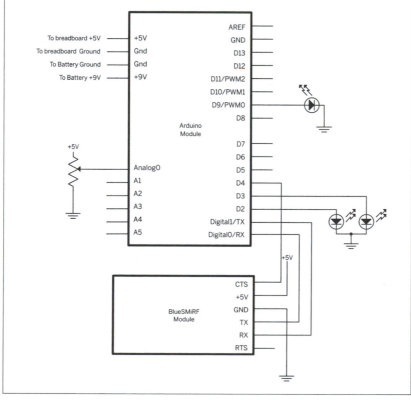

▸▸ The setup() method just sets the states of the pins, initializes serial, and blinks an LED, as usual. The clear-to-send pin is taken low here so that the BlueSMiRF can start sending serial data to the microcontroller. Then an initial attempt to connect the radios is made, using a method called BTConnect():

```
void setup() {
  // configure serial communications:
  Serial.begin(9600);

  // configure output pins:
  pinMode(txLed, OUTPUT);
  pinMode(rxLed, OUTPUT);
  pinMode (analogLed, OUTPUT);
  pinMode(CTSpin, OUTPUT);

  // set CTS low so BlueSMiRF can send you serial data:
  digitalWrite(CTSpin, LOW);

  // attempt a connection:
  BTConnect();

  // blink the tx LED to say that you're done with setup:
  blink(3);

}
```

▸▸ Here's the BTConnect() method. It sends +++ followed by ATDH to break any existing connection, then sends the ATDM command, which requests a connection to the other radio.

```
void BTConnect() {
  Serial.print("+++\r");
  delay(250);
  Serial.print("ATDH\r");
  Serial.print("ATDM");
  Serial.print(remoteAddress);
  Serial.print(",1101\r");
}
```

▸▸ The readSensor() method checks the value of the potentiometer:

```
int readSensor() {
  int message = 0;
  // read the sensor:
  int sensorReading = analogRead(sensorPin);

  // look for a change from the last reading
  // that's greater than the threshold:
  if (abs(sensorReading - lastSensorReading) > threshold) {
    message = sensorReading/4;
    lastSensorReading = sensorReading;
  }
  return message;
}
```

▶▶ The blink() method is the same as it was in the earlier XBee example:

```
void blink(int howManyTimes) {
  for (int i=0; i< howManyTimes; i++) {
    digitalWrite(txLed, HIGH);
    delay(200);
    digitalWrite(txLed, LOW);
    delay(200);
  }
}
```

▶▶ The main loop listens for incoming serial data and handles it. If more than five seconds have passed and the radio's still not connected to the other radio, the microcontroller attempts to connect again:

```
void loop() {
  if (Serial.available() > 0) {
    // signal that there's incoming data using the rx LED:
    digitalWrite(rxLed, HIGH);
    // do something with the incoming byte:
    handleSerial();
    // turn the rx LED off.
    digitalWrite(rxLed, LOW);
  }

  // if you're not connected and 5 seconds have passed in that state,
  // make an attempt to connect to the other radio:
  if (!connected && millis() - lastConnectTry > connectTimeout) {
    BTConnect();
    lastConnectTry = millis();
  }
}
```

The handleSerial() method is similar to the one in the XBee project, but there are some important differences. First, because there's a dedicated connection between the two radios, you need to keep track of the connection status. When a new connection is made, the BlueSMiRF will send a serial message like this before dropping into data mode:

CONNECT,0016CB202BF3

When the connection's broken, it will send this message, and stay in command mode:

DISCONNECT

In addition, when it's searching, there are a couple of other messages it might send:

NO CARRIER
NO ANSWER

Now that you know all the messages that you might get, you can establish what messages to look for. If you want to be thorough, you'd need to wait for the whole message each time and confirm that it's the right message. Parsing strings in most microcontroller languages is tricky, because of their limited memory, so it's simpler to look for unique characters in the various strings, because then you have to check for just one byte each time. It's not as thorough, but in this case, it works very consistently.

The only time a comma shows up is in the CONNECT message, so you can use that as a sign of connection. The only time a S shows up is in the DISCONNECT message, so you can use that as a sign of disconnection. You might be tempted to use D, but remember that D is a hexadecimal digit, so it might show up in the CONNECT message. Likewise C, which also shows up in three of the four messages. Finally, R shows up only in the other two messages, and they both only show up when you're disconnected, so you can use them in case your microcontroller misses a DISCONNECT message.

The sequence for this handleSerial()
method is a bit complicated, so Figure
6-18 shows it in a flowchart. The actual
code follows:

```
void handleSerial() {
  inByte = Serial.read();
  delay(2);
  // comma comes only in the CONNECT,<address> message:
  if (inByte == ',') {
    // send an initial message:
    sendData();
    // update the connection status:
    connected = true;
  }


  //S comes only in the DISCONNECT message:
  if (inByte == 'S') {
    // turn off the analog LED:
    analogWrite(analogLed, 0);
    connected = false;
  }
  //R comes only in the NO CARRIER and NO ANSWER messages:
  if (inByte == 'R') {
    // turn off the analog LED:
    analogWrite(analogLed, 0);
    connected = false;
  }

  if (connected) {
    // save only ASCII numeric characters (ASCII 0 - 9):
    if ((inByte >= '0') && (inByte <= '9')){
      inString[stringPos] = inByte;
      stringPos++;
    }
    // if you get an asterisk, it's the end of a string:
    if (inByte == '*') {
      // convert the string to a number:
      int brightness = atoi(inString);
      // set the analog output LED:
      analogWrite(analogLed, brightness);

      // put zeroes in the array
      for (int c = 0; c < stringPos; c++) {
        inString[c] = 0;
      }
      // reset the string pointer:
      stringPos = 0;
      // as this  byte (*) is the end of an incoming string,
      // send out your reading in response:
      sendData();
    }
  }
}
```

▶▶ handleSerial() calls the sendData() method to read the sensor and send it out. Here it is:

```
void sendData() {
  // indicate that we're sending using the tx LED:
  digitalWrite(txLed, HIGH);
  Serial.print(readSensor(), DEC);
  // string termination:
  Serial.print("*");
  // turn off the tx LED:
  digitalWrite(txLed, LOW);
}
```

❝❝ That's the whole program. Run this on your microcontroller, filling in the address of your second radio for the address in the remoteAddress array above. Then connect your second radio to your USB-to-serial adaptor, if it's not there already, and open a serial terminal window to it. The microcontroller will continue to try to connect to this radio every five seconds until a connection is established, and then it will start sending sensor values through. Your initial messages should look like this in the serial terminal:

CONNECT,00A096152B36
105*

You can respond as if you were sending your own sensor values, and the microcontroller will fade the LED on pin 9 accordingly. Try this:

12*
120*
255*
1*

The LED should start dim, get brighter, then brightest, then get very dim. You should get four sensor readings in response.

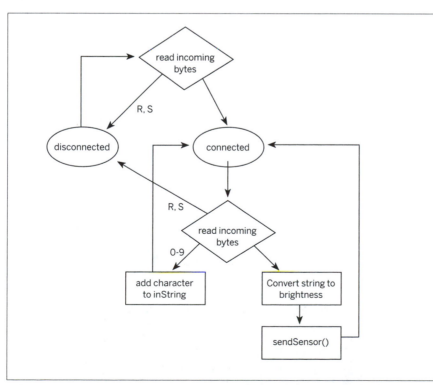

Figure 6-18
Flowchart of the handleSerial() method.

→ Step 3: Connecting Two Microcontrollers Via Bluetooth

If you've been following the parallels between the XBee example and this one, you probably know what's coming. Build the same circuit for your second microcontroller, using the second radio. Then change the Bluetooth address in the earlier program to be the address of the first radio, and program the second microcontroller. Then reset both microcontrollers. They will both attempt to connect to the other, and when either connects, they'll begin exchanging data. If you have trouble getting them to connect, change the connectTimeout variable so that they don't have the same value. This program won't work with every Bluetooth connection you have to make. When connecting to personal computers or mobile phones, you have to take different approaches, depending on the specific messages that those devices use. But the basic sequence should be similar enough to this that it will serve as a useful starting place.

X

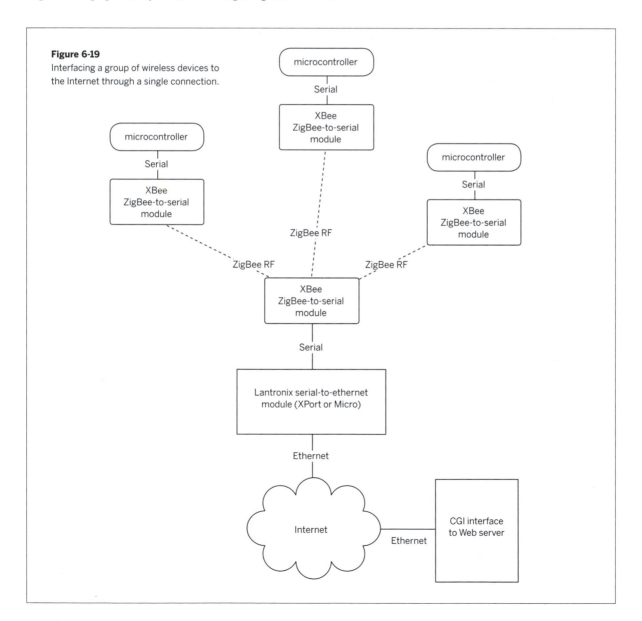

Figure 6-19
Interfacing a group of wireless devices to the Internet through a single connection.

❝ What About Wi-Fi?

So far, you've seen the most basic serial radios in action in the transmitter-receiver project, and more advanced radios in the transceiver projects. If you're thinking about networks of microcontrollers, you're probably wondering whether you can connect your projects to the Internet and to each other using Wi-Fi. The answer is: yes, you can.

In Project #5, you connected a microcontroller to the internet using a Lantronix Micro serial-to-Ethernet module. You could replace the Micro with a WiMicro and build the exact project, with only some minor configuration changes on the WiMicro.

It's worth mentioning why Wi-Fi isn't more pervasive in embedded wireless projects. First, there's the cost. Most of the serial-to-Wi-Fi modules on the market are more expensive than equivalent transceivers implementing other protocols. For example, the WiMicro costs about $165. DigiConnect's equivalent module, the plaintively named Wi-ME, costs about $130. Other wireless Ethernet-to-serial modules on the market are in the same price range — over $100. When compared to $20 for XBee and other serial transceivers, or even the $60 price range typical for many Bluetooth modules, Wi-Fi isn't exactly a bargain.

Besides the cost, however, there's another factor to consider before going Wi-Fi. Most Wi-Fi modules consume more electrical power than the other radio types mentioned here. Because one of the main reasons for going wireless is to go mobile, you'll be eating up battery life with Wi-Fi radios. So they're great when they're conveniently already built into a product, but if you're building from the ground up, it's worth considering other alternatives. One common solution for wireless projects that need Internet access is to make an RF-to-Ethernet bridge. For example, one of the XBee radios from the earlier project could be interfaced to a Lantronix XPort or Micro module to act as the Internet connection for a whole collection of XBee-enabled objects. Figure 6-19 shows a typical network setup for such a system.
X

❝ Buying Radios

You've seen a few different kinds of wireless modules in this chapter. Though they do the job well, they're not the only options on the market. You should definitely shop around for modules that suit your needs. Following are a few things to consider in choosing your radios.

The wisest thing you can do when buying your radios is to buy them as a set. Matching a transmitter from one company to a receiver from another is asking for headaches. They may say that they operate in the same frequency range, but there's no guarantee. Likewise, trying to hack an analog radio, such as that from a baby monitor or a walkie-talkie, may seem like a cheap and

easy solution, but in the end, it'll cost you time and eat your soul. When looking for radios, look for something that can take the serial output of your microcontroller. Most microcontrollers send serial data at TTL levels, with 0V for logic 0 and 3.3V or 5V for logic 1. Converting the output to RS-232 levels is also fairly simple, so radios that can take those signals are good for your purposes.

Consider the data rate you need for your application — and, more specifically, for the wireless part of it. You may not need high-speed wireless. One common use for wireless communication in the performance world is to get data off the bodies of performers without a wired connection, in order to control MIDI performance devices like samplers and lighting dimmers. You might think that you need your radios to work at MIDI data rates to do this, but you don't. You can send the sensor data from the performers wirelessly at a low data rate to a stationary microcontroller, then have the microcontroller send the data on via MIDI at a higher data rate.

Most of the inexpensive radio transmitters mentioned previously send data at relatively low rates (under 9600 bps). Given the noisy nature of RF, it's wise to not attempt to send at the top speed if you don't need to. In the transmitter-receiver project, the radio pair can operate at up to 4800 bps, but you are sending at only 2400 bps. Try it at 4800 bps, and you'll notice more errors. The 2.4Ghz radios used for Bluetooth, ZigBee, and wireless Ethernet are exceptions to this rule. They generally operate reasonably at much higher data rates, because they've got a microcontroller on board to manage the data flow.

Consider the protocols of the devices that you already have at your disposal. For example, if you're building an object to speak to a mobile phone or a laptop computer, and there's only one object involved, consider Bluetooth. Most laptops and many mobile phones already have Bluetooth radios onboard, so you'll need only one radio to do the job. It may take some work to make your object compatible with the commands specific to the existing devices you're working with, but if you can concentrate on that instead of on getting the RF transmission consistent, you'll save yourself a lot of time.
X

❝ Conclusion

Wireless communication involves some significant differences from wired communication. Because of the complications, you can't count on the message getting through like you can with a wired connection, so you have to decide what you want to do about it.

If you opt for the least expensive solutions, you can just implement a one-way wireless link with transmitter-receiver pairs and send the message again and again, hoping that it's eventually received. If you spend a little more money, you can implement a duplex connection, so that each side can query and acknowledge the other. Regardless of which method you choose, you have to prepare for the inevitable noise that comes with a wireless connection. If you're using infrared, incandescent light and heat act as noise, and if you're using radio, all kinds of electromagnetic sources act as noise, from microwave ovens to generators to cordless phones. You can write your own error-checking routines, but increasingly, wireless protocols like Bluetooth and ZigBee are making it possible for you to forget about that, because the modules that implement these protocols include their own error correction.

Just as you started learning about networks by starting with the simplest one-to-one network in Chapter 2, you started with wireless connections by looking at simple pairs in this chapter. In the next chapter, you'll look at peer-to-peer networks, in which there is no central controller, and each object on the network can talk to any other object. You'll see both Ethernet and wireless examples.
X

▸▸ **Urban Sonar by Kate Hartman, Kati London, and Sai Sriskandarajah.**
The jacket contains four ultrasonic sensors and two pulse sensors. a microcontroller in the jacket communicates via Bluetooth to your mobile phone. The personal space bubble as measured by the sensors and your changing heart rate as a result of your changing personal space paint a portrait of you that is sent over the phone to a visualizer on the internet.

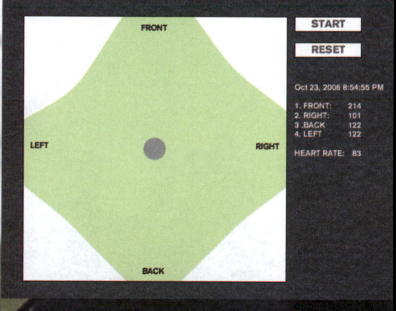

FRONT

START

RESET

Oct 23, 2006 8:54:55 PM

1. FRONT: 214
2. RIGHT: 101
3 .BACK 122
4. LEFT 122

HEART RATE: 83

LEFT

RIGHT

BACK

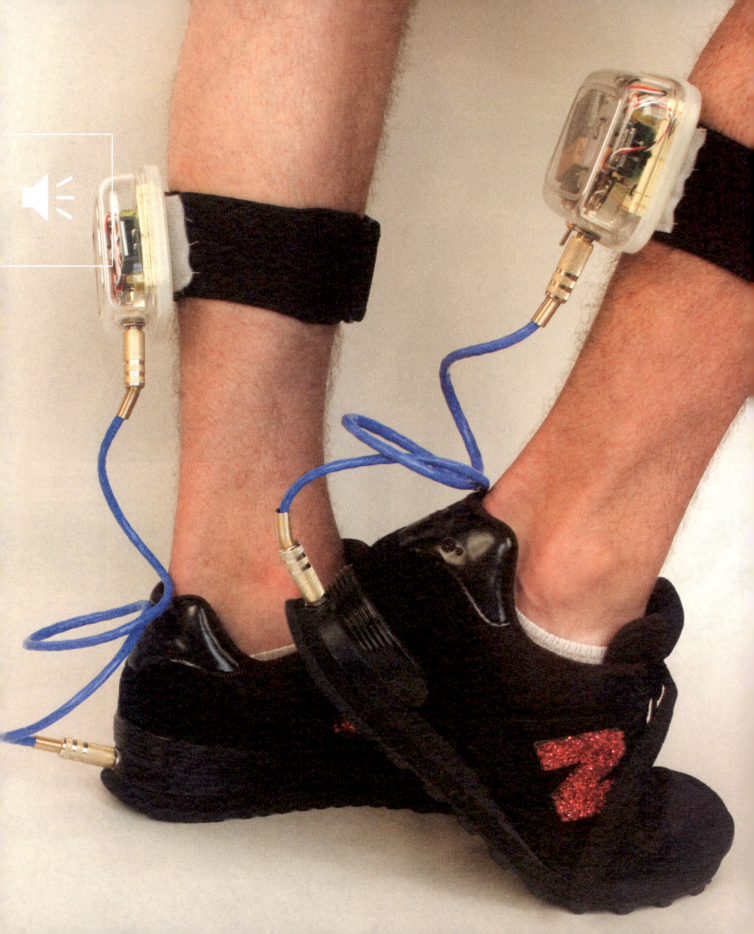

7

Sessionless Networks

So far, the network connections you've seen in this book have mostly been dedicated connections between two objects. Serial communications involve the control of a serial port. Mail, web, and telnet connections involve a network port. In all of these cases, there's a device that makes the port available (generally a server), and a client that requests access to the port (a client). The networked pong application in Chapter 5 was a classic example of this. In that application, the server handled all the communications between the other devices. In this chapter, you'll learn how to make multiple devices on a network talk to each other directly, or talk to all the other devices at once.

◀◀ **Perform-o-shoes by Andrew Schneider.**
The shoes exchange messages with a multimedia computer via XBee radio. When you moonwalk in the shoes, your pace and rhythm controls the playback of music from the computer.

❝ Look, Ma: No Microcontroller!

Since the beginning of the book, you've been working with programmable micro-controllers, writing the whole program yourself. You don't always have to do this. The various network devices you've been working with — the Lantronix devices, and XBee and Bluetooth Radios — all have their own microcontrollers built in. Some of them have their own digital and analog input and output pins. You can configure these devices to activate and respond to these I/O pins with network messages, but you need to learn their protocols first. To give you some examples of how you can use these network modules to their full potential, none of the projects in this chapter use programmable microcontrollers.

Sessions versus Messages

In Chapter 5, you learned about the Transmission Control Protocol, TCP, which is used for much of the communication on the Internet. To use TCP, your device has to request a connection to another device. The other device opens a network port, and the connection is established. Once the connection is made, information is exchanged, then the connection is closed. The whole request-connect-converse-disconnect sequence constitutes a session. If you want to talk to multiple devices, you have to open and maintain multiple sessions. Sessions characterize TCP communications.

Sometimes you want to make a network in which objects can talk to each other more freely, switching conversational partners on the fly, or even addressing the whole group if the occasion warrants. For this kind of communication, there's another protocol used on the Internet, called the User Datagram Protocol, or UDP.

Unlike the session-based TCP, UDP communication is all about messages. UDP messages are called datagrams. Each datagram to be sent is given a destination address and is sent on its merry way. Once the sender sends a message, it forgets about it. There is no two-way socket connection between the sender and receiver. It's the receiver's responsibility to decide what to do if some of the datagram packets don't arrive, or if they arrive in the wrong order.

Because UDP doesn't rely on a dedicated one-to-one connection between sender and receiver, it's possible to send a broadcast UDP message that's sent to every other object on a given subnet, For example, if your address is 192.168.1.45, and you send a UDP message to 192.168.1.255, everybody on your subnet receives the message. Because this is such a handy thing to do, a special address is reserved for this purpose: 255.255.255.255, which is the limited broadcast address, goes only to addresses on the same LAN, and does not require you to know your subnet address. This address is useful for tasks like finding out who's on the subnet.

The advantage of UDP is that data moves faster, because there's no error checking. It's also easier to switch the end device that you're addressing on the fly. The disadvantage is that it's less reliable byte-for-byte, as dropped packets aren't resent. UDP is useful for streams of data where there's a lot of redundant information, like video or audio. If a packet is dropped in a video or audio stream, you may notice a blip, but you can still make sense of the image or sound.

The relationship between TCP and UDP is similar to the relationship between Bluetooth and 802.15.4. Bluetooth devices have to establish a session to each other to communicate, whereas 802.15.4 radios like the XBee radios in Chapter 6 communicate simply by sending addressed messages out to the network without waiting for a result. Like TCP, Bluetooth is reliable for byte-critical applications, but less flexible in its pairings than 802.15.4.

X

🦆 Who's Out There? Broadcast Messages

The first advantage to sessionless protocols like UDP and 802.15.4 is that they allow for broadcasting messages to everyone on the network at once. Although you don't want to do this all the time, because you'd flood the network with messages that not every device needs, it's a handy ability to have when you want to find out who else is on your network. You simply send out a broadcast message asking "Who's there?" and wait for replies. You could write your own methods for doing this, but most of the time you won't have to. Broadcast querying is such a useful technique that most manufacturers of network devices include it as part of their products' functionality. Lantronix uses a specific UDP message to query a subnet for any of their devices. Similarly, the XBee devices from Maxstream have a special broadcast query command.

Querying for Lantronix Devices Using UDP

All the Lantronix devices are preprogrammed to respond via UDP if they receive a particular UDP message. Knowing this, you can find out the IP address of any Lantronix device on your subnet by sending this message. They reserve a special port for status queries: port 30718. When you send UDP messages to that port, you get back a status report from the device. This is handy if you've got a few Lantronix devices on the network and need to know their addresses.

To test this, all you need is a Lantronix device that's powered and connected to your Ethernet or Wi-Fi network, and a program that sends UDP datagrams. The network query messages don't involve any communication over

the devices' serial ports, so it doesn't matter what you've got connected to the serial port. You can reuse the pong client you built in Chapter 5 or the air quality meter from Chapter 4. In fact, it would work if you just provided power to the Lantronix device.

There's no way to send UDP messages using the Processing Network library, but there's a good free UDP library available from the Hypermedia Atelier at hypermedia.loeil org/processing/. You can also find it linked from the Libraries page of the main Processing site, at www.processing.org/reference/libraries/index.html. To use it, make a new directory called **udp/** in the **libraries/** subdirectory of your Processing application directory. Then unzip the contents of the download and drop them in the directory you created. After that, restart Processing and you're ready to use the UDP library.

Try It   Here's a Processing sketch using that library that sends out a search string for Lantronix devices on a subnet, waits for responses, and then prints them. Run the program, make sure the applet window has focus, and press any key to send the UDP broadcast message.

```
/*
  Lantronix UDP Device Query
  Language: Processing

  Sends out a UDP broadcast packet to query a subnet for Lantronix
  serial-to-ethernet devices.
  Lantronix devices are programmed to respond to UDP messages
  received on port 30718.  If a Lantronix device receives the string
  0x00 0x00 0x00 0xF6, it responds with a UDP packet containing the
  status message on port 30718.

  When the program starts, press any key on the keyboard and watch
```

»

The response is stored in an array called inData[], and you can see in the code how that array breaks down. Byte 3, for example, is a byte that tells us what follows. If that byte's value is 0xF7, then the next 16 bytes contain the device's basic configuration, including its firmware version, checksum and device type. Following that, in bytes 24 to 30 of the array, is the device's MAC address. Because the MAC address is usually on a sticker on the side of the device, this is a handy way to find out who's who.

Continued from previous page.

```
the message pane for responses.

See the Lantronix integration guide from http://www.lantronix.com
for the details.

This program uses the Hypermedia UDP library, available from
http://hypermedia.loeil.org/processing/.

*/

// import UDP library
import hypermedia.net.*;


UDP udp;                         // define the UDP object
int queryPort = 30718;           // the port number for the device query

void setup() {
  // create a new connection to listen for
  // UDP datagrams on query port;
  udp = new UDP(this, queryPort);

  // listen for incoming packets:
  udp.listen( true );
}

//process events
void draw() {
  // Twiddle your thumbs. Everything is event-generated.
}

/*
 send the query message when any key is pressed:
 */
void keyPressed() {
  byte[] queryMsg = new byte[4];
  queryMsg[0] = 0x00;
  queryMsg[1] = 0x00;
  queryMsg[2] = 0x00;
  // because 0xF6 (decimal value 246) is greater than 128
  // you have to explicitly convert it to a byte:
  queryMsg[3] = byte(0xF6);

  // send the message
  udp.send( queryMsg, "255.255.255.255", queryPort );
  println("UDP Query sent");
}

/*
```

»

The responses you get from the query message will look like this:

```
UDP Query sent
response from 192.168.1.128 on port 30718
Received response: F6


response from 192.168.1.47 on port 30718
Received response: F7
MAC Addr:  00 20 4A 8A 1E 48


response from 192.168.1.116 on port 30718
Received response: F7
MAC Addr:  00 20 4A 8F A1 6F


response from 192.168.1.236 on port 30718
Received response: F7
MAC Addr:  00 20 4A 66 A9 DD
```

NOTE: Notice that the first response is from the IP address of your computer. When you send a broadcast message, it comes back to you as well!

Continued from opposite page.

```
    listen for responses via UDP
  */
void receive( byte[] data, String ip, int port ) {
  String inString = new String(data);  // incoming data converted to string
  int[] intData = int(data);           // data converted to ints
  int i = 0;                           // counter

  // print the result:
  println( "response from "+ip+" on port "+port );

  // parse the response for the appropriate data.
  // if the fourth byte is <F7>, we got a status reply:
  print("Received response: ");
  println(hex(intData[3],2));
  if (intData[3] == 0xF7) {
    // MAC address of the sender is bytes 24 to 30 (the end):
    print("MAC Addr: ");
    for (i=24; i < intData.length; i++) {
      print(" " + hex(intData[i], 2));
    }
  }
  // print two blank lines to separate messages from multiple responders:
  print("\n\n");
}
```

“ Querying for XBee Radios Using 802.15.4 Broadcast Messages

Like the Lantronix devices, the XBee radios have a command for querying the air for any available radios. This is referred to as node discovery. When given the AT command ATND\r, the XBee radio sends out a broadcast message requesting that all other radios on the same personal area network (PAN) identify themselves. If a radio receives this message, it responds with its source address, serial number, received signal strength, and node identifier.

NOTE: To do node discovery, your radios must have version 10A1 of the XBee firmware or later. See the sidebar on upgrading the firmware on XBee radios for more details.

For the purposes of this exercise, you'll need at least two XBee radios connected to serial ports on your computer. The easiest way to do this is by using the USB-to-serial converter you've been using all along. The circuit from Figure 6-5 will work for this.

Once you've got the radios connected and working, open a serial terminal connection to one of them and issue the following command (you can use the XBee Terminal Processing program from Chapter 6 to communicate more easily with the XBee): +++ then wait for the radio to respond with OK. Then type (remember, \r means carriage return, so press Enter or Return instead of \r): ATND\r.

If there are other XBee radios on the same personal area network in range, the radio will respond after a few seconds with a string like this:

```
1234
13A200
400842A7
28
TIG0E1

5678
13A200
400842A9
```

1E
TIGOE3

Each grouping represents a different radio. The first number is the radio's source address (the number you get when you send it the command string ATMY). The second is the high word of the radio's serial number, the third is the low word. The fourth number is a measurement of the radio's received signal strength; in other words, it tells you how strong the radio signal of the query message was when it arrived at the receiving radio. The final line gives the radio's node identifier. This is a text string, up to 20 characters long, that you can enter into the radio to give it a name you can remember. You didn't use this function in Chapter 6, so your radios may not have node identifier strings. If you want to set the node identifier for further use, type: ATNI myname, WR\r

Replace myname with the name you want.

Broadcast messages can be useful for reasons other than for identification queries like the ones shown here, but they should be used sparingly, because they create more traffic than is necessary. In the next project, you'll use broadcast messages to reach all the other objects in a small, closed network.

Upgrading the Firmware on XBee Radios

To use the node discover and node identifier and some of the other XBee AT commands covered in this chapter, your XBee radios need to be upgraded to at least version 10A1. To check the firmware version of your radios, send the following command: ATVR\r. The radio will respond: 10A2. If the number is 10A1 or above (remember, it's in hexadecimal), you're good to go. If not, go to www.maxstream.net/support/downloads.php and download the X-CTU software. Bad news, Mac OS X users: it only runs on Windows (though you can run it under Parallels, if your Mac runs Parallels).

Before you can download software, you'll need to add a couple of connections between your serial port and your radio. Specifically, connect the DTR and RTS connections from the XBee (pins 9 and 16, respectively) to the same pins of your serial port. Figure 7-2 shows how do to this on the SparkFun FTDI board. Once you've made these connections, you're ready to run the software.

Once you've installed the software, launch it. On the PC Settings tab, you'll be able to select the serial port that your XBee radio is attached to. Pick a port, and leave the settings at their defaults. Click the Modem Configuration tab and you'll get to the tab where you can update the firmware. Click the Read button to read the current firmware on your radio. You'll get a screenful of the settings of your radio, similar to that in Figure 7-1. The firmware version is shown in the upper righthand corner. You can pull down that menu to see the latest versions available. Pick the latest one (anything after 10A1), then check the Always Update Firmware checkbox. Leave the Function Set menu choice set

to XBEE 802.15.4. Then click the Write button. The software will download the new firmware to your radio, and you're ready to go. The X-CTU software is useful to keep around, because it also lets you change and record your radio's settings without having to use the AT commands.

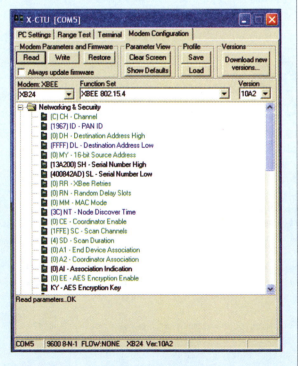

Figure 7-1. The X-CTU Modem Configuration tab.

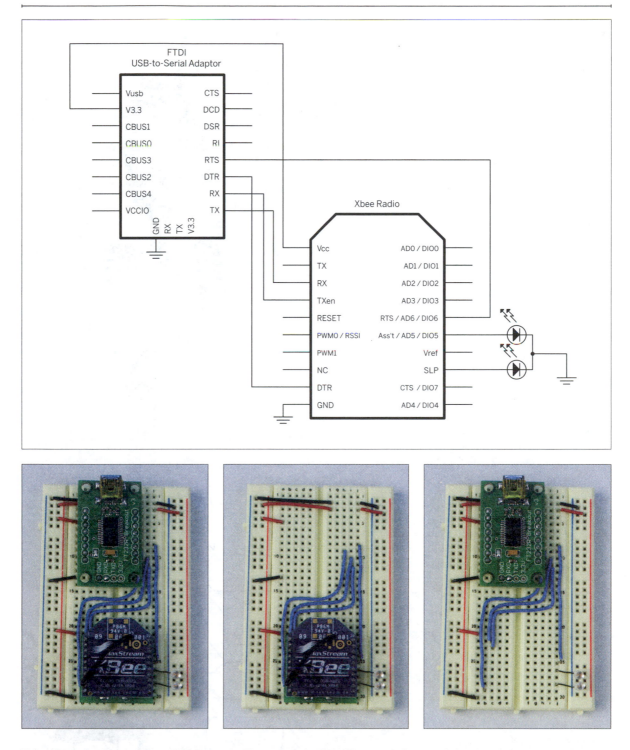

Figure 7-2. Connecting the DTR and RTS pins on the XBee radio to the FTDI USB-to-serial adaptor, including the wiring under the radio and the FTDI adaptor.

Reporting Toxic Chemicals in the Shop

If you've got a workshop to take care of, you'll appreciate this project. You're going to attach a volatile organic compound (VOC) sensor to an XBee radio to sense the concentration of organic solvents in the air in your shop. All too often, when you're working in the shop by yourself, you become insensitive to the fumes of the chemicals you're working with. This project is an attempt to remedy that issue.

The sensor values are sent to two other radios: one is attached to an XPort, which is connected to the Internet. From there, a PHP script reads the data and stores it in a web document. The other radio is attached to a cymbal-playing toy monkey elsewhere in the house that makes an unholy racket when the organic solvent levels in the shop get high. That way, the rest of the family will know immediately if your shop is toxic. If you don't share my love of monkeys, anything that can be switched on from a transistor can be controlled by this circuit. Figure 7-4 shows the network for this project. And Figure 7-3 shows the completed elements of the project.

> ⚠️ **WARNING: This project is designed for demonstration purposes only. The sensor circuit hasn't been calibrated. It won't save your life; it'll just make you a bit more aware of the solvents in your environment. Don't rely on this circuit if you need an accurate measurement of the concentration of organic compounds. Check with Figaro Sensor (www. figarosensor.com) to learn how to build a properly calibrated sensor circuit.**

» at right, above
Figure 7-3
The completed toxic sensor system: sensor, monkey, and network connection.

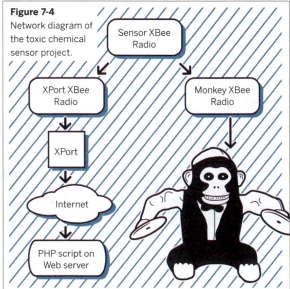

Figure 7-4
Network diagram of the toxic chemical sensor project.

Sensor XBee Radio → XPort XBee Radio → XPort → Internet → PHP script on Web server

Sensor XBee Radio → Monkey XBee Radio

MATERIALS

» **1 USB-to-TTL serial adaptor** SparkFun's (www.sparkfun.com) BOB-00718 from Chapter 2 will do the job. If you use a USB-to-RS-232 adaptor such as a Keyspan or Iogear dongle, refer to Chapter 2 for the schematics to convert RS-232-to-5V TTL serial. You'll use this for configuring the radios only.

Sensor Circuit

» **1 solderless breadboard** such as Digi-Key (www.digikey.com) part number 438-1045-ND, or Jameco (www.jameco.com) part number 20601

» **1 MaxStream XBee OEM RF module** available from www.maxstream.net or www.gridconnect.com, part number GC-WLM-XB24-A

» **1 5V regulator** The LM7805 series (SparkFun part number COM-00107, Digi-Key part number LM7805CT-ND) work well.

» **1 3.3V regulator** The LD1117-33V (SparkFun part number COM-00526) or the MIC2940A-3.3WT (Digi-Key part number 576-1134-ND) work well.

» **1 2mm breakout board** The XBee modules listed here have pins spaced 2mm apart. To use them on a breadboard, you'll need a breakout board that shifts the spacing to 0.1 inches. You could solder wires on to every pin, or you could make or purchase a printed circuit board that shifts the pins. SparkFun's Breakout Board for XBee Module (BOB-08276) works.

» **2 rows of 0.1-inch header pins** as available from most electronics retailers

» **2 2mm female header rows** Samtec (www.samtec.com) part number MMS-110-01-L-SV. Samtec, like many part makers, supplies free samples of this part in small quantities. SparkFun sells these as part number PRT-08272.

» **1 1µF capacitor** Digi-Key part number P10312-ND

» **1 10µF capacitor** SparkFun part number COM-00523, Digi-Key part number P11212-ND

» **1 Figaro Sensors TGS2620 sensor** for the detection of solvent vapors. You can order this directly from Figaro (www.figarosensor.com or +1-847-832-1701).

» **2 LEDs**

» **1 4.7KΩ resistor**

Internet Connection Circuit

» **1 Lantronix embedded device server** Available from many vendors, including Symmetry Electronics (www.semiconductorstore.com) as part number CO-E1-11AA (Micro) or WM11A0002-01 (WiMicro), or XP1001001-03R (XPort). This example uses an XPort.

» **1 RJ45 breakout board** SparkFun part number BOB-00716 (needed only if you're using an XPort).

» **1 solderless breadboard** such Digi-Key part number 438-1045-ND, or Jameco part number 20601

» **1 MaxStream XBee OEM RF module** MaxStream part number GC-WLM-XB24-A

» **1 3.3V regulator** SparkFun part number COM-00526 or Digi Key part number 576-1134-ND

» **1 2mm breakout board** SparkFun BOB-08276

» **2 rows of 0.1-inch header pins**

» **2 2mm female header rows** Samtec part number MMS-110-01-L-SV. SparkFun part number PRT-08272.

» **1 1µF capacitor** Digi-Key part number P10312-ND

» **1 10µF capacitor** SparkFun part number COM-00523, Digi-Key part number P11212-ND

» **2 LEDs**

» **1 momentary reset switch** SparkFun part number COM-00097, Digi-Key part number SW400-ND.

Cymbal Monkey Circuit

» **1 solderless breadboard** such as Digi-Key part number 438-1045-ND, or Jameco part number 20601

» **1 MaxStream XBee OEM RF module** MaxStream part number GC-WLM-XB24-A

» **1 cymbal monkey** The one used here is a Charlie Chimp, ordered from the Aboyd Company (aboyd.com), part number ABC 40-1006.

NOTE: If your Monkey uses a 3V power supply (such as 2 D batteries), you won't need the LD1117-33V regulator. Make sure that there's adequate amperage supplied for the radios. If you connect the circuit as shown and the radios behave erratically, the monkey's motor may be drawing all the power. If so, use a separate power supply for the radio circuit.

» **1 2mm breakout board** SparkFun BOB-08276

» **2 rows of 0.1-inch header pins**

» **2 2mm female header rows** Samtec part number MMS-110-01-L-SV. SparkFun part number PRT-08272.

» **2 LEDs**

» **1 10K trimmer potentiometer** SparkFun part number COM-00104, Digi-Key part number D4AA14-ND

» **1 TIP120 Darlington NPN transistor**. Digi-Key part number 497-2539-5-ND.

» **1 1N4004 power diode.** Digi-Key part number 1N4004-E3/54GICT-ND.

» **1 1KΩ resistor**

» **1 100µF capacitor.** SparkFun part number COM-00096, Digi-Key part number P10195-ND

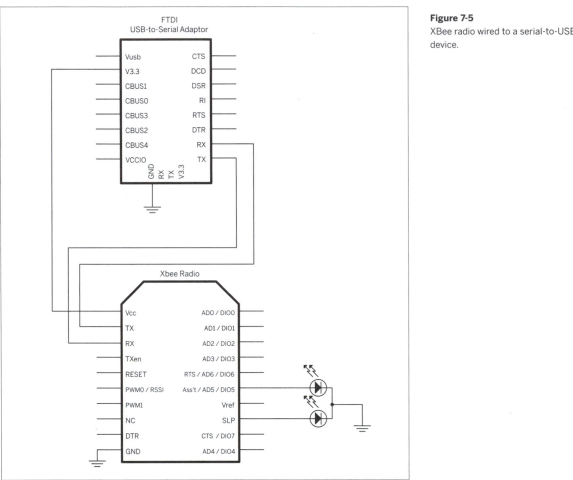

Figure 7-5
XBee radio wired to a serial-to-USB
device.

You'll be building three separate circuits for this project, so the parts list is broken down for each one. Most of these items are available at retailers other than the ones listed here, if you can't find them at the places mentioned in the materials list.

Radio Settings

Solder the XBee breakout boards as you did in Chapter 6. Connect one of the radio breakout boards to the FTDI USB-to-serial adaptor, as shown in Figure 7-5. You'll use this circuit for configuring the radios only. Notice that the FTDI module is supplying 3.3V for the radio, so no regulator is needed. If you're using a different USB-to-serial adaptor, you must supply 3.3V for the radio.

You've got three radios: the sensor's radio, the monkey's radio, and the XPort's radio. You know from Chapter 5 that you can configure the radios' addresses, destination addresses, and Personal Area Network (PAN) IDs. In addition, you can also configure some of their behavior. For example, you can configure the digital and analog I/O pins to operate as inputs, outputs, or to turn off. You can also set them to be digital or analog inputs, or digital or pulse width modulation (PWM) outputs. You can even link an output pin's behavior to the signals it receives from another radio.

The sensor radio is the center of this project. You'll configure it to read an analog voltage on its first analog input (AD0, pin 20) and broadcast the value that it reads to all other radios on the same PAN. Its settings are as follows:

- ATMY01 – Sets the sensor radio's source address
- ATDLFFFF – Sets the destination address to broadcast to the whole PAN
- ATID1111 – Sets the Personal Area Network (PAN)
- ATD02 – Sets I/O pin 0 (D0) to act as an analog input
- ATIR64 – Sets the analog input sample rate to 100 milliseconds (0x64 hex)
- ATIT5 – Sets the radio to gather five samples before sending, so it will send every 500 milliseconds (5 samples x 100 milliseconds sample rate = 500 milliseconds)

The monkey radio will listen for messages on the PAN, and if any radio sends it a packet of data with an analog sensor reading formatted the way it expects, it will set the first pulse width modulation output (PWM0) to the value of the received data. In other words, the monkey radio's PWM0 output will be linked to the sensor radio's analog input. Its settings are as follows:

- ATMY02 – Sets the monkey radio's source address
- ATDL01 – Sets the destination address to send only to the sensor radio (address 01). Doesn't really matter, as this radio won't be sending.
- ATID1111 – Sets the Personal Area Network (PAN)
- ATP02 – Sets PWM pin 0 (P0) to act as a PWM output
- ATIU1 – Sets the radio to send any I/O data packets out the serial port. This is used for debugging purposes only; you won't actually attach anything to this radio's serial port in the final project.
- ATIA01 or ATIAFFFF – Sets the radio to set its PWM outputs using any I/O data packets received from address 01 (the sensor radio's address). If you set this parameter to FFFF, the radio sets its PWM outputs using data received from any radio on the PAN.

The XPort radio listens for messages on the PAN and sends them out its serial port to the XBee. This radio's settings are the simplest, as it's doing the least. Its settings are as follows:

- ATMY03 – Sets the XPort radio's source address
- ATDL01 – Sets the destination address to send only to the sensor radio (address 01). Again, doesn't matter, as this radio won't be sending.
- ATID1111 – Sets the Personal Area Network (PAN)
- ATIU1 – Sets the radio to send any I/O data packets out the serial port. This data will go to the attached XPort.

Here's a summary of all of the settings:

Sensor Radio	Monkey Radio	XPort Radio
MY = 01	MY = 02	MY = 03
DL = FFFF	DL = 01	DL = 01
ID = 1111	ID = 1111	ID = 1111
D0 = 2	P0 = 2	IU = 1
IR = 64	IU = 1	
IT = 5	IA = 01 (or FFFF)	

NOTE: If you want to reset your XBee radios to the factory default settings before configuring for this project, send them the command ATRE\r

Make sure to save the configuration to each radio's memory by finishing your commands with WR. To set the whole configuration of these, you can do it line by line, or all at once. For example, to set the sensor radio, type:

+++

Then wait for the radio to respond with OK. Then type the following (the 0 in D02 is the number 0):

```
ATMY1, DLFFFF\r
ATID1111, D02, IR64\r
ATIT5, WR\r
```

For the monkey radio, the configuration is:

```
ATMY2, DL1\r
ATID1111, P02\r
ATIU1, IA1, WR\r
```

And for the XPort radio, it's:

```
ATMY3, DL1\r
ATID1111, IU1, WR\r
```

The Circuits

Once you've got the radios configured, set up the circuits for the sensor, the monkey, and the XPort. In all of these circuits, make sure to include the decoupling capacitors on either side of the voltage regulator. The XPort and the XBee radios tend to be unreliable without them.

The Sensor Circuit

The VOC sensor takes a 5V supply voltage, so you need a 5V regulator for it, a 3.3V regulator for the XBee, and a power supply that's at least 9V to supply voltage to the circuit. Figure 7-6 shows the circuit. The VOC sensor should output between 0 and 3.3V under the most likely shop conditions, but test it before you go too much further. Connect and power the circuit, but leave out the wire connecting the sensor's output to the XBee's analog input. Power up the circuit, and let it heat for a minute or two. The circuit takes time to warm up, because there's a heater element in the sensor. Measure the voltage between the sensor's output and ground. You should get about 1 volt if the air is free of VOCs. While still measuring the voltage, take a bottle of something that has an organic solvent (I used hand sanitizer, which has a lot of alcohol in it), and gently waft the fumes over the sensor. Be careful not to breathe it in yourself. You should get something considerably higher — up to 3 volts. If the voltage exceeds 3.3V, change the fixed resistor until you get results in a range below 3.3V, even when the solvent's fumes are high. Once you've got the sensor reading in an acceptable range, connect its output to the XBee's analog input pin, which is pin 20. Make sure to connect the XBee's voltage reference pin (pin 14) to 3.3 volts as well.

NOTE: Make sure to air out your workspace as soon as you've tested the sensor. You don't want to poison yourself making a poison sensor!

To test whether the XBee is reading the sensor correctly, connect its TX pin to the USB-to-serial adaptor's RX pin, its RX pin to the adaptor's TX pin, and connect their ground lines together. Then plug the adaptor into your computer and open a serial connection to it. Type +++, and wait for the OK. Then type ATIS\r (this command forces the XBee to read the analog inputs and return a series of values). You'll get a reply like this:

```
1
200
3FF
```

Don't worry about what the values are for now, as long as you're getting something. You'll see the actual values as the project develops later.

The Monkey Circuit

To control the monkey, disconnect the monkey's motor from its switch and connect the motor directly to the circuit shown in Figure 7-7. The monkey's battery pack supplies 3V, which is enough for the XBee radio, so you can power the whole radio circuit from the monkey. Connect leads from the battery pack's power and ground to the board. If your monkey runs on a different voltage, make sure to adapt the circuit accordingly, so that your radio circuit is getting at least 3V. Figure 7-8 shows the modifications in the monkey's innards. I used an old telephone cord to wire the monkey to the board, for convenience.

The cymbal monkey circuit takes the variable output that the radio received and turns it into an on-off switch. The PWM output from the XBee radio controls the base of a TIP120 transistor. The monkey itself has a motor built into it, which is controlled by a TIP120 Darlington transistor in this circuit. When the transistor's base goes high, the motor turns on. When it goes low, the motor turns off. The motor has physical inertia, however, so if the length of the pulse is short and the length of the pause between pulses is long, the motor doesn't turn. When the duty cycle of the pulse width (the ratio of the pulse and the pause) is high enough, the motor starts to turn.

To test this circuit, make sure that the sensor radio is working, and turn it on. When the sensor's value is low, the motor should be turned off, and when the sensor reads a high concentration of VOCs, the motor will turn on and the

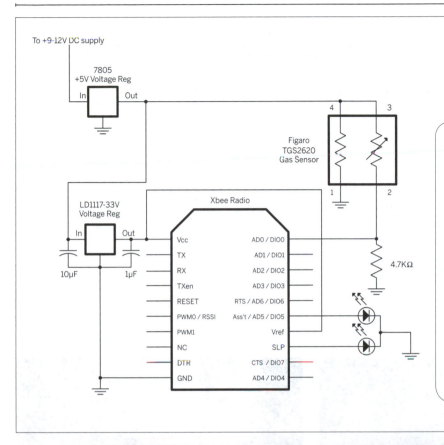

To +9-12V DC supply

7805
+5V Voltage Reg

In   Out

Figaro
TGS2620
Gas Sensor

4   3

1   2

LD1117-33V
Voltage Reg

In   Out

10µF   1µF

Xbee Radio

Vcc   AD0 / DIO0
TX   AD1 / DIO1
RX   AD2 / DIO2
TXen   AD3 / DIO3
RESET   RTS / AD6 / DIO6
PWM0 / RSSI   Ass't / AD5 / DIO5
PWM1   Vref
NC   SLP
DTR   CTS / DIO7
GND   AD4 / DIO4

4.7KΩ

Figure 7-6
XBee radio connected to a Figaro Sensors VOC sensor. The detail photo shows the wiring underneath the XBee radio.

▶▶ **All the projects in this chapter** are made using the LD1117-33V 3.3V voltage regulator. The pins on this regulator are configured differently from the pins on the other regulators used in the book. Be sure to check the data sheet for your regulator to be sure you have the pins correct. You should make a habit of checking this because the same catalog number may be supplied as slightly different parts. For example, SparkFun part number COM-00526 (Voltage Regulator—3.3V) can arrive either as an LD1117-33V or an LM7833, which do not have the same pin configuration.

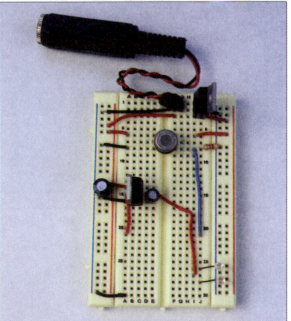

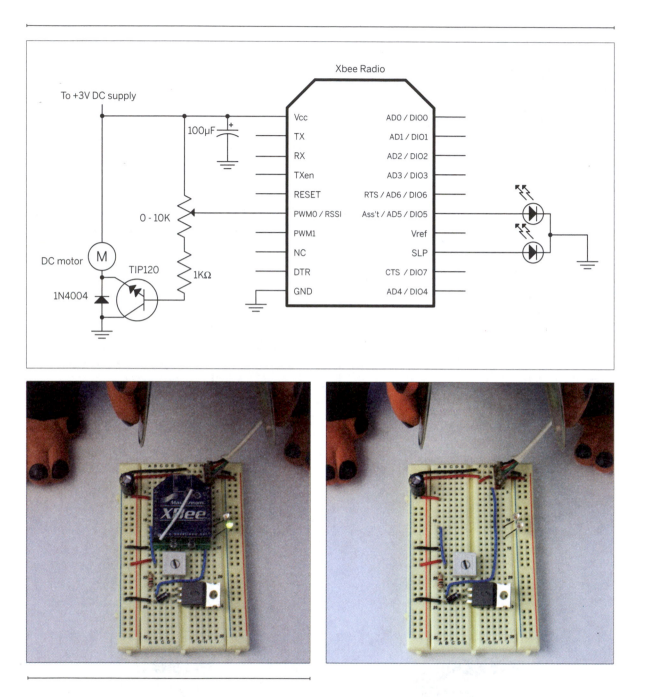

Figure 7-7
XBee radio connected to a Cymbal Monkey. The detail shows
the circuit without the XBee, to reveal the wiring underneath.

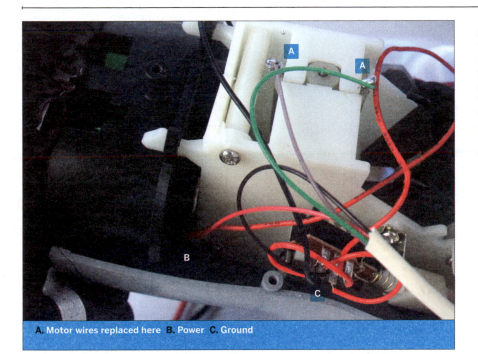

Figure 7-8
The insides of the monkey, showing the wiring modifications. Solder the power to the breadboard to the positive terminal of the battery. Solder the ground wire to the ground terminal. Cut the existing motor leads, and add new ones that connect to the breadboard.

A. Motor wires replaced here B. Power C. Ground

monkey will play his cymbals in warning. Use the potentiometer to affect the motor's activation threshold. Start with the potentiometer set very high, then slowly turn it down until the motor turns off. At that point, expose the sensor to some alcohol. The motor should turn on again, and should go off when the air around the sensor is clear. If you're unsure that the motor circuit is working correctly, connect an LED from 3V to the collector of the transistor instead of the motor. It should grow brighter when the sensor reading is higher, and dimmer when the sensor reading is lower. The LED has no physical inertia like the motor does, so it turns on at a much lower duty cycle.

The XPort Circuit
The XPort, like the XBee radios, takes a 3.3V supply voltage, so you can run both from a 3.3V regulator, as shown in Figure 7-9. Before you connect this circuit, connect the XPort to your serial port using the circuit in Figure 7-10, and configure it as follows. See "Configuring the Micro" in Chapter 4 for detailed configuration instructions.

Server settings:

```
IP Address : as appropriate for your network
Set Gateway IP Address Y
Gateway IP addr as appropriate for your network
Netmask: Number of Bits for Host Part  8
```

Channel 1 settings:

```
Baudrate:  9600
I/F Mode: 4C
Flow: 00
Port No: 10001
ConnectMode: D4
Send '+++' in Modem Mode:  N
Auto increment source port:  N
Remote IP Address : 0.0.0.0
Remote Port  0
DisConnMode 00
FlushMode   00
DisConnTime 00:00
SendChar 1  00
SendChar 2  00
```

Figure 7-10 shows an XPort connected to an FTDI USB-to-serial adaptor. This circuit can be used to set the XPort's settings. Even though the FTDI adaptor can supply 3.3V, it's worthwhile to use a regulator, because the XPort performs inconsistently when powered directly from the FTDI adaptor's 3.3V supply. To test this circuit, connect your XPort to your local area network and open a telnet session to its IP address on port 10001. If you're on Linux or Mac OS X, make one change now. When you're logged in, type Control-] and you'll get a telnet prompt like this:
telnet>

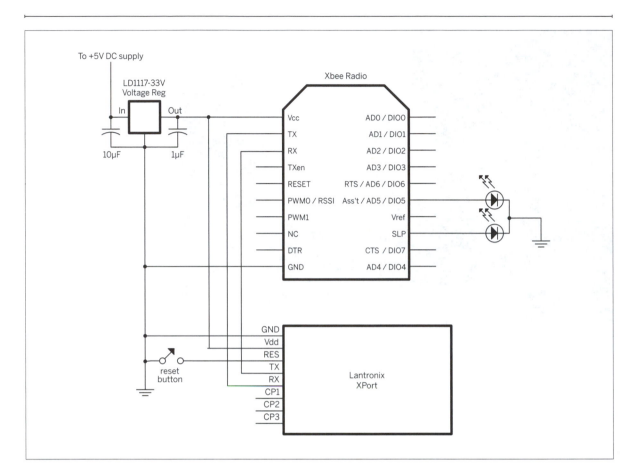

Figure 7-9
XBee radio connected to an XPort. The detail photos show the wiring under the XBee radio and the XPort.

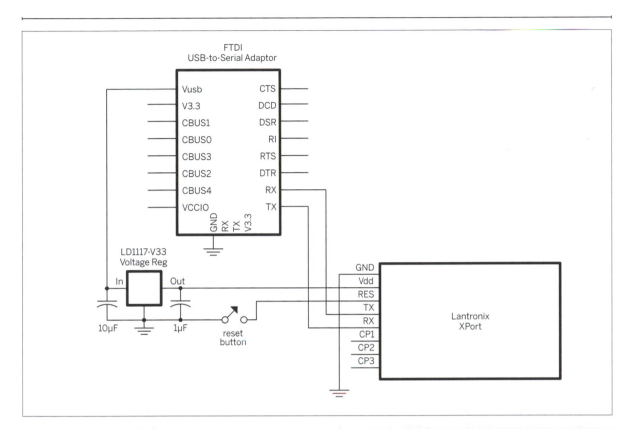

Figure 7-10
XPort connected to a USB-to-serial adaptor. The detail photo shows the wiring under the XPort.

Then type: `mode char\r`

This command puts telnet into character mode, meaning that it will send every character as you type it. You'll need to be in this mode in order to send the +++ string (by default, the Windows telnet program is in the correct mode).

Now try typing XBee commands to read the configuration. Start with the usual +++ and wait for the OK, then ATMY\r, ATDL\r and so forth. If you've wired the circuit correctly, you should get responses from the XBee just as if you were connected to its serial port — because you are!

Once you know that you've got serial data transmitting from the XPort to the XBee, power up the sensor radio while you're still logged in to the XPort. Once it starts up, it should be transmitting regularly, and you should see the data coming into your telnet window. It's being transmitted from the sensor's radio, then to the XPort's radio, on to the XPort, and to your window via the network. Likewise, if you plug the monkey radio in now, you should see the monkey clashing his cymbals as the data changes from the sensor. Now all of your hardware works.

The Server Code

Once you have all of the circuits working, it's time to get the data onto the Web. To do this, you're going to write a PHP script that logs into the XPort, retrieves the data, and displays the results. It will display a summary value telling you the sensor's average reading over 10 packets of data, and it will write that value to a file on the server, so you can see the sensor readings over time if you want.

So far, you've been able to rely on the XBee radios to do their work without having to understand their message protocol. Now it's time to interpret that protocol. The XBee radios format the readings from their analog-to-digital converters into a packet before they transmit. The format of the packet is explained in the MaxStream XBee 802.15.4 user's manual. It works like this:

- Byte 1: 0x7E, the start byte value.
- Byte 2-3: packet size, a 2-byte value. This depends on your other settings.
- Byte 4: API identifier value, a code that says what this response is.
- Byte 5-6: XBee sender's address.
- Byte 7: RSSI, Received Signal Strength Indicator.
- Byte 8: Broadcast options (not used here).
- Byte 9: Number of samples in the packet (you set it to 5 using the IT command shown earlier).
- Byte 10–11: Which I/O channels are currently being used. This example assumes only one analog channel, AD0, and no digital channels are in use.
- Byte 12–21: 10-bit values, each ADC sample from the sender. Set this to 5 using the IT command.

Because every packet starts with a constant value, 0x7E (that's decimal value 126), you can start your PHP program looking for that value.

> ⚠️ **If your PHP script is running on a different network than your XPort (such as on a web hosting company's server), you'll need to find a way to put your XPort on the Internet. See "Making a Device Visible to the Internet When It Has a Private IP Address," later in this chapter, for more information.**

Connect It The following program opens a socket to the XPort, reads bytes and puts them in an array until it's seen the value 0x7E ten times, then closes the socket. In other words, it attempts to read ten packets. Save this file to your server as **toxic_report.php**.

NOTE: In the following code, set $ip to the IP address of your XPort.

```php
<?php
/*  toxic_report.php
    Socket connection string reader
    Language: PHP
    This program opens a socket connection to an XPort
    and reads bytes from the socket.
*/

// Global variables.  These can be used by any of the script's functions:
global $ip, $port, $packetsToRead, $timeStamp, $messageString;
$ip = "192.168.1.236";      // IP adddress to connect to.
                            // Change this to your XPort's IP address.

$port = 10001;              // port number of IP
```

»

```
Continued from opposite page.

$packetsToRead = 10;        // total number of packets to read
$packetCounter = 0;         // counter for packets when you're reading them
$bytes = array();           // array for bytes when you're reading them

// open a socket to the XPort:
$mySocket = fsockopen ($ip, $port, $errorno, $errorstr, 30);
if (!$mySocket) {
    //if the socket didn't open, return an error message
    return "Error $errorno: $errorstr<br>";
} else {
    // if the socket exists, read packets until you reach $packetsToRead:
    while ($packetCounter < $packetsToRead) {
        // read a character from the socket connection,
        // and convert it to a numeric value using ord(),
        $char = ord(fgetc($mySocket));

        // if you got a header byte, deal with the last array
        // of bytes first:
        if ($char == 0x7E) {
            // increment the packet counter:
            $packetCounter++;
        }
        // push the current byte onto the end of the byte array:
        array_push($bytes, $char);
    }
    // iterate over the array of bytes and print them out:
    foreach ($bytes as $thisByte) {
        // if the current byte = 0x7E, it starts a new packet;
        // print a break first, so you see each packet on a new line
        // in the browser:
        if ($thisByte == 0x7E) {
            echo "<br>";
        }
        echo "$thisByte ";
    }
    // close the socket:
    fclose ($mySocket);
}
?>
```

When you save this to your server and open the script in a browser, you'll get a result like this:

NOTE: If you're getting weird numbers, power off the sensor and Lantronix circuits, wait about a minute, and power them back on. Devices sometimes get confused.

```
201 1 201 1 200 1 197 91
126 0 18 131 0 1 43 0 5 2 0 1 197 1 196 1 198 1 198 1 197 106
126 0 18 131 0 1 43 0 5 2 0 1 197 1 193 1 193 1 192 1 192 125
126 0 18 131 0 1 44 0 5 2 0 1 194 1 194 1 193 1 190 1 190 130
126 0 18 131 0 1 43 0 5 2 0 1 189 1 189 1 191 1 190 1 190 143
126 0 18 131 0 1 43 0 5 2 0 1 190 1 186 1 186 1 186 1 188 156
126 0 18 131 0 1 43 0 5 2 0 1 187 1 187 1 186 1 183 1 183 166
126 0 18 131 0 1 43 0 5 2 0 1 182 1 182 1 184 1 183 1 183 178
126 0 18 131 0 1 43 0 5 2 0 1 181 1 180 1 179 1 179 1 182 191
126 0 18 131 0 1 43 0 5 2 0 1 181 1 181 1 180 1 178 1 177 195
126
```

Refine It It'd be handy to have each packet in its own array. To make that happen, add a new global array variable called $packets before you open the socket:

```php
$packets = array();   // array to hold the arrays of bytes
```

» Then change the while() loop, adding code to push the byte array on to the packet array when a new header byte arrives, and then to empty the byte array to receive a new packet:

Most of the lines have 22 bytes, corresponding to the packet format described earlier. You may wonder why the first line of the output shown above didn't have a full complement of bytes. It's simply because there's no way to know what byte the Lantronix XBee radio is receiving when the PHP script connects to it.

You want only full packets, so add a function to parse the array and read only full packets. This function also extracts the XBee address of the sender, and averages the ADC readings in bytes 12 to 21 of the packet.

```php
while ($packetCounter < $packetsToRead) {
    // read a character from the socket connection,
    // and convert it to a numeric value using ord(),
    $char = ord(fgetc($mySocket));

    // if you got a header byte, deal with the last array
    // of bytes first:
    if ($char == 0x7E) {
        // push the last byte array onto the end of the packet array:
        array_push($packets, $bytes);
        // clear the byte array:
        $bytes = array();
        // increment the packet counter:
        $packetCounter++;
    }
    // push the current byte onto the end of the byte array:
    array_push($bytes, $char);
}
```

» Add this at the end of the program (but before the closing ?>):

```php
/*-------------------------------------*/

function parsePacket($whichPacket) {
    $adcStart = 11;                  // ADC reading starts at 12th byte
    $numSamples = $whichPacket[8];   // number of samples in the packet
    $total = 0;                      // sum of ADC readings for averaging

    // if you got all the bytes, find the average ADC reading:
    if( count($whichPacket) == 22) {
        // read the address -- it's a two-byte value, so you
        // add the two bytes as follows:
        $address = $whichPacket[5] + $whichPacket[4] * 256;

        // read $numSamples 10-bit analog values, two at a time,
        // because each reading is two bytes long:
        for ($i = 0; $i < $numSamples * 2;  $i=$i+2) {
            // 10-bit value = high byte * 256 + low byte:
            $thisSample = ($whichPacket[$i + $adcStart] * 256) +
                $whichPacket[($i + 1) + $adcStart];
            // add the result to the total for averaging later:
            $total = $total + $thisSample;
```

»

Continued from opposite page.

```
        }
        // average the result:
        $average = $total / $numSamples;
        return $average;
    } else {
        return -1;
    }
}
```

▸▸ To call this routine, add another variable at the beginning of the program called $totalAverage:

```
$totalAverage = 0;   // average of sensor readings in each packet
```

▸▸ Next, replace the for() loop that iterates over the byte array and prints the bytes with the following one that iterates over the array of packets:

```
// iterate over the array of arrays and print them out:
foreach ($packets as $thisPacket) {
    $packetAverage = parsePacket($thisPacket);
    echo "Average sensor reading in this packet: $packetAverage<br>";
}
```

You should get a result like this:

```
Average sensor reading in this packet: -1
Average sensor reading in this packet: 368.2
Average sensor reading in this packet: 368.8
Average sensor reading in this packet: 368.2
Average sensor reading in this packet: 368
Average sensor reading in this packet: 368.6
Average sensor reading in this packet: 367.6
Average sensor reading in this packet: 366.6
Average sensor reading in this packet: 368.2
Average sensor reading in this packet: 367.2
```

When there's not a complete packet, parsePacket() returns −1, so you know if you've got a good reading or not.

▸▸ Now you've got ten packets of data coming in, and you're averaging the sensor readings from each packet. To display an overall reading, you need a function to average the results from all of the packets. Here's a function to do it:

```
/*--------------------------------------*/

function averagePackets($whichArray) {
    $packetAverage = 0;          // average of all the sensor readings
    $validReadings = 0;          // number of valid readings
    $readingsTotal = 0;          // total of all readings, for averaging

    // iterate over the packet array:
    foreach ($whichArray as $thisPacket) {
        // parse each packet to get the average sensor reading:
        $thisSensorReading = parsePacket($thisPacket);
```

»

Continued from previous page.

```php
        if ($thisSensorReading > 0 && $thisSensorReading < 1023) {
            // if the sensor reading is valid, add it to the total:
            $readingsTotal = $readingsTotal + $thisSensorReading;
            // increment the total number of valid readings:
            $validReadings++;
        }
    }
    if ($validReadings > 0) {
        // round the packet average to 2 decimal points:
        $packetAverage = round($readingsTotal / $validReadings, 2);
        return $packetAverage;
    } else {
        return -1;
    }

}
```

▶▶ This function replaces the for() loop that you just added to print the results, so you can take that loop out now, and just write:

```php
// average the readings from all the packets to get a final
// sensor reading:
$totalAverage = averagePackets($packets);

echo "Sensor Reading :" . $totalAverage;
```

Now you've got a web page that gives you a snapshot of the air quality in your shop. The page should read something like this:

Sensor Reading :349.98

❝❝ But Wait! That's Not All!

Perhaps you'd like to set up several sensors, each attached to its own XBee/XPort combination, or perhaps you'd like to save the sensor data to a file so that you can see the levels over time. To do that, you need to add a form so you can change the variables from the Web, and you need to add a routine to write the sensor reading to a file. While you're at it, you need to check the time of the reading so that you can add a time stamp to the saved readings.

▶▶ First, add the form at the end of the script. This is just HTML, and it comes at the very end, outside your closing PHP ?> tag:

```html
<html>
    <head>
    </head>
    <body>
        <h2>
        <?=$messageString?>
        </h2>
        <hr>
        <form name="message" method="post" action="toxic_report.php">
            IP Address: <input type="text" name="ip" value="<?=$ip?>"
```

»

```
Continued from opposite page.

                          size="15" maxlength="15">
            Port: <input type="text" name="port" value="<?=$port?>"
                          size="5" maxlength="5">  <br>
            Number of readings to take: <input type="text"
              name="packetsToRead" value="<?=$packetsToRead?>" size="6">
            <input type="submit" value="Send It">
          </form>
        </body>
      </html>
```

You can see a few PHP tags in the HTML. These add the PHP variables to the HTML. Next, you need some code in the script to read the form. Add the following near the beginning of the program, after the global variables, but before you open the socket to the XPort:

```
//if a filled textbox was submitted, get the values:
if ((isset($_POST["ip"])) &&
    (isset($_POST["port"])) &&
    (isset($_POST["packetsToRead"]))) {
        $ip = $_POST["ip"];
        $port = $_POST["port"];
        $packetsToRead = $_POST["packetsToRead"];
}
```

Add two new variables to the beginning of the program, one to get the time, and one to make the HTML code simpler to write:

```
// $messageString is used to return messages for printing in the HTML:
$messageString = "No Sensor Reading Taken";
// Get the time and date:
$timeStamp =  $date = date("m-d-Y H:i:s");
```

To use these two variables, change the lines that average and print the sensor reading like so. You'll get a page that looks like Figure 7-11.

```
// average the readings from all the packets to get a
// final sensor reading:
$totalAverage = averagePackets($packets);

// update the message for the HTML:
$messageString =
  "Sensor Reading at: ". $timeStamp . ": " . $totalAverage;
```

▼ **Figure 7-11**
The final web page of the toxic report.

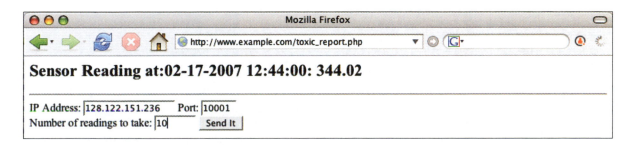

Now you can add some code to save the sensor data to a server. Add one more function to do this:

```
/*-------------------------------------*/

function writeToFile($whichReading) {
    global $timeStamp, $messageString;

    // combine the reading and the timestamp:
    $logData = "$timeStamp $whichReading\n";
    $myFile = "datalog.txt";    // name of the file to write to:

    // check to see whether the file exists and is writable:
    if (is_writable($myFile)) {
        // try to write to the file:
        if (!($fh = fopen($myFile, "a"))) {
            $messageString = "Couldn't open file $myFile";
        } else {
            // if you could open the file but not write to it, say so:
            if (!fwrite($fh, $logData)) {
                $messageString = "Couldn't write to $myFile";
            }
        }
    } else {
        //if it's not writeable:
        $messageString = "The file $myFile is not writable";
    }
}
```

Finally, just before the socket closing at the end of the main script, add the following to call this function:

```
// if you got a good reading, write it to the datalog file:
if ($totalAverage > 0) {
    writeToFile($totalAverage);
}
```

You can find a complete listing in Appendix C.

" To enable the PHP script to write to the data log file, you'll need to create the file on your server first. Make a blank text file called **datalog.txt** in the same directory as the PHP script (at the Linux or Mac OS X terminal, you can use the command touch datalog.txt). Change its permissions so that it's readable and writable by others. From the command line of a Linux or Mac OS X system, you'd type:

```
chmod o+rw datalog.txt
```

If you're creating the file using a GUI-based program, get info on the file and set the permissions that way. Figure 7-12 shows the Get Info window from BBEdit, which is

similar to many others. Once you've made this file and viewed the web page a few times, open the datalog.txt file. You'll see something like this:

```
02-17-2007 13:01:38 338.98
02-17-2007 13:01:44 338.93
02-17-2007 13:09:57 338.31
02-17-2007 13:10:03 338.2
02-17-2007 13:10:09 338.62
```

Now that you've got the data, you can work with it in interesting ways. For example, you could write another PHP script to read the sensor regularly and graph the results. **X**

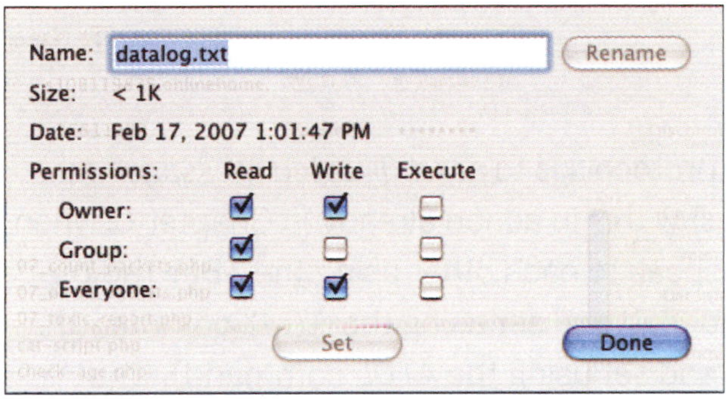

Name:	datalog.txt				Rename
Size:	< 1K				
Date:	Feb 17, 2007 1:01:47 PM				
Permissions:		Read	Write	Execute	
Owner:		☑	☑	☐	
Group:		☑	☐	☐	
Everyone:		☑	☑	☐	
		Set		Done	

Figure 7-12
Setting the read-write permissions for a file from a GUI-based program.

Making a Private IP Device Visible to the Internet

Up until now, all of the Internet-related projects in this book have either worked only on a local subnet, or only sent data outbound and waited for a reply. This is the first project in which your Lantronix device needs to be visible to the Net at large (or at least to the PHP script). If it's connected to your home router and has a private IP address, however, that won't be the case. To get around this, you need to arrange for one of your router's ports to forward incoming messages and connection requests to your XPort.

To do this, open your router's administrator interface and look for controls for "port forwarding" or "port mapping."

The interface will vary depending on the make and model of your router, but the settings generally go by one of these names. It's easiest if the forwarded port on the router is the same as the open port on the XPort, so configure it so that port 10001 on your router connects to port 10001 on the XPort. Once you've done this, any incoming requests to connect to your router's public IP address on that port will be forwarded to the XPort's private IP address on the same port. Figures 7-13 and 7-14 show the settings on a Linksys wireless router and an Apple Airport Express router. On the Linksys router, Port Forwarding can be found under the Advanced tab.

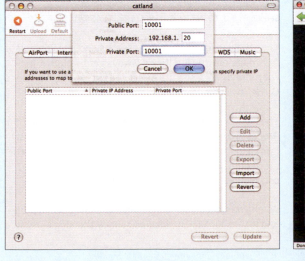

Figure 7-13. Port mapping tab on an Apple Airport Express router.

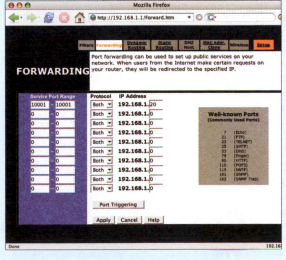

Figure 7-14. Port forwarding on a Linksys wireless router.

❝ Directed Messages

The more common way to use sessionless protocols is to send *directed messages* to the object to which you want to speak. You saw this in action already in Chapter 6, when you programmed your microcontrollers to speak to each other using the XBee radios. Each radio had a source address (which you read and set using the *ATMY* command) and a destination address (which you read and set using the *ATDL* command). One radio's destination was another's source, and vice versa. Though there were only two radios in that example, you could have included many more radios, and decided which one to address by changing the destination address on the fly.

Sending UDP Datagrams To and From a Lantronix Device

So far, you've used the Lantronix devices to communicate via TCP, but they can also send and receive UDP packets. To do this, you have to set the connectMode appropriately (see "Configuring the Micro" in Chapter 4 for configuration instructions) and set an address to which the datagrams will be sent. You can also control when datagrams are sent; for example, the default is 12 milliseconds after a serial byte is received, but you can change the time delay, or you can set the device to send after it receives a specific string of characters.

To send directed UDP packets, you have to set the connect Mode to 0xCC, which sets your device to accept any incoming UDP packets. It also allows you to send UDP packets to the address and port number that you set for the remote IP address. Once you've set the connectMode to 0xCC, set the Datagram Type to 01. With these settings, your XPort, Micro, or WiPort will send only to the remote IP specified in your configuration. Here's a summary of the appropriate settings:

```
Baudrate: 9600
I/F Mode: 4C
Flow: 00
Port No: 10001
ConnectMode: CC
Datagram Type: 01
Remote IP Address : fill in the address of your personal computer
Remote Port : 10002
Pack Cntrl : 00
SendChar 1 : 00
```

Whatever bytes you send into the device's serial port are sent out as a datagram. There is a limit on the delay between bytes, but as long as you're sending all your bytes at once, you should be fine. If you have a problem, you can control it by changing the way datagrams are sent. You can set the device to send only after it gets a specific two-byte sequence, like \n\r. To do this, change the channel 1 configuration as follows:

```
packControl : 30
SendChar 1 : 0A (that's 10, or linefeed in ASCII)
SendChar 2 : 0D (13, or carriage return in ASCII)
```

Then make sure all of your messages end in a linefeed and a carriage return, and they'll always get through intact. For more on this, see the XPort, WiPort, or Micro's User's Guide, available from www.lantronix.com.

The next sketch demonstrates how UDP works using Processing and an XPort. In it, the sketch and the XPort form a loop, as shown in Figure 7-15: when you type a u, the sketch sends UDP packets to the XPort's Ethernet connection, and listens on its serial port.

When you type an s, it sends via the XPort's serial port, and listens for UDP messages sent by the XPort.

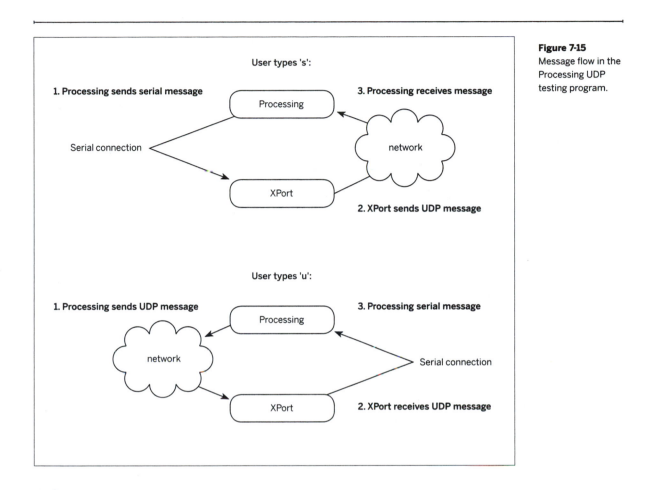

Figure 7-15
Message flow in the Processing UDP testing program.

Test It Here is the Processing sketch to test UDP sending and receiving. To use it, connect an XPort, WiPort, or Micro to a USB-to-serial adaptor as shown in Figure 7-10. Then run this program:

```
/*
Lantronix UDP Tester
language: Processing

Sends and receives UDP messages from  Lantronix
serial-to-Ethernet devices.

Sends a serial message to a Lantronix device connected to the
serial port when you type "s".

Sends a UDP message to the Lantronix device when you type "u".

Listens for both UDP and serial messages and prints them out.

*/

// import UDP library
import hypermedia.net.*;
// import serial library:
import processing.serial.*;
```

»

Continued from previous page.

```
UDP udp;                      // define the UDP object
int queryPort = 10002;        // the port number for the device query
Serial myPort;
```

>> **You'll need to change this number.**

```
String xportIP = "192.168.1.20";   // fill in your XPort's IP here
int xportPort = 10001;        // the XPort's receive port
String inString = "";         // incoming serial string

void setup() {
  // create a new connection to listen for
  // UDP datagrams on query port;
  udp = new UDP(this, queryPort);

  // listen for incoming packets:
  udp.listen( true );

  println(Serial.list());
  // make sure the serial port chosen here is the one attached
  // to your XPort:
  myPort = new Serial(this, Serial.list()[0], 9600);
}

//process events
void draw() {
  // a nice blue background:
  background(0,0,255);
}

/*
 send messages when s or u key is pressed:
 */
void keyPressed() {
  switch (key) {
  case 'u':
    udp.send("Hello UDP!\r\n", xportIP, xportPort);
    break;
  case 's':
    String messageString = "Hello Serial!";
    for (int c = 0; c < messageString.length(); c++) {
      myPort.write(messageString.charAt(c));
    }
    break;
  }
}
```

>>

Continued from opposite page.

```
/*
  listen for UDP responses
 */
void receive( byte[] data, String ip, int port ) {
  String inString = new String(data); // incoming data converted to string
  println( "received "+inString +"  from "+ip+" on port "+port );

  // print two blank lines to separate messages from multiple responders.
  print("\n\n");
}


/*
  listen for serial responses
 */
void serialEvent(Serial myPort) {
  // read any incoming bytes from the serial port and print them:
  char inChar = char(myPort.read());

  // if you get a linefeed, the string is ended; print it:
  if (inChar == '\n') {
    println("received " + inString + "  in the serial port\r\n");
    // empty the string for the next message:
    inString = "";
  }
  else {
    // add the latest byte to inString:
    inString += inChar;
  }
}
```

Project 13

Relaying Solar Cell Data Wirelessly

In this project, you'll relay data from a solar cell via two XBee radios and an XPort to a Processing sketch that graphs the result. This project is almost identical to the previous one in terms of hardware, but instead of using broadcast messages, you'll relay the data from the first to the second to the third using directed messages. In addition, the XPort uses directed UDP datagrams to send messages to the Processing program.

This project comes from Gilad Lotan and Angela Pablo (Figure 7-16), students at the Interactive Telecommunications Program (ITP) at New York University. The ITP is on the fourth floor of a twelve-story building in Manhattan, and maintains an 80-watt solar panel on the roof of the building. The students wanted to watch how much useful energy the cell receives each day. Because it's used to charge a 12-volt battery, it's useful only when the output voltage is higher than 12V. In order to monitor the cell's output voltage on the fourth floor, Gilad and Angela (advised by a third student, Robert Faludi), arranged three XBee radios to relay the signal down the building's stairwell from the roof to the fourth floor. From there, the data went over the local network via an XPort, and on to an SQL database. This example, based on their work, uses a smaller solar cell from SparkFun and a Processing program to graph the data instead of an SQL database.

There are three radios in this project: one attached to the solar cell, one relay radio standing on its own, and one attached to the XPort. Figure 7-17 shows the network.

Radio Settings
The radio settings are similar to the settings for the previous project. The only difference is in the destination addresses. You won't be using broadcast addresses this time. Instead, the solar cell radio (address = 1) will send to the relay radio (address = 2), and that radio will send to the XPort radio (address = 3). Instead of forming a broadcast network, they form a chain, extending the distance the message travels. Their settings are shown in

Sensor Radio	Relay Radio	XPort Radio
MY = 01	MY = 02	MY = 03
DL = 02	DL = 03	DL = 01
ID = 1111	ID = 1111	ID = 1111
DO = 2	PO = 2	IU = 1
IR = 0x64	IU = 1	
IT = 5	IA = 01 (or 0xFFFF)	

the table above. Here are the command strings to set them. For the solar cell radio:

```
ATMY1, DL02\r
ATID1111, D02, IR64\r
ATIT5, WR\r
```

For the relay radio:

```
ATMY2, DL03\r
ATID1111, P02\r
ATIU1, IA1, WR\r
```

And for the XPort radio:

```
ATMY3, DL01\r
ATID1111, IU1, WR\r
```

The Circuits
The solar cell circuit runs off the solar cell itself, because the cell can produce the voltage and amperage in daylight needed to power the radio. The LD1117-33V regulator can take up to 15V input, and the solar panel's maximum output is 12V, so you're safe there. The MAX8212 IC is a voltage trigger. When the input voltage on its threshold pin goes above a level determined by the resistors attached to the circuit, the output pin switches from high to low. This change turns on the 2N3906 transistor. The transistor then allows voltage and current from the solar cell to power the regulator. When the solar cell isn't producing enough voltage, the radio will simply turn off. It's okay if the radio doesn't transmit when the cell is dark, because there's nothing worth reporting then. The two resistors attached to the XBee's AD0 pin form a voltage divider that drops the voltage from the solar cell proportionally to something within the 3.3V range of the radio's analog-to-digital converter. The 4700μF capacitors store the charge

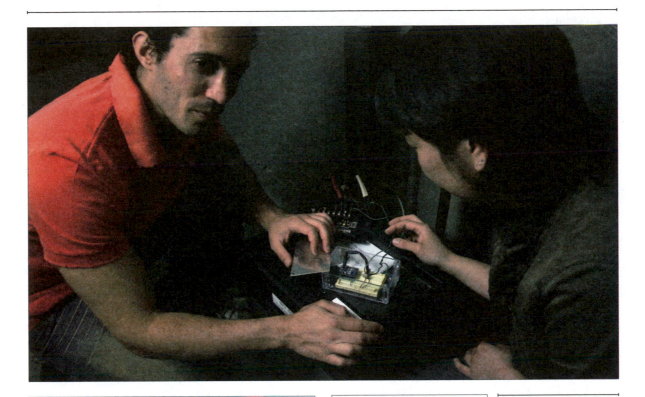

⬆ **Figure 7-16**
ITP students Angela Pablo
and Gilad Lotan with the
solar battery pack and
XBee monitor radio.

Mesh Networking

The XBee radios can be configured as a mesh network,
using the ZigBee protocol. In a mesh network, some radios
function as routers, similar to how the relay radio works
in this project. Routers can not only relay messages,
but can also store and forward them when the radios
at the end node are not on. This provides the whole
network with net power saving, as the end nodes can be
turned off most of the time. At the time of this writing,
MaxStream's implementation of the ZigBee protocol
was not fully finished, so this simpler solution was used.
MaxStream recently announced a second generation
of the XBee radios, which uses a different chipset and
implements the ZigBee protocol better than the original
did. For more information, see www.maxstream.net.

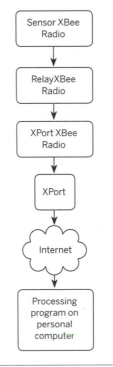

◀◀ **Figure 7-17**
Network diagram for the
solar project.

from the solar cell like batteries, to keep the radio's supply
constant. Figure 7-18 shows the circuit.

The XPort radio circuit is identical to the one used in the
last project. Build it as shown in Figure 7-9.

MATERIALS

» **1 USB-to-TTL serial adaptor** You'll use this for testing only, just as you did in the last project.

Solar cell Circuit

» **1 solderless breadboard** such as Digi-Key part number 438-1045-ND, or Jameco part number 20601
» **1 MaxStream XBee OEM RF module** part number GC-WLM-XB24-A
» **1 3.3V regulator** The LD1117-33V (SparkFun part number COM-00526) or the MIC2940A-3.3WT (Digi-Key part number 576-1134-ND) work well.
» **1 2mm breakout board** The XBee modules listed here have pins spaced 2mm apart. To use them on a breadboard, you'll need a breakout board that shifts the spacing to 0.1 inches. SparkFun's Breakout Board for XBee Module (BOB-08276) does the trick.
» **2 rows of 0.1-inch header pins** as available from most electronics retailers.
» **2 2mm female header rows** Samtec part number MMS-110-01-L-SV. Samtec, like many part makers, supplies free samples of this part in small quantities. SparkFun sells these as part number PRT-08272.
» **1 1µF capacitor** Digi-Key part number P10312-ND
» **1 10µF capacitor** SparkFun part number COM-00523, Digi-Key part number P11212-ND
» **3 4700µF electrolytic capacitors** Digi-Key part number 493-1088-ND. Other vendors carry these, too.
» **1 MAX8212 voltage monitor.** You can order free samples from Maxim (www.maxim-ic.com) or order it from Digi-Key, part number MAX8212CPA+-ND.
» **1 10kΩ resistor**
» **3 100kΩ resistors**
» **1 4.7kΩ resistor**
» **1 1kΩ resistor**
» **1 2N3906 PNP-type transistor** such as Digi-Key part number 2N3906D26ZCT-ND, or SparkFun part number COM-00522
» **2 LEDs**
» **1 solar cell** SparkFun part number PRT-07840 works at an acceptable voltage, and can produce enough current on its own to power the radio.

XPort radio circuit

This is identical to the radio circuit in the previous project.

» **1 Lantronix embedded device server** Available from many vendors, including Symmetry part number CO-E1-11AA (Micro), WM11A0002-01 (WiMicro), or XP1001001-03R (XPort). This example uses an XPort.

» **1 RJ45 breakout board** SparkFun part number BOB-00716 (needed only if you're using an XPort)
» **1 solderless readboard** such as Digi-Key part number 438-1045-ND, or Jameco part number 20601
» **1 MaxStream XBee OEM RF module** part number GC-WLM-XB24-A
» **1 3.3V regulator** The LD1117-33V (SparkFun part number COM-00526) and the MIC2940A-3.3WT (Digi-Key part number 576-1134-ND) work well.
» **1 2mm breakout board** SparkFun's Breakout Board for XBee Module (BOB-08276)
» **2 rows of 0.1-inch header pins**
» **2 2mm female header rows** Samtec part number MMS-110-01-L-SV. SparkFun sells these as part number PRT-08272.
» **1 1µF capacitor** Digi-Key part number P10312-ND
» **1 10µF capacitor** SparkFun part number COM-00523, or Digi-Key part number P11212-ND
» **2 LEDs**
» **1 reset switch** Any momentary switch such as SparkFun's COM-00097 or Digi-Key's SW400-ND.

Relay radio circuit

This circuit is just an XBee radio by itself, powered by a 9V battery.

» **1 solderless breadboard** such as Digi-Key part number 438-1045-ND, or Jameco part number 20601
» **1 Maxstream XBee OEM RF module** available from http://www.maxstream.net, or http://www.gridconnect.com, part number GC-WLM-XB24-A
» **1 3.3V regulator.** The LD1117-33V (SparkFun part number COM-00526) or the MIC2940A-3.3WT (Digi-Key part no. 576-1134-ND) will work well.
» **1 2mm breakout board.** SparkFun's Breakout Board for XBee Module (BOB-08276)
» **2 rows of 0.1-inch header pins**
» **2 2mm female header rows** Samtec part number MMS-110-01-L-SV. SparkFun sells these as part number PRT-08272.
» **2 LEDs**
» **2 1µF capacitors** Digi-Key part number P10312-ND
» **1 10µF capacitor** SparkFun part number COM-00523, or Digi-Key part number P11212-ND
» **1 9V battery clip**
» **1 9V battery** You can use 3 or 4 AA batteries as well, if you have a battery holder for them.

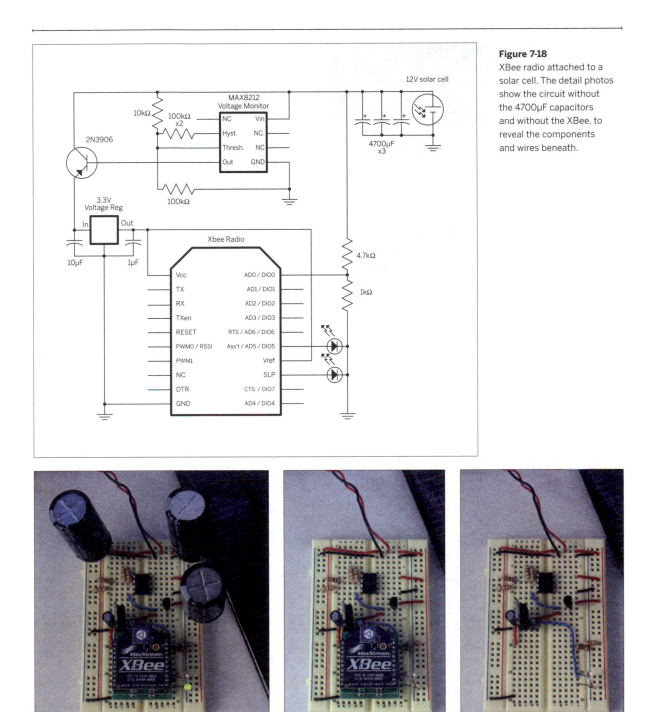

Figure 7-18
XBee radio attached to a solar cell. The detail photos show the circuit without the 4700µF capacitors and without the XBee, to reveal the components and wires beneath.

Figure 7-19
The XBee radio relay circuit.

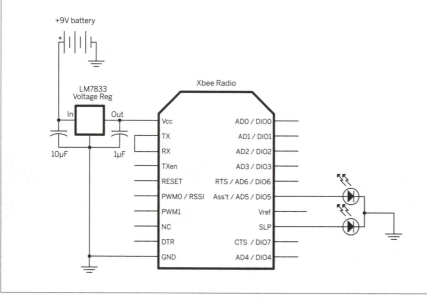

The relay radio circuit is very simple. It's just a radio on a battery with its transmit pin and receive pin connected together. This is how it will relay the messages. Any incoming messages will get sent out the serial transmit pin, then back into the receive pin, where they will be sent out again as transmissions. Figure 7-19 shows the circuit.

Once you've got the radios configured and working, you need to configure the XPort so that it can pass the messages received from its radio on to the Processing

program. The configuration is identical to that shown earlier in the "Sending UDP Datagrams to and from a Lantronix Device" section. The connect Mode is 0xCC, the datagramType is 01, the remote IP address is the address of your personal computer, and the remote port number is 10002. Set SendChar 1 and 2 both to 00.

The Graphing Program
Now that all the hardware is ready, it's time to write a Processing sketch to graph the data. The beginning of the program looks a lot like the UDP tester program shown earlier.

First you need to import the UDP library, initialize it, and write a method to listen for incoming datagrams:

This program will print out strings of numbers that look a lot like the initial ones from the PHP program in the VOC sensor project. That's because the datagrams the program is receiving are the same protocol — the XBee protocol for sending analog readings.

```
/*  XBee Packet Reader and Graphing Program
      Reads a packet from an XBee radio via UDP and parses it.
      Graphs the results over time.
    language: Processing


      Reads a packet from an XBee radio
 */

import hypermedia.net.*;
import processing.serial.*;


UDP udp;                            // define the UDP object
int queryPort = 10002;              // the port number for the device query


void setup() {
  // create a new connection to listen for
  // UDP datagrams on query port:
  udp = new UDP(this, queryPort);

  // listen for incoming packets:
  udp.listen( true );
}


void draw() {
    // nothing happens here.
}


/*
  listen for UDP responses
 */
void receive( byte[] data, String ip, int port ) {
  int[] inString = int(data);     // incoming data converted to string
  print(inString);
  println();
}
```

The next thing to do is to add a method to interpret the protocol. Not surprisingly, this looks a lot like the parsePacket() function from the PHP program in the previous project. Add this method to the end of your program.

To call it, replace the print() and println() statements in the receive() method with this:

```
parseData(inString);
```

```
void parseData(int[] thisPacket) {
  int adcStart = 11;                       // ADC reading starts at byte 12
  int numSamples = thisPacket[8];          // number of samples in packet
  int[] adcValues = new int[numSamples];   // array to hold the 5 readings
  int total = 0;                           // sum of all the ADC readings
  int rssi = 0;                            // the received signal strength

  // read the address -- a two-byte value, so you
  // add the two bytes as follows:
  int address = thisPacket[5] + thisPacket[4] * 256;

  // read the received signal strength:
  rssi = thisPacket[6];
```

»

Continued from previous page.

```
// read <numSamples> 10-bit analog values, two at a time
// because each reading is two bytes long:
for (int i = 0; i < numSamples * 2;  i=i+2) {
  // 10-bit value = high byte * 256 + low byte:
  int thisSample = (thisPacket[i + adcStart] * 256) +
    thisPacket[(i + 1) + adcStart];
  // put the result in one of 5 bytes:
  adcValues[i/2] = thisSample;
  // add the result to the total for averaging later:
  total = total + thisSample;
}
// average the result:
int average = total / numSamples;
print("Average reading:" + average + "\t");
// print the received signal strength:
println("Signal Strength:" + rssi);
}
```

Now that you've got the average reading printing out, add some code to graph the result. For this, you'll need a new global variable before the setup() method that keeps track of where you are horizontally on the graph:

```
int hPos = 0;               // horizontal position on the graph
```

You'll also need to add a line at the beginning of the setup() method to size the window:

```
// set the window size:
size(400,300);
```

Now add a new method, drawGraph(), to the end of the program:

Call this from the parseData() method, replacing the println() statement that prints out the average, as well as the println() statement that prints out the signal strength (rssi), like so:

```
// draw a line on the graph:
drawGraph(average/4);
```

Now when you run the program, it should draw a graph of the sensor readings, updating every time it gets a new datagram.

```
/*
  update the graph
 */
void drawGraph(int graphValue) {
  // draw the line:
  stroke(0,255,0);
  line(hPos, height, hPos, height - graphValue);
  // at the edge of the screen, go back to the beginning:
  if (hPos >= width) {
    hPos = 0;
    //wipe the screen:
    background(0);
  }
  else {
    // increment the horizontal position to draw the next line:
    hPos++;
  }
}
```

» Finally, add some code to add a time stamp. This task requires one new global variable before the setup() to set the size of a font to draw text on the screen:

```
int fontSize = 14;                // size of the text font
```

» Then add two lines to the setup() method to initialize the font, The first line picks a font from the list of available system fonts, and the second initializes the font (I didn't like the first font in my system's list, so I went with the second — choose your own as you see fit):

```
// create a font with the second font available to the system:
PFont myFont = createFont(PFont.list()[1], fontSize);
textFont(myFont);
```

» Add two methods to the end of the program, eraseTime() and drawTime(). The latter draws the date and time, and the former draws a black block over the previous date and time:

You're going to call these methods from a few different places in the program. The first is at the end of the setup() method, to show the initial time:

```
// show the initial time and date:
background(0);
eraseTime(hPos, 0);
drawTime(hPos, 0);
```

The next is at the end of the parseData() method, to draw the time of the current line:

```
// draw a line on the graph:
drawGraph(average/4);
eraseTime (hPos - 1, fontSize * 2);
drawTime(hPos, fontSize * 2);
```

```
/*
 Draw a black block over the previous date and time strings
 */

void eraseTime(int xPos, int yPos) {
  // use a rect to block out the previous time, rather than
  // redrawing the whole screen, which would mess up the graph:
  noStroke();
  fill(0);
  rect(xPos,yPos, 120, 80);
  // change the fill color for the text:
  fill(0,255,0);
}

/*
 print the date and the time
 */
void drawTime(int xPos, int yPos) {
  // set up an array to get the names of the months
  // from their numeric values:
  String[] months = {
    "Jan", "Feb", "Mar", "Apr", "May", "Jun", "Jul", "Aug",
    "Sep", "Oct", "Nov", "Dec"              };

  String date = "";         // string to hold the date
  String time = "";         // string to hold the time

  // format the date string:
  date += day();
  date += " ";
  date += months[month() -1];
  date += " ";
  date += year();

  // format the time string:
  time += hour();
```

Continued from previous page.

```
time += ":";
if (minute() < 10) {
  time += "0";
  time += minute();
}
else {
  time +=minute();
}
time += ":";
if (second() < 10) {
  time += "0";
  time += second();
}
else {
  time +=second();
}

// print both strings:
text(date, xPos, yPos + fontSize);
text(time, xPos, yPos + (2 * fontSize));
}
```

Finally, call these methods from the drawGraph() method, in the part where you reset the whole graph. This is inside the if() statement that checks to see where the horizontal position is. This way, each time the graph reaches the edge of the window, it erases the whole screen, and updates the initial time:

```
if (hPos >= width) {
  hPos = 0;
  //wipe the screen:
  background(0);
  // wipe the old date and time, and draw the new:
  eraseTime(hPos, 0);
  drawTime(hPos, 0);
}
```

That's the whole program. When it's running, it should look like Figure 7-20.

To view the program in its entirety, see Appendix C.

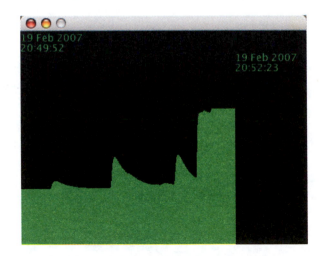

Figure 7-20
The output of the solar graph program. These sensor values were faked with a flashlight! Your actual values may differ.

❝ Conclusion

Sessionless networks can be really handy when you're just passing short messages around and don't need a lot of acknowledgment. They involve a lot less work, because you don't have to maintain the connection. They also give you a lot more freedom in how many devices you want to address at once.

As you can see by comparing the two projects in this chapter, there's not a lot of work to be done to switch from directed messages and broadcast messages when you're making a sessionless network. It's best to default to directed messages when you can, in order to reduce the traffic for those devices that don't need to get every message.

Now that you've got a good grasp of both session-based and sessionless networks, the next chapters switch direction slightly to talk about two other activities connecting networks to the physical world: location and identification.
X

⬆ The solar energy display, by Gilad Lotan and Angela Pablo.

How to Locate (Almost) Anything

By now, you've got a pretty good sense of how to make things talk to each other over networks. You've learned about packets, sockets, datagrams, clients, servers, and all sorts of protocols. Now that you know how to talk, the last two chapters deal with two common questions: where am I, and who am I talking to? Location technologies and identification technologies share some important properties. As a result, it's not uncommon to confuse the two, and to think that a location technology can be used to identify a person or an object, and vice versa. These are two different tasks in the physical world, however, and often in the network environment as well. Systems for determining physical location aren't always very good at determining identity, and identification systems don't do a good job of determining precise location. Likewise, knowing who's talking on a network doesn't always help you to know where the speaker is. In the examples that follow, you'll see methods for determining location and identification in both physical and network environments.

◀◀ **Address 2007 by Mouna Andraos and Sonali Sridhar**
This necklace contains a GPS module. When activated, it displays the distance between the necklace and your home location. *Photo by J. Nordberg.*

❝❝ Network Location and Physical Location

Locating things is one of the most common tasks people want to achieve with sensor systems. Once you understand the wide range of things that sensors can detect, it's natural to get excited about the freedom this affords. All of a sudden, you don't have to be confined to a chair to interact with computers. You're free to dance, run, jump — and it's still possible for a computer to read your action and respond in some way.

The downside of this freedom is the perception that in a networked world, you can be located anywhere. Ubiquitous surveillance cameras and systems like Wireless E911, a system for locating mobile phones on a network, make it seem as if anyone or anything can be located anywhere and at any time, whether you want to be located or not. The reality of location technologies lies somewhere in between these extremes.

Locating things on a network is different than locating things in physical space. As soon as a device is connected to a network, you can get a general idea of its location using a variety of means, from address lookup to measuring its signal strength, but that doesn't mean that you know its physical location. You just know its relationship to other nodes of the network. You might know that a cell phone is closest to a given cell transmitter tower, or that a computer is connected to a particular Wi-Fi access point. You can use that information along with other data to build up a picture of the person using the device. If you know that the cell transmitter tower is less than a kilometer from you, then you'd know that the person with the cell phone is going to reach you soon, and you can act appropriately in response. For many network applications, you don't need to know physical location as much as you need to know relationship to other nodes in the network.

➲ Step 1: Ask a Person

People are really good at locating things. At the physical level, we have a variety of senses to throw at the problem and a brain that's wonderful at matching patterns of shapes and determining distances from different sensory clues. At the behavioral level, we've got thousands of patterns of behavior that make it easier to determine why you might be looking for something. Computer systems don't have these same advantages, so when you're designing an interactive system to locate things or people, the best tool you have to work with, and the first one you

should consider, is the person for whom you're making your system.

Getting a good location starts with cultural and behavioral cues. If you want to know where you are, ask another person near you. In an instant, she's going to sum up all kinds of things, like your appearance, your behavior, the setting you're both in, the things you're carrying, and more, in order to give you a reasonably accurate and contextually relevant answer. No amount of technology can do that, because the connection between where we are and why we want to know is always an abstract thing. As a result, the best thing you can do when you're designing a locating system is to harness the connection-making talents of the person who will be using that system. Providing him with cues as to where to position himself when he should take action, and what actions he can take, helps eliminate the need for a lot of technology. Asking him to tell your system where things are, or to position them so that the system can easily find them, makes for a more effective system.

For example, imagine you're making an interactive space that responds to the movements of its viewers. This is popular among interactive artists, and often they begin by imagining a "body-as-cursor" project, in which the viewer is imagined as a body moving around in the space of the gallery. Some sort of tracking system is needed to determine his position and report it back in two dimensions, like the position of a cursor on a computer screen.

What's missing here is the reason why the viewer might be moving in the first place. If you start by defining what the viewer's doing, and give him cues as to what you expect him to do at each step, you can narrow down the space in which you need to track him. Perhaps you only need to know when he's approaching one of several sculptures in the space, so that you can trigger the sculpture to move in response. If you think of the sculptures as nodes in a network, the task gets easier. Instead of tracking the viewer in an undefined two-dimensional space, now all you have to do is to determine his proximity to one of several points in the room. Instead of building a tracking system, you can now just place a proximity sensor near each object and look up which he's near, and read how near he is. You're using a combination of spatial organization and technology to simplify the task. You can make your job even easier by giving him visual, auditory, and behavioral cues to interact appropriately. He's no longer passive; he's now an active participant in the work.

Or take a different example: let's say you're designing a mobile phone city guide application for tourists that relies on knowing the phone's position relative to nearby cell towers to determine the phone's position. What do you do when you can't get a reliable signal from the cell towers? Perhaps you ask the tourist to input the address she's at, or the postal code she's in, or some other nearby cue. Then your program can combine that data with the location based on the last reliable signal it received, and determine a better result. In these cases, and in all location-based systems, it's important to incorporate human talents in the system to make it better.

→ Step 2: Know the Environment

Before you can determine where you are, you need to determine your environment. For any location, there are several ways to describe it. For example, you could describe a street corner in terms of its address, its latitude and longitude, its postal code, or the businesses nearby. Which of these coordinates you choose depends in part on the technology you have on hand to determine it. If you're making the mobile city guide described earlier, you might use several different ones: the nearest cell transmitter ID, the street address, and the nearby businesses might all work to define the location. In this case, as in many, your job in designing the system is to figure out how to relate one system of coordinates to another in order to give some meaningful information.

Mapping places to coordinate systems is a lot of work, so most map databases are incomplete. Geocoding allows you to look up the latitude and longitude of most any U.S. street address. It doesn't work everywhere in the U.S., and it doesn't work most places outside the U.S. because the data hasn't been gathered and put in the public domain for everywhere. Geocoding depends on having an accurate database of names mapped to locations. If you don't agree on the names, you're out of luck. The Virtual Terrain Project (www.vterrain.org) has a good list of geocoding

resources for the US and international locations at www.vterrain.org/Culture/geocoding.html. Geocoder.net offers a free US-based lookup at www.geocoder.net, and Worldkit offers an extended version that also looks up international cities, at www.worldkit.org/geocoder.

Street addresses are the most common coordinates that are mapped to latitude and longitude, but there are other systems that'd be useful to have physical coordinates for as well. For example, mobile phone cell transmitters all have physical locations. It would be handy to have a database of physical coordinates for those towers. However, cell towers are privately owned by mobile telephone carriers, so detailed data about the tower locations is proprietary, and the data is not in the public domain. Projects such as CellSpotting (www.cellspotting.com) attempt to map cell towers by using GPS-equipped mobile phones running custom software. As there are many different mobile phone operating systems, even developing the software to do the job is a huge challenge. Open source cell geocoding is still in its infancy, so finding a complete database is difficult.

IP addresses don't map exactly to physical addresses, because computers can move. Nevertheless, there are several geocoding databases for IP addresses. These work on the assumption that routers don't move a lot, so if you know the physical location of a router, then the devices gaining access to the Net through that router can't be too far away. The accuracy of IP geocoding is limited, but it can help you determine a general area of the world, and sometimes even a neighborhood or city block, where a device on the Internet is located. Of course, IP lookup doesn't work on private IP addresses. In the next chapter, you'll see an example that combines network identity and geocoding.

You can develop your own database relating physical locations to cultural or network locations, if the amount of information you need is small, or you have a large group of people to do the job. But generally, it's better to rely on existing infrastructures when you can.

→ Step 3: Acquire and Refine

Once you know where you're going to look, there are two tasks that you have to do continually: acquire a new position, and refine the position's accuracy. Acquisition gives a rough position. Acquisition usually starts by identifying which device on a network is the center of activity. In the interactive installation example described earlier, you could acquire a new position by determining that the viewer tripped a sensor near one of the objects in the room. Once you know roughly where he is, you can refine the position by measuring his distance with the proximity sensor attached to the object.

Refining doesn't have to mean getting a more accurate physical position. When you have a rough idea of where something's happening, you need to know about the activity at that location in order to provide a response. In the interactive installation example, you may never need to know the viewer's physical coordinates in feet and inches (or meters and centimeters). When you know which object he's close to in the room, and whether he's close enough to relate to it, you can make that object respond. You might be changing the graphics on an LCD display when he walks close to it, or activating an animatronic sculpture as he walks by. In both cases, you don't need to know the precise distance; you just need to know he's close enough to pay attention. Sometimes distance ranging sensors are used as motion detectors to define general zones of activity rather than to measure distance.

Determining proximity doesn't always give you enough information to take action. Refining can also involve determining the orientation of one object relative to another. If you're giving directions from one location to another, you need to know which way you're oriented. It's also valuable information when two people or objects are close to each other. You don't want to activate the animatronic sculpture if the viewer has his back to the thing!

X

35 Ways to Find Your Location

At the 2004 O'Reilly Emerging Technology Conference, Interaction designer and writer Chris Heathcote gave an excellent presentation on cultural and technological solutions to finding things entitled *35 Ways to Find Your Location*. He outlined a number of important factors to keep in mind before you choose tools to do the job. He pointed out that the best way to locate someone or something involves a combination of technological methods and interpretation of cultural and behavioral cues. His list is a handy tool for inspiring solutions when you need to develop a system to find locations. A few of the more popular techniques that Chris listed are:

- Assume: the Earth. Or a smaller domain, but assume that's the largest space you have to look in.
- Use the time.
- Ask someone.
- Association: who or what are you near?
- Proximity to phone boxes, public transport stops, and utility markings.
- Use a map.
- Which cell phone operators are available? Public phone operators?
- Phone number syntax?
- Newspapers available?
- Language being spoken?
- Post codes/ZIP codes
- Street names.
- Street corners/intersections.
- Street numbers.
- Business names.
- Mobile phone location, through triangulation or trilateration.
- Triangulation and trilateration on other radio infrastructures, like TV, radio, and public Wi-Fi.
- GPS, assisted GPS, WAAS, and other GPS enhancements.
- Landmarks and "littlemarks."
- Dead reckoning.

❝ Determining Distance

Electronic locating systems like GPS, mobile phone location, and sonar seem magical at first, because there's no visible evidence as to how they work. When you break the job down into its components, it becomes relatively straightforward. Most physical location systems are based on the same principle. They determine distance from several known and fixed locations by measuring the energy of an electromagnetic or acoustic wave coming from the object to be located. Then they combine those measurements to determine a position in two or three dimensions.

For example, a GPS receiver determines its position on the surface of the planet by measuring the strength of received radio signals from several geosynchronous satellites. Similarly, mobile phone location systems measure the signal strength of the phone at several cell towers. Sonar and infrared ranging sensors work by sending out an acoustic signal (sonar) or an infrared signal (IR rangers) and measuring the strength of that signal when it's reflected off the target.

Distance ranging techniques can be classified as active or passive. In active systems, the target has a radio, light, or acoustic source on it, and the receiver just listens for the signal from the target. In passive systems, the target doesn't have to have any technology on board. The receiver emits a signal, and the signal bounces off the target. Mobile phone location is active, because it relies on the phone sending out a radio signal. Sonar and infrared ranging are passive, because the sensor has to emit a signal in order to measure the reflection. GPS is an active locating technology, because although the receiver doesn't emit a signal, it has an electronic receiver onboard to receive satellites' signals.

Sometimes distance ranging is used for acquiring a position, and other times it's used for refining it. In the following examples, the passive distance rangers deliver a measurement of physical distance, but the radio ranging tell you only when another radio is in transmission range of your radio, and whether it's near or far within the range.

Passive Distance Ranging

Ultrasonic rangers like the Devantech SRF02 and infrared rangers like the Sharp GP2D12, shown in Figure 8-1, are examples of distance rangers. The Devantech sensor sends an ultrasonic signal out and listens for an echo; it's basically a sonar device. The Sharp sensor sends out an infrared light beam, and senses the reflection of that beam. These sensors only work in a short range. The Sharp sensor can read about 10 cm to 80 cm, and the Devantech sensor reads from about 15 cm to 6.4 m; these are useful only for very local measurements. Passive sensors like these are handy, though, when you want to measure the distance of a person in a limited space, and you don't want to have to put any hardware on the person. They're also handy when you're building moving objects that need to know their proximity to other objects in the same space as they move.

Figure 8-1
Devantech SRF02 and Sharp GP2D12 sensors. The Devantech sensor can read a range from 15 cm to 6 m. The Sharp sensor can read a range from 10 cm to 80cm.

◀€ **Project 14**

Infrared Distance Ranger Example

The Sharp GP2xx series of infrared ranging sensors give a decent measurement of short-range distance by bouncing an infrared light signal off the target and measuring the returned brightness. They're very simple to use. Shown in Figure 8-2 is a circuit for a Sharp GP2D12 IR ranger, which can detect an object in front of it within about 10 cm to 80 cm. The sensor requires 5V power, and outputs an analog voltage from 0 to 5V, depending on the distance to the nearest object in its sensing area.

MATERIALS

» **1 solderless breadboard** such as Digi-Key (www.digikey.com) part number 438-1045-ND, or Jameco (www.jameco.com) part number 20601. The breadboard is optional; as shown in the photo, you can assemble this without it.

» **1 Arduino module** or other microcontroller

» **1 Sharp GP2D12 IR ranger** Acroname (www.acroname.com) part number R48-IR12; SparkFun (www.sparkfun.com) part number SEN-00242 for the Sharp GP2Y0A21YK, a similar model; Trossen Robotics (www.trossenrobotics.com) part number S-10-GP2D12; Digi-Key part number 425-2469-ND. It's best to buy the connector and cable needed with the sensor, as they are difficult to make. Acroname sells these as part number R47-JSTCON-2, Trossen Robotics as part number S-10-GP2D12C.

» **1 10µF capacitor**

▸▸ The Sharp sensors' outputs are not linear, so if you want to get a linear range, you need to make a graph of the voltage over distance, and do some math. Fortunately, the good folks at Acroname Robotics have done the math for you. For the details, see www.acroname.com/robotics/info/articles/irlinear/irlinear.html.

The next program reads the sensor and outputs the distance measured in centimeters. The conversion formula gives only an approximation, but it's accurate enough for general purposes.

```
/*
  Sharp GP2D12 IR ranger reader
  language: Wiring/Arduino

  Reads the value from a Sharp GP2D12 IR ranger and sends it
  out serially.
*/

int sensorPin = 0;      // Analog input pin
int sensorValue = 0;    // value read from the pot

void setup() {
  // initialize serial communications at 9600 bps:
  Serial.begin(9600);
}

void loop() {
  sensorValue = analogRead(sensorPin); // read the pot value

  // the sensor actually gives results that aren't linear.
  // this formula converts the results to a linear range.
  int range = (6787 / (sensorValue - 3)) - 4;

  Serial.println(range, DEC);    // print the sensor value
  delay(10);                     // wait 10 milliseconds
                                 // before the next loop

}
```

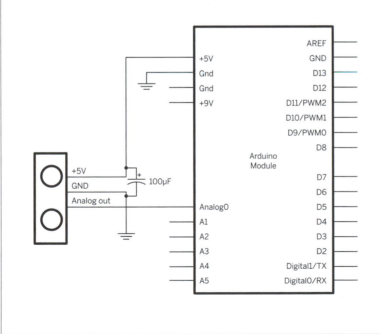

Figure 8-2
The Sharp GP2D12 IR ranger attached to a microcontroller. The capacitor attached to the body of the sensor smoothes out fluctuations due to the sensor's current load.

Ultrasonic Distance Ranger Example

The Devantech SRFxx ultrasonic sensors measure distance using a similar method to the Sharp sensors, but have a greater sensing range. They send an ultrasonic signal out and wait for the echo to return, and measure the distance based on the time required for the echo to return. These sensors require 5V power, and return their results via an I2C synchronous serial protocol. The SRF02 sensors and other SRFxx sensors like the SRF08 and SRF10, which use the same protocol, are available from the sites www.acroname.com and robot-electronics.co.uk. The MaxBotix EZ1 and LV-EZ1 (available from www. sparkfun.com) are ultrasonic rangers that are similar to the Devantech ones, but that use TTL serial, pulsewidth output, or analog voltage output instead of I2C.

I2C is comparable to RS-232 or USB, in that it doesn't define the application — just the way that data is sent. Every I2C device uses two wires to send and receive data: a serial clock pin, called the SCL pin, that the microcontroller pulses at a regular interval, and a serial data pin, called the SDA pin, over which data is transmitted. For each serial clock pulse, a bit of data is sent or received. When the clock changes from low to high (known as the rising edge of the clock), a bit of data is transferred from the microcontroller to the I2C device. When the clock changes from high to low (known as the falling edge of the clock), a bit of data is transferred from the I2C device to the microcontroller.

The Arduino module uses analog pin 4 as the SDA pin, and analog pin 5 as the SCL pin. Figure 8-3 shows the SRF02 sensor connected to an Arduino.

Distance rangers have a limited conical field of sensitivity, so they're not great for determining location over a large two-dimensional area. The Devantech SRF02 sensor, for example, has a cone-shaped field of sensitivity that's about 55 degrees wide and 6 meters from the sensor to the edge of the range. In order to use it to cover a room, you'd need to use several of them and get creative about how you arrange them. Figure 8-4 shows one way to cover a 4m x 4m space using five of the SRF02 rangers. In this case, you'd need to make sure that no two of the sensors were operating at the same instant, because their signals would interfere with each other. The sensors would have to be activated one after another in sequence. Because each one takes up to 36 milliseconds to return a result, you'd need up to 180 milliseconds to make a complete scan of the space.

MATERIALS

» **1 solderless breadboard** such as Digi-Key part number 438-1045-ND, or Jameco part number 20601
» **1 Arduino module** or other microcontroller
» **1 Devantech SRF02 ultrasonic ranger** Acroname Robotics part number R287-SRF02
» **1 100µF capacitor** SparkFun part number COM-00096, or Digi-Key part number P10195-ND

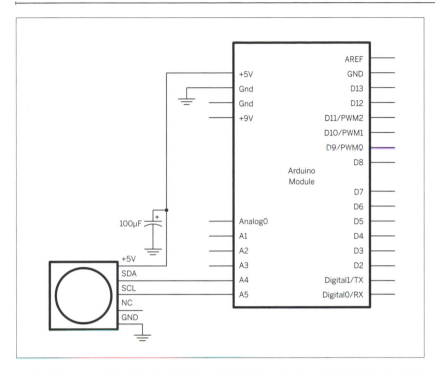

Figure 8-3
SRF02 ultrasonic sensor connected to an an Arduino Mini 04 module. Female headers have been soldered to the Arduino Mini's analog 4-7 holes to make them easier to use.

» Bottom right

Figure 8-4
Measuring distance in two dimensions using ultrasonic distance rangers. The square in each drawing is a 4m × 4m floor plan of a room. In order to cover the whole of a rectangular space, you need several sensors placed around the side of the room.

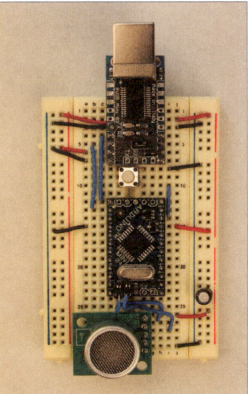

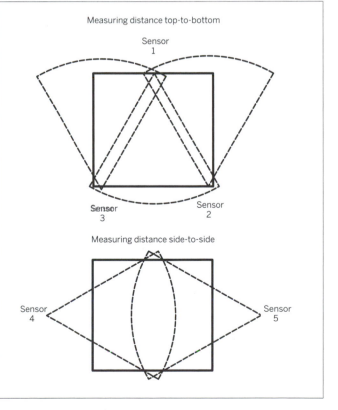

Try It This sketch sends commands to the SRF02 sensor to take distance readings and return them to the microcontroller.

NOTE: If you have trouble compiling this sketch, you might need to delete the compiled version of the Wire library, and let Arduino recompile it the next time you compile your program. The file you need to delete is called Wire.o, and it's in a subdirectory of the Arduino application directory: lib/targets/libraries/Wire/. In general, for any library you want to recompile, you can delete the object file (the .o file), and Arduino will recompile it.

```
/*
  SRF02 sensor reader
 language: Wiring/Arduino

 Reads data from a Devantech SRF02 ultrasonic sensor.
 Should also work for the SRF08 and SRF10 sensors as well.

 Sensor connections:
 SDA - Analog pin 4
 SCL - Analog pin 5

 */
// include Wire library to read and write I2C commands:
#include <Wire.h>

// the commands needed for the SRF sensors:
#define sensorAddress 0x70
#define readInches 0x50
// use these as alternatives if you want centimeters or microseconds:
#define readCentimeters 0x51
#define readMicroseconds 0x52
// this is the memory register in the sensor that contains the result:
#define resultRegister 0x02


void setup()
{
  // start the I2C bus
  Wire.begin();
  // open the serial port:
  Serial.begin(9600);
}

void loop()
{
  // send the command to read the result in inches:
  sendCommand(sensorAddress, readInches);
  // wait at least 70 milliseconds for a result:
  delay(70);
  // set the register that you want to read the result from:
  setRegister(sensorAddress, resultRegister);

  // read the result:
  int sensorReading = readData(sensorAddress, 2);
  // print it:
  Serial.print("distance: ");
  Serial.print(sensorReading);
  Serial.println(" inches");
  // wait before next reading:
  delay(70);
}
```

»

Continued from opposite page.

```
/*
  SendCommand() sends commands in the format that the SRF sensors expect
*/
void sendCommand (int address, int command) {
  // start I2C transmission:
  Wire.beginTransmission(address);
  // send command:
  Wire.send(0x00);
  Wire.send(command);
  // end I2C transmission:
  Wire.endTransmission();
}
/*
  setRegister() tells the SRF sensor to change the address
  pointer position
 */
void setRegister(int address, int thisRegister) {
  // start I2C transmission:
  Wire.beginTransmission(address);
  // send address to read from:
  Wire.send(thisRegister);
  // end I2C transmission:
  Wire.endTransmission();
}
/*
readData() returns a result from the SRF sensor
 */
int readData(int address, int numBytes) {
  int result = 0;          // the result is two bytes long

  // send I2C request for data:
  Wire.requestFrom(address, numBytes);
  // wait for two bytes to return:
  while (Wire.available() < 2 )  {
    // wait for result
  }
  // read the two bytes, and combine them into one int:
  result = Wire.receive() * 256;
  result = result + Wire.receive();
  // return the result:
  return result;
}
```

❝❝ Active Distance Ranging

The ultrasonic and infrared rangers in the preceding sections are passive distance sensing systems. Mobile phones and the Global Positioning System measure longer distances by using ranging as well. These systems include a radio beacon (the cell tower or GPS satellite) and a radio receiver (the phone or GPS receiver). The receiver determines its distance from the beacon based on the received signal from the beacon. These systems can measure much greater distances, on an urban or global scale. The disadvantage of active distance ranging is that you must have both a sending device and receiving device. You can't measure a person's distance from somewhere using active distance ranging unless you attach a receiver to the person.

GPS and cellular location systems don't actually give you the distance from their radio beacons, just the relative signal strength of the radio signal. Bluetooth, 802.15.4,

ZigBee, and Wi-Fi radios all provide data about signal strength as well. In order to relate this to distance, you need to be able to calculate that distance as a function of signal strength. The main function of a GPS receiver is to calculate distances to the GPS satellites based on signal strength and determine a position using those distances. The other radio systems mentioned here don't do those calculations for you.

In many applications, though, you don't need to know the distance — you just need to know how relatively near or far one person or object is to another. For example, if you're making a pet door lock that opens in response to the pet, you could imagine a Bluetooth beacon on the pet's collar, and a receiver on the door lock. When the signal strength from the pet's collar is strong enough, the door lock opens. In this case, and in others like it, there's no need to know the actual distance.
X

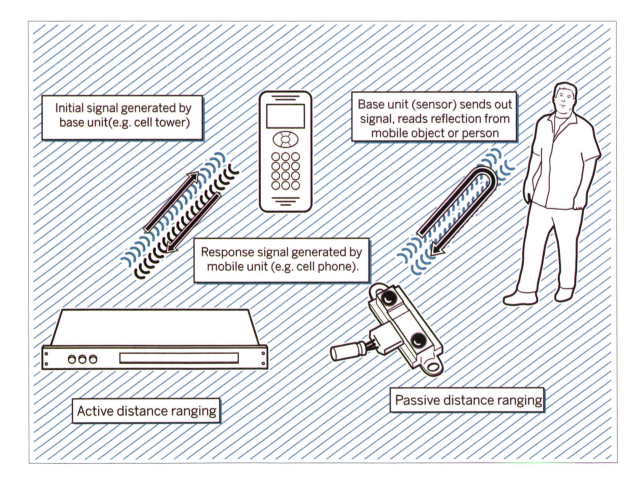

Initial signal generated by base unit(e.g. cell tower)

Base unit (sensor) sends out signal, reads reflection from mobile object or person

Response signal generated by mobile unit (e.g. cell phone).

Active distance ranging

Passive distance ranging

Project 16

Reading Received Signal Strength Using XBee Radios

In the last chapter, you saw the received signal strength, but you didn't do anything with it. The Processing code that read the solar cell's voltage output parsed the XBee packet for the received signal strength (RSSI). Here's a simpler variation on it that just reads the signal strength. To test it, you can use the same radio settings from the solar cell project and attach the receiving XBee radio to a USB-to-serial adaptor. See Figure 7-5 for the receiving circuit, and Figure 7-6 (the VOC sensor circuit) or Figure 7-18 (the solar cell circuit) for circuits that work well as transmitters.

Run this Processing sketch to connect to the receiver radio via the USB-to-serial device. When you run this program, you'll get a graphing bar like that in Figure 8-5.

```
/*  XBee Signal Strength Reader
    Language: Processing

Reads a packet from an XBee radio and parses it.  The packet
should be 22 bytes long. It should be made up of the following:
byte 1:     0x7E, the start byte value
byte 2-3:   packet size, a 2-byte value  (not used here)
byte 4:     API identifier value, a code that says what this response
            is (not used here)
byte 5-6:   Sender's address
byte 7:     RSSI, Received Signal Strength Indicator (not used here)
byte 8:     Broadcast options (not used here)
byte 9:     Number of samples to follow
byte 10-11: Active channels indicator (not used here)
byte 12-21: 5 10-bit values, each ADC samples from the sender

*/
import processing.serial.*;

Serial XBee ;                   // input serial port from the XBee Radio
int[] packet = new int[22];     // with 5 samples, the XBee packet is
                                // 22 bytes long
int byteCounter;                // keeps track of where you are in
                                // the packet
int rssi = 0;                   // received signal strength
int address = 0;                // the sending XBee 's address

Serial myPort;                  // The serial port

int fontSize = 18;              // size of the text on the screen
int lastReading = 0;            // value of the previous incoming byte

void setup () {
  size(400, 300);       // window size
```

»

Continued from previous page.

```
  // create a font with the third font available to the system:
  PFont myFont = createFont(PFont.list()[2], fontSize);
  textFont(myFont);

  // get a list of the serial ports:
  println(Serial.list());
  // open the serial port attached to your XBee radio:
  XBee = new Serial(this, Serial.list()[0], 9600);
}

void draw() {
  // if you have new data and it's valid (>0), graph it:
  if ((rssi > 0 ) && (rssi != lastReading)) {
    // set the background:
    background(0);
    // set the bar height and width:
    int rectHeight = rssi;
    int rectWidth = 50;
    // draw the rect:
    stroke(23, 127, 255);
    fill (23, 127, 255);
    rect(width/2 - rectWidth, height-rectHeight, rectWidth, height);
    // write the number:
    text("XBee Radio Signal Strength test", 10, 20);
    text("From: " + hex(address), 10, 40);

    text ("RSSI: -" + rssi + " dBm", 10, 60);
    // save the current byte for next read:
    lastReading = rssi;
  }
}

void serialEvent(Serial XBee ) {
  // read a byte from the port:
  int thisByte = XBee .read();
  // if the byte = 0x7E, the value of a start byte, you have
  // a new packet:
  if (thisByte == 0x7E) {   // start byte
    // parse the previous packet if there's data:
    if (packet[2] > 0) {
      parseData(packet);
    }
    // reset the byte counter:
    byteCounter = 0;
  }
  // put the current byte into the packet at the current position:
  packet[byteCounter] = thisByte;
  //  increment the byte counter:
  byteCounter++;
}
```

»

Continued from opposite page.

```
/*
 Once you've got a packet, you need to extract the useful data.
 This method gets the address of the sender and RSSI.
 */
void parseData(int[] thisPacket) {

  // read the address -- a two-byte value, so you
  // add the two bytes as follows:
  address = thisPacket[5] + thisPacket[4] * 256;
  // get RSSI:
  rssi = thisPacket[6];
}
```

" Radio signal strength is measured in decibel-milliwatts (dBm). You might wonder why the signal reads −65dBm. How can the signal strength be negative? The relationship between milliwatts of power and dBm is logarithmic. To get the dBm, take the log of the milliwatts. So, for example, if you receive 1 milliwatt of signal strength, you've got log 1 dBm. Log 1 = 0, so 1 mW = 0 dBm. When the power drops below 1 mW, the dBm drops below 0, like so: 0.5 mW = (log 0.5) dBm or −3.01 dBm. 0.25mW = (log 0.25) dBm, or −6.02 dBm. If logarithms confuse you, just remember that 0 dBm is the maximum transmission power, which means that signal strength is going to start at 0 dBm and go down from there. The minimum signal that the XBee radios can receive is −92 dBm. Bluetooth radios and Wi-Fi radios typically have a similar range of sensitivity. In a perfect world with no obstructions to create errors, relationship between signal strength and distance would be a logarithmic curve.

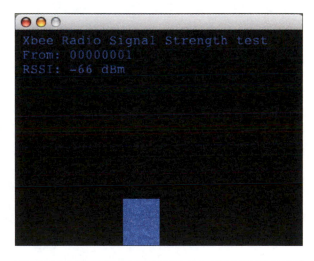

Figure 8-5
Output of the XBee RSSI test program.

Reading Received Signal Strength Using Bluetooth Radios

The BlueRadios modules used in Chapters 2 and 6 can also give you an RSSI reading. To see this, the radio needs to be connected to another Bluetooth radio. The simplest way to see this is to pair your radio with your laptop as shown in Project #3 in Chapter 2.

Once you've done this, open a serial connection to the radio via Bluetooth, not via the radio's hardware serial interface. Once you're connected, drop out of data mode into command mode by typing the following (\r indicates that you should type a carriage return; press Enter or Return when you see \r):

```
+++AT\r
```

You'll get an OK prompt from the radio. Next type:

```
ATRSSI\r
```

The radio will respond like so:

```
OK
+0.6
```

As you move the radio closer to or further from your computer, type the ATRSSI command again. You'll see the signal strength change just as it did in the XBee example in the preceding project.

❝ The Multipath Effect

The biggest source of error in distance ranging is what's called the multipath effect (see Figure 8-6). When electromagnetic waves radiate, they bounce off things. Your phone may receive multiple signals from a nearby cell tower if you're positioned near a large obstacle such as a building. The reflected waves off the building create "phantom" signals that look to the receiver as real as the original signal. This issue makes it impossible for the receiver to calculate the distance from the beacon accurately and causes degradation in the signal quality of mobile phone reception, as well as errors in locating the phones. For GPS receivers, multipath results in a much wider range of possible locations, as the error means that you can't calculate the position as accurately. It is possible to filter for the reflected signals, but not all radios incorporate such filtering.

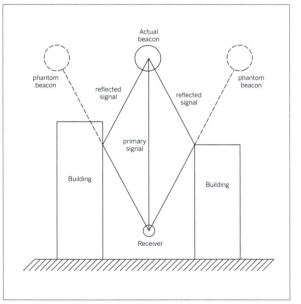

Figure 8-6
Multipath. Reflected radio waves create phantom beacons that the receiver can't tell from the real beacon, causing errors in calculating the distance based on signal strength.

❝ Determining Position Through Trilateration

Distance ranging tells you how far away an object is from your measuring point in one dimension, but it doesn't define the whole position. The distance between your position and the target object determines a circle around your position (or a sphere, if you're measuring in three dimensions). Your object could be anywhere on that circle.

In order to locate it within a two- or three-dimensional space, though, you need to know more than distance. The most common way to do this is by measuring the distance from at least three points. This method is called trilateration. If you measure the object's distance from two points, you get two possible places it could be on a plane, as shown in Figure 8-7. When you add a third circle, you have one distinct point on the plane where your object could be. A similar method, triangulation, uses two known points and calculates the position using the distance between the two known points and the angles of the triangle formed by those points and the position you want to know.

The Global Positioning System uses trilateration to determine an object's position. GPS uses a network of geosynchronous satellites circling the globe. The position of each satellite can be calculated at any given moment. Each one is broadcasting its position, and GPS receivers pick up that broadcast. When a receiver has at least three satellites, it can determine a rough position. Most receivers use at least six satellite signals to calculate their position, in order to correct any errors. Cell phone location systems like Wireless E911 calculate a phone's approximate position in a similar fashion, by measuring the distance from multiple cell towers based on the time difference of arrival of signals from those towers.

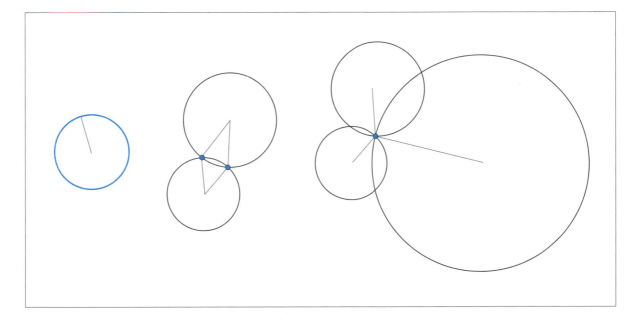

Figure 8-7
Trilateration on a two-dimensional plane. Knowing the distance from one point defines a circle of possible locations. Knowing the distance from two points narrows it to two possible points. Knowing the distance from three points determines a single point on the plane.

🔊 **Project 18**

Reading the GPS Serial Protocol

The good news is that if you're using GPS, you never have to do trilateration or triangulation calculations for yourself. GPS receivers do the work for you. They then give you the position in terms of latitude and longitude. There are several data protocols for GPS receivers, but the most widely used is the NMEA 0183 protocol established by the National Marine Electronics Association in the United States. Just about all receivers on the market output NMEA 0183, and usually one or two other protocols as well.

NMEA 0183 is a serial protocol that operates at 4800 bits per second, 8 data bits, no parity, 1 stop bit (4800-8-N-1). Most receivers send this data using either RS-232 or TTL serial levels. The receiver used for this example, an EM-406A SiRF III receiver available from SparkFun, sends NMEA data at 5V TTL levels. Figure 8-8 shows the module connected to BlueSMiRF radio, for testing. The data is sent back over Bluetooth to a personal computer running Processing. You can pair the BlueSMiRF to your personal computer using the instructions from Project #2 in Chapter 2, if it's not already paired.

Once your personal computer recognizes the Bluetooth radio, open a serial connection to it at 9600 bits per second. You're opening a serial connection over Bluetooth, not over USB as you've done with most of the projects in this book. The GPS module operates at 4800 bits per second, so you need to reset the Bluetooth radio's serial data rate in order to get data from the GPS module through it. If you do see any data, it'll be illegible, because the radio's serial connection to the GPS module is set to 9600 bps, and the GPS module's sending at 4800 bps. To change this, type: +++\r This command takes the radio out of data mode and puts it in command mode. The radio will respond: OK

Next, type:

```
ATSW20,20,0,0,1\r
ATMD\r
```

▶▶ This changes the data rate to 4800 bits per second

▶▶ This puts the radio back into data mode.

After that, you should see data in the NMEA protocol, like what you see here, below:

MATERIALS

» **1 solderless breadboard** such as Digi-Key part number 438-1045-ND, or Jameco part number 20601
» **1 GPS receiver module** SparkFun part number GPS-00465 or Parallax (www.parallax.com) part number 28146 (the Parallax module, developed by Grand Design Studio, comes mounted on a breadboard-ready breakout board)
» **1 BlueSMiRF Bluetooth Modem module** from SparkFun
» **1 5V voltage regulator** Digi-Key part number LM7805CT-ND; Jameco part number 51262; SparkFun part number COM-00107

```
$GPGGA,155123.000,4043.8432,N,07359.7653,W,1,05,1.7,49.7,M,-34.2,M,,0000*5F
$GPGSA,A,3,10,24,29,02,26,,,,,,,,6.2,1.7,6.0*3C
$GPGSV,3,1,12,10,62,038,38,29,57,160,38,24,52,311,32,06,52,273,29*77
$GPGSV,3,2,12,26,43,175,39,02,40,106,38,07,40,294,36,15,30,301,*77
$GPGSV,3,3,12,21,14,298,,08,10,078,,27,10,051,,04,04,112,*7B
$GPRMC,155123.000,A,4043.8432,N,07359.7653,W,0.15,83.25,200407,,*28
$GPGGA,155124.000,4043.8432,N,07359.7653,W,1,05,1.7,49.8,M,-34.2,M,,0000*57
$GPGSA,A,3,10,24,29,02,26,,,,,,,,6.2,1.7,6.0*3C
$GPRMC,155124.000,A,4043.8432,N,07359.7653,W,0.15,79.50,200407,,*28
$GPGGA,155125.000,4043.8432,N,07359.7654,W,1,05,1.7,49.7,M,-34.2,M,,0000*5E
$GPGSA,A,3,10,24,29,02,26,,,,,,,,6.2,1.7,6.0*3C
$GPRMC,155125.000,A,4043.8432,N,07359.7654,W,0.10,11.88,200407,,*20
```

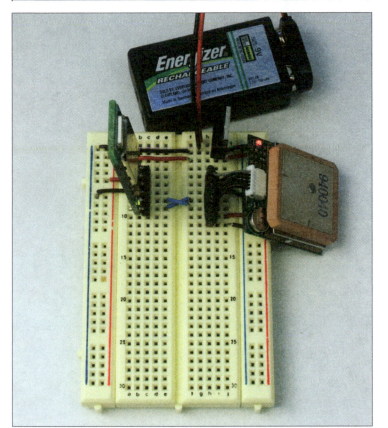

Figure 8-8
EM-406A GPS receiver attached to a Bluetooth radio. In order to get a real GPS signal, you'll have to go outside, so wireless data and a battery power source are handy.

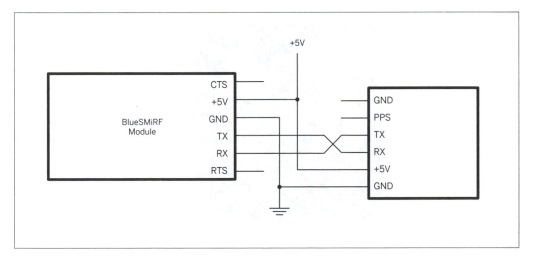

There are several different types of sentences within the NMEA protocol. Each sentence serves a different function. Some tell you your position, some tell you about the satellites in view of the receiver, some deliver information about your course heading, and so on. Each sentence begins with a dollar sign ($) followed by five letters that identify the type of sentence. After that come each of the parameters of the sentence, separated by commas. An asterisk comes after the parameters, then a checksum, then a carriage return and a linefeed.

↠ Take a look at the $GPRMC sentence as an example:

`$GPRMC,155125.000,A,4043.8432,N,07359.7654,W,0.10,11.88,200407,,*20`

RMC stands for Recommended Minimum specifiC global navigation system satellite data. It gives the basic information almost any application might need. This sentence contains the information shown in the table.

Using the NMEA protocol in a program is just a matter of deciding which sentence gives you the information you need, reading the data in serially, and converting the data into values you can use. In most cases, the RMC sentence gives you all the data you need about position.

The Processing sketch shown next reads NMEA serial data in and parses out the time, date, latitude, longitude, and heading. It draws an arrow on the screen to indicate heading. The output looks like Figure 8-9. (Be sure to use the correct serial port when opening myPort; you may need to modify the code before you can run it.)

NOTE: Extra credit: Figure out where I was when I wrote this chapter.

Message identifier	$GPRMC
Time	155125.000 or 15:51:25 GMT
Status of the data (valid or not valid)	A = valid data (V = not valid)
Latitude	4043.8432 or 40°43.8432'
North/South Indicator	N = North (S = South)
Longitude	07359.7654 or 73°59.7654'
East/West indicator	W = West (E = East)
Speed over ground	0.10 knots
Course over ground	11.88° from north
Date	200407 or April 20, 2007
Magnetic Variation	none
Mode	none
Checksum (there is no comma before the checksum; magnetic variation would appear to the left of that final comma, and mode would appear to the right)	*20

```
4/21/2007
22:18:38 GMT
55.47087 N, 12.34531 E
heading 325.0 degrees
```

Figure 8-9
The output of the Processing GPS parser.

Find It   First, set up your global variables as usual:

```
/*
GPS parser
language: Processing

This program takes in NMEA 0183 serial data and
parses out the date, time, latitude, and longitude
using the GPRMC sentence.
*/

// import the serial library:
import processing.serial.*;

Serial myPort;            // the serial port
float latitude = 0.0;     // the latitude reading in degrees
String northSouth;        // north or south?
float longitude = 0.0;    // the longitude reading in degrees
String eastWest;          // east or west?
float heading = 0.0;      // the heading in degrees

int hrs, mins, secs;      // time units
int thisDay,  thisMonth, thisYear;
```

The setup() method sets the window size, defines the font and the drawing parameters, and opens the serial port.

```
void setup() {
  size(300, 300);         // window size

  // create a font with the third font available to the system:
  PFont myFont = createFont(PFont.list()[2], 14);
  textFont(myFont);

  // settings for drawing arrow:
  noStroke();
  smooth();

  // list all the available serial ports:
  println(Serial.list());

  // I know that the first port in the serial list on my mac
  // is always my Keyspan adaptor, so I open Serial.list()[0].
  // Open whatever port you're using.
  myPort = new Serial(this, Serial.list()[0], 4800);

  // read bytes into a buffer until you get a carriage
  // return (ASCII 13):
  myPort.bufferUntil('\r');
}
```

» The draw() method prints the readings in the window, and calls another method, drawArrow() to draw the arrow and circle.

```
void draw() {
  background(0);
  // make the text white:
  fill(255);

  // print the date and time from the GPS sentence:
  text(thisMonth+ "/"+ thisDay+ "/"+ thisYear , 50, 30);
  text(hrs+ ":"+ mins+ ":"+ secs + " GMT  ", 50, 50);
  // print the position from the GPS sentence:
  text(latitude + " " + northSouth + ", " +longitude +" "+ eastWest,
      50, 70);
  text("heading " + heading + " degrees", 50,90);

  // draw an arrow using the heading:
  drawArrow(heading);
}
```

» The serialEvent() method gets any incoming data as usual, and passes it off to a method called parseString(). That method splits the incoming string into all the parts of the GPS sentence. If it's a GPRMC sentence, it passes it to a method, getRMC() to handle it. If you were writing a more universal parser, you'd write similar methods for each type of sentence.

```
void serialEvent(Serial myPort) {
  // read the serial buffer:
  String myString = myPort.readStringUntil('\n');

  // if you got any bytes other than the linefeed, parse it:
  if (myString != null) {
    parseString(myString);
  }
}

void parseString (String serialString) {
  // split the string at the commas:
  String items[] = (split(serialString, ','));

  // if the first item in the sentence is the identifier, parse the rest
  if (items[0].equals("$GPRMC")) {
    // get time, date, position, course, and speed
    getRMC(items);
  }
}
```

» The getRMC() method converts the latitude, longitude, and other numerical parts of the sentence into numbers.

```
void getRMC(String[] data) {
  // move the items from the string into the variables:
  int time = int(data[1]);
  // first two digits of the time are hours:
  hrs = time/10000;
  // second two digits of the time are minutes:
  mins = (time%10000)/100;
  // last two digits of the time are seconds:
  secs = (time%100);
```

»

Continued from opposite page.

```
// if you have a valid reading, parse the rest of it:
if (data[2].equals("A")) {
    latitude = float(data[3])/100.0;
    northSouth = data[4];
    longitude = float(data[5])/100.0;
    eastWest = data[6];
    heading = float(data[8]);
    int date = int(data[9]);
    // last two digits of the date are year.  Add the century too:
    thisYear = date%100 + 2000;
    // second two digits of the date are month:
    thisMonth =  (date%10000)/100;
    // first two digits of the date are day:
    thisDay = date/10000;
  }
}
```

>> drawArrow() is called by the draw() method. It draws the arrow and the circle.

```
void drawArrow(float angle) {
  // move whatever you draw next so that (0,0) is centered on the screen:
  translate(width/2, height/2);

  // draw a circle in light blue:
  fill(80,200,230);
  ellipse(0,0,50,50);
  // make the arrow black:
  fill(0);
  // rotate using the heading:
  rotate(radians(angle));

  // draw the arrow.  center of the arrow is at (0,0):
  triangle(-10, 0, 0, -20, 10, 0);
  rect(-2,0, 4,20);
}
```

❝❝ Determining Orientation

People have an innate ability to determine their orientation relative to the world around them, but objects don't. So orientation sensors are usually used for refining the position of objects rather than of people. In this section, you'll see two types of orientation sensors: a digital compass for determining heading relative to the Earth's magnetic field, and an accelerometer for determining orientation relative to the Earth's gravitational field. Using these two sensors, you can determine which way is north and which way is up.

🔊 **Project 19**

Determining Heading Using a Digital Compass

Calculating heading can be done using a compass if you are in a space that doesn't have a lot of magnetic interference. There are many digital compasses on the market. These acquire a heading by measuring the change in the earth's magnetic field along two axes, just as an analog compass does. Like analog compasses, they are subject to interference from other magnetic fields, including those generated by strong electrical induction.

This example uses a digital compass from Devantech, model CMPS03. It's available from www.acroname.com, and www.robot-electronics.co.uk. It measures its orientation using two magnetic field sensors placed at right angles to each other, and reports the results via two interfaces: a changing pulse width corresponding to the heading, or synchronous serial data sent over an I2C connection. You'll recognize some of the I2C methods used here from the SRF02 distance ranger example shown earlier. Both are made by the same company, and both use similar protocols.

The interface to the microcontroller is similar to that of the distance ranger. The Arduino module uses analog pin 4 as the SDA pin, and analog pin 5 as the SCL pin. Figure 8-10 shows the compass connected to an Arduino.

The compass operates on 5V. Its pins are as follows:

1. +5V
2. SCL – I2C serial clock
3. SDA – I2C serial data
4. PWM – Pulsewidth output. Pulsewidth is from 1 millisecond to 36.99 milliseconds, and each degree of compass heading is 100 microseconds of pulsewidth.
5. No connection.
6. Calibrate.
7. 50/60Hz select — Take this pin high or leave unconnected for 60Hz operation, take it low for 50Hz.
8. No connection
9. Ground

MATERIALS

» **1 solderless breadboard** such as Digi-Key part number 438-1045-ND, or Jameco part number 20601
» **1 Arduino module** or other microcontroller
» **2 4.7kΩ resistors**
» **1 digital compass, Devantech model CMPS03** available from Acroname Robotics, part number R117-COMPASS, or Robot Electronics CMPS03

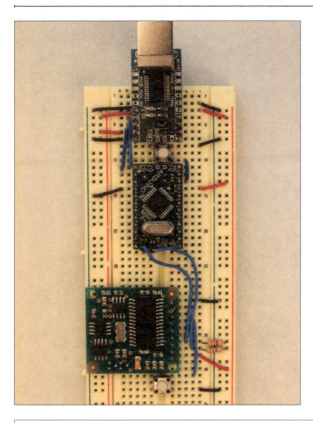

Figure 8-10
Devantech CMPS03 compass connected to an Arduino Mini 04 module. Female headers have been soldered to the Arduino Mini's analog 4-7 holes to make them easier to use. Note that the SDA and SCL lines need to have 4.7KΩ pull-up resistors connecting them to 5V.

NOTE: To calibrate the compass, take pin 6 low and rotate the compass slowly through 360 degrees on a flat, level surface. When calibrating the compass, you need to know the cardinal directions precisely. Get a magnetic needle compass and check properly. You should calibrate away from lots of electronic equipment and sources of magnetic energy (except the Earth). For example, in my office, needle compasses tend to point west-southwest, so I calibrate outside, powering the whole Arduino circuit from a battery. For more on calibrating the CMPS03, see www.robot-electronics.co.uk/htm/cmps_cal.shtml.

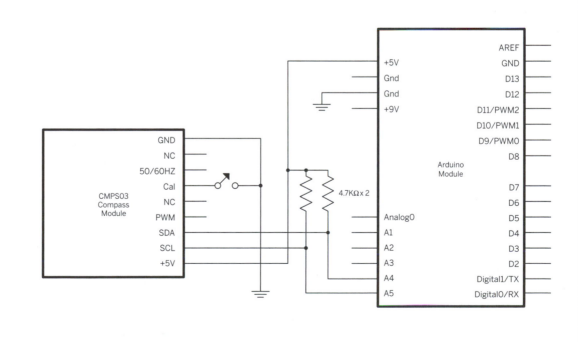

Try It This program uses the Wire library to communicate via I2C with the compass. There are no global variables, but before the setup() method, you have to include the library and define a couple of constants that are operational codes for the compass module.

```
/*
  CMPS03 compass reader
  language: Wiring/Arduino

  Reads data from a Devantech CMPS03 compass sensor.

  Sensor connections:
  SDA - Analog pin 4
  SCL - Analog pin 5
  */


// include Wire library to read and write I2C commands:
#include <Wire.h>

// the commands needed for the SRF sensors:
#define sensorAddress 0x60
// this is the memory register in the sensor that contains the result:
#define resultRegister 0x02
```

▸▸ The setup() method initializes the Wire and Serial libraries.

```
void setup()
{
  Wire.begin();        // start the I2C bus
  Serial.begin(9600);  // open the serial port
}
```

▸▸ The main loop calls a method called setRegister() to read from the compass' registers. Then it prints what it read. The compass needs about 68 milliseconds between readings, so the loop delays after the readings.

```
void loop()
{
  // send the command to read the result in inches:
  setRegister(sensorAddress, resultRegister);
  // read the result:
  int bearing = readData(sensorAddress, 2);
  // print it:
  Serial.print("bearing: ");
  Serial.print(bearing/10);
  Serial.println(" degrees");
  delay(70);  // wait before next reading
}
```

▸▸ The compass has memory registers and function registers. The compass heading is stored in a memory register. To read it, you send an initial transmission of the address of the register you want to read from, then you request however many bytes you want to read.

```
/*
  setRegister() tells the SRF sensor to change the address
  pointer position
  */
void setRegister(int address, int thisRegister) {
  Wire.beginTransmission(address);  // start I2C transmission
  // send address to read from:
  Wire.send(thisRegister);
  Wire.endTransmission();           // end I2C transmission
}
```

» readData() makes the request for two bytes of data from the compass' memory register, waits until those bytes have been returned, reads them, and returns the result as a single integer.

```
/*
readData() returns a result from the SRF sensor
 */

int readData(int address, int numBytes) {
  int result = 0;          // the result is two bytes long

  // send I2C request for data:
  Wire.requestFrom(address, numBytes);
  // wait for two bytes to return:
  while (Wire.available() < 2 )   {
    // wait for result
  }
  // read the two bytes, and combine them into one int:
  result = Wire.receive() * 256;
  result = result + Wire.receive();
  // return the result:
  return result;
}
```

Determining Attitude Using an Accelerometer

Compass heading is an excellent way to determine orientation if you're level with the Earth, but sometimes you need to know how you're tilted. In navigation terms, this is called your attitude, and there are two major aspects to it: roll and pitch. Roll refers to how you're tilted side-to-side. Pitch refers how you're tilted front-to-back. If you've ever used an analog compass, you know how important it is to control your roll and pitch in order to get an accurate reading. Rotation on the axis perpendicular to the horizon is called yaw, and for our purposes, it's easiest to measure with a compass.

MATERIALS
» **1 solderless breadboard** such as Digi-Key part number 438-1045-ND, or Jameco part number 20601 » **1 Arduino module** or other microcontroller » **1 Analog Devices ADXL320 accelerometer** SparkFun sells a module with this accelerometer mounted on a breakout board, part number SEN-00847

Measuring roll and pitch is relatively easy to do using an accelerometer. You used one of these already in Chapter 5, in the seesaw ping pong client. Accelerometers measure changing acceleration. At the center of an accelerometer is a tiny mass that's free to swing in one, two, or three dimensions. As the accelerometer tilts relative to the earth, the gravitational force exerted on the mass changes. Because force equals mass times acceleration, and because the mass of the accelerometer is constant, the change is read as a changing acceleration.

In the following example, you'll use an accelerometer to control the pitch and roll of a disk onscreen in Processing. The numeric values from the sensor are written on the disk as it tilts.

▶▶ Connect the accelerometer to the Arduino as shown in Figure 8-11. Then program it using the following code:

```
/*
Accelerometer reader
language: Wiring/Arduino

Reads 2 axes of an accelerometer and sends the
values out the serial port
*/

int accelerometer[2];      // variable to hold the accelerometer values

void setup() {
  // open serial port:
  Serial.begin(9600);
  // send out some initial data:
  Serial.println("0,0,");
}
```

»

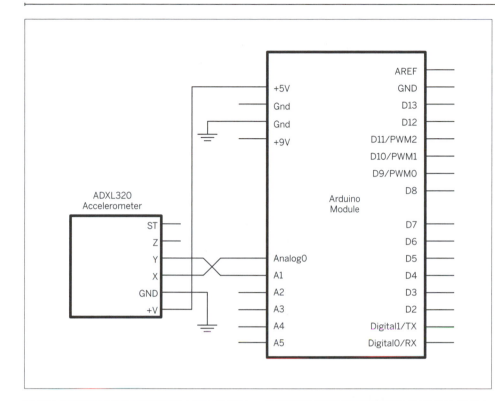

Figure 8-11
ADXL320 accelerometer connected to an Arduino Mini 04 module. The detail photo shows the board with the accelerometer removed to show the wiring underneath.

Continued from previous page.

```
void loop() {
  // read 2 channels of the accelerometer:
  for (int i = 0; i < 2; i++) {
    accelerometer[i] = analogRead(i);
    // delay to allow analog-to-digital converter to settle:
    delay(10);
  }

  // if there's serial data in, print sensor values out:
  if (Serial.available() > 0) {
    // read incoming data to clear serial input buffer:
    int inByte = Serial.read();
    for (int i = 0; i <  2; i++) {
      // values as ASCII strings:
      Serial.print(accelerometer[i], DEC);
      // print commas between values:
      Serial.print(",");
    }
    // print \r and \n after values are sent:
    Serial.println();
  }
}
```

Connect It   This sketch uses a call-and-response serial method, so you won't see any data coming out unless you send it a character serially. You can test it using your favorite serial terminal program. With the serial port open in the serial terminal program, type any key to make the microcontroller send a response. Once you've got it working, run the following sketch in Processing, making sure that the serial port opened by the program matches the one to which your microcontroller is connected:

```
/*
  accelerometer tilt
  language: Processing

  Takes the values from an accelerometer
  and uses it to set the attitudeof a disk on the screen.
*/

import processing.serial.*;       // import the serial lib

int graphPosition = 0;           // horizontal position of the graph
int[] vals = new int[2];         // raw values from the sensor
int[] maximum = new int[2];      // maximum value sensed
int[] minimum = new int[2];      // minimum value sensed
int[] range = new int[2];        // total range sensed
float[] attitude = new float[2]; // the tilt values
float position;                  // position to translate to

Serial myPort;                   // the serial port
boolean madeContact = false;     // whether there's been serial data sent in

void setup () {
  // draw the window:
  size(400, 400, P3D);

  // set the background color:
```

Continued from opposite page.

```
  background(0);
  // set the maximum and minimum values:
  for (int i = 0; i < 2; i++) {
    maximum[i] = 600;
    minimum[i] = 200;
    // calculate the total current range:
    range[i] = maximum[i] - minimum[i];
  }
  position = width/2;  // calculate position

  // create a font with the third font available to the system:
  PFont myFont = createFont(PFont.list()[2], 18);
  textFont(myFont);

  // list all the available serial ports:
  println(Serial.list());
  // Open whatever port you're using.
  myPort = new Serial(this, Serial.list()[0], 9600);
  // generate a serial event only when you get a return char:
  myPort.bufferUntil('\r');

  // set the fill color:
  fill(90,250,250);
}
```

▶▶ The draw() method just refreshes the screen in the window, as usual. It calls a method, setAttitude(), to calculate the tilt of the plane. Then it calls a method called tilt() to actually tilt the plane.

```
void draw () {
  // clear the screen:
  background(0);
  // print the values:
  text(vals[0] + " " + vals[1], -30, 10);

  // if you've never gotten a string from the microcontroller,
  // keep sending carriage returns to prompt for one:
  if (madeContact == false) {
    myPort.write('\r');
  }
  setAttitude(); // set the attitude
  tilt();        // draw the plane
}
```

▶▶ The 3D system in Processing works on rotations from zero to 2*PI. setAttitude() converts the accelerometer readings into that range, so the values can be used to set the tilt of the plane.

```
void setAttitude() {
  for (int i = 0; i < 2; i++) {
    // calculate the current attitude as a percentage of 2*PI,
    // based on the current range:
    attitude[i] = (2*PI) * float(vals[i] - minimum[i]) /float(range[i]);
  }
}
```

The tilt() method uses Processing's translate() and rotate() methods to move and rotate the plane of the disc to correspond with the accelerometer's movement.

```
void tilt() {
  // translate from origin to center:
  translate(position, position, position);

  // X is front-to-back:
  rotateX(-attitude[1]);
  // Y is left-to-right:
  rotateY(-attitude[0] - PI/2);

  // set the fill color:
  fill(90,250,250);
  // draw the rect:
  ellipse(0, 0, width/4, width/4);
  // change the fill color:
  fill(0);
  // draw some text so you can tell front from back:
  // print the values:
  text(vals[0] + " " + vals[1], -30, 10,1);

}
```

The serialEvent() method reads all the incoming serial bytes and parses them as comma-separated ASCII values just as you did in Monski pong in Chapter 2.

Figure 8-12
The output of the Processing accelerometer sketch.

```
// The serialEvent method is run automatically by the Processing applet
// whenever the buffer reaches the byte value set in the bufferUntil()
// method in the setup():

void serialEvent(Serial myPort) {
  // if serialEvent occurs at all, contact with the microcontroller
  // has been made:
  madeContact = true;
  // read the serial buffer:
  String myString = myPort.readStringUntil('\n');

  // if you got any bytes other than the linefeed:
  if (myString != null) {
    myString = trim(myString);
    // split the string at the commas
    //and convert the sections into integers:
    int sensors[] = int(split(myString, ','));
    // if you received all the sensor strings, use them:
    if (sensors.length >= 2) {
      vals[0] = sensors[0];
      vals[1] = sensors[1];

      // send out the serial port to ask for data:
      myPort.write('\r');
    }
  }
}
```

❝❝ Conclusion

When you start to develop projects that use location systems, you usually find that less is more. It's not unusual to start a project thinking you need to know position, distance, and orientation, then pare away systems as you develop the project. The physical limitations of the things you build and the spaces you build them in solve many problems for you.

This effect, combined with your users' innate ability to locate and orient themselves, makes your job much easier. Before you start to solve all problems in code or electronics, put yourself physically in the place you're building for, and do what you intend your users to do. You'll learn a lot about your project, and save yourself time, aggravation, and money.

The examples in this chapter are all focused on a solitary person or object. As soon as you introduce multiple participants, location and identification become more tightly connected, because you need to know whose signal is coming from a given location, or what location a given speaker is at. In the next chapter, you'll see methods crossing the line from physical identity to network identity.

X

9

Identification

In the previous chapters, you've assumed that identity equals address. Once you knew a device's address on the network, you started talking. Think about how disastrous this would be if you used this formula in everyday life: you pick up the phone, dial a number, and just start talking. What if you dialed the wrong number? What if someone other than the person you expected answers the phone?

Networked objects mark the boundaries of networks, but not of the communications that travel across them. We use these devices to send messages to other people. The network identity of the device and the physical identity of the person are two different things. Physical identity generally equates to presence (is it near me?) or address (where is it?), but also takes into consideration network capabilities of the device and the state it's in when you contact it. In this chapter, you'll learn some methods for giving physical objects network identities. You'll also learn ways that devices on a network can learn each other's capabilities though the messages they send and the protocols they use.

◀◀ **Sniff, a toy for sight-impaired children, by Sara Johansson.**
The dog's nose contains an RFID reader. When he detects RFID-tagged objects, he gives sound and tactile feedback, a unique response for each object. Designed by Sara Johansson, a student in the Tangible Interaction course at the Oslo School of Architecture and Design, under the instruction of tutors Timo Arnall and Mosse Sjaastad. *Photo courtesy of Sara Johansson.*

❝ Physical Identification

The process of identifying physical objects is such a fundamental part of our experience that we seldom think about how we do it. We use our senses, of course: we look at, feel, pick up, shake and listen to, smell, and taste objects until we have a reference for them — then we give them a label. The whole process relies on some pretty sophisticated work by our brains and bodies, and anyone who's ever dabbled in computer vision or artificial intelligence in general can tell you that teaching a computer to recognize physical objects is no small feat. Just as it's easier to determine location by having a human being narrow it down for you, it's easier to distinguish objects computationally if you can limit the field, and if you can label the important objects.

Just as we identify things using information from our senses, so do computers. They can identify physical objects only by using information from their sensors. Two of the best-known digital identification techniques are optical recognition and radio frequency identification, or RFID. Optical recognition can take many forms, from video color tracking and shape recognition to the ubiquitous bar code. Once an object has been recognized by a computer, the computer can give it an address on the network.

The network identity of a physical object can be centrally assigned and universally available, or it can be provisional. It can be used only by a small subset of devices on a larger network or used only for a short time. RFID is an interesting case in point. The RFID tag pasted on the side of a book may seem like a universal marker, but what it means depends on who reads it. The owner of a store may assign that tag's number a place in his inventory, but to the consumer who buys it, it means nothing unless she has a tool to read it and a database in which to categorize it. She has no way of knowing what the number meant to the store owner unless she has access to his database. Perhaps he linked that ID tag number to the book's title, or to the date on which it arrived in the store. Once it leaves the store, he may delete it from his database, so it loses all meaning to him. The consumer, on the other hand, may link it to entirely different data in her own database, or she may choose to ignore it entirely, relying on other means to identify it. In other words, there is no central database linking RFID tags and the things they're attached to, or who's possessed them.

Like locations, identities become more uniquely descriptive as the context they describe becomes larger. For example, knowing that my name is Tom doesn't give you much to go on. Knowing my last name narrows it down some more, but how effective that is depends on where you're looking. In the United States, there are dozens of Tom Igoes. In New York, there are at least three. When you need a unique identifier, you might choose a universal label, like using my Social Security number, or you might choose a provisional label, like calling me "Frank's son Tom." Which you choose depends on your needs in a given situation. Likewise, you may choose to identify physical objects on a network using universal identifiers, or you might choose to use provisional labels in a given temporary situation.

The capabilities assigned to an identifier can be fluid as well. Taking the RFID example again: in the store, a given tag's number might be enough to set off alarms at the entrance gates or to cause a cash register to add a price to your total purchase. In another store, that same tag might be assigned no capabilities at all, even if it's using the same protocol as other tags in the store. Confusion can set in when different contexts use similar identifiers. Have you ever left a store with a purchase and tripped the alarm, only to be waved on by the clerk who forgot to deactivate the tag on your purchase? Try walking into a Barnes & Noble bookstore with jeans you just bought at a Gap store and you're likely to trip the alarms because the two companies use the same RFID tags, but don't always set their security systems to filter out tags that are not in their inventory.

Video color recognition in Processing, using the code in Project 21. This simple sketch works well with vibrantly pink monkeys.

Video Identification

All video identification relies on the same basic method: the computer reads a camera's image and stores it as a two-dimensional array of pixels. Each pixel has a characteristic brightness and color that can be measured using any one of a number of palettes: red-green-blue is a common scheme for video and screen-based applications, as is hue-saturation-value. Cyan-magenta-yellow-black is common in print applications. The properties of the pixels, taken as a group, form patterns of color, brightness, and shape. When those patterns resemble other patterns in the computer's memory, it can identify those patterns as objects.

Color Recognition

Recognizing objects by color is a relatively simple process, if you know that the color you're looking for is unique in the camera's image. This technique is used in film and television production to make superheroes fly. The actor is filmed against a screen of a unique color, usually green, as green isn't a natural color for human skin. Then the pixels of that color are removed, and the image is combined with a background image.

Color identification can be an effective way to track physical objects in a controlled environment. Assuming that you've got a limited number of objects in the camera's view, and each object's color is unique and doesn't change as the lighting conditions change, you can identify each object reasonably well. Even slight changes in lighting can change the color of a pixel, however, so lighting conditions need to be tightly controlled, as the following project illustrates.
x

Color Recognition Using a Webcam

In this project, you'll get a firsthand look at how computer vision works. The Processing sketch shown here uses a video camera to generate a digital image, looks for pixels of a specific color, and then marks them on the copy of the image that it displays onscreen for you. Processing has a video library that enables you to capture the image from a webcam attached to your computer and manipulate the pixels.

> **MATERIALS**
>
> » **Personal computer with USB or FireWire port**
> » **USB or FireWire webcam**
> » **Colored objects**

The following Processing sketch is an example of color tracking using the video library. To use this, you'll need to have a camera attached to your computer, and have the drivers installed. The one you used in Chapter 3 for the cat camera should do the job fine. You'll also need some small colored objects. Stickers or toy balls can work well.

First, import the video library and write a program to read the camera. Every time a new frame of video is available, the video library generates a captureEvent. You can use this to read the video, then paint it to the stage:

Run this sketch and you should see yourself onscreen.

```
/*
    Color Sensor
    Language: Processing
*/
import processing.video.*;

Capture myCamera;                    // instance of the Capture class

void setup()
{
  // set window size:
  size(320, 240);

  // List all available capture devices. Macintoshes generally
  // identify three cameras, and the first or second is the built-in
  // iSight of the laptops.  Windows machines need a webcam
  // installed before you can run this program.
  println(Capture.list());

  // capture from the second device in the list (in my case,
  // my iSight).
  //
  // change this to match your own camera:
  String myCam = Capture.list()[1];
  myCamera = new Capture(this, myCam, width, height, 30);
}
```

»

Continued from opposite page.

```
void draw(){
  // draw the current frame of the camera on the screen:
  image(myCamera, 0, 0);
}


void captureEvent(Capture myCamera) {
  // read the myCamera and update the pixel array:
  myCamera.read();
}
```

▸▸ Now, add a method to capture the color of a pixel at the mouse location. First, add two new global variables at the top of the program for the target color and the pixel location where you find it:

```
color targetColor = color(255,0,0);    // the initial color to find
int[] matchingPixel = new int[2];       // matching pixel's coordinate
```

▸▸ Then add the following mouse Released() method at the end of the sketch:

```
/* when the mouse is clicked, capture the
 color of the pixel at the mouse location
 to use as the tracking color:
*/
void mouseReleased() {
  // get the color of the mouse position's pixel:
  targetColor = myCamera.pixels[mouseY*width+mouseX];
  // get the pixel location
  matchingPixel[0] = mouseX;
  matchingPixel[1] = mouseY;
}
```

▸▸ Then add two lines of code at the end of the draw() method to draw the ball:

When you run the sketch this time, you can click anywhere on the image and you'll get a dot at that location matching the color of the video at the spot.

```
// draw a dot at the matchingPixel:
fill(targetColor);
ellipse(matchingPixel[0], matchingPixel[1], 10, 10);
```

▸▸ To find other colors matching this color, you have to scan through all the pixels in the image to see which one's red, blue, and green matches yours. To do this, add a method called findColor() that takes the target color as a parameter, and returns the pixel matching that color as a return value:

```
int[] findColor(color thisColor) {
  // initialize the matching position with impossible numbers:
  int[] bestPixelYet = {
    -1,-1 };
  // intialize the smallest acceptable color difference:
  float smallestDifference = 1000.0;

  // scan over the pixels  to look for a pixel
  // that matches the target color:
  for(int row=0; row<height; row++) {
```

»

Continued from previous page.

```
for(int column=0; column<width; column++) { //for each column
  //get the color of this pixel
  // find pixel in linear array using formula:
  // pos = row*rowWidth+column
  color pixelColor = myCamera.pixels[row*width+column];

  // determine the difference between this pixel's color
  // and the target color:
  float diff = abs(red(targetColor) - red(pixelColor)) +
    abs(green(targetColor) - green(pixelColor)) +
    abs(blue(targetColor) - blue(pixelColor))/3;

  // if this is closest to our target color, take note of it:
  if (diff<= smallestDifference){
    smallestDifference = diff;
    // save the position so you can return it:
    bestPixelYet[0] = row;
    bestPixelYet[1] = column;
  }
 }
}
return bestPixelYet;
}
```

▶▶ Add these lines to the end of captureEvent():

```
// look for a pixel matching the target color
matchingPixel = findColor(targetColor);
```

For the sketch in its entirety, see Appendix C.

“ As you can see when you run it, it's not the most robust color tracker! You can get it to be more precise by controlling the image and the lighting very carefully. Day-Glo colors under ultraviolet fluorescent lighting tend to be the easiest to track, but they lock you into a very specific visual aesthetic. Objects that produce their own light are easier to track, especially if you put a filter on the camera to block out stray light. A black piece of 35mm film negative (if you can still find 35mm film!) works well as a visible light filter, blocking most everything but infrared light. Two polarizers, placed so that their polarizing axes are perpendicular, also work well. Infrared LEDs track very well through this kind of filter, as do incandescent flashlight lamps. Regular LEDs don't always work well as color tracking objects, unless they're relatively dim.

Brighter LEDs tend to show up as white in a camera image because their brightness overwhelms the camera.

Color recognition doesn't have to be done with a camera. There are color sensors that can do the same job. Parallax (www.parallax.com) sells a color sensor, the TAOS TCS230. This sensor contains four photodiodes, three of which are covered with color filters, and the fourth of which is not, so it can read red, green, blue, and white light. It outputs the intensity of all four channels as a changing pulse width.

Challenges of Identifying Physical Tokens

Designer Durrell Bishop's marble telephone answering machine is an excellent example of the challenges of identifying physical tokens. With every new message the machine receives, it drops a marble into a tray on the front of the machine. The listener hears the messages played back by placing a marble on the machine's "play" tray. Messages are erased and the marbles recycled when the marble is dropped back into the machine's hopper. Marbles become physical tokens representing the messages, making it very easy to tell at a glance how many messages there are.

Bishop tried many different methods to reliably identify and categorize physical tokens representing the messages:

> "I first made a working version with a motor and large screw (like a vending machine delivery mechanism), with pieces of paper tickets hung on the screw and had different color gray levels on the back. When it got a new message the machine read the next gray before it rotated once and dropped the ticket.
>
> It was a bit painful so I bought beads and stuffed resistors in to the hole which was capped (soldered) with sticky backed copper tape. When I went to Apple and worked with Jonathan Cohen we built a properly hacked version for the Mac with networked bar codes.
>
> Later again with Jonathan but this time at Interval Research, we used the Dallas ID chips."

Color by itself isn't enough to give you identity in most cases, but there are ways in which you can design a system to use color as a marker of physical identity. However, it has its limitations. In order to tell the marbles apart, Bishop could have used color recognition to read the marbles, but that would limit the design in at least two ways. First, there would be no way to tell the difference between multiple marbles of the same color. If, for example, he wanted to use color to identify the different people who received messages on the same answering machine, there would then be no way to tell the difference between multiple messages for each person. Second, the system would be limited by the number of colors between which the color recognition can reliably differentiate.

Shape and Pattern Recognition

Recognizing a color is relatively simple computationally, but recognizing a physical object is more challenging. To do this, you need to know the two-dimensional geometry of the object from every angle, so that you can compare any view you get of the object.

A computer can't actually "see" in three dimensions using a single camera. The view it has of any object is just a two-dimensional shadow. Furthermore, it has no way of distinguishing one object from another in the camera view without some visual reference. The computer has no concept of a physical object. It can only compare patterns. It can rotate the view, stretch it, and do all kinds of mathematical transformations on the pixel array, but the computer doesn't understand an object as a discrete entity the same way a human does. It just matches patterns. You could use two or more cameras to get a stereoscopic view, or write an AI program to give the computer a concept of a physical object, but a simpler solution is usually to restrict the view to a single two-dimensional plane, and to simplify the pattern. This is where bar codes come in handy.

Bar Code Recognition

A bar code (see Figure 9-1) is simply a pattern of dark and light lines or cells used to encode an alphanumeric string. A computer reads a bar code by scanning the image and interpreting the widths of the light and dark bands as zeroes or ones. This scanning can be done using a camera, or even a single photodiode, if the bar code can be passed over the photodiode at a constant speed. Many handheld bar code scanners work by having the user run a wand with an LED and a photodiode in the tip over the bar code, and reading the pattern of light and dark that the photodiode detects.

Figure 9-1
A one-dimensional bar code. This is the ISBN bar code for this book.

The best known bar code application is the Universal Product Code, or UPC, used by nearly every major manufacturer on the planet to label goods. There are many dozen different bar code symbologies, used for a wide range of applications. POSTNET is used by the U.S. Postal Service to automate mail sorting. European Article Numbering, or EAN, and Japanese Article Numbering, or JAN, are supersets of the UPC system developed to facilitate international exchange of goods. Each symbology represents a different mapping of bars to alphanumeric characters. The symbologies are not interchangeable, so you can't properly interpret a POSTNET bar code if you're using an EAN interpreter. This means that either you have to write a more comprehensive piece of software that can interpret several symbologies, or you have to know the symbology in advance if you want to get a reliable reading. There are numerous software libraries for generating bar codes, and even several bar code fonts for some of the more popular symbologies.

Bar codes such as the one shown earlier are called one-dimensional bar codes because the scanner or camera needs to read the image only along one axis. There are also two-dimensional bar codes that encode data in a two-dimensional matrix for more information density. As with

Figure 9-2
A two-dimensional bar code.

one-dimensional bar codes, there are a variety of symbologies. Figure 9-2 shows a typical two-dimensional bar code. This type of code, the QR (Quick Response) code, was originally created in Japan for tracking vehicle parts, but it's since become popular for all kinds of product labeling. The inclusion of software to read these tags on many camera phones in Japan has made the tags more popular. The following example uses an open source Java library to read QR codes in Processing. The Java library used here was originally developed for use with the Java 2 Mobile Edition (J2ME) on mobile phones.

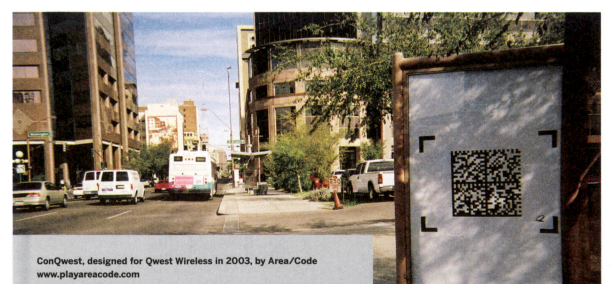

ConQwest, designed for Qwest Wireless in 2003, by Area/Code
www.playareacode.com

The first ever use of semacode, 2D bar codes scanned by phonecams. A city-wide treasure-hunt designed for high school students, players went through the city "shooting treasure" with Qwest phonecams and moving their totem pieces to capture territory. Online, a web site showed the players' locations and game progress, turning it into a spectacular audience-facing event.
Photo courtesy Area/Code and Kevin Slavin

2D Bar Code Recognition Using a Webcam

In this project, you'll generate some two-dimensional bar codes from text using an online QR Code generator. Then you'll decode your tags using a camera and a computer. Once this works, try decoding the QR Code illustrations in this book.

MATERIALS

» **Personal computer with USB or FireWire port**
» **USB or FireWire Webcam**
» **Printer**

This sketch reads QR Codes using a camera attached to a personal computer. The video component is very similar to the color tracking example earlier. Before you start on the sketch, though, you'll need some QR Codes to read. Fortunately, there are a number of QR Code generators available online. Just type the term into a search engine and see how many pop up. There's a good one at qrcode.kaywa.com, from which you can generate URLs, phone numbers, or plain text. The more text you enter, the larger the symbol is. Generate a few codes and print them out for use later. Save them as **.jpg** or **.png** files as well, because you'll need them for the sketch.

To run this sketch, you'll need to download the pqrcode library for Processing by Daniel Shiffman, It's based on the qrcode library from qrcode.sourceforge.jp. You can download the pqrcode library from www.shiffman.net/p5/pqrcode. Unzip it, and you'll get a directory called **pqrcode/**. Drop it into the **libraries/** subdirectory of your Processing application directory and restart Processing. Make a new sketch, and within the sketch's directory, make a subdirectory called **data/** and put the **.jpg** or **.png** files of the QR Codes that you generated earlier there. Now you're ready to begin writing the sketch.

▶▶ In the setup() for this sketch, you'll import the pqrcode and video libraries, initialize a few global variables, and establish a text font for printing on the screen:

```
/*
   QRCode reader
   Language: Processing
*/
import processing.video.*;
import pqrcode.*;

Capture video;                              // video capture object
String statusMsg = "Waiting for an image"; // a string for messages

// decoder object from prdecoder library
Decoder decoder;

// make sure to generate your own image here:
String testImageName = "qrcode.png";

void setup() {
  size(400, 320);
  video = new Capture(this, width, height-20, 30);
  // create a decoder object:
  decoder = new Decoder(this);

  // create a font with a font available to the system:
  PFont myFont = createFont(PFont.list()[2], 14);
  textFont(myFont);
}
```

⏩ The draw() method draws the camera image and prints a status message to the screen, and the captureEvent() updates the camera as in the previous project. Once you've entered this much, you can run the sketch to make sure that you got the libraries in the right places, and that the video works:

```
void draw() {
  background(0);

  // Display video
  image(video, 0, 0);
  // Display status
  text(statusMsg, 10, height-4);
}


void captureEvent(Capture video) {
  video.read();
}
```

⏩ The pqrcode library has a method called decodeImage(). In order to use it, you pass it an image. You'll do this in the keyReleased() method. A switch statement checks to see which key has been pressed. If you type f, it passes the decoder a file called **qrcode.png** from the **data/** subdirectory. If you press the spacebar, it passes the camera image. If you type s, it brings up a camera settings dialog box:

```
void keyReleased() {
  String code = "";
  // Depending on which key is hit, do different things:
  switch (key) {
  case ' ':            // Spacebar takes a picture and tests it:
    // copy it to the PImage savedFrame:
    PImage savedFrame = createImage(video.width,video.height,RGB);
    savedFrame.copy(video, 0,0,video.width,video.height,0,0,
      video.width,video.height);
    savedFrame.updatePixels();
    // Decode savedFrame
    decoder.decodeImage(savedFrame);
    break;
  case 'f':    // f runs a test on a file
    PImage preservedFrame = loadImage(testImageName);
    // Decode file
    decoder.decodeImage(preservedFrame);
    break;
  case 's':        // s opens the settings for this capture device:
    video.settings();
    break;
  }
}
```

⏩ Once you've given the decoder an image, you wait. When it's decoded the image, it generates a decoderEvent(), and you can read the tag's ID using the getDecodedString() method:

```
// When the decoder object finishes
// this method will be invoked.
void decoderEvent(Decoder decoder) {
  statusMsg = decoder.getDecodedString();
}
```

⏩ Finally, add an if() statement to the end of the draw() method to update the user as to the status of an image being decoded:

```
// If we are currently decoding
if (decoder.decoding()) {
  // Display the image being decoded
  PImage show = decoder.getImage();
```

»

Continued from opposite page.

```
image(show,0,0,show.width/4,show.height/4);
statusMsg = "Decoding image";
// fancy code for drawing dots as a progress bar:
for (int i = 0; i < (frameCount/2) % 10; i++)
{
  statusMsg += ".";
}
}
```

When you run this, notice how the **.jpg** or **.png** images scan much more reliably than the camera images. The distortion from the analog-to-digital conversion through the camera causes many errors. This error is made worse by poor optics or low-end camera imaging chips in mobile phones and web cams. Even with a good lens, if the code to be scanned isn't centered, the distortion at the edge of an image can throw off the pattern-recognition routine. You can improve the reliability of the scan by guiding the user to center the tag before taking an image. Even simple graphic hints like putting crop marks around the tag, as shown in Figure 9-3, can help. When you do this, users framing the image tend to frame to the crop marks, which ensures more space around the code, and a better scan. Methods like this help with any optical pattern recognition through a camera, whether it's one- or two-dimensional bar codess, or another type of pattern altogether.

Optical recognition forces one other limitation on you besides various limitations mentioned earlier: you have to be able to see the bar code. By now most of the world is familiar with bar codes, because they decorate everything we buy or ship. This limitation is not only aesthetic. If you've ever turned a box over and over looking for the bar code to scan, you know that it's also a functional limitation. A system that allowed for machine recognition of physical objects, but didn't rely on a line of sight to the identifying tag would be an improvement. This is one of the main reasons that RFID is beginning to supersede bar codes in inventory control and other ID applications.

Radio Frequency Identification

Like bar code recognition, RFID relies on tagging objects in order to identify them. Unlike bar codes, however, RFID tags don't need to be visible to be read. An RFID reader sends out a short-range radio signal, which is picked up by

Figure 9-3

A two-dimensional bar code (a QR Code, to be specific) with crop marks around it. The image parsers won't read the crop marks, but they help users center the tag for image capture.

an RFID tag. The tag then transmits back a short string of data. Depending on the size and sensitivity of the reader's antenna and the strength of the transmission, the tag can be several feet away from the reader, enclosed in a book, box, or item of clothing. In fact, some large clothing manufacturers are now sewing RFID tags into their merchandise, to be removed by the customer.

There are two types of RFID system: passive and active, just like distance ranging systems. Passive RFID tags contain an integrated circuit that has a basic radio transceiver and a small amount of nonvolatile memory. They are powered by the current that the reader's signal induces in their antennas. The received energy is just enough to power the tag to transmit its data once, and the signal is relatively weak. Most passive readers can only read tags a few inches to a few feet away.

In an active RFID system, the tag has its own power supply and radio transceiver, and transmits a signal in response to a received message from a reader. Active systems can transmit for a much longer range than passive systems, and are less error-prone. They are also much more expensive. If you're a regular automobile commuter and you have to pass through a toll gate in your commute, you're probably an active RFID user. Systems like E-ZPass use active RFID tags so that the reader can be placed several meters away from the tag.

You might think that because RFID is radio-based, you could use it to do radio distance ranging as well, but that's not the case. Neither passive nor active RFID systems are typically designed to report the signal strength received from the tag. Without this information, it's impossible to use RFID systems to determine the actual location of a tag. All the reader can tell you is that the tag is within reading range. Although some high-end systems can report the tag signal strength, the vast majority of readers are not made for location as well as identification.

RFID systems vary widely in cost. Active systems can cost tens of thousands of dollars to purchase and install. Commercial passive systems can also be expensive. A typical passive reader that can read a tag a meter away from the antenna typically costs a few thousand dollars. At the low end, short-range passive readers can come as cheap as $30 or less. As of this writing, $100 gets you a reader that can read no more than a few inches. Anything that can read a longer distance will be more expensive.

There are many different RFID protocols, just as with bar codes. Short-range passive readers come in at least three common frequencies: two low-frequency bands at 125 and 134.2Khz, and high-frequency readers at 13.56MHz. The higher-frequency readers allow for faster read rates and longer-range reading distances. In addition to different frequencies, there are also different protocols. For example, in the 13.56 band alone, there are the ISO 15693 and ISO 14443 and 14443-A standards; within the ISO 15693 standard, there are different implementations by different manufacturers: Philips' I-Code, Texas Instruments' Tag-IT HF, Picotag, and implementations by Infineon, STMicro-

electronics, and others. Within the ISO 14443 standard, there's Philips' Mifare, Mifare UL, ST's SR176, and others. So you can't count on one reader to read every tag. You can't even count on one reader to read all the tags in a given frequency range. You have to match the tag to the reader.

There are a number of inexpensive and easy-to-use readers on the market now, covering the range of passive RFID frequencies and protocols. Parallax (www.parallax. com) sells a 125KHz reader that can read EM Microelectronic tags such as EM4001 tags. It has a built-in antenna, and the whole module is about 2.5" x 3.5", on a flat circuit board. ID Innovations makes a number of small low-frequency readers less than 1.5 inches on a side, capable of reading the EM4001 protocol tags. SparkFun (www.sparkfun.com) and CoreRFID (www.rfidshop.com) both sell the ID Innovations readers and matching tags. The ID Innovations readers and the Parallax readers can read the same tags. Trossen Robotics (www.trossenrobotics.com) sells a range of readers, the least expensive of which is the APSX RW-210, a 13.56MHz module that can read and write to tags using the ISO 15693 protocol. Trossen's also got a wide range of tags for everyone's readers, including the EM tags that match the Parallax and ID Innovations readers. SkyeTek (www.skyetek.com) makes a number of small readers like the M1 and the M1-mini that operate in the 13.56MHz range as well. Though their readers are moderately priced, SkyeTek generally doesn't sell them until you've bought their development kit, which is priced considerably higher. Texas Instruments (www.ti.com/rfid/shtml/rfid.shtml) makes a 134.2KHz reader, the RI-STU-MRD1. The Texas Instruments reader and the SkyeTek readers are the only ones mentioned here that don't come with a built-in antenna. You can make your own, however, and TI helpfully provides advice on how to do it in the reader's data sheet.

RFID tags come in a number of different forms, as shown in Figure 9-4: sticker tags, coin discs, key fobs, credit cards, playing cards, even capsules designed for injection under the skin. The last are used for pet tracking and are not designed for human use, though there are some adventurous hackers who have had these tags inserted under their own skin. Like any radio signal, RFID can be read through a number of materials, but is blocked by any kind of RF shielding, like wire mesh, conductive fabric lamé, metal foil, or adamantium skeletons. This feature means that you can embed it in all kinds of projects, as long as your reader has the signal strength to penetrate.

Before picking a reader, think about the environment in which you plan to deploy it, and how that affects both the tags and the reading. Will the environment have a lot of RF noise? In what range? Consider a reader outside that range. Will you need a relatively long-range read? If so, look at the high-frequency readers, if possible. If you're planning to read existing tags rather than tags you purchase yourself, research carefully in advance, because not all readers will read all tags. Pet tags can be some of the trickiest, as many of them operate in the 134.2KHz range, in which there are fewer readers to choose from.

In picking a reader, you also have to consider how it behaves when tags are in range. For example, even though the Parallax reader and the ID Innovations readers can read the same tags, they behave very differently when a tag is in range. The ID Innovations reader reports the tag ID only once. The Parallax reader reports it continually until the tag is out of range. The behavior of the reader can affect your project design, as you'll see later on.

All of the readers mentioned here have TTL serial interfaces, so they can be connected to a microcontroller or a

Figure 9-4
RFID tags in all shapes and sizes.

> ⚠ **Most RFID capsules are not sanitized for internal use in animals (humans included), and they're definitely not designed to be inserted without qualified medical supervision. Besides, insertion hurts. Don't RFID-enable yourself or your friends. Don't even do it to your pets—let your vet do it for you. If you're really gung-ho to be RFID-tagged, make yourself a nice set of RFID tag earrings.**

USB-to-serial module very easily. Sketches in Processing for the APSX reader, the Parallax reader, and the ID Innovations reader follow. All of these readers have a similar operating scheme. The APSX is the only one you need to send a serial command to; all of the others simply transmit a tag ID whenever a tag is in range.

X

Reading RFID Tags in Processing

In this project, you'll read some RFID tags and get a sense of how the readers behave. You'll see how far away from your reader a tag can be read. This is a handy test program for use any time you're adding RFID to a project.

The Circuits
The circuits for all three readers are fairly similar. Connect the module to 5V and ground, and connect the reader's serial transmit line to the serial adaptor's serial receive line, and vice versa. For the Parallax reader, you'll also need to attach the enable pin to ground. For the ID12, connect the reset pin to 5V, and connect an LED from the Card Present pin to ground as well. Figures 9-6, 9-7, and 9-8 show the circuits for the Parallax, ID Innovations, and ASPX readers, respectively.

Parallax RFID Reader
The Parallax reader is the simplest of the three readers to read. It communicates serially at 2400 bps. When the Enable pin is held low, it sends a reading whenever a tag is in range. The tag ID is a 12-byte string starting with a carriage return (ASCII 13) and finishing with a newline (ASCII 10). The ten digits in the middle are the unique tag ID. The EM4001 tags format their tag IDs as ASCII-encoded hexadecimal values, so the string will never contain anything but the ASCII digits 0 through 9 and the letters A through F.

MATERIALS

» **RFID reader** Either the RFID Reader Module from Parallax, part number 28140; the ID Innovations ID-12 from CoreRFID or from SparkFun as part number SEN-08419; or the APSX RW-210 from Trossen Robotics.
» **Two 2mm female header rows** If you're using the ID12 reader, you'll need Samtec (www.samtec.com) part number MMS-110-01-L-SV. Samtec, like many part makers, supplies free samples of this part in small quantities. SparkFun sells these as part number PRT-08272. They also sell a breakout board for the module, part number SEN-08423.
» **RFID tags** Get the tags that match your reader. All three of the retailers listed earlier in this list sell tags that match their readers in a variety of physical packages, so choose the ones you like the best.
» **1 USB-to-TTL serial adaptor** SparkFun's BOB-00718 from Chapter 2 can do the job. If you use a USB-to-RS232 adaptor such as a Keyspan or logear dongle, refer to Chapter 2 for the schematics to convert RS-232-to-5V TTL serial.

Try It The following sketch waits for twelve serial bytes, strips out the carriage return and the newline, and prints the rest to the screen:

```
/*
 Parallax RFID Reader
 language: Processing
*/

// import the serial library:
import processing.serial.*;

Serial myPort;      // the serial port you're using
String tagID = "";  // the string for the tag ID

void setup() {
  size(600,200);
```
»

Figure 9-6
The Parallax RFID reader connected to an FTDI USB-to-serial adaptor.

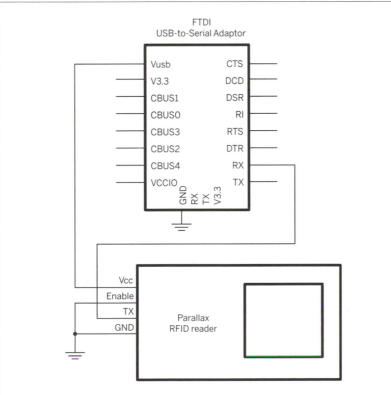

Continued from previous page.

```
  // list all the serial ports:
  println(Serial.list());

  // based on the list of serial ports printed from the
  // previous command, change the 0 to your port's number:
  String portnum = Serial.list()[0];
  // initialize the serial port:
  myPort = new Serial(this, portnum, 2400);
  // incoming string from reader will have 12 bytes:
  myPort.buffer(12);

  // create a font with the third font available to the system:
  PFont myFont = createFont(PFont.list()[2], 24);
  textFont(myFont);
}

void draw() {
  // clear the screen:
  background(0);
  // print the string to the screen:
  text(tagID, width/4, height/2 - 24);
}

/*
 this method reads bytes from the serial port
 and puts them into the tag string.
 It trims off the \r and \n
 */
void serialEvent(Serial myPort) {
  tagID = trim(myPort.readString());
}
```

ID Innovations ID12 Reader

The ID Innovations reader (see Figure 9-7) is slightly more complex than the Parallax reader. It operates at 9600 bps. It has an output pin that goes high when a tag is present, which is a handy way to know if it's reading your tag, even if you haven't got it connected to anything. It reads the same tags as the Parallax reader, but doesn't format the data the same way. All the ID Innovations readers use the same protocol. It starts with a start-of-transmission (STX) byte (ASCII 02) and ends with an end-of-transmission (ETX) byte (ASCII 03). The STX is followed by the ten-byte tag ID. A checksum follows that, then a carriage return (ASCII 13) and linefeed (ASCII 10), then the ETX. The EM4001 tags format their tag IDs as ASCII-encoded hexadecimal values, so the string will never contain anything but the ASCII digits 0 through 9 and the letters A through F.

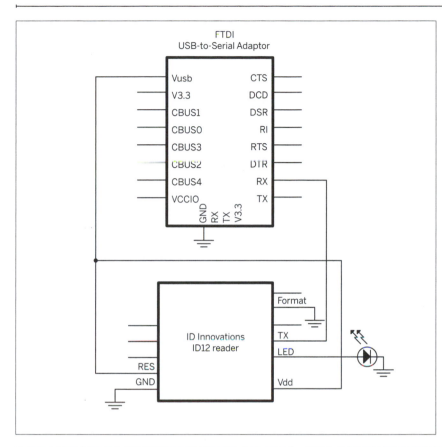

FTDI
USB-to-Serial Adaptor

Vusb	CTS
V3.3	DCD
CBUS1	DSR
CBUS0	RI
CBUS3	RTS
CBUS2	DTR
CBUS4	RX
VCCIO	TX

GND RX TX V3.3

ID Innovations
ID12 reader

Format

TX

LED

RES

GND

Vdd

Figure 9-7
The ID Innovations ID12 RFID reader attached to an FTDI USB-to-serial adaptor. The ID12 has pins spaced 2mm apart, so you'll need to solder wires onto them to fit them on a breadboard. You can also use the 2mm female sockets used with the XBee modules, or you can use SparkFun's breakout board.

The sketch shown here is a modification of the Parallax sketch, with a new method, parseString(). It reads the entire string, confirms that the start and end bytes are there, and strips out all but the ten-byte tag ID. The changes to the previous sketch are shown in blue:

```
/*
ID Innovations RFID Reader
language: Processing

*/

// import the serial library:
import processing.serial.*;

Serial myPort;      // the serial port you're using
String tagID = "";  // the string for the tag ID

void setup() {
  size(600,200);
  // list all the serial ports:
  println(Serial.list());

  // based on the list of serial ports printed from the
  // previous command, change the 0 to your port's number:
  String portnum = Serial.list()[0];
  // initialize the serial port:
  myPort = new Serial(this, portnum, 9600);
  // incoming string from reader will have 16 bytes:
  myPort.buffer(16);

  // create a font with the third font available to the system:
  PFont myFont = createFont(PFont.list()[2], 24);
  textFont(myFont);
}

void draw() {
  // clear the screen:
  background(0);
  // print the string to the screen:
  text(tagID, width/4, height/2 - 24);
}

/*
 this method reads bytes from the serial port
 and puts them into the tag string
 */

void serialEvent(Serial myPort) {
  // get the serial input buffer in a string:
  String inputString = myPort.readString();
  // filter out the tag ID from the string:
  tagID = parseString(inputString);
}
```

»

Continued from opposite page.

```
/*
  This method reads a string and looks for the 10-byte
  tag ID. It assumes that it gets an STX byte (0x02)
  at the beginning and an ETX byte (0x03) at the end.
*/
String parseString(String thisString) {
  String tagString = "";    // string to put the tag ID into

  // first character of the input:
  char firstChar = thisString.charAt(0);
  // last character of the input:
  char lastChar = thisString.charAt(thisString.length() -1);

  // if the first char is STX (0x02) and the last char is ETX (0x03),
  // then put the next ten bytes into the tag string:
  if ((firstChar == 0x02) && (lastChar == 0x03)) {
    tagString = thisString.substring(1, 11);
  }
  return tagString;
}
```

APSX RW-210 Reader

The APSX reader (Figure 9-8) has a totally different format than the previous two. First, you have to send it a command byte to start it reading. You can send it either a byte of value 250 (0xFA), which causes it to read once, or a byte of value 251 (0xFB), which causes it to read continually. The read-once option saves power, as it powers the reader down once a tag is read. The tag ID returned is 12 bytes long. The byte values are not limited to alphanumeric values, so the following sketch converts them to ASCII-encoded hexadecimal values and separates them by spaces for easy reading. Despite the different format, the code is very similar to the Parallax reader sketch.

Try It Changes from the Parallax reader sketch are shown in blue:

```
/*
 APSX RFID Reader
 language: Processing

*/

// import the serial library:
import processing.serial.*;

Serial myPort;       // the serial port you're using
String tagID = "";  // the string for the tag ID

void setup() {
  size(600,200);
  // list all the serial ports:
  println(Serial.list());
```

»

Continued from previous page.

```
  // based on the list of serial ports printed from the
  // previous command, change the 0 to your port's number:
  String portnum = Serial.list()[0];
  // initialize the serial port:
  myPort = new Serial(this, portnum, 19200);
  // incoming string from reader will have 12 bytes:
  myPort.buffer(12);

  // create a font with the third font available to the system:
  PFont myFont = createFont(PFont.list()[2], 24);
  textFont(myFont);

  // send the continual read command:
  myPort.write(0xFB);
}

void draw() {
  // clear the screen:
  background(0);
  // print the string to the screen:
  text(tagID, width/8, height/2 - 24);
}

/*
  this method reads bytes from the serial port
  and puts them into the tag string
*/
  void serialEvent(Serial myPort) {
    int thisByte = 0;
    tagID = "";
    while(myPort.available() > 0) {
      int newByte = myPort.read();
      tagID += hex(newByte, 2);
      tagID += " ";
    }
}
```

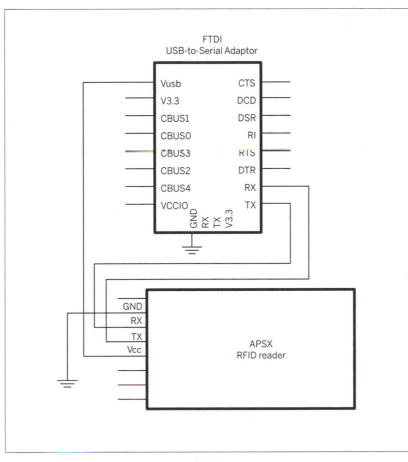

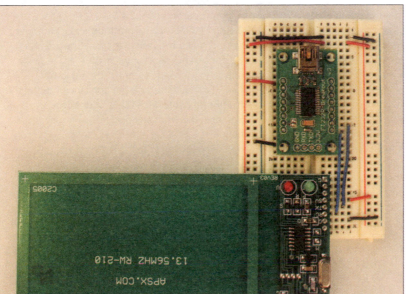

Figure 9-8
The APSX RW-210 RFID reader
attached to an FTDI USB-to-serial
adaptor.

RFID Meets Home Automation

Between my officemate and me, we have dozens of devices drawing power in our office: two laptops, two monitors, four or five lamps, a few hard drives, a soldering iron, Ethernet hubs, speakers, and so forth. Even when we're not here, the room is drawing a lot of power. What devices are turned on at any given time depends largely on which of us is here, and what we're doing. This project is a system to reduce our power consumption, particularly when we're not there.

When either of us comes into the room, all we have to do is throw our keys on a side table by the door, and the room turns on or off what we normally use. Each of us has a key ring with an RFID-tag key fob. The key table has an RFID reader in it, and reads the presence or absence of the tags.

The reader is connected to a microcontroller module that communicates over the AC power lines using the X10 protocol. Each of the various power strips is plugged into an X10 appliance module. Depending on which tag is read, the microcontroller knows which modules to turn on or off. Figure 9-9 shows the system.

The Circuit

The RFID module is connected to the microcontroller as you might expect: the module's transmit pin connects to the microcontroller's receive. It's basically the same circuit as shown in the previous project with the X10 module added. The X10 interface module connects to the microcontroller via the phone cable. Clip one end of the cable and solder headers onto the four wires. Then connect them to the microcontroller as shown in Figure 9-10. The schematic shows the phone jack (an RJ-11 jack) on the interface module as you're looking at it from the bottom. Make sure the wires at the header ends correspond with the pins on the jack from right to left.

MATERIALS

» **1 solderless breadboard** such as Digi-Key (www.digikey.com) part number 438-1045-ND, or Jameco (www.jameco.com) part number 20601. For the photos in this example, I used an Arduino-compatible Protoshield module from SparkFun, part number DEV-07914.

» **1 Arduino module** or other microcontroller

» **RFID reader** Either the RFID Reader Module from Parallax, part number 28140; the ID Innovations ID-12 from CoreRFID or SparkFun part number SEN-08419; or the APSX RW-210 from Trossen Robotics.

» **Two 2mm female header rows** if you're using the ID12 reader, Samtec part number MMS-110-01-L-SV. Samtec, like many part makers, supplies free samples of this part in small quantities. SparkFun sells these as part number PRT-08272. They also sell a breakout board for the module, SparkFun part number SEN-08423.

» **RFID tags** Get the tags that match your reader. All three of the retailers listed sell tags that match their readers in a variety of physical packages, so choose the ones you like the best.

» **Interface module: X10 One-Way Interface Module** from Smarthome (www.smarthome.com), part number 1134B.

» **2 X10 modules** *Either:* 2 Appliance Modules from Smarthome, part number 2002, or 2 Powerhouse X10 Lamp Modules from Smarthome, part number 2000. You'll need two modules total. Choose one of each, or two of one as you see fit. If you're going to control only incandescent lamps, get lamp modules. For anything else, get appliance modules.

» **4-wire phone cable with RJ-11 connector** You can take this from any discarded phone, or get one at your local electronics shop.

I used an extra few inches of the phone cable to make an extension cable for the RFID reader. You may or may not need to, depending on how you plan to enclose the electronics. Separating the two makes it easier to hide the microcontroller and reader in two separate places, so the antenna can get closer to what you need to read.

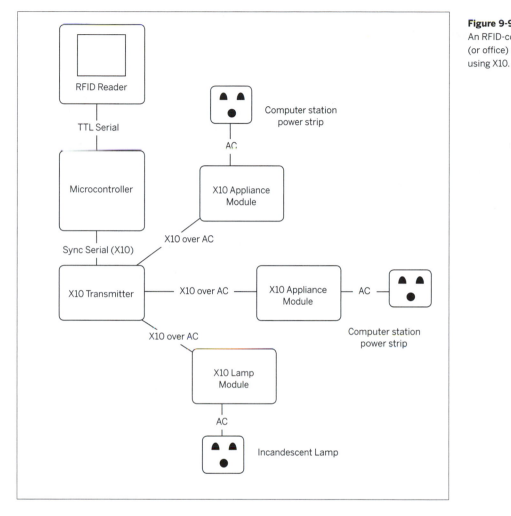

Figure 9-9
An RFID-controlled home
(or office) automation system
using X10.

To send X10 commands, use the X10 library for Arduino. You can download it from www.arduino.cc/en/Tutorial/ X10. Unzip it and place the resulting directory in the **lib/ targets/libraries/** subdirectory of your Arduino application directory. Then restart the Arduino program.

X10 device addresses have a two-tier structure. There are 16 house codes, labeled A through P, and within each house code, you can have 16 individual units. These are assigned unit codes. Each X10 module has two click-wheels to set the house code and the unit code. For this project, get at least two appliance or lamp modules. Set the first module to house code A, unit 1, and the second code A, unit 2.

NOTE: The X10 library may be already included with later versions of Arduino, after version 0009. Check the Arduino website at **www.arduino.cc** to be sure.

The Code

Once you've got the circuit connected, program the micro-controller to read the RFID tags, just to make sure that works. A test sketch is shown next.

NOTE: You'll probably need to disconnect the serial line between the RFID reader and the Arduino in order to program the module, as you did with the XPort and XBee modules in earlier chapters.

NOTE: You also need to set the serial monitor speed to 2400 bps to match the speed this program uses. The default for the Arduino serial monitor is 9600, and you can change it from a pop-up menu in the serial monitor.

What is X10?

X10 is a communications protocol that works over AC power lines. It's designed for use in home automation. Companies such as Smarthome (www.smarthome.com) and X10.com (www.x10.com) sell various devices that communicate over power lines using X10: cameras, motion sensors, switch control panels, and more. It's a slow and limited protocol, but has been popular with home automation enthusiasts for years, because the equipment is relatively inexpensive and easy to obtain.

X10 is basically a synchronous serial protocol, like I2C and SPI. Instead of sending bits every time a master clock signal changes, X10 devices send a bit every time the AC power line crosses zero volts. This means that X10's maximum data rate is 120 bits per second in the U.S., as the AC signal crosses the zero point twice per cycle, and AC signals are 60Hz in the U.S. The protocol is tricky to program if you have to do it yourself, but many microcontroller development systems include libraries to send X10 signals.

There are four devices that come in handy for developing X10 projects: an interface module, an appliance control module, a lamp control module, and a control panel module. You'll be building your own controllers, but the control panel module is useful as a diagnostic tool, because it already works. When you can't get the appliance or lamp modules to respond to your own projects, you can at least get them to respond to the control panel module — that way, you know whether the bits are passing over the power lines. Smarthome sells versions of all four of these:

- Interface module: X10 One-Way Interface Module, part number 1134B. You'll see two common versions of this, the PL513 and the TW523. They both work essentially the same way. The TW523 is a two-way module, and can send and receive X10 signals, while the PL513 can only send.

- Appliance control module: X10 Appliance Module 3-Pin, part number 2002. These can control anything you can plug into an AC socket, up to 15 Amps.

- Lamp control module: Powerhouse X10 Lamp Module, part number 2000. These can control only incandescent (not fluorescent or neon) lamps.

- Control panel module: X10 Mini Controller, part number 4030

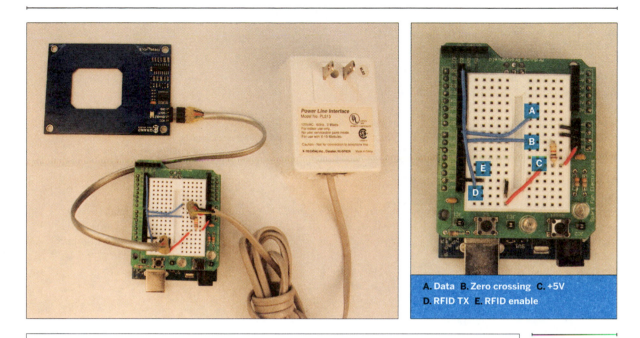

A. Data B. Zero crossing C. +5V
D. RFID TX E. RFID enable

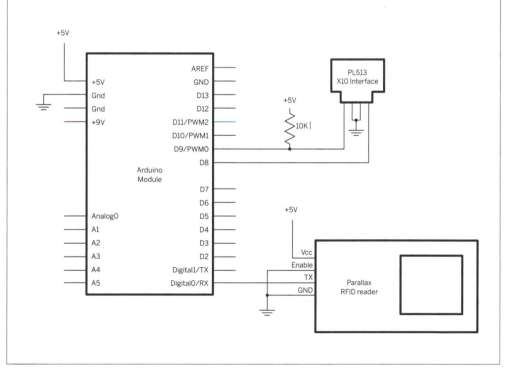

Figure 9-10
The circuit for
the RFID-to-X10
project. The detail
shows the con-
nections on the
breadboard.

Test It   This sketch reads in bytes similar to the Processing sketches earlier. The readByte() method does all the work with the serial data. It reads the first byte, and if it's the correct value, it resets an array called tagID. It saves the next ten bytes into the array. When it gets the final byte, it changes a variable called tagComplete so that the rest of the program knows it can use the tag array. You can use the same code for the Parallax reader or the ID Innovations reader; all you have to do is change the startByte and endByte values and the data rate.

```
/*
RFID Reader
language: Wiring/Arduino

*/

#define tagLength 10    // each tag ID contains 10 bytes
#define startByte 0x0A  // for the ID Innovations reader, use 0x02
#define endByte 0x0D    // for the ID Innovations reader, use 0x03
#define dataRate 2400   // for the ID Innovations reader, use 9600


char tagID[tagLength];        // array to hold the tag you read
int tagIndex = 0;             // counter for number of bytes read
int tagComplete = false;      // whether the whole tag's been read

void setup() {
  // begin serial:
  Serial.begin(dataRate);
}

void loop() {
  // read in and parse serial data:
  if (Serial.available() > 0) {
    readByte();
  }
  if(tagComplete == true) {

    Serial.println(tagID);
  }
}

/*
  This method reads the bytes, and puts the
  appropriate ones in the tagID

 */
void readByte() {
  char thisChar = Serial.read();
Serial.print(thisChar, HEX);
  switch (thisChar) {
  case startByte:      // start character
    // reset the tag index counter
    tagIndex = 0;
    break;
  case endByte:           // end character
    tagComplete = true;  // you have the whole tag
    break;
  default:                // any other character
    tagComplete = false; // there are still more bytes to read
    // add the byte to the tagID
```

»

Continued from opposite page.

```
    if (tagIndex < tagLength) {
      tagID[tagIndex] = thisChar;
      // increment the tag byte counter
      tagIndex++;
    }
    break;
  }
}
```

▸▸ When you know that works, run this sketch to test the X10:

```
/*
 X10 test
 language: Wiring/Arduino

*/
// include the X10 library files:
#include <x10.h>
#include <x10constants.h>

#define zcPin 9          // the zero crossing detect pin
#define dataPin 8        // the X10 data out pin
#define repeatTimes 1    // how many times to repeat each X10 message
                         // in an electrically noisy environment, you
                         // can set this higher.

// set up a new x10 library instance:
x10 myHouse =  x10(zcPin, dataPin);

void setup() {
  // turn off all lights:
  myHouse.write(A, ALL_UNITS_OFF,repeatTimes);
}

void loop() {
      // turn on first module:
      myHouse.write(A, UNIT_1,repeatTimes);
      myHouse.write(A, ON,repeatTimes);
      myHouse.write(A, UNIT_2,repeatTimes);
      myHouse.write(A, OFF,repeatTimes);
    delay(500);
      // turn on second module:
      myHouse.write(A, UNIT_1,repeatTimes);
      myHouse.write(A, OFF,repeatTimes);
      myHouse.write(A, UNIT_2,repeatTimes);
      myHouse.write(A, ON,repeatTimes);
      delay(500);


}
```

It's unlikely that this will work the first time. X10 is notorious for having synchronization problems, and it doesn't work when the transmitter and receiver are on different circuits. Some of the more expensive surge protectors might filter out X10 as well. If your lights don't turn on correctly, start by unplugging everything, then set the addresses, then plug everything in, then reset the Arduino. If that fails, make sure that your units are on the same circuit, and eliminate surge protectors, if you're using them. Try to turn the modules using a control panel module. Once you've got control over your modules, you can combine the RFID and the X10 programs.

Refine It First, combine the initialization and setup routines like so (be sure to set tagOne and tagTwo to the values of your tags):

```
/*
 RFID –to-X10 translator
 language: Wiring/Arduino

*/

// include the X10 library files:
#include <x10.h>
#include <x10constants.h>

#define zcPin 9          // the zero crossing detect pin
#define dataPin 8        // the X10 data out pin
#define repeatTimes 1    // how many times to repeat each X10 message
                         // in an electrically noisy environment, you
                         // can set this higher.

#define tagLength 10     // each tag ID contains 10 bytes
#define startByte 0x0A   // for the ID Innovations reader, use 0x02
#define endByte 0x0D     // for the ID Innovations reader, use 0x03
#define dataRate 2400    // for the ID Innovations reader, use 9600

// set up a new x10  library instance:
x10 myHouse =  x10(zcPin, dataPin);

char tagID[tagLength];         // array to hold the tag you read
int tagIndex = 0;              // counter for number of bytes read
int tagComplete = false;       // whether the whole tag's been read
char tagOne[] = "0415AB6FB7";  // put the values for your tags here
char tagTwo[] = "0415AB5DAF";
char lastTag = 0;              // value of the last tag read

void setup() {
  // begin serial:
  Serial.begin(dataRate);
  // turn off all lights:
  myHouse.write(A, ALL_LIGHTS_OFF,repeatTimes);
}
```

The loop() method is a bit more complex now. You need to add a block to compare the RFID tag to the two existing tag numbers. You'll call a method called compareTags() to do this. This method just iterates over the arrays and compares them byte by byte. Once you've got a match, you send the appropriate X10 commands. Here's the rest of the sketch:

```
void loop() {
  // read in and parse serial data:
  if (Serial.available() > 0) {
    readByte();
  }

  // if you've got a complete tag, compare your tag
  // to the existing values:

  if (tagComplete == true) {
    if (compareTags(tagID, tagOne) == true) {

      if (lastTag != 1) {
        // if the last tag wasn't this one,
        // send commands:
        myHouse.write(A, UNIT_1,repeatTimes);
        myHouse.write(A, ON,repeatTimes);
        myHouse.write(A, UNIT_2,repeatTimes);
        myHouse.write(A, OFF,repeatTimes);
        // note that this was the last tag read:
        lastTag = 1;
      }
    }
    if (compareTags(tagID, tagTwo) == true) {
      if (lastTag != 2) {
        // if the last tag wasn't this one,
        // send commands:
        myHouse.write(A, UNIT_1,repeatTimes);
        myHouse.write(A, OFF,repeatTimes);
        myHouse.write(A, UNIT_2,repeatTimes);
        myHouse.write(A, ON,repeatTimes);
        // note that this was the last tag read:
        lastTag = 2;
      }
    }
  }
}


/*
  this method compares two char arrays, byte by byte:
*/
char compareTags(char* thisTag, char* thatTag) {
  char match = true;  // whether they're the same

    for (int i = 0; i < tagLength; i++) {
    // if any two bytes don't match, the whole thing fails:
    if (thisTag[i] != thatTag[i]) {
      match = false;
    }
  }
  return match;
}
```

Continued from previous page.

```
/*
  This method reads the bytes, and puts the
  appropriate ones in the tagID

*/
void readByte() {
  char thisChar = Serial.read();

  switch (thisChar) {
  case startByte:            // start character
    // reset the tag index counter
    tagIndex = 0;
    break;
  case endByte:              // end character
    tagComplete = true;   // you have the whole tag
    break;
  default:                   // any other character
    tagComplete = false;  // there are still more bytes to read
    // add the byte to the tagID
    if (tagIndex < tagLength) {
      tagID[tagIndex] = thisChar;
      // increment the tag byte counter
      tagIndex++;
    }
    break;
  }
}
```

When you run this code, you'll see that the RFID signals are slow enough that you can actually see one complete before the other begins. It's not a good protocol for real-time interaction. The assumption in this application is that the RFID tag is going to remain in place for a long time, so a few seconds' delay is not a problem. However, this is where the reader's behavior in the presence of a tag makes a difference. The ID Innovations reader doesn't continue reporting tags if they remain in the field, while the Parallax one does. With the Parallax reader, you can detect not only the presence of a tag, but also the absence. In this application, it means that you can leave your key tag in the bowl as long as you want the lights on, then remove it when you want them off.

None of the readers shown here features the ability to read multiple tags if more than one tag is in the field. That's an important limitation. It means that you have to design the interaction so that the person using the system places only one tag at a time, then removes it before the second one is placed. In effect, it means that two people can't place their key tags in the bowl at the same time. In other words, users of the system need to take explicit action to make something happen. Presence isn't enough.

X

Figure 9-11
The finished RFID reader bowl. A bamboo box
and dessert plate from a nearby gift shop made a
nice housing. Double-stick tape holds the reader
to the top of the box. A hole drilled in the back of
the box provides access for the X10 and power
cables.

❝ Network Identification

So far, you've identified network devices computationally by their address. For devices on the Internet, you've seen both IP addresses and MAC addresses. Bluetooth and 802.15.4 devices have standard addresses as well. The address of a device doesn't tell you anything about what the device is or what it does.

Recall the networked air quality project in Chapter 4. The microcontroller made a request via HTTP and the PHP script sent back a response. Because you already knew the microcontroller's capabilities, you could send a response that was short enough for it to process efficiently, and format it in a way that made it easy to read. But what if that same PHP script had to respond to HTTP requests from an XPort, a desktop browser like Safari or Internet Explorer, and a mobile phone browser? How would it know how to format the information?

Most net communications protocols include a basic exchange of information about the sender's and receiver's identity and capabilities as part of the initial header messages. You can use these to your advantage when designing network systems like the ones you've seen here. There's not room here to discuss this concept comprehensively, but following are two examples that use HTTP and mail.

HTTP Environment Variables

When a server-side program, such as a PHP script, receives an HTTP request, it has access to a lot more information than you've seen thus far about the server, the client, and more.

▸▸ To see some of it, save the following PHP script to your web server, then open it in a browser. Call it **env.php**:

```php
<?php
/*
    Environment Variable Printer
    Language: PHP

    Prints out the environment variables
*/
    foreach ($_REQUEST as $key => $value)
    {
        echo "$key: $value<br>\n";
    }
    foreach ($_SERVER as $key => $value)
    {
        echo "$key: $value<br>\n";
    }
?>
```

You should get something like this in your browser.

```
DBENTRY: /home/youraccountname/:d0000#CPU 6 #MEM 10240 #CGI
16734 #NPROC 12 #TAID 36811298 #WERB 0 #LANG 3 #PARKING 1
#STAT 1
DOCUMENT_ROOT: /home/youraccountname/
HTTP_ACCEPT: text/xml,application/xml,application/
xhtml+xml,text/html;q=0.9,text/plain;q=0.8,image/png,*/
*;q=0.5
HTTP_ACCEPT_CHARSET: ISO-8859-1,utf-8;q=0.7,*;q=0.7
HTTP_ACCEPT_ENCODING: gzip,deflate
HTTP_ACCEPT_LANGUAGE: en-us,en;q=0.5
HTTP_CONNECTION: keep-alive
HTTP_COOKIE: __utmz=152494652.1182194862.12.12.utmccn=(r
eferral)|utmcsr=www.someserver.com|utmcct=/~youraccount/
|utmcmd=referral; __utma=152494652.116689300.1180965223.1181
918391.1182194862.12; __utmc=152494652
HTTP_HOST: www.example.com
HTTP_KEEP_ALIVE: 300
HTTP_USER_AGENT: Mozilla/5.0 (Macintosh; U; Intel Mac OS X;
en-US; rv:1.8.1.4) Gecko/20070515 Firefox/2.0.0.4
PATH: /bin:/usr/bin
REDIRECT_DBENTRY: /home/youraccountname/:d0000#CPU 6 #MEM
10240 #CGI 16734 #NPROC 12 #TAID 36811298 #WERB 0 #LANG 3
#PARKING 1 #STAT 1
REDIRECT_SCRIPT_URI: http://www.example.com/php/09_env.php
REDIRECT_SCRIPT_URL: /php/09_env.php
REDIRECT_STATUS: 200
REDIRECT_UNIQUE_ID: RnfW1UrQECcAAFcpZ2w
REDIRECT_URL: /php/09_env.php
REMOTE_ADDR: 66.168.47.40
REMOTE_PORT: 39438
SCRIPT_FILENAME: /home/youraccountname/php/09_env.php
SCRIPT_URI: http://www.example.com/php/09_env.php
SCRIPT_URL: /php/09_env.php
SERVER_ADDR: 77.248.128.3
SERVER_ADMIN: webmaster@example.com
SERVER_NAME: example.com
SERVER_PORT: 80
SERVER_SIGNATURE:
SERVER_SOFTWARE: Apache/1.3.33 (Unix)
UNIQUE_ID: RnfW1UrQECcAAFcpZ2w
GATEWAY_INTERFACE: CGI/1.1
SERVER_PROTOCOL: HTTP/1.1
REQUEST_METHOD: GET
QUERY_STRING:
REQUEST_URI: /php/09_env.php
SCRIPT_NAME: /php/09_env.php
PATH_INFO: /php/09_env.php
PATH_TRANSLATED: /home/youraccountname/php/09_env.php
STATUS: 200
```

As you can see, there's a lot of information there: the web server's IP address, the client's IP address, the browser type, the directory path to the script, and more. You probably never knew you were giving up so much information when you make a simple HTTP request, and this is only a small part of it! This is very useful when you want to write CGI scripts that can respond to different clients in different ways.

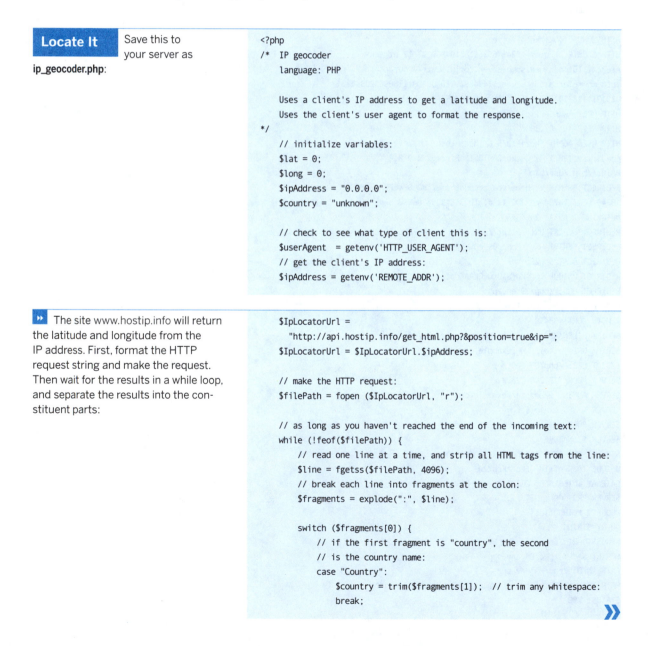

Project 25

IP Geocoding

The next example uses the client's IP address to get its latitude and longitude. It gets this information from www.hostip.info, a community-based IP geocoding project. The data there is not always the most accurate, but it is free. This script also uses the HTTP user agent to determine whether the client is a desktop browser or a Lantronix device. It then formats its response appropriately for each device.

Locate It

Save this to your server as **ip_geocoder.php**:

```php
<?php
/*  IP geocoder
    language: PHP

    Uses a client's IP address to get a latitude and longitude.
    Uses the client's user agent to format the response.
*/
    // initialize variables:
    $lat = 0;
    $long = 0;
    $ipAddress = "0.0.0.0";
    $country = "unknown";

    // check to see what type of client this is:
    $userAgent  = getenv('HTTP_USER_AGENT');
    // get the client's IP address:
    $ipAddress = getenv('REMOTE_ADDR');
```

The site www.hostip.info will return the latitude and longitude from the IP address. First, format the HTTP request string and make the request. Then wait for the results in a while loop, and separate the results into the constituent parts:

```php
    $IpLocatorUrl =
      "http://api.hostip.info/get_html.php?&position=true&ip=";
    $IpLocatorUrl = $IpLocatorUrl.$ipAddress;

    // make the HTTP request:
    $filePath = fopen ($IpLocatorUrl, "r");

    // as long as you haven't reached the end of the incoming text:
    while (!feof($filePath)) {
        // read one line at a time, and strip all HTML tags from the line:
        $line = fgetss($filePath, 4096);
        // break each line into fragments at the colon:
        $fragments = explode(":", $line);

        switch ($fragments[0]) {
            // if the first fragment is "country", the second
            // is the country name:
            case "Country":
                $country = trim($fragments[1]);  // trim any whitespace:
                break;
```

»

Continued from opposite page.

```
            // if the first fragment is "Latitude", the second
            // is the latitude:
            case "Latitude":
                // trim any whitespace:
                $lat = trim($fragments[1]);
                break;
            // if the first fragment is "Longitude", the second
            //is the longitude:
            case "Longitude":
                // trim any whitespace:
                $long = trim($fragments[1]);
                break;
        }
    }
    // close the connection:
    fclose($filePath);
```

Now that you've got the location, it's time to find out who you're sending the results to, and format your response appropriately. The information you want is in the HTTP user agent:

```
    // decide on the output based on the client type:
    switch ($userAgent) {
        case "lantronix":
            // Lantronix device wants a nice short answer:
            echo "<$lat,$long,$country>\n";
            break;
        case "processing":
            // Processing does well with lines:
            echo "Latitude:$lat\nLongitude:$long\nCountry:$country\n\n";
            break;
        default:
            // other clients can take a long answer:
            echo <<<END
<html>
<head></head>

<body>
    <h2>Where You Are:</h2>
        Your country: $country<br>
        Your IP: $ipAddress<br>
        Latitude: $lat<br>
        Longitude: $long<br>
</body>
</html>
END;
    }
?>
```

" If you call this script from a browser, you'll get the HTML version. If you want to get the "processing" or "lantronix" responses, you'll need to send a custom HTTP request. Try calling it from your terminal program as follows:

First. connect to the server as you did before:

```
telnet example.com 80
```

Then send the following (press Enter one extra time after you type that last line):

```
GET /~yourAccount/ip_geocoder.php HTTP/1.1
HOST: example.com
USER-AGENT: lantronix
```

You should get a response like this:

```
HTTP/1.1 200 OK
Date: Thu, 21 Jun 2007 14:44:11 GMT
Server: Apache/2.0.52 (Red Hat)
Content-Length: 38
Connection: close
Content-Type: text/html; charset=UTF-8

<40.6698,-73.9438,UNITED STATES (US)>
```

If you change the user agent from lantronix to processing, you'll get:

```
HTTP/1.1 200 OK
Date: Thu, 21 Jun 2007 14:44:21 GMT
Server: Apache/2.0.52 (Red Hat)
Content-Length: 64
Connection: close
Content-Type: text/html; charset=UTF-8

Latitude:40.6698
Longitude:-73.9438
Country:UNITED STATES (US)
```

As you can see, this is a powerful feature, and all you need to do to use it is to add one line to your HTTP requests from Processing or the microcontroller (see Chapter 3). Just add an extra *print* statement to send the user agent, and you're all set. In Processing, the HTTP request would now look like this:

```
// Send the HTTP GET request:
String requestString = "/~yourAccount/ip_geocoder.php";
```

```
client.write("GET  " + requestString + " HTTP/1.0\r\n");
client.write("HOST: example.com\r\n");
client.write("USER-AGENT: processing\r\n\r\n");
```

The equivalent for Arduino would look like this:

```
// Make HTTP GET request. Fill in the path to your version
// of the CGI script:
Serial.print("GET/~yourAccount/ip_geocoder.php HTTP/1.0\
r\n");
// Fill in your server's name:
Serial.print("HOST:example.com\r\n");
// Print the user agent:
Serial.print("USER-AGENT: lantronix\r\n\r\n");
```

Using the user agent variable like this can simplify your development a great deal, because it means that you can easily use a browser or the command line to debug programs that you're writing for any type of client.

Mail Environment Variables

Email can be a very flexible way to exchange messages between objects, as well. It affords a more flexible relationship between objects than you get with IP addresses, because it gives you the ability to structure complex conversations. An object can communicate not only who it is (the from: address), but who it would like you to reply to (using the reply-to: field), and whom you should include in the conversation (cc: and bcc: fields). All of that information can be communicated without even using the subject or the body of the messages. PHP gives you simple tools to do the parsing. Because so many devices communicate via email (mobile phone text messaging can interface with email as well), it expands the range of possible devices you can add to a system.

Like HTTP, email protocols have environment variables that you can take advantage of as well. If you've ever viewed the full headers of an email in your favorite mail client, you've seen some of these. To look at mail in more depth, there's a useful PHP extension library you can use, called Net_POP3. It lets you retrieve mail from a mail server and parse the whole exchange from server to client. To use it, download it from pear.php.net/package/Net_POP3. Unzip the downloaded file and copy the file **POP3. php** to your server. (Depending on your server's configuration, you may need additional files; check the documentation for Net_POP3.)

Send It Put the following PHP script on your server:

```php
<?php
/*
    mail reader
    language: PHP
*/


include('POP3.php');

// keep your personal info in a separate file:
@include_once("pwds.php");

// new instance of the Net_POP3 class:
$pop3 =& new Net_POP3();

// connect to the mail server:
$pop3->connect($host , $port);

// send login info:
$pop3->login($user , $pass , 'APOP');

// get a count of the number of new messages waiting:
$numMsgs = $pop3->numMsg();

echo "<pre>\n";
echo "Checking mail...\n";
echo "Number of messages: $numMsgs\n";

// get the headers of the first message:
echo($pop3->getRawHeaders(1));
echo "\n\n\n";
echo "</pre>\n";

// disconnect:
$pop3->disconnect();
?>
```

▸▸ Next, make a separate file called **pwds.php** on your server. This file contains your username and password info. Keep it separate from the main PHP file so that you can protect it. Format it like this:

```php
<?php
$user='username';        // your mail login
$pass='password';         // exactly as you normally type it --
$host='pop.example.com'; // usually pop.yourmailserver.com --
$port="110";             // this won't work on gmail.com and
                         // other servers using SSL
?>
```

As soon as you've saved the **pwd.php** file, change its permissions so that only the owner (you) can read and write from it. From the command line, type:

```
chmod go-rwx pwd.php
```

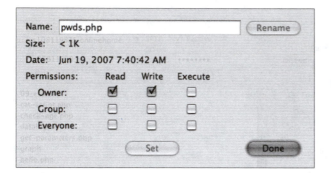

Figure 9-12
Permissions for the **pwds.php** file. Make sure that no one can read from and write to it — besides you.

NOTE: If you're using a graphic SFTP or FTP client, your settings for this file will look like Figure 9-12. This protection will deter anyone who doesn't have access to your account from accessing your account info. It isn't an ideal security solution, but serves for demonstration purposes, and can be made more secure by changing your password frequently.

You'll need to make sure that you have at least one unread mail message on your server for that code to work. When you do, you should get something like this when you open the script in a browser:

```
Checking mail...
Number of messages: 1
Return-Path:
Delivery-Date: Tue, 19 Jun 2007 15:08:33 -0400
Received-SPF: none (mxus2: 12.34.56.78 is neither
permitted nor denied by domain of www.example.com) client-
ip=12.34.56.78; envelope-from=apache@www.example.com;
helo=mx.example.com;
Received: from [12.34.56.78] (helo=mx.example.com)
    by mx.yourserver.com (node=mxus2) with ESMTP (Nemesis),
    id 0MKobQ-1I0j432Ui8-0002oD for youraccount@yourserver.
com; Tue, 19 Jun 2007 15:08:32 -0400
Received: from www.example.com (localhost [127.0.0.1])
    by www.example.com (8.13.1/8.13.1) with ESMTP id
l5JJ8UuJ029983
    for ; Tue, 19 Jun 2007 15:08:31 -0400
Received: (from apache@localhost)
    by www.example.com (8.13.1/8.13.1/Submit) id
l5JJ8Ua2029982;
    Tue, 19 Jun 2007 15:08:30 -0400
Date: Tue, 19 Jun 2007 15:08:30 -0400
Message-Id: <200706191908.l5JK8Ub2129982@www.example.com>
To: youraccount@yourserver.com
Subject: the cat
From: cat@catmail.com
Envelope-To: youraccount@yourserver.com
```

There's a lot of useful information in this header. You can see though the mail says it's from cat@catmail.com, it's actually from a server that's run by example.com. It's common to put an alias on the from: address, or to assign a different reply-to: address than the from: address, or both. It allows sending from a script such as the **cat** script in Chapter 4, yet the reply goes a real person who can answer it. It's important to keep this in mind if you're writing scripts that reply to each other. If you were using email to communicate between networked devices, the program for each device must be able to tell the from: address from the reply-to: address — otherwise, they might not get each other's messages.

This particular message doesn't have a field called X-Mailer:, though many do. X-Mailer tells you which program sent the mail. For example, Apple Mail messages always show up with an x-mailer of Apple Mail, followed by a version number such as (2.752.3). Like the HTTP User Agent, the X-Mailer field can help you to decide how to format mail messages. You could use it in a similar fashion, to tell something about the device that's mailing you, so you can format messages appropriately when mailing back.

Email from RFID

This project shows you some of the possibilities of email for communication, and of using email headers for identification. It's an RFID reader that emails you when it's seen one of three tags. It can be used to notify you when certain RFID-embedded objects have been seen at a particular location. For example, if the RFID reader opened a door latch, you'd know whenever people with the appropriate RFID-enabled door tag had been at the door. For simplicity's sake, the system consists of an RFID reader and a Lantronix module — in this case, an XPort. You could easily add a microcontroller to control other things as well.

NOTE: You'll need an XPort, WiMicro, WiPort, or later for this project; the Lantronix Micro can't send mail by itself.

By sending an email notification, you get a lot of information all at once, including:

- Which person you're dealing with (based on the RFID tag number)
- Which reader the person was at (based on the IP address of the XPort that sends the mail)
- What time the person's tag was read (based on the time stamp of the email)

Though only one unit is described here, this project is designed to be duplicated, so that you can get messages from multiple locations. The system is shown in Figure 9-13. The RFID reader is connected to a Lantronix module. The RFID reader sends serial data to the XPort, which sends an email. The output is a PHP script that reads the emails and displays the results.

MATERIALS

- » **1 solderless breadboard** such as Digi-Key part number 438-1045-ND, or Jameco part number 20601
- » **1 RFID reader module** from Parallax, part number 28140. With a little extra work, the project could be modified to use one of the other readers mentioned in this chapter.
- » **3 RFID tags** Get the tags that match your reader. All three of the retailers listed here sell tags that match their readers in a variety of physical packages, so choose the ones you like the best.
- » **1 Lantronix embedded device server** Available from many vendors, including Symmetry Electronics (www.semiconductorstore.com) as part number WM11A0002-01 (WiMicro) or XP1001001-03R (XPort). This example uses an XPort.
- » **1 RJ45 breakout board** SparkFun part number BOB-00716
- » **1 3.3V regulator** The LD1117-33V (SparkFun part number COM-00526) or the MIC2940A-3.3WT (Digi-Key part number 576-1134-ND) work well.
- » **1 1µF capacitor** Digi-Key part number P10312-ND
- » **1 10µF capacitor** SparkFun part number Comp-10uF, or Digi-Key part number COM-00523
- » **1 reset switch** Any momentary switch will do. The ones used here are SparkFun part number COM-00097, or Digi-Key part number SW400-ND.
- » **1 5V regulator** The LM7805 series (SparkFun part number COM-00107, Digi-Key part number LM7805CT-ND) work well.
- » **1 USB-to-TTL serial adaptor** SparkFun's BOB-00718 from Chapter 2 can do the job. If you use a USB-to-RS-232 adaptor such as a Keyspan or logear dongle, refer to Chapter 2 for the schematics to convert RS-232-to-5V TTL serial. You'll use this for configuring the XPort only. If you've got more than one, it'll be handy for troubleshooting, but you won't need one for the final project.

Figure 9-14
The RFID emailer circuit.

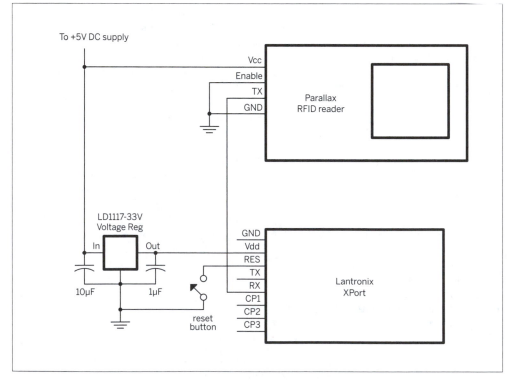

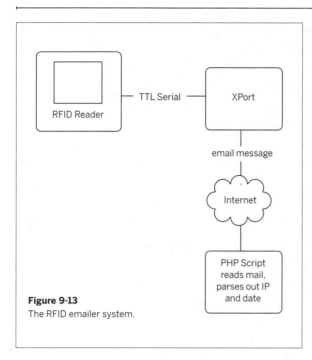

Figure 9-13
The RFID emailer system.

The Circuit

The circuit is fairly straightforward. The RFID reader's serial output is connected to the XPort's serial receive pin. The reader's enable pin is connected to ground. That's it. Figure 9-14 shows the circuit.

To make this work, you'll configure the XPort to send emails. It can automatically generate an email to a preset address when you send it a given serial string. To determine the strings to send, you'll need to read the tags with the RFID reader first. To do this, connect the RFID reader's output to the USB-to serial adaptor's input and connect the reader's enable pin to ground, as shown back in Figure 9-6. Then connect the USB-to-serial adaptor to your computer and open a serial terminal connection to it at 2400 bps. When you wave the tags in front of it, you should see strings like this:

0415AB6FB7
0415AB5DAF
0415AB5DAF
0F008F7CE8
0F008F7CE8

As you know from the previous projects, each unique string represents a unique tag. Pick two characters that are unique to each tag. In the example, you could use the last two characters — B7, AF, and E8. The values will be different for your tags. Write them down.

Now disconnect the RFID reader and connect the XPort to the USB-to-serial adaptor as shown in Figure 9-15. Open a serial terminal connection at 9600bps.

Hold down the x key on your keyboard and press the reset button on the breadboard to reset the XPort. You'll get the usual configuration menu. Type 1 to get the serial setup menu, and enter the following settings:

```
Baudrate (2400) ?
I/F Mode (4C) ?
Flow (00) ?
Port No (10001) ?
ConnectMode (D4) ?
Send '+++' in Modem Mode  (N) ?
Auto increment source port  (N) ?
Remote IP Address : (0) .(0) .(0) .(0)
Remote Port  (0) ?
DisConnMode (00) ?
FlushMode (00) ?
DisConnTime (00:00) ?:
SendChar 1  (00) ?
SendChar 2  (00) ?
```

Then choose menu item 3 to set the email settings. The XPort can be configured with your email address and SMTP server, and can send up to three different email notifications based on various events. It can send mail based on incoming serial messages, or based on changes on its configurable I/O pins. For this project, you'll use serial messages.

Unfortunately, the XPort expects the bytes you'll send it as hexadecimal values. This means that if you're sending the bytes shown earlier, for example, you'd need to convert them from ASCII to hexadecimal as follows:

ASCII characters	Hexadecimal values
"B7"	0x42, 0x37
"AF"	0x41, 0x46
"E8"	0x45, 0x38

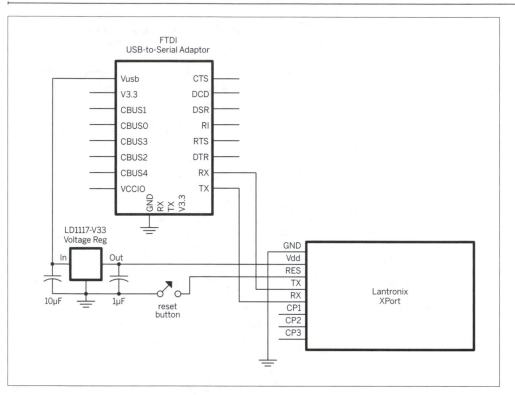

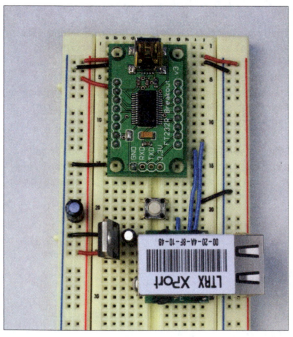

Figure 9-15
XPort connected to a USB-to-serial adaptor.

The first items you'll need to set for menu item 3 are the SMTP mail server IP and your login info. To get your mail server's numeric IP address, you can ping it. For example, if your mail server is smtp.yahoo.com, open a terminal window and type:

```
ping -c 2 smtp.yahoo.com
```

You'll get a reply starting with a line containing the IP you need:

```
PING smarthost.yahoo.com (216.145.54.172): 56 data bytes
```

Here are some initial mail settings for the XPort. Replace these values with the appropriate ones for your server:

```
Mail server () ? (216) .(145) .(54) .(172)
Unit name () ? myAccountName
Domain name () ? example.com
Recipient 1 () ? myAccountName@example.com
Recipient 2 () ?
```

Once you've got the account set up, it's time to set the serial bytes that will trigger the messages, and the messages themselves. Replace the hexadecimal values shown here with your own values:

```
- Trigger 1
Enable serial trigger input (N) ? Y
  No. of bytes (2) ? 2
  Match (,) ? 42,37
Trigger input1 [A/I/X] (X) ?
Trigger input2 [A/I/X] (X) ?
Trigger input3 [A/I/X] (X) ?
Message () ? Tag one
Priority (L) ?
```

Next, set the minimum notification interval and the re-notification interval. The former sets how many seconds have to elapse at minimum between email messages. Because the RFID reader reads repeatedly, set this interval fairly high, so as not to flood the network with emails. The renotification interval sets how soon the XPort should repeat an email if it gets the same trigger string twice. Again, set this fairly high:

```
Min. notification interval (1 s) ? 10
Re-notification interval (0 s) ? 20
```

Repeat the operation for messages 2 and 3, changing the message itself and the trigger strings appropriately. Here

are my settings for messages 2 and 3:

```
Enable serial trigger input (N) ? Y
  No. of bytes (2) ? 2
  Match (,) ? 41,46
Message () ? Tag Two
```

```
Enable serial trigger input (N) ? Y
  No. of bytes (2) ? 2
  Match (,) ? 45,38
Message () ? Tag Three
```

When you're finished, choose menu item 9 to save your settings and reset the XPort.

NOTE: The XPort listens for the serial reset message (xxx) only at 9600 bps. So if you're trying to get to the setup menu, make sure that you're connected to the serial port at 9600 bps. Because the RFID reader needs to be at 2400 bps, you might accidentally open the port at the wrong rate.

Now connect the RFID reader to the XPort, as shown in Figure 9-14. Connect it to the Internet, power it up, and wave a tag in front of the reader. Then check your email. You should see a message like this:

```
From:    myAccountName@example.com
Subject: Notification: Tag one
Date:    June 21, 2007 6:11:59 PM EDT
To:      myAccountName@example.com
```

When you get this email, you know everything's working. Try the other two tags. You should get a unique message for each one.

You could duplicate this circuit for several locations, but unless you set up an email address for each XPort, the email from the XPorts all comes from the same account. How would you know which XPort sent the mail? Easy: check the IP address of the sender. Open the full header and look for this string:

```
Received: from myAccountName ( [12.34.56.78])
```

That IP address will be the IP address of your XPort. To distinguish between different XPorts, you'd need a program to look for the IP address of the sender. You could get the identity of the person with the RFID tag from the subject, and the time of the tag read from the email's timestamp. This gives you a pretty good picture of who was where at what time.

Try It   Following is a PHP script to
look for these messages.
It filters out all other mail messages
and just reports the notifications from
the XPort. It needs the same **POP3.php**
library and the same **pwd.php** file as the
previous program. Save it in the same
directory as **rfid_mail_reader.php**:

```php
<?php
/*
    RFID mail reader
    language: PHP

    Parses a POP email box for a specific message from an XPort.
    The message looks like this:

    From:     myAccountName@myMailhost.com
    Subject: Notification: Tag one
    Date:     June 21, 2007 6:11:59 PM EDT
    To:       myAccountName@myMailhost.com


*/
include('POP3.php');

// keep your personal info in a separate file:
@include_once("pwds.php");

echo "Checking mail...";

// New instance of the Net_POP3 class:
$pop3 =& new Net_POP3();

// Connect to the mail server:
$pop3->connect($host , $port);

// Send login info:
$pop3->login($user , $pass , 'APOP');

// Get a count of the number of new messages waiting:
$numMsgs = $pop3->numMsg();

echo "<pre>\n";
echo "Number of messages: $numMsgs\n";

// iterate over the messages:
for ($thisMsg = 1; $thisMsg <= $numMsgs; $thisMsg++) {
    // parse the headers for each message into
    // an array called $header:
    $header = $pop3->getParsedHeaders($thisMsg);

    // print the subject header:
    $subject = $header["Subject"];
    // look for the word "Notification" before a colon
    // in the subject:
    $words = explode(":", $subject);
```

»

When you open this in a browser, you should get output like this:

```
Checking mail...

Number of messages: 234
Tag three showed up at address
12.34.56.78 at
     Thu, 21 Jun 2007 17:16:56 -0400 (EDT)
Tag one showed up at address
12.34.56.89 at
     Thu, 21 Jun 2007 17:17:10 -0400 (EDT)
Tag two showed up at address
12.34.56.78 at
     Thu, 21 Jun 2007 17:17:11 -0400 (EDT)
Tag two showed up at address
12.34.56.89 at
     Thu, 21 Jun 2007 18:11:59 -0400 (EDT)
Tag two showed up at address
12.34.56.89 at
     Thu, 21 Jun 2007 18:12:12 -0400 (EDT)
That's all folks
```

Continued from opposite page.

```php
// only do the rest if this mail message is a notification:
if ($words[0] == "Notification"){
    // get the second half of the subject; that's the tag ID:
    $idTag = $words[1];
    // print it;
    echo "$idTag showed up at address\t";

    /*
        the IP address is buried in the "Received" header.
        That header is an array. The second element contains
        who it's from.  In that string, the IP is the first
        thing contained in square brackets. So:
    */

    // get the stuff in the right array element after the
    // opening square bracket:
    $receivedString = explode("[", $header["Received"][1]);
    // throw away the stuff after the closing bracket:
    $recdString2 = explode("]", $receivedString[1]);
    // what's left is the IP address:
    $ipAddress = $recdString2[0];

    // print the IP address:
    echo "$ipAddress at \t";

    // print the date header:
    $date = $header["Date"];
    echo "$date\t";
    echo "\n";
}


}

echo "That's all folks";
echo "</pre>";

// disconnect:
$pop3->disconnect();
?>
```

> You can see that there were many more messages than the script printed out (234 messages, only 5 shown here). You can also see that there were two different XPorts reporting (12.34.56.78 and 12.34.56.89). Finally, you've got the time, location, and ID of every tag that showed up in your system. You've got a information about both identity and activity, just using the headers of email messages.
>
> **X**

❝❝ Conclusion

The boundary between physical identity and network identity always introduces the possibility for confusion and miscommunication. No system for moving information across that boundary is foolproof. Establishing identity, capability, and activity are all complex tasks, and the more that you can incorporate human input into the situation, the better your results will be.

Security is essential when you're transmitting identifying characteristics, in order to maintain the trust of the people using what you make and to keep them and yourself safe. Once you're connected to the Internet, nothing's truly private, and nothing's truly closed, so learning to work with the openness makes your life easier. In the end, keep in mind that clear, simple ways of marking identity are the most effective, whether they're universal or not. Many beginners and experienced network professionals often get caught on this point, because they feel that identity has to be absolute, and clear to the whole world. Don't get caught up in how comprehensively you can identify things at first. It doesn't matter if you can identify someone or something to the whole world — it only matters that you can identify them for your own purposes. Once that's established, you've got a foundation on which to build.

When you start to develop projects that use location systems, you usually find that less is more. It's not unusual to start a project thinking you need to know position, distance, and orientation, then pare away systems as you develop the project. The physical limitations of the things you build and the spaces you build them in will solve many problems for you.

x

And Another Thing

This book only touches the tip of the iceberg in terms of how you can connect physical devices to networks. There are many tools and applications that were left out because there wasn't enough space to explain them adequately. Other tools came on the market as I was writing, leaving not enough time to try them out thoroughly enough to write about them. Still others were left out because they were similar to the main tools described already. Following is a collection of pieces that didn't make the main text, but that still may be useful to you as you're networking physical objects.

❝ Other Useful Protocols

There are many more useful protocols than have been covered. Here are a few that you might run across, along with some notes on where to begin learning about them.

MIDI

The Musical Instrument Digital Interface (MIDI) protocol is a protocol for real-time communication between digital musical instruments. It's the granddaddy of digital synthesizer protocols. Most music synthesizers, sequencers, samplers, keyboards, and workstations on the market today speak MIDI. If you plan to make music using hardware, you're going to run across it. It's a serial protocol running at 31,250 bps. There's a standard MIDI connector called a DIN5 connector that you'll find on all MIDI gear. All the connectors on the gear are female plugs, and the cables all have male connectors on both ends. Figure A-1 shows the MIDI connector and a simple MIDI output circuit from an Arduino board. You can find hundreds of examples of how to send and receive MIDI data online.

MIDI messages are divided into three or more bytes. The first byte, a command byte, is always greater than 127 in value. Its value depends on the command. The bytes that follow it are called status bytes. All status bytes have values less than 128. This makes it possible to tell a command byte from a status byte by the value alone.

There are a number of different MIDI commands. The most basic, note on and note off messages, control the playing of notes on 16 different channels of a synthesizer. Each note on or note off command contains two status bytes, specifying the pitch in a range from 0 to 127, and the velocity (how hard the note should be struck) from 0 to 127. Pitch value 69 is defined as A above middle C (A440) by the general MIDI specification. The general MIDI spec also covers the instruments that you're likely to find on each channel.

As MIDI instruments, channels, and banks of sounds are grouped in groups of 16, MIDI messages are generally written in hexadeximal notation. This makes it easy to read commands based on the value. For example, 0x80 to 0x8F are all note off messages, 0x90 to 0x9F are all note on messages. 0x90 is note on channel 1, 0x91 is note on channel 2, and so forth.

For more information on MIDI, see Paul D. Lehrman and Tim Tully's book *MIDI for the Professional* (Amsco, 1993).

▸▸ Here is the "Hello World!" of MIDI, a program to send MIDI notes to a synthesizer. It plays notes. To use it, build the circuit as shown, connect it to a MIDI synth, and connect the synth to an amplifier and speakers.

```
/*
   MIDI
   Language: Wiring/Arduino

   plays MIDI notes from 30 to 90 (F#-0 to F#-5)
*/

char note = 0;      // The MIDI note value to be played

void setup() {
 // Set MIDI baud rate:
 Serial.begin(31250);
}

void loop() {
 // play notes from F#-0 (30) to F#-5 (90):
 for (note = 0; note < 127; note ++) {
 // Note on channel 1 (0x90), some note value (note), middle velocity
 // (0x45):
```

»

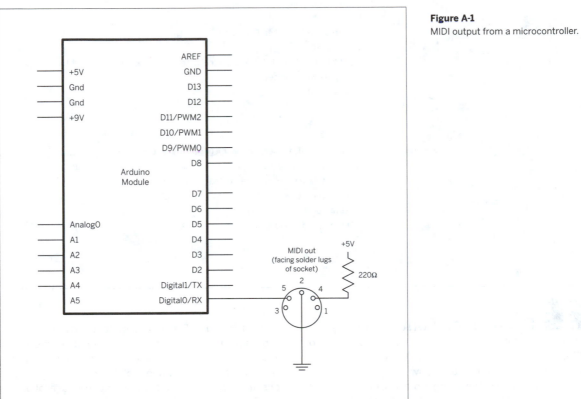

Continued from previous page.

```
noteOn(0x90, note, 0x70);
delay(10);
//Note on channel 1 (0x90), some note value (note), silent velocity (0x00):
noteOn(0x90, note, 0x00);
delay(10);
}
}

// plays a MIDI note. Doesn't check to see that
// cmd is greater than 127, or that data values are less than 127:
void noteOn(char cmd, char data1, char data2) {
  Serial.print(cmd, BYTE);
  Serial.print(data1, BYTE);
  Serial.print(data2, BYTE);
}
```

OpenSound Control (OSC)

OpenSound Control (OSC) was created as a successor to MIDI. MIDI is aging as a protocol. As it's been expanded to other uses, MIDI's limitations have become more apparent. Compared to modern protocols, MIDI's data rate is relatively low. Furthermore, MIDI doesn't travel well over packet networks. OSC was designed to be implemented over many transport protocols, from serial to UDP to whatever comes next. When formatting OSC messages, you define an address space to define the device. For example, you can use OSC to control the MAKE controller (described later in this appendix). Each set of functions has an address. For example, to read the third analog input channel, the address space would be:

`/analogin/2/value`

The controller would then send you back the value of that analog channel. OSC is designed to be flexible enough to allow for control of devices that haven't even been invented yet. Because you define the address space, you can define any set of devices and functions that you want.

OSC has been implemented on many different platforms, including Flash, PHP, C, C++, Java, Max/MSP, PD, Processing and more. Though there's not yet an official library for OSC in Wiring or Arduino, there may be soon. For more information on OSC, see the OSC homepage at www.cnmat.berkeley.edu/OpenSoundControl/.

Exemplar (shown in Figure A-2) is a toolkit for prototyping physical devices that uses OSC to communicate with various microcontroller modules. It allows you to read data from the microcontroller and prototype onscreen applications that use that data without having to write a lot of code. The Exemplar firmware for Arduino is a good simple example of how to implement OSC in code. For more on Exemplar, including code to communicate from Wiring and Arduino to Exemplar using OSC, see hci.stanford.edu/research/exemplar/. It's both an analysis tool and a proxy tool, like those covered further on.

DMX512

DMX512 is a real-time serial protocol for communicating between stage-lighting control systems and lighting dimmers. It has been the industry standard for stage lighting and show control equipment for a couple of decades now. It's also used to control special effects machines, moving lights, projection systems, and more. It's fast for a serial protocol, at 250 kbps; fast enough that you can't just send regular serial data from a microcontroller. There are a few examples online as to how to send DMX512 from microcontrollers, though. Numerous examples for the PIC microcontrollers exist, and pointers for implementing it on Arduino can be found on the Arduino playground site at www.arduino.cc/playground/Learning/DMX. For more on DMX, see www.opendmx.net. Like MIDI, DMX is aging as a protocol. The lighting industry has started to develop its successor, Advanced Controller

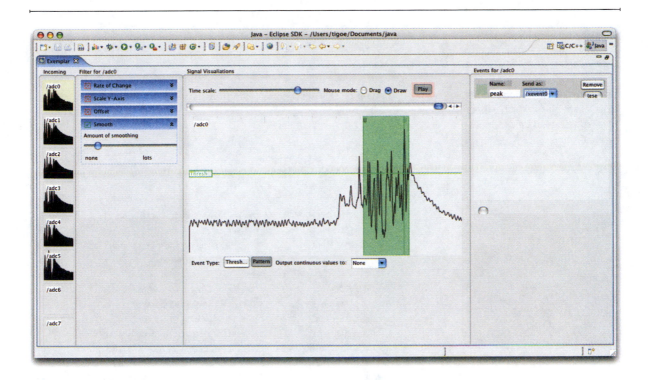

▲ **Figure A-2**
Network, or ACN, which can run over Ethernet. Over the next few years, you can expect to see it grow in prominence. For more on show control protocols in general, John Huntington's book *Control Systems for Live Entertainment* (Focal Press, 2007) can't be beat.

X

Figure A-2
The Exemplar interface. You can view the outputs of sensors on time graphs, filter them, match patterns, and have those patterns generate messages that can be sent to other applications.

❝ Proxies of All Kinds

Many of the software programs you've written in this book are basically proxies, converting one form of communication to another. There are a number of useful programs on the market that convert from one protocol to another in order to enable two devices that don't speak the same language to communicate. Here are a few examples.

Network Serial Proxy

One of the most common tasks in networked projects is converting a stream of serial data to a network TCP stream. Most developers of physical computing projects have written their own network serial proxy, so there are many examples to look at. It's a particularly useful thing to do when you want to communicate between applications that can't access a serial port, like Adobe Flash, and a microcontroller. The next page shows just such a proxy.

▶▶ Here's a very basic proxy sketch written in Processing that works with Flash. It will work with other applications, too, but it's optimized for ActionScript's XMLSocket class, which expects every message to be wrapped in bytes of value 0.

```
/*
 Serial Server
 language: processing

 This program makes a connection between a serial port
 and a network socket.

*/

import processing.serial.*;
import processing.net.*;

int socketNumber = 9001; // the port the server listens on
Server myServer;          // the server
Client thisClient;        // the reference to the client that logs
char terminationString = '\0'; // zero terminator byte

Serial myPort;            // the serial port you're using
String portnum;           // name of the serial port
String outString = "";    // the string being sent out the serial port
String inString = "";     // the string coming in from the serial port
String socketString = ""; // string of bytes in from the socket
int receivedLines = 0;    // how many serial lines have been received
int bufferedLines = 5;    // number of incoming lines to keep

void setup() {
  size(400, 300);         // window size

  // create a font with a font available to the system:
  PFont myFont = createFont(PFont.list()[2], 14);
  textFont(myFont);

  // list all the serial ports:
  println(Serial.list());

  // based on the list of serial ports printed from the
  //previous command, change the 0 to your port's number:
  portnum = Serial.list()[0];
  // initialize the serial port:
  myPort = new Serial(this, portnum, 9600);
  // buffer until a newLine:
  myPort.bufferUntil('\n');
  // start the server:
  myServer = new Server(this, socketNumber); // Starts a server

}

void draw() {
  // clear the screen:
  background(0);
  // print the name of the serial port:
```

Continued from opposite page.

```
text("Serial port: " + portnum, 10, 20);
// Print out what you get:
text("From serial port:\n" + inString, 10, 80);
text("From socket:\n" + socketString, 200, 80);

// if the client is not null, and says something, display
// what it said:
if (thisClient !=null) {
 // print out the current client:
 text("Active client: " + thisClient.ip(), 10, 60);
 // read what the client said:
 String whatClientSaid = thisClient.readString();
 if (whatClientSaid != null) {
  // save what it said to print to the screen:
  socketString = whatClientSaid;
  // send what it said out the serial port:
  myPort.write(socketString);
 }
}
}


// this method runs when bytes show up in the serial port:
void serialEvent(Serial myPort) {
 // read the String from the serial port:
 String whatSerialSaid = myPort.readStringUntil('\n');
 if (whatSerialSaid != null) {
  // save what it said to print to the screen:
  inString = whatSerialSaid;
  // if there is a netClient, send the serial stuff to them:
  if (thisClient != null) {
   // put a zero byte before and after everything you send to Flash:
   thisClient.write(terminationString);
   // send the actual text string:
   thisClient.write(inString);
   // add the end zero byte:
   thisClient.write(terminationString);
  }
 }
}


void serverEvent(Server myServer, Client someClient) {
 if (thisClient == null) {
  // don't accept the client if we already have one:
  thisClient = someClient;
 }
}
```

<table>
<tr><td>

Try It   Here's a sample of Action-
Script to test it with. Paste
this into the action window in the first
frame of a new Flash movie and run it.
Thanks to Dan O'Sullivan for this code:

</td><td>

```
/*
    Socket Test
    Language: ActionScript 2.0

    Exchanges strings through an XMLSocket
*/

var i = 0;        // counter for the number of clicks

createSocket();

function createSocket() {
    socket = new XMLSocket();
    // 127.0.0.1 is the same as "localhost"
    // i.e. an alias to your local machine
    socket.connect("127.0.0.1",9001);
    // define the functions that get called when these events happen:
    socket.onConnect = success;
    socket.onClose = closed;
    socket.onData = newData;
}

// when you click on the screen, Flash sends a click out
// the server port:
function onMouseUp() {
    trace("click");
    socket.send("click ");
    socket.send(i);
    i++;
}

function success() {
    trace("socket opened");
    socket.send("F\n"); // tell proxy it is talking to Flash
}

function closed() {
    trace("socket closed");
    socket.send("Q\n"); // tell proxy that Flash is closing socket
}

function newData(inString) {
    trace(inString); // trace the packet of data to the Flash
                     // output screen
}
```

</td></tr>
</table>

◀◀ **Figure A-3**
The Tinker.it AppleScript proxy. Any character coming in the serial port can be assigned to an AppleScript command.

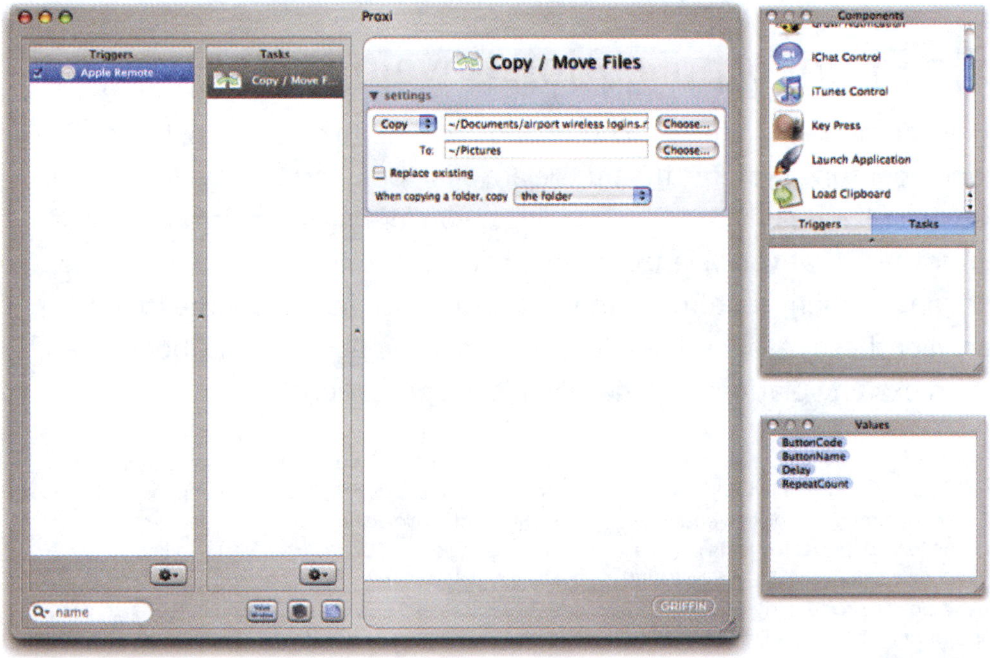

⤓ **Figure A-4**
Griffin Proxi. Connections are made by pulling triggers and tasks from their bins to the main window and setting their characteristics.

❝ Other Proxy Programs

There are numerous programs on the Web that act as proxies, receiving messages from one source and passing it to another. Following are a few that are popular among physical computing enthusiasts.

TinkerProxy

The folks at Tinker.it have written a useful application for Mac OS X that receives serial information and generates AppleScript events for Mac OS X. This app (Figure A-3) allows you to control nearly any application on a Macintosh, as most applications have at least rudimentary AppleScript controls. They've also written TinkerProxy, a TCP-to-serial proxy for Windows. See tinker.it/now/category/software/ for more details.

NADA

Sketchtools NADA is a proxy tool that takes in MIDI, serial OSC, and other messages and sends them out to various development environments like Flash, or Java. Originally designed to work with the Phidgets line of hardware tools, it can work with the MAKE Controller, MakingThings' earlier Teleo tools, any MIDI device, and many others as well. See www.sketchtools.com for more details.

Griffin Proxi

Griffin Proxi (Figure A-4, preceding page) is a tool that runs various operating system tasks in Mac OS X in response to events like a mouse click, keyboard hit, incoming email, and more. You can use it to generate screen messages, make sounds, run AppleScripts, write to files and send email and test messages from various hardware devices connected to your computer. See proxi.griffintechnology. com for more details.

Girder

Girder is an operating system automator for Windows that lets you generate serial, network and X10 events from operating system events. Like the others, it makes it possible to connect various operating system events with network and serial messages without programming. See www.girder.nl for details.

X

❝ Mobile Phone Application Development

Mobile phone development is limited by a number of factors. To begin with, there are many more phone operating systems than there are desktop operating systems. This makes portability of software difficult. The learning curve for beginners is an order of magnitude greater than what you've encountered here. In addition to that, access to both the network and to many features of the phones is often limited by the mobile service providers. For these reasons, I didn't include mobile phones in this book, even though they are an exciting platform for these kinds of applications.

If you're interested in mobile phone application development, look into phones running the Symbian Series 60 operating system. Linux is beginning to make a strong showing on phones, too. Most of these are Nokia phones. They can run the Java Micro Edition (formerly called J2ME, now Java ME), which is a powerful and fairly accessible toolkit for phone programming. There is a limited variation of Processing called Mobile Processing that runs on these phones as well as most Java-capable phones. In addition, there is a version of the Python scripting language. Python for Series 60 is exciting, because it allows you access to features of the phone that Java and Mobile Processing don't. For example, you can make phone calls and find the cell tower ID using Python. If you know Adobe's Flash programming environment, you should look into Flash Lite, which runs on mobile phones as well.

The most productive approaches to mobile phone development lie in three directions: developing for the browser, for SMS, and for voice and touchtone connections. For the browser, you can use WAP/WML (Wireless Application Protocol/Wireless Markup Language), or you can use HTML. Because SMS messages can travel across email servers, you can use the POP, IMAP, and SMTP mail protocols you saw earlier in this book to send and transmit them. Asterisk is an open-source private branch exchange (PBX) for managing telephony, allowing you to make and receive audio phone calls from a server.

Browsers on the Phone

Because most mobile phones on the market as of this writing have at least a rudimentary web browser, you can develop web applications for them. Some of them use WAP/WML only, but increasingly many of them can read plain old HTML. The functionality of low-end phones is limited, so it's not wise to do lots of graphics-heavy pages, but you can easily browse text pages with a few small graphics on a phone. Any of the HTML pages generated by the PHP scripts in this book should be viewable on most mobile phones. You can even customize the HTML output for mobile phones by reading the HTTP User Agent as you saw in Chapter 9, and outputting a special page for mobile phone browsers.

HTTP User Agent for Phones

Here's a PHP script that runs on most web-enabled phones. It identifies the user agent and IP address and mails it back to you. It's a useful diagnostic tool for finding phones and knowing their browsers. To use this, save this PHP script to your server, then open the script in a browser on your phone:

```php
<?php
/*
    Phone Finder
    Language: PHP

    Identifies the user agent and IP address and sends an email
    notification. Runs on mobile phones.

*/
$userAgent = getenv('HTTP_USER_AGENT');
$ipAddress = getenv('REMOTE_ADDR');
sendMessage('you@example.com', 'user agent',
    "$userAgent $ipAddress");

    echo <<<END
<html>
<head></head>

<body>
    <h2>Hi There</h2>
        Your IP: $ipAddress<br>
        Your browser: $userAgent<br>
        Thanks!
</body>
</html>
END;

 end;

function sendMessage($to, $subject, $message) {
    $from = "phone@example.com";
    mail($to, $subject, $message, "From: $from");
}
 ?>
```

You'll get a number of different replies. Here are some examples:

```
Mozilla/5.0 (SymbianOS/9.1; U; en-us) AppleWebKit/413
(KHTML, like
   Gecko) Safari/
NokiaN73-1/2.0628.0.0.1 S60/3.0 Profile/MIDP-2.0
Configuration/
   CLDC-1.1
NokiaN93-1/20.0.058 SymbianOS/9.1 Series60/3.0 Profile/
MIDP-2.0
   Configuration/CLDC-1.1
Nokia6230/2.0 (05.51) Profile/MIDP-2.0 Configuration/
CLDC-1.1
   UP.Link/6.3.0.0.0
BlackBerry8100/4.2.0 Profile/MIDP-2.0 Configuration/CLDC-1.1
   VendorID/100
BlackBerry7290/4.1.0 Profile/MIDP-2.0 Configuration/CLDC-1.1
   VendorID/100 216.9.250.99
LGE-PM325/1.0 UP.Browser/6.2.3.2 (GUI) MMP/2.0
Palm680/RC1 Mozilla/4.0 (compatible; MSIE 6.0; Windows 98;
   PalmSource/Palm-D053; Blazer/4.5) 16;320x320
UP.Link/6.3.0.0.
Mozilla/2.0 (compatible; MSIE 3.02; Windows CE; PPC;
240x320)
   BlackBerry8100/4.2.0 Profile/MIDP-2.0 Configuration/
CLDC-1.1
   VendorID/100
Mozilla/4.0 (compatible; MSIE 6.0; Windows 98; PalmSource/
Palm-D052;
   Blazer/4.5) 16;320x320 68.28.123.118
SAMSUNG-SGH-A707/1.0 SHP/VPP/R5 NetFront/3.3 SMM-MMS/1.2.0
   profile/MIDP-2.0 configuration/CLDC-1.1 UP.Link/6.3.0.0.0
209.183.32.17
Mozilla/4.0 (MobilePhone RL-4920/US/1.0) NetFront/3.1
MMP/2.0
Mozilla/4.0 Sprint:MotoQ (compatible; MSIE 4.01; Windows CE;
   Smartphone; 176x220)
```

As you can see, there's a wide variety of mobile phone browsers out there, so telling what's a phone and what's not can be a challenge. That's a good reason to keep your display output simple if you're planning for it to be seen on mobile phones. Some of the browsers conveniently report their screen size. For example, the final one here, a MotoQ, has a screen size of 176 x 220. For more information on the capabilities of various handsets, check out the WURFL project at wurfl.sourceforge.net.

SMS Text Messaging

SMS is an easy way to get and receive messages from mobile phones, because it's just email, from a server's point of view. Sending an email from a mobile phone via SMS varies with each carrier, but it generally works like this. Type in the short code that your carrier uses for sending email via SMS. You can get this from the carrier's website. For example, T-Mobile in the United States uses the shortcode 500. Verizon just requires you to send directly to the email address. Each carrier is different, but here's a general approach:

1. Type the email address you want to send to, followed by a space.
2. Type in the subject line, followed by a space.
3. Type # then the body of the message.
4. Hit send.
5. Check your email for the message.

So on my T-mobile phone, I type:

```
To: 500
you@yourmailserver.com hello there #this is the body
```

In your mail, you should receive:

```
From: 19175555555@tmomail.net
To: you@yourmailserver.com
Subject: hello

this is the body
```

You can parse these messages just like mail using the PHP NET_POP3 class.

Sending text messages is just as easy. You need to know the carrier's mail domain, which you can get from the carrier's website. Here are a few of the U.S. carriers' mail domains, as of this week. Mergers and acquisitions could make these domains incorrect by the time you read this, so check with your carrier. Replace the number with your own:

```
T-Mobile: 12225555555@tmomail.net
Sprint: 12225555555@messaging.sprintpcs.com
Verizon: 12225555555@vtext.com
AT&T: 12225555555@txt.att.net
Nextel: 12225555555@messaging.nextel.com
```

Try It   To send an SMS, just send mail to the ten-digit phone number at the recipient's carrier. Here's a PHP script to send yourself an SMS. Save this as **sms.php**:

> ⚠ Consider password-protecting this script, or removing it after you're done testing. It could become the target of abuse if it's found by a roving spambot with a pocket full of phone numbers.

There's an extra carrier in the list of carriers in that code that you may not be familiar with. Teleflip (www.teleflip.com) is a text message aggregator service. It allows you to send to any U.S. 10-digit phone number by sending to number@teleflip.com. This frees you from having to look up the carriers' mail host names.

```php
<?php
/*
    SMS messenger
    Language: PHP

    Sends SMS messages

*/
    $phoneNumber = $_GET["phoneNumber"];    // get the phone number
    $carrier    = $_GET["carrier"];         // get the carrier
    $message    = $_GET["message"];         // get the message
    $recipient = $phoneNumber."@".$carrier; // compose the recipient

    // if there's a phone number in the form, you can send:
    if ($phoneNumber != null) {
        // send the message:
        $from = "you@yourmailhost.com";
        mail($recipient, "Mail message", $message, $from);
    }

    // finally, print the browser form:
    echo <<<END
<html>
<head></head>

<body>
    <h2>SMS Messenger</h2>
        <form name="txter" lookupMethod="post" action="sms.php">

    Phone number: <input type="text" name="phoneNumber"
        size='15' maxlength='15'><br>
    Message: <input type="text" name="message" size='30'
        maxlength='128'><br>
    Carrier:      $to<br>

        <select name="carrier">
            <option value="teleflip.com">Teleflip</option>
            <option value="tmomail.net">T-Mobile</option>
            <option value="messaging.sprintpcs.com">Sprint</option>
            <option value="txt.att.net">AT&T</option>
            <option value="vtext.com">Verizon</option>
            <option value="messaging.nextel.com">Nextel</option>
        </select>

        <input type="submit" name="Submit" value="submit">

    </form>
</body>
</html>

END;

?>
```

❝ Asterisk

Asterisk is an open source private branch telephone exchange (PBX). It allows you to manage a phone exchange over an IP network. It can make and take phone calls, save messages, play prerecorded messages to people who call in, and offers most of the usual features a phone account does, like caller ID, call waiting, call blocking, and so forth. You can also make connections between the phone and the Internet. For example, you can allow users to control the output of a PHP script using their touchtone keypad. It's not a large step from there to having a mobile phone keypad controlling a physical object through a Lantronix device, XBee radio, or any of the other tools you've seen here. It runs on a Unix or Linux server. Asterisk isn't easy for the beginner, but it's manageable by anyone comfortable with server-side programming like the PHP you've seen here. For more details on Asterisk, see www.asterisk.org.

The mobile phone development landscape is changing rapidly at the moment, and by the time you're reading this, there are likely many more tools for developing on phones, and for using phones as a user interface to networks in nontraditional ways. If you've enjoyed making embedded systems talk to each other, then by all means, jump into mobile phone programming as well. **X**

❝ Other Microcontrollers

Though the examples in this book have all been done using Arduino and Wiring, there are many other microcontroller platforms that you can use to do the same work. This section is an introduction to a few others on the market, and what they're good for. Some of these are standalone controllers that you program yourself, as you've done with the controllers in this book. Others are designed to be connected to a personal computer at all times. You don't have to program these, you just configure them via serial or Ethernet, then read from their inputs and write to their outputs from your desktop-based development environment.

Basic Stamp

Parallax (www.parallax.com) Basic Stamp and Basic Stamp 2 (BS-2) are probably the most common microcontrollers in the hobbyist market. Programmed in PBASIC, they are easy to use, and include the same basic functions as Wiring and Arduino: digital in and out, serial in and out, PWM out, and a form of analog in. Their analog in is slower than an analog-to-digital converter, however. In addition, PBASIC lacks the ability to pass parameters to functions, which makes programming many of the examples shown in this book more difficult. It's possible to do everything you've seen here on a Basic Stamp, however. And there are more code samples available on the Net for the BS-2 than for just about any other controller.

BX-24

NetMedia's BX-24 controller (www.basicx.com) affords everything that Wiring and Arduino do; in fact, it's even based on the same microcontroller family that those two are (the Atmel AVR controllers). It's programmed in a variant of Visual BASIC (BasicX), and even includes limited support for multitasking. The programming environment for it is available only on Windows, however. Of the various Basic Stamp–like modules on the market, it's arguably the best, especially for tasks like the ones found in this book. It's a decent alternative for networked objects for beginners.

The BX-24 and the Basic Stamp both cost around $50 apiece, and by the time you've bought the starter kit, around $100.

PIC and AVR

Microchip's PIC and Atmel's AVR microcontrollers are excellent microcontrollers. You'll find the AVRs at the heart of Arduino, Wiring, and BX-24 controllers, and the PICs at the heart of the Basic Stamps. The BX-24, Basic Stamp, Wiring, and Arduino environments are essentially wrappers around these controllers, making them easier to work with. To use PICs or AVRs on their own, you need a hardware programmer that connects to your computer, and you need to install a command-line compiler. There are BASIC and C compilers available for both microcontroller families. The commercial PIC C and BASIC compilers tend to be far more thoroughly developed and supported than any open source compilers for that family. In contrast, avr-gcc, the open source compiler for the AVR controllers, is an excellent tool, and has been expanded enthusiastically by the community using it. In fact, it's the engine that runs Wiring and Arduino.

If you're looking to expand to other compilers, or you want to learn about the technical details underlying what you've seen here, www.atmel.com and www.avrfreaks. net are the best places to start. In addition, Pascal Stang's AVRlib libraries for the AVR controllers offer many useful functions: hubbard.engr.scu.edu/avr/avrlib/. If you want to learn more about the PIC, start at the source: www. microchip.com. If you want a good BASIC compiler for the PIC, check out MicroEngineering Labs PicBasic Pro at www.melabs.com, and if you want a good commercial C compiler for it, try CCS C: www.ccsinfo.com.

Though the microcontrollers themselves are cheap (between $1 and $10 apiece), getting all the tools set up for yourself will cost you some money. It's generally cheaper on the AVR side, as the avr-gcc is a good free compiler, and the hardware programmers for the AVR can be gotten for less than $100. On the PIC side, you could spend a few hundred dollars by the time you get a good programmer and compiler. There's also a pretty significant time investment in getting set up, as the tools for pro-gramming these controllers from scratch assume more knowledge than any of the others listed here.

Make Controller

The MAKE Controller from *Make Magazine*, made by Making Things (www.makingthings.com) is a powerful controller. It's got built-in Ethernet, high-current drivers for motors on its outputs, and support for multitasking and communication via OSC. At $150, it's not the least expensive controller here, and at 3.5" x 4.5", it's not the smallest, but it is highly capable. With built-in Ethernet, it can replace the Arduino plus Lantronix combination handily, if your project has room for its footprint.

There are a few different ways to work with the Make module. If you're an experienced programmer, you can set up the compiler and development environment on your own machine and program it in C. If you're not, you can interface to it from other environments by sending it OSC commands, either via USB or via Ethernet. In addition, there are some built-in functions called Poly functions that allow you to build basic applications. Expect to see many exciting new developments in terms of its interface in the near future as well.

Propeller

The Parallax Propeller controller (www.parallax.com/ propeller) is similar to the Make controller, in that it's a more powerful controller that affords multitasking. The programming environment for it is not for the beginner, and it's only available for Windows. The Propeller is capable of generating video, handling input from keyboard and mouse, and other tasks simultaneously. In fact, Uncommon Projects have made the YBox (ybox.tv), a device that overlays text from a website on a TV signal using a Propeller and an XPort. Though there are not yet generic examples using the Propeller to communicate over Ethernet, there undoubtedly will be soon.

As advanced processors continue to fall in price, you can expect to see more modules like the Make controller and the Propeller on the market for hobbyists and beginners.

Phidgets

Phidgets (www.phidgets.com) is a set of sensor and actuator modules that connect to your computer via USB. You don't program them, you just read their inputs and outputs from your desktop environment using Flash, Max/MSP, Java, or other tools. The NADA proxy tool mentioned earlier is designed to interface with Phidgets, among other things. Among the Phidgets modules are a number of useful sensors and actuators that can be used with other microcontroller and desktop environments. Their parts are well-designed and their connectors are solid, so if you know your project is going to take some abuse, you may want to spend a little more and buy at least your sensors from them.

SitePlayer

NetMedia's SitePlayer is an alternative to the Lantronix devices. It's basically a web server with telnet on a chip. Its form factor isn't quite as compact as the Lantronix units, and the tools for downloading new configurations for it are available only for Windows. Its web interface is handy, though, if you're looking to build a project in which users control a physical device through a web interface, because the interface can live directly on the chip, with no need for an external server.
X

66 New Tools

There is no such thing as the technology book that's fully up-to-date, and this book is no exception. New tools are coming out for networking physical devices every day. Here are a few of the ones that excited me most that came out as I was finishing this book:

- Lantronix announced two new products: the XPort Direct, a lower cost version of the XPort; and the MatchPort, a lower-cost and smaller version of the WiPort. With these two, both serial-to-Ethernet and serial-to-WiFi connections get ever cheaper.
- The Arduino Bluetooth board is now available, allowing both programming and communication wirelessly from an Arduino board. An Arduino Ethernet board is in the works as well. In addition to Arduino modules made by the original developers, there are many Arduino derivatives coming on the market from the community as well.
- MaxStream announced the next generation of the XBee radios, which will include real ZigBee mesh networking, beyond what the examples in this book have demonstrated.

- IOgear, Netgear, Actiontec, and many others have released Powerline Ethernet modules. These devices enable you to send Ethernet signals over AC powerlines at speeds up to 200 Mbps, several orders of magnitude faster than X10. Powerline Ethernet control modules won't be far behind this.

More tools will follow these. Though some specifics of the examples you've read may be out of date in a few years, the principles will give you the foundations to learn not only the tools you've seen here, but also new ones as they come along.
X

Where to Get Stuff

Many different hardware suppliers and software sources are mentioned in this book. This appendix provides a summary of all of them, along with a brief description of each. It's organized in two sections: hardware and software, sorted alphabetically by source.

Hardware

KEY
☏ Phone / * Toll Free
📠 Fax
✉ Mailing address

Abacom Technologies
Abacom sells a range of RF transmitters, receivers, and transceivers and serial-to-Ethernet modules.
www.abacomdirect.com
email: info@abacomdirect.com
✉ 383 Bering Avenue
   Toronto, ON M8Z 3B1, Canada

Aboyd Company
The Aboyd Company sells art supplies, costumes, novelties, cardboard standups, home décor, and more. They're also a good source of Charley Chimp cymbal-playing monkeys.
www.aboyd.com
email: info@aboyd.com
☏ +1-888-458-2693
☏ +1-601-948-3477 International
📠 +1-601-948-3479
✉ P.O. Box 4568
   Jackson, MS 39296, USA

Acroname Easier Robotics
Acroname sells a wide variety of sensors and actuators for robotics and electronics projects. They've got an excellent range of esoteric sensors like UV flame sensors, cameras, and thermal array sensors. They've got a lot of basic distance rangers as well. They also have a number of good tutorials on how to use their parts on their site.
www.acroname.com
email: info@acroname.com
☏ +1-720-564-0373
📠 +1-720-564-0376
✉ Acroname Inc.
   4822 Sterling Dr.
   Boulder, CO 80301-2350, USA

Adafruit Industries
Adafruit makes a number of useful open source DIY electronics kits, including an AVR programmer, an MP3 player, and more.
www.adafruit.com
email: sales@adafruit.com

Atmel
Atmel makes the AVR microcontrollers that are at the heart of the Arduino, Wiring, and BX-24 modules. They also make the ARM microcontroller that runs the Make controller.
www.atmel.com
☏ +1-408-441-0311
✉ 2325 Orchard Parkway
   San Jose, CA 95131, USA

Blue Radios
Blue Radios makes and sells Bluetooth radio modules for electronics manufacturers. Their radios are at the heart of SparkFun's BlueSMiRF dongles.
www.blueradios.com
email: sales@blueradios.com
☏ +1-303-957-1003
📠 +1-303-845-7134
✉ 7173 S. Havana Street, Suite 600
   Englewood, CO 80112, USA

Devantech/Robot Electronics
Devantech makes ultrasonic ranger sensors, electronic compasses, LCD displays, motor drivers, relay controllers, and other useful add-ons for microcontroller projects.
robot-electronics.co.uk
e-mail: sales@robot-electronics.co.uk
☏ +44 (0)1379 640450 or 644285
📠 +44 (0)1379 650482
✉ Unit 2B Gilray Road
   Diss, Norfolk, IP22 4EU, England

Digi-Key Electronics
Digi-Key is one of the U.S.'s largest retailers of electronics components. They're a staple source for things you use all the time — resistors, capacitors, connectors, some sensors, breadboards, wire, solder, and more.
www.digikey.com
☏ +1-800-344-4539 or
☏ +1-218-681-6674
📠 +1-218-681-3380
✉ 701 Brooks Avenue South
   Thief River Falls, MN 56701, USA

ELFA
ELFA is one of Northern Europe's largest electronics components suppliers.
www.elfa.se
email: export@elfa.se
☏ +46 8 580 941 30
✉ S-175 80 Järfälla, Sweden

Farnell
Farnell supplies electronics components for all of Europe. Their catalog part numbers are consistent with Newark in the U.S., so if you're working on both sides of the Atlantic, sourcing Farnell parts can be convenient.
www.farnell.co.uk
email: sales@farnell.co.uk
☏ +44-8701-200-200
📠 +44-8701-200-201
✉ Canal Road,
   Leeds, LS12 2TU, United Kingdom

Figaro USA, Inc.
Figaro Sensor sells a range of gas sensors, including volatile organic compound sensors, carbon monoxide sensors, oxygen sensors, and more.
www.figarosensor.com
email: figarousa@figarosensor.com
☏ +1-847-832-1701
📠 +1-847-832-1705
✉ 3703 West Lake Ave., Suite 203
   Glenview, IL 60026, USA

Future Technology Devices International, Ltd. +(FTDI)

FTDI makes a range of USB-to-serial adaptor chips, including the FT232RL that's on many of the modules in this book.

www.ftdichip.com

email: admin1@ftdichip.com

(+44 (0) 141 429 2777

▢ 373 Scotland Street
  Glasgow, G5 8QB, United Kingdom

Glolab

Glolab makes a range of electronic kits and modules including several useful RF and IR transmitters, receivers, and transceivers.

www.glolab.com

email: lab@glolab.com

Gridconnect

Gridconnect distributes networking products, including those from Lantronix and Maxstream.

www.gridconnect.com

email: sales@gridconnect.com

(+1 630 245 1445

✆ +1 630 245 1717

(* +1 800 975 GRID (4743) U.S. toll-free

▢ 1630 W. Diehl Road
  Naperville, IL 60563, USA

Images SI Inc.

Images SI sells robotics and electronics parts. They carry a range of RFID parts, force-sensing resistors, stretch sensors, gas sensors, electronic kits, speech recognition kits, solar energy parts, and microcontrollers.

www.imagesco.com

email: imagesco@verizon.net

(+1-718-966-3694

✆ +1-718-966-3695

▢ 109 Woods of Arden Road
  Staten Island, NY 10312, USA

Interlink Electronics

Interlink makes force-sensing resistors, touchpads, and other input devices.

www.interlinkelectronics.com

email: specialty@interlink
         electronics.com

(+1-805-484-8855

✆ +1-805-484-8989

▢ 546 Flynn Road
  Camarillo, CA 93012, USA

IOGear

IOGear make computer adaptors. Their USB-to-serial adaptors are good, and they carry Powerline Ethernet products.

www.iogear.com

email: sales@iogear.com

(* +1-866-946-4327 Toll-free

(+1-949-453-8782

✆ +1-949-453-8785

▢ 23 Hubble Drive
  Irvine, CA 92618, USA

Jameco Electronics

Jameco carries bulk and individual electronics components, cables, breadboards, tools, and other staples for the electronics hobbyist or professional.

www.jameco.com

    1355 Shoreway Road
    Belmont, CA 94002, USA

email:
domestic@jameco.com
international@jameco.com
custservice@jameco.com

(+1-800-831-4242
  Toll-free 24-hour order line

(+1-650-592-8097
  International order line

✆ +1-650-592-2503 International

✆ +1-800-237-6948* Toll-free fax

✆ +001-800-593-1449*
  Mexico toll-free fax

✆ +1-803-015-237-6948*
  Indonesia toll-free fax

Keyspan

Keyspan makes computer adaptors. Their USA-19xx series of USB-to-serial adaptors are very handy for micro-controller work.

www.keyspan.com

email: info@keyspan.com

(+1-510-222-0131 Info/sales

(+1-510-222-8802 Support

✆ +1-510-222-0323

▢ 4118 Lakeside Dr
  Richmond, CA 94806, USA

Lantronix

Lantronix makes the serial-to-Ethernet modules used in this book: the XPort, the WiPort, the WiMicro, the Micro, and many others.

www.lantronix.com

email: sales@lantronix.com

(+1-800-526-8766

(+1-949-453-3990

✆ +1-949-450-7249

▢ 5353 Barranca Parkway
  Irvine, CA 92618, USA

Libelium

Libelium makes an XBee shield for Arduino and other wireless products.

www.libelium.com

email: info@libelium.com

▢ Libelium Comunicaciones
  Distribuidas S.L.
  Maria de Luna 11, Instalaciones
  CEEIARAGON, C.P: 50018
  Zaragoza, Spain

Linx Technologies

Linx makes a number of RF receivers, transmitters, and transceivers.

www.linxtechnologies.com

email: info@linxtechnologies.com

(+1-800-736-6677 U.S.

(+1-541-471-6256 International

✆ +1-541-471-6251

▢ 159 Ort Lane
  Merlin, OR 97532, USA

Low Power Radio Solutions

LPRS makes a number of RF receivers, transmitters, and transceivers.

www.lprs.co.uk

email: info@lprs.co.uk

(+44-1993-709418

(+44-1993-708575

▣ *Two Rivers Industrial Estate*
Station Lane, Witney
Oxon, OX28 4BH, United Kingdom

Making Things

Making Things makes the MAKE controller, and originated the now-discontinued Teleo controllers. They do custom hardware engineering solutions.

www.makingthings.com

email: info@makingthings.com

(+1-415-255-9513

▣ 1020 Mariposa Street, #2
San Francisco, CA 94110, USA

Mannings RFID Shop

Mannings sells RFID tools and bar code readers and printers. They sell the ID Innovations RFID readers.

www.rfidshop.com

email: info@manningsrfid.com

(+44-1704-538-202

(+44-1704-514-713

▣ Units 1–5, Russell Road
Southport, Merseyside, England
PR9 7SY, United Kingdom

Maxim Integrated Products

Maxim makes sensors, communications chips, power management chips, and more. They also own Dallas Semiconductor. Together, they're one of the major sources for chips related to serial communication, temperature sensors, LCD control, and much more.

www.maxim-ic.com

email: info2@maxim-ic.com

(+1-408-737-7600

(+1-408-737-7194

▣ 120 San Gabriel Drive
Sunnyvale, CA 94086, USA

Maxstream

Maxstream makes ZigBee radios, radio modems, and Ethernet bridges.

www.maxstream.net

(+1-866-765-9885

(+1-801-765-9885 *International*

(+1-801-765-9895

▣ 355 South 520 West Suite 180
Lindon, UT 84042, USA

Microchip

Microchip makes the PIC family of microcontrollers. They have a very wide range of microcontrollers, for just about every conceivable purpose.

www.microchip.com

(+1-480-792-7200

▣ 2355 West Chandler Blvd.
Chandler, AZ, 85224-6199, USA

Mouser

Mouser is a large retailer of electronic components in the U.S. They stock most of the staple parts used in the projects in this book, like resistors, capacitors, and some sensors. They also carry the FTDI USB-to-serial cable.

www.mouser.com

email: help@mouser.com

▣ 1000 North Main Street
Mansfield, TX 76063, USA

NetMedia

NetMedia makes the BX-24 micro-controller module and the SitePlayer Ethernet module.

www.basicx.com

siteplayer.com

email: sales@netmedia.com

(+1-520-544-4567

(+1-520-544-0800

▣ 10940 N. Stallard Place
Tucson, AZ 85737, USA

Newark In One Electronics

Newark supplies electronics components in the U.S. Their catalog part numbers are consistent with Farnell in the Europe, so if you're working on both sides of the Atlantic, sourcing parts from Farnell and Newark can be convenient.

www.newark.com

email: somewhere@something.com

(+1-773-784-5100

(+1-888-551-4801

▣ 4801 N. Ravenswood
Chicago, IL 60640-4496, USA

New Micros

New Micros sells a number of micro-controller modules. They also sell a USB-XBee dongle that allows you to connect Maxstream's XBee radios to a computer really easily. Their dongles also have all the necessary pins connected for reflashing the XBee's firmware serially.

www.newmicros.com

email: nmisales@newmicros.com

(+1-214-339-2204

Parallax

Parallax makes the Basic Stamp family of microcontrollers. They also make the Propeller microcontroller, and a wide range of sensors, beginners' kits, robots, and other useful tools for people interested in electronics and microcontroller projects.

www.parallax.com

email: sales@parallax.com

(* +1-888-512-1024 *Toll-free sales*

(+1-916-624-8333
Office/international

(+1-916-624-8003

▣ 599 Menlo Drive
Rocklin, California 95765, USA

Phidgets

Phidgets makes input and output modules that connect desktop and laptop computers to the physical world.
www.phidgets.com
email: sales@phidgets.com
℡ +1-403-282-7335
℻ +1402-282-7332
✉ 2715A 16A NW
   Calgary, Alberta T2M3R7, Canada

RadioShack

You've got questions, they've got a cell phone plan for you. Despite their increasing focus on mobile phone plans, they still do carry some useful parts. Check the website for part numbers and call your local store first to see if they've got what you need. It'll save you time.
www.radioshack.com

Reynolds Electronics

Reynolds Electronics makes a number of small kits and modules for RF and infrared communications, IR remote control, and other useful add-on functions for microcontroller projects.
www.rentron.com
email: sales@rentron.com
℡ +1-772-589-8510
℻ +1-772-589-8620
✉ 12300 Highway A1A
   Vero Beach, Florida, 32963, USA

Samtec

Samtec makes electronic connectors. They have a very wide range of connectors, so if you're looking for something odd, they probably make it.
www.samtec.com
email: info@samtec.com
℡ +1-800-SAMTEC-9

Skyetek

Skyetek makes RFID readers, writers, and antennas.
www.skyetek.com
℡ +1-720-565-0441
℻ +1-720-565-8989
✉ 11030 Circle Point Road, Suite 300
   Westminster, CO 80020, USA

Smarthome

Smarthome makes a wide variety of home automation devices, including cameras, appliance controllers, X10, and INSTEON devices.
www.smarthome.com
email: custsvc@smarthome.com
℡ 1-800-762-7846
℡ + 1-800-871-5719 Canada
℡ +1-949-221-9200 International
✉ 16542 Millikan Avenue
   Irvine, CA 92606, USA

Smart Projects/PCB Europe

Smart Projects/PCB Europe makes Arduino modules and shields, kits for building your own modules. They also make custom electronics projects.
www.pcb-europe.net/catalog
email: info@pcb-europe.net
℡ +39-339-296-5590
✉ Via Siccardi, 12
   10034 Chivasso TO, Italy

SparkFun Electronics

SparkFun makes it easier to use all kinds of electronic components. They make breakout boards for sensors, radios, power regulators, and sell a variety of microcontroller platforms.
www.sparkfun.com
email: spark@sparkfun.com
✉ 2500 Central Avnue, Suite Q
   Boulder, CO 80301, USA

Symmetry Electronics

Symmetry sells ZigBee and Bluetooth radios, serial-to-Ethernet modules, wi-fi modules, cellular modems, and other electronic communications devices.
www.semiconductorstore.com
℡ +1-877-466-9722
℡ +1-310-643-3470 International
℻ +1-310-297-9719
✉ 5400 West Rosecrans Avenue
   Hawthorne, CA 90250, USA

TI-RFID

TIRIS is Texas Instruments' RFID division. They make tags and readers for RFID in many bandwidths and protocols.
www.tiris.com
℡ +1-800-962-RFID (7343)
℻ +1-214-567-RFID (7343)
✉ Radio Frequency
   Identification Systems
   6550 Chase Oaks Blvd., MS 8470
   Plano, TX 75023, USA

Trossen Robotics

Trossen Robotics sells a range of RFID supplies and robotics. They have a number of good sensors, including Interlink force-sensing resistors, linear actuators, Phidgets kits, RFID readers, and tags for most RFID ranges.
www.trossenrobotics.com
email: jenniej@trossenrobotics.com
℡ +1-877-898-1005
℻ +1-708-531-1614
✉ 1 Westbrook Co. Center, Suite 910
   Westchester, IL 60154, USA

Uncommon Projects

Uncommon Projects make the YBox, a text overlay device that puts text from web feeds on your TV.
www.uncommonprojects.com
ybox.tv
email: info@uncommonprojects.com
✉ 68 Jay Street #206
   Brooklyn New York 11201, USA

Software

Most of the software listed in this book is open source. In the following listings, anything that's not open source is noted explicitly as a commercial application. If there's no note, you can assume it's open.

Arduino

Arduino is a programming environment for AVR microcontrollers. It's based on Processing's programming interface. It runs on Mac OS X, Linux, and Windows operating systems.
www.arduino.cc

Asterisk

Asterisk is a software private branch exchange (PBX) manager for telephony. It runs on Linux and Unix operating systems.
www.asterisk.org

AVRlib

AVRlib is a library of C functions for a variety of tasks using AVR processors. It runs on Mac OS X, Linux, and Windows operating systems as a library for the avr-gcc compiler.
hubbard.engr.scu.edu/avr/avrlib/

avr-gcc

The GNU avr-gcc is a C compiler and assembler for AVR microcontrollers. It runs on Mac OS X, Linux, and Windows operating systems.
www.avrfreaks.net/AVRGCC/

CCS C

CCS C is a commercial C compiler for the PIC microcontroller. It runs on Windows and Linux operating systems.
www.ccsinfo.com

Dave's Telnet

Dave's Telnet is a telnet application for Windows.
dtelnet.sourceforge.net

Eclipse

Eclipse is an integrated development environment (IDE) for programming in many different languages. It's extensible through a plugin architecture, and there are compiler links to most major programming languages. It runs on Mac OS X, Linux, and Windows.
www.eclipse.org

Evocam

Evocam is a commercial webcam application for Mac OS X.
evological.com

Exemplar

Exemplar is a tool for authoring sensor applications through behavior rather than through programming. It runs on Mac OS X, Linux, and Windows operating systems as a plugin for Eclipse.
hci.stanford.edu/research/exemplar/

Fwink

Fwink is a webcam application for Windows.
lundie.ca/fwink

Girder

Girder is a commercial home automation application for Windows.
www.girder.nl

Java

Java is a programming language. It runs on Mac OS X, Linux, and Windows operating systems, and many embedded systems as well.
java.sun.com

Macam

Macam is a webcam driver for Mac OS X.
https://sourceforge.net/projects/webcam-osx/

Max/MSP

Max is a commercial graphic data flow authoring tool. It allows you to program by connecting graphic objects rather than writing text. Connected with Max are MSP, a realtime audio signal processing library, and Jitter, a realtime video signal processing library. It runs on Mac OS X, Linux, and Windows operating systems.
www.cycling74.com

Puredata (PD)

Puredata (PD) is a graphic data flow authoring tool. It allows you to program by connecting graphic objects rather than writing text. It runs on Mac OS X, Linux, and Windows operating systems.
puredata.info

PEAR

PEAR is the PHP Extension and Application Repository. It hosts extension libraries for the PHP scripting language, including NET_POP3 (pear.php.net/package/Net_POP3), which is used in this book.
pear.php.net

PHP

PHP is a scripting language that is especially suited for web development and can be embedded into HTML. It runs on Mac OS X, Linux, and Windows operating systems.
www.php.net

PicBasic Pro

PicBasic Pro is a commercial BASIC compiler for PIC microcontrollers. It runs on Windows.
www.melabs.com

Processing

Processing is a programming language and environment designed for the non technical user who wants to program images, animation, and interaction. It runs on Mac OS X, Linux, and Windows.
www.processing.org

Proxi

Proxi is a free (but not open source) application for automating operating system tasks based on events. It runs on Mac OS X.
proxi.griffintechnology.com

Putty SSH

Putty is a telnet/SSH/serial port client for Windows.
www.puttyssh.org

QRcode Library

QRcode library is a set of libraries for encoding and decoding QRcode 2-D barcodes. It runs on Mac OS X, Linux, and Windows as a library for Java.
qrcode.sourceforge.jp

Dan Shiffman's Processing Libraries

Dan Shiffman has written a number of useful libraries for Processing, including the pqrcode library used in this book (www.shiffman.net/p5/pqrcode). He's also got a SFTP library (www.shiffman.net/2007/06/04/sftp-with-java-processing/) and a sudden-motion sensor library for Mac OS X (www.shiffman.net/2006/10/28/processingsms/).

Sketchtools NADA

NADA is a commercial proxy tool for connecting programming environments with hardware devices.
www.sketchtools.com

TinkerProxy

TinkerProxy is a TCP-to-serial proxy application. It runs on Windows.
tinker.it/now/category/software/

UDP Library for Processing

Hypermedia's UDP library for Processing enables you to communicate via UDP from Processing. It runs on Mac OS X, Linux, and Windows as a library for Processing.
hypermedia.loeil.org/processing/

Wiring

Wiring is a programming environment for AVR microcontrollers. It's based on Processing's programming interface. It runs on Mac OS X, Linux, and Windows operating systems.
www.wiring.org.co

```php
    $char = ord(fgetc($mySocket));

    // if you got a header byte, deal with t
    if ($char == 0x7E) {
        // push the last byte array onto the
        array_push($packets, $bytes);
        // clear the byte array:
        $bytes = array();
        // increment the packet counter:
        $packetCounter++;

    push the current byte onto the end of
    ay_push($bytes, $char);

    verage the readings from all the packets
    totalAverage = averagePackets($packets);
    print_r($packets);
    echo "hi there";
    // if you got a good reading, write it to th
    if ($totalAverage > 0) {
        writeToFile($totalAverage);
    }
    //close the socket:
    fclose ($mySocket);
    // update the message for the HTML:
    essageString = "Sensor Reading at:". Stime


    ------------------------------*/

    ets($whichArray) {
                    // average of all th
                    // number of valid r
                    // total of all read


    ket) {
                    e average
```

```c
void setup() {
    // make pin 13 an output pin. You'll pu
    pinMode(13, OUTPUT);
}


void loop() {
    // read an analog input, 0 - 1023:
    int pulse = analogRead(0);
    // use that value to pulse an LED o0n p
    pulseOut(13, pulse, HIGH);

}

void pulseOut(int pinNumber, int pulseWidt
    // only pulse if the pulseWidth value is
    if (pulseWidth > 0) {
        // if the pulse should be high, go hig
        if (state == HIGH) {
            digitalWrite(pinNumber, HIGH);
            delayMicroseconds(pulseWidth);
            digitalWrite(pinNumber, LOW);
            delayMicroseconds(pulseWidth);
        }
        // if the pulse should be low, go low
        else {
            digitalW        mber, LOW);
            delayM        s(pulseWidth);
```

Appendix C 🔊

MAKE: PROJECTS

Program Listings

This Appendix contains the complete code listings for all of the programs in the book. You can find a link to download the source code at www.makezine.com/go/MakingThingsTalk.

Chapter 1

Hello World!
Language: Processing
Prints out "Hello World!"

```
println("Hello World!\n");
```

Triangle drawing program
Language: Processing
Draws a triangle whenever the mouse button is not pressed. Erases when the mouse button is pressed.

```
// declare your variables:
float redValue = 0;     // variable to hold the red color
float greenValue = 0;   // variable to hold the green color
float blueValue = 0;    // variable to hold the blue color

// the setup() method runs once at the beginning of the program:

void setup() {
  size(320, 240);      // sets the size of the applet window
  background(0);       // sets the background of the window to black
  fill(0);             // sets the color to fill shapes with (0 = black)
  smooth();            // draw with antialiased edges
}

// the draw() method runs repeatedly, as long as the applet window
// is open.  It refreshes the window, and anything else you program
// it to do:

void draw() {

  // Pick random colors for red, green, and blue:
  redValue = random(255);
  greenValue = random(255);
  blueValue = random(255);

  // set the line color:
  stroke(redValue, greenValue, blueValue);

  // draw when the mouse is up (to hell with conventions):
  if (mousePressed == false) {
    // draw a triangle:
    triangle(mouseX, mouseY, width/2, height/2,pmouseX, pmouseY);
  }
  // erase when the mouse is down:
  else {
    background(0);
    fill(0);
  }
}
```

Hello World!
Language: PHP
Prints out a "Hello World!" HTML page

```
<?php
echo "<html><head></head><body>\n";
echo "hello world!\n";
echo "</body></html>\n";
?>
```

Date printer
Language: PHP
Prints the date and time in an HTML page.

```
<?php
//    Get the date, and format it:
$date = date("Y-m-d h:i:s\t");

// print the beginning of an HTML page:
echo "<html><head></head><body>\n";
echo "hello world!<br>\n";
// Include the date:
echo "Today's date: $date<br>\n";
// finish the HTML:
echo "</body></html>\n";

?>
```

Blink (aka Hello World! In Arduino/Wiring):

Language: Arduino/Wiring
Blinks an LED attached to pin 13 every half second.
Connections: Pin 13: + leg of an LED (- leg goes to ground)

```
int LEDPin = 13;

void setup() {
  pinMode(LEDPin, OUTPUT);    // set pin 13 to be an output
}

void loop() {
  digitalWrite(LEDPin, HIGH);    // turn the LED on pin 13 on
  delay(500);                    // wait half a second
  digitalWrite(LEDPin, LOW);     // turn the LED off
  delay(500);                    // wait half a second
}
```

Simple Serial

Language: Arduino/Wiring

Listens for an incoming serial byte, adds one to the byte and sends the result back out serially. Also blinks an LED on pin 13 every half second.

```
int LEDPin = 13;          // you can use any digital I/O pin you want
int inByte = 0;           // variable to hold incoming serial data
long blinkTimer = 0;      // keeps track of how long since the LED
                          // was last turned off
int blinkInterval = 1000; // a full second from on to off to on again

void setup() {
  pinMode(LEDPin, OUTPUT);   // set pin 13 to be an output
  Serial.begin(9600);        // configure the serial port for 9600 bps
                             // data rate.
}

void loop() {
  // if there are any incoming serial bytes available to read:
  if (Serial.available() > 0) {
    // then read the first available byte:
    inByte = Serial.read();
    // and add one to it, then send the result out:
    Serial.print(inByte+1, BYTE);
  }

  // Meanwhile, keep blinking the LED.
  // after a quarter of a second, turn the LED on:
  if (millis() - blinkTimer >= blinkInterval / 2) {
    digitalWrite(LEDPin, HIGH);      // turn the LED on pin 13 on
  }
  // after a half a second, turn the LED off and reset the timer:
  if (millis() - blinkTimer >= blinkInterval) {
    digitalWrite(LEDPin, LOW);       // turn the LED off
    blinkTimer = millis();           // reset the timer
  }
}
```

Chapter 2

Sensor Reader

Language: Wiring/Arduino

Reads two analog inputs and two digital inputs and outputs their values.

Connections:

- analog sensors on analog input pins 0 and 1
- switches on digital I/O pins 2 and 3

```
int leftSensor = 0;    // analog input for the left arm
int rightSensor = 1;   // analog input for the right arm
int resetButton = 2;   // digital input for the reset button
int serveButton = 3;   // digital input for the serve button

int leftValue = 0;     // reading from the left arm
int rightValue = 0;    // reading from the right arm
int reset = 0;         // reading from the reset button
int serve = 0;         // reading from the serve button

void setup() {
  // configure the serial connection:
  Serial.begin(9600);
  // configure the digital inputs:
  pinMode(resetButton, INPUT);
  pinMode(serveButton, INPUT);
}

void loop() {
  // read the analog sensors:
  leftValue = analogRead(leftSensor);
  rightValue = analogRead(rightSensor);

  // read the digital sensors:
  reset = digitalRead(resetButton);
  serve = digitalRead(serveButton);

  // print the results:
  Serial.print(leftValue, DEC);
  Serial.print(",");
  Serial.print(rightValue, DEC);
  Serial.print(",");
  Serial.print(reset, DEC);
  Serial.print(",");
  // print the last sensor value with a println() so that
  // each set of four readings prints on a line by itself:
  Serial.println(serve, DEC);
}
```

Serial String Reader

Language: Processing

Reads in a string of characters from a serial port until it gets a linefeed (ASCII 10). Then splits the string into sections separated by commas. Then converts the sections to ints, and prints them out.

```
import processing.serial.*;      // import the Processing serial library

int linefeed = 10;               // Linefeed in ASCII
Serial myPort;                   // The serial port

void setup() {
  // List all the available serial ports
  println(Serial.list());

  // I know that the first port in the serial list on my mac
  // is always my  Arduino module, so I open Serial.list()[0].
  // Change the 0 to the appropriate number of the serial port
  // that your microcontroller is attached to.
  myPort = new Serial(this, Serial.list()[0], 9600);

  // read bytes into a buffer until you get a linefeed (ASCII 10):
  myPort.bufferUntil(linefeed);
}

void draw() {
  // twiddle your thumbs
}

// serialEvent  method is run automatically by the Processing applet
// whenever the buffer reaches the  byte value set in the bufferUntil()
// method in the setup():

void serialEvent(Serial myPort) {
  // read the serial buffer:
  String myString = myPort.readStringUntil(linefeed);

  // if you got any bytes other than the linefeed:
  if (myString != null) {
    myString = trim(myString);

    // split the string at the commas
    // and convert the sections into integers:
    int sensors[] = int(split(myString, ','));

    // print out the values you got:
    for (int sensorNum = 0; sensorNum < sensors.length; sensorNum++) {
      print("Sensor " + sensorNum + ": " + sensors[sensorNum] + "\t");
    }
    // add a linefeed after all the sensor values are printed:
    println();
  }
}
```

Monski Pong

Language: Processing

Uses the values from four sensors to animate a game of pong. Expects a serial string from the serial port in the following format:

leftPaddle, rightPaddle, resetButton, serveButton, linefeed

- leftPaddle: ASCII numeric string from 0 - 1023
- rightPaddle: ASCII numeric string from 0 - 1023
- resetButton: ASCII numeric string from 0 - 1
- serveButton: ASCII numeric string from 0 - 1

```
import processing.serial.*;      // import the serial library

int linefeed = 10;                    // Linefeed in ASCII
Serial myPort;                        // The serial port

float leftPaddle, rightPaddle;   // variables for the flex sensor values
int resetButton, serveButton;    // variables for the button values
int leftPaddleX, rightPaddleX;   // horizontal positions of the paddles
int paddleHeight = 50;           // vertical dimension of the paddles
int paddleWidth = 10;            // horizontal dimension of the paddles

float leftMinimum = 250;         // minimum value of the left flex sensor
float rightMinimum = 260;        // minimum value of the right flex sensor
float leftMaximum = 450;         // maximum value of the left flex sensor
float rightMaximum = 460;        // maximum value of the right flex sensor

int ballSize = 10;      // the size of the ball
int xDirection = 1;     // the ball's horizontal direction.
                        // left is -1, right is 1.
int yDirection = 1;     // the ball's vertical direction.
                        // up is -1, down is 1.
int xPos, yPos;  // the ball's horizontal and vertical positions

boolean ballInMotion = false; // whether the ball should be moving
int leftScore = 0;
int rightScore = 0;

PFont myFont;
int fontSize = 36;

void setup() {
  // set the window size:
  size(640, 480);

  // initialize the ball in the center of the screen:
  xPos = width/2;
  yPos = height/2;

  // List all the available serial ports
  println(Serial.list());

  // Open whatever port is the one you're using.
  myPort = new Serial(this, Serial.list()[0], 9600);
```

```
  // read bytes into a buffer until you get a linefeed (ASCII 10):
  myPort.bufferUntil(linefeed);

  // initialize the sensor values:
  leftPaddle = height/2;
  rightPaddle = height/2;
  resetButton = 0;
  serveButton = 0;

  // initialize the paddle horizontal positions:
  leftPaddleX = 50;
  rightPaddleX = width - 50;

  // set no borders on drawn shapes:
  noStroke();

  // create a font with the third font available to the system:
  PFont myFont = createFont(PFont.list()[2], fontSize);
  textFont(myFont);
}

void draw() {
  background(0);
  // draw the left paddle:
  rect(leftPaddleX, leftPaddle, paddleWidth, paddleHeight);
  // draw the right paddle:
  rect(rightPaddleX, rightPaddle, paddleWidth, paddleHeight);

  // calculate the ball's position and draw it:
  if (ballInMotion == true) {
    animateBall();
  }
  // if the serve button is pressed, start the ball moving:
  if (serveButton == 1) {
    ballInMotion = true;
  }
  // if the reset button is pressed, reset the scores
  // and start the ball moving:
  if (resetButton == 1) {
    leftScore = 0;
    rightScore = 0;
    ballInMotion = true;
  }
  // print the scores:
  text(leftScore, fontSize, fontSize);
  text(rightScore, width-fontSize, fontSize);
}

// serialEvent  method is run automatically by the Processing applet
// whenever the buffer reaches the  byte value set in the bufferUntil()
// method in the setup():

void serialEvent(Serial myPort) {
  // read the serial buffer:
  String myString = myPort.readStringUntil(linefeed);
```

```
  // if you got any bytes other than the linefeed:
  if (myString != null) {

    myString = trim(myString);
    // split the string at the commas
    //and convert the sections into integers:
    int sensors[] = int(split(myString, ','));
    // if you received all the sensor strings, use them:
    if (sensors.length == 4) {
      // calculate the flex sensors' ranges:
      float leftRange = leftMaximum - leftMinimum;
      float rightRange = rightMaximum - rightMinimum;

      // scale the flex sensors' results to the paddles' range:
      leftPaddle =  height * (sensors[0] - leftMinimum) / leftRange;
      rightPaddle = height * (sensors[1] - rightMinimum) / rightRange;

      // assign the switches' values to the button variables:
      resetButton = sensors[2];
      serveButton = sensors[3];

      // print the sensor values:
      print("left: "+ leftPaddle + "\tright: " + rightPaddle);
      println("\treset: "+ resetButton + "\tserve: " + serveButton);
    }
  }
}

void animateBall() {
  // if the ball is moving left:
  if (xDirection < 0) {
    // if the ball is to the left of the left paddle:
    if  ((xPos <= leftPaddleX)) {
      // if the ball is in between the top and bottom
      // of the left paddle:
      if((leftPaddle - (paddleHeight/2) <= yPos) &&
        (yPos <= leftPaddle + (paddleHeight /2))) {
        // reverse the horizontal direction:
        xDirection =-xDirection;
      }
    }
  }
  // if the ball is moving right:
  else {
    // if the ball is to the right of the right paddle:
    if  ((xPos >= ( rightPaddleX + ballSize/2))) {
      // if the ball is in between the top and bottom
      // of the right paddle:
      if((rightPaddle - (paddleHeight/2) <=yPos) &&
        (yPos <= rightPaddle + (paddleHeight /2))) {
        // reverse the horizontal direction:
        xDirection =-xDirection;
      }
    }
  }
}
```

```
  // if the ball goes off the screen left:
  if (xPos < 0) {
    rightScore++;
    resetBall();
  }
  // if the ball goes off the screen right:
  if (xPos > width) {
    leftScore++;
    resetBall();
  }

  // stop the ball going off the top or the bottom of the screen:
  if ((yPos - ballSize/2 <= 0) || (yPos +ballSize/2 >=height)) {
    // reverse the y direction of the ball:
    yDirection = -yDirection;
  }
  // update the ball position:
  xPos = xPos + xDirection;
  yPos = yPos + yDirection;

  // Draw the ball:
  rect(xPos, yPos, ballSize, ballSize);
}

void resetBall() {
  // put the ball back in the center
  xPos = width/2;
  yPos = height/2;
}
```

Monski Pong with Handshake

Language: Processing

Uses the values from four sensors to animate a game of pong. Expects a serial string from the serial port in the following format:

leftPaddle, rightPaddle, resetButton, serveButton, linefeed

- leftPaddle: ASCII numeric string from 0 - 1023
- rightPaddle: ASCII numeric string from 0 - 1023
- resetButton: ASCII numeric string from 0 - 1
- serveButton: ASCII numeric string from 0 - 1

Uses software handshaking by sending a carriage return for the microcontroller to respond to.

```
import processing.serial.*;    // import the serial library

int linefeed = 10;             // Linefeed in ASCII
Serial myPort;                 // The serial port
boolean madeContact = false;   // whether you've made initial contact
                               // with the microcontroller
float leftPaddle, rightPaddle; // variables for the flex sensor values
int resetButton, serveButton;  // variables for the button values
int leftPaddleX, rightPaddleX; // horizontal positions of the paddles
```

```
int paddleHeight = 50;         // vertical dimension of the paddles
int paddleWidth = 10;          // horizontal dimension of the paddles

float leftMinimum = 250;       // minimum value of the left flex sensor
float rightMinimum = 260;      // minimum value of the right flex sensor
float leftMaximum = 450;       // maximum value of the left flex sensor
float rightMaximum = 460;      // maximum value of the right flex sensor

int ballSize = 10;             // the size of the ball
int xDirection = 1;            // the ball's horizontal direction.
// left is -1, right is 1.
int yDirection = 1;            // the ball's vertical direction.
// up is -1, down is 1.
int xPos, yPos;                // the ball's horizontal and vertical positions

boolean ballInMotion = false;  // whether or not the ball should be moving
int leftScore = 0;
int rightScore = 0;

PFont myFont;
int fontSize = 36;

void setup() {
  // set the window size:
  size(640, 480);

  // initialize the ball in the center of the screen:
  xPos = width/2;
  yPos = height/2;

  // List all the available serial ports
  println(Serial.list());
  // Open whatever port is the one you're using.
  myPort = new Serial(this, Serial.list()[0], 9600);

  // read bytes into a buffer until you get a linefeed (ASCII 10):
  myPort.bufferUntil(linefeed);

  // initialize the sensor values:
  leftPaddle = height/2;
  rightPaddle = height/2;
  resetButton = 0;
  serveButton = 0;

  // initialize the paddle horizontal positions:
  leftPaddleX = 50;
  rightPaddleX = width - 50;

  // set no borders on drawn shapes:
  noStroke();

  // create a font with the third font available to the system:
  PFont myFont = createFont(PFont.list()[2], fontSize);
  textFont(myFont);
}
```

```
void draw() {
  // if you've never gotten a string from the microcontroller,
  // keep sending carriage returns to prompt for one:
  if (madeContact == false) {
    myPort.write('\r');
  }
  background(0);
  // draw the left paddle:
  rect(leftPaddleX, leftPaddle, paddleWidth, paddleHeight);

  // draw the right paddle:
  rect(rightPaddleX, rightPaddle, paddleWidth, paddleHeight);

  // calculate the ball's position and draw it:
  if (ballInMotion == true) {
    animateBall();
  }
  // if the serve button is pressed, start the ball moving:
  if (serveButton == 1) {
    ballInMotion = true;
  }
  // if the reset button is pressed, reset the scores
  // and start the ball moving:
  if (resetButton == 1) {
    leftScore = 0;
    rightScore = 0;
    ballInMotion = true;
  }
  // print the scores:
  text(leftScore, fontSize, fontSize);
  text(rightScore, width-fontSize, fontSize);
}


// serialEvent  method is run automatically by the Processing applet
// whenever the buffer reaches the  byte value set in the bufferUntil()
// method in the setup():

void serialEvent(Serial myPort) {
  // if serialEvent occurs at all, contact with the microcontroller
  // has been made:
  madeContact = true;

  // read the serial buffer:
  String myString = myPort.readStringUntil(linefeed);

  // if you got any bytes other than the linefeed:
  if (myString != null) {

    myString = trim(myString);
    // split the string at the commas
    //and convert the sections into integers:
    int sensors[] = int(split(myString, ','));
    // if you received all the sensor strings, use them:
    if (sensors.length == 4) {
```

```
      // calculate the flex sensors' ranges:
      float leftRange = leftMaximum - leftMinimum;
      float rightRange = rightMaximum - rightMinimum;

      // scale the flex sensors' results to the paddles' range:
      leftPaddle = height * (sensors[0] - leftMinimum) / leftRange;
      rightPaddle = height * (sensors[1] - rightMinimum) / rightRange;

      // assign the switches' values to the button variables:
      resetButton = sensors[2];
      serveButton = sensors[3];

      // print the sensor values:
      print("left: "+ leftPaddle + "\tright: " + rightPaddle);
      println("\treset: "+ resetButton + "\tserve: " + serveButton);

      // send out the serial port to ask for data:
      myPort.write('\r');
    }
  }
}
void animateBall() {
  // if the ball is moving left:
  if (xDirection < 0) {
    // if the ball is to the left of the left paddle:
    if ((xPos <= leftPaddleX)) {
      // if the ball is in between the top and bottom
      // of the left paddle:
      if((leftPaddle - (paddleHeight/2) <= yPos) &&
        (yPos <= leftPaddle + (paddleHeight /2))) {
        // reverse the horizontal direction:
        xDirection =-xDirection;
      }
    }
  }
  // if the ball is moving right:
  else {
    // if the ball is to the right of the right paddle:
    if ((xPos >= ( rightPaddleX + ballSize/2))) {
      // if the ball is in between the top and bottom
      // of the right paddle:
      if((rightPaddle - (paddleHeight/2) <=yPos) &&
        (yPos <= rightPaddle + (paddleHeight /2))) {

        // reverse the horizontal direction:
        xDirection =-xDirection;
      }
    }
  }

  // if the ball goes off the screen left:
  if (xPos < 0) {
    rightScore++;
    resetBall();
  }
```

```
// if the ball goes off the screen right:
if (xPos > width) {
  leftScore++;
  resetBall();
}


// stop the ball going off the top or the bottom of the screen:
if ((yPos - ballSize/2 <= 0) || (yPos +ballSize/2 >=height)) {
  // reverse the y direction of the ball:
  yDirection = -yDirection;
}
// update the ball position:
xPos = xPos + xDirection;
yPos = yPos + yDirection;

// Draw the ball:
  rect(xPos, yPos, ballSize, ballSize);
}


void resetBall() {
  // put the ball back in the center
  xPos = width/2;
  yPos = height/2;
}
```

Chapter 3

Modified Date page
Language: PHP
Prints the date. But no HTML.

```php
<?php
//    Get the date, and format it:
$date = date("Y-m-d h:i:s\t");
// Include the date:
echo "< $date >\n";
?>
```

Parameter reader
Language: PHP
Prints any parameters sent in using an HTTP GET command.

```php
<?php
// print the beginning of an HTML page:
echo "<html><head></head><body>\n";

// print out all the variables:
foreach ($_REQUEST as $key => $value)
    {
        echo "$key: $value<br>\n";
    }
// finish the HTML:
echo "</body></html>\n";
?>
```

Age checker
Language: PHP
Expects two parameters from the HTTP request:
• name (a text string)
• age (an integer)
Prints a personalized greeting based on the name and age.

```php
<?php
// print the beginning of an HTML page:
echo "<html><head></head><body>\n";

// read all the parameters and assign them to local variables:
foreach ($_REQUEST as $key => $value) {
    if ($key == "name") {
        $name = $value;
    }
    if ($key == "age") {
        $age = $value;
    }
}
```

```php
if ($age < 21) {
    echo "<p> $name, You're not old enough to drink.</p>\n";
} else {
    echo "<p> Hi $name. You're old enough to have a drink, but do ";
    echo "so responsibly.</p>\n";
}
// finish the HTML:
echo "</body></html>\n";
?>
```

Analog sensor reader

Language: Arduino/Wiring

Reads an analog input on Analog in 0, prints the result as an ASCII-formatted decimal value.

Connections:

- FSR analog sensor on Analog in 0

```
int sensorValue;          // outgoing ADC value
void setup()
{
  // start serial port at 9600 bps:
  Serial.begin(9600);
}

void loop()
{
  sensorValue = analogRead(0); // read analog input.

  // send analog value out in ASCII decimal format:
  Serial.println(sensorValue, DEC);

  delay(10);  // wait 10ms for next reading.
}
```

Serial String Reader

Language: Processing

Reads in a string of characters until it gets a linefeed (ASCII 10). Then converts the string into a number. Then graphs it.

```
import processing.serial.*;

int graphPosition = 0;  // the horizontal position of the latest
                        // line to be drawn on the graph
int linefeed = 10;      // linefeed in ASCII
Serial myPort;          // The serial port
int sensorValue = 0;    // the value from the sensor
```

```
void setup() {
  size(400,300);
  // List all the available serial ports
  println(Serial.list());

  // I know that the first port in the serial list on my Mac
  // is always my Arduino, so I open Serial.list()[0].
  // Open whatever port is the one you're using (the output
  // of Serial.list() can help, the are listed in order
  // starting with the one that corresponds to [0]).
  myPort = new Serial(this, Serial.list()[0], 9600);

  // read bytes into a buffer until you get a linefeed (ASCII 10):
  myPort.bufferUntil(linefeed);
}

void draw() {
  // twiddle your thumbs
}

// serialEvent  method is run automatically by the Processing applet
// whenever the buffer reaches the  byte value set in the bufferUntil()
// method in the setup():
void serialEvent(Serial myPort) {
  // read the serial buffer:
  String myString = myPort.readStringUntil(linefeed);

  // if you got any bytes other than the linefeed:
  if (myString != null) {
    // trim the carriage return and convert the string to an integer:
    sensorValue = int(trim(myString));

    println(sensorValue); // print it.
    drawGraph();
  }
}

void drawGraph() {
  // adjust this formula so that lineHeight is always less than
  // the height of the window:
  int lineHeight = sensorValue /2;

  stroke(0,255,0); // draw the line.
  line(graphPosition, height, graphPosition, height - lineHeight);
  // at the edge of the screen, go back to the beginning:
  if (graphPosition >= width) {
    graphPosition = 0;
    background(0);
  }
  else {
    graphPosition++;
  }
}
```

Cat graphing program
Language: Processing
Reads in a string of characters until it gets a linefeed (ASCII 10). Then converts the string into a number. Then graphs it. If the number has changed significantly, and there hasn't been a big change in more than a minute, the program prints a text string in place of an email message.

```
import processing.serial.*;

int linefeed = 10;         // linefeed in ASCII
Serial myPort;             // The serial port
int sensorValue = 0;       // the value from the sensor
int graphPosition = 0;     // the horizontal position of the latest
                           // line to be drawn on the graph
int prevSensorValue = 0;   // the previous sensor reading
boolean catOnMat = false;  // whether or not the cat's on the mat
int threshold = 320;       // above this number, the cat is on the mat.
```

▶▶ **Change this number to reflect the threshold of your own sensor.**

▶▶ **Adjust this to an acceptable frequency for sending emails.**

```
int timeThreshold = 1;    // minimum number of minutes between emails
int timeLastSent[] = {
  hour(), minute() - 1 }; // time the last message was sent

void setup() {
  size(400,300);
  // List all the available serial ports
  println(Serial.list());
  // I know that the first port in the serial list on my Mac
  // is always my Arduino, so I open Serial.list()[0].
  // Open whatever port is the one you're using (the output
  // of Serial.list() can help; the are listed in order
  // starting with the one that corresponds to [0]).
  myPort = new Serial(this, Serial.list()[0], 9600);

  // read bytes into a buffer until you get a linefeed (ASCII 10):
  myPort.bufferUntil(linefeed);
  println(hour() + ":" + minute());
}

void draw() {
  if (sensorValue > threshold ) {
    // if the last reading was less than the threshold,
    // then the cat just got on the mat.
    if (prevSensorValue <= threshold) {
      delay(100);
      if (sensorValue > threshold) {
        catOnMat = true;
        sendMail();
      }
    }
  }
```

```
  } else {
    // if the sensor value is less than the threshold,
    // and the previous value was greater, then the cat
    // just left the mat
    if (prevSensorValue >= threshold) {
      catOnMat = false;
    }
  }
  // save the sensor value as the previous value
  // so you can take new readings:
  prevSensorValue = sensorValue;
}


// serialEvent method is run automatically by the Processing applet
// whenever the buffer reaches the byte value set in the bufferUntil()
// method in the setup():
void serialEvent(Serial myPort) {
  // read the serial buffer:
  String myString = myPort.readStringUntil(linefeed);
  // if you got any bytes other than the linefeed:
  if (myString != null) {
    // trim the carriage return and convert the string to an integer:
    sensorValue = int(trim(myString));
    drawGraph(); // call this method instead of println()
  }
}


void drawGraph() {
  int lineHeight = sensorValue /2;
  // draw the line:
  if (catOnMat) {
    stroke(0,255,0); // draw green
  }
  else {
    stroke(255,0,0); // draw red
  }
  line(graphPosition, height, graphPosition, height - lineHeight);
  // at the edge of the screen, go back to the beginning:
  if (graphPosition >= width) {
    graphPosition = 0;
    background(0);
  }
  else {
    graphPosition++;
  }
}

void sendMail() {
  // calculate the current time in minutes:
  int[] presentTime = { hour(), minute() };

  // print the current time and the last time you sent a message:
  print(sensorValue + "\t");
  print( presentTime[0] + ":" + presentTime[1] +"\t");
  println(timeLastSent[0] + ":" + timeLastSent[1]);
```

```
  // if you're still in the same hour as the last message,
  // then make sure at least the minimum number of minutes has passed:
  if (presentTime[0] == timeLastSent[0]) {
    if (presentTime[1] - timeLastSent[1] >= timeThreshold) {
      println("This is where you'd send a mail.");
      // take note of the time this message was sent:
      timeLastSent[0] = hour();
      timeLastSent[1] = minute();
    }
  }


  // if the hour has changed since the last message,
  // then the difference in minutes is a bit more complex.
  // Use != rather than > to make sure the shift
  // from 23:59 to 0:00 is covered as well:
  if (presentTime[0] != timeLastSent[0]) {
    // calculate the difference in minutes:
    int minuteDifference = (60 - timeLastSent[1]) + presentTime[1];


    if (minuteDifference >= timeThreshold) {
      println("This is where you'd send a mail.");

      // take note of the time this message was sent:
      timeLastSent[0] = hour();
      timeLastSent[1] = minute();
    }
  }
}
```

Cat On Mat

Language: PHP

Expects a parameter called SensorValue, an integer. Prints a custom message depending on the value of SensorValue.

```php
<?php

$threshold = 320;    // minimum sensor value to trigger action

// print the beginning of the HTML page:
echo "<html><head></head><body>\n";

// read all the parameters and assign them to local variables:
foreach ($_REQUEST as $key => $value) {
    if ($key == "sensorValue") {
        $sensorValue = $value;
    }
}
// Respond depending on the sensor value:
if ($sensorValue > $threshold) {
    echo "<p> The cat is on the mat.</p>\n";
} else {
    echo "<p> the cat is not on the mat.</p>\n";
}
```

```php
// finish the HTML:
echo "</body></html>\n";
?>
```

Mail sender

Language: PHP

Expects a parameter called SensorValue, an integer. Sends an email if sensorValue is above a threshold value. This is an extension of the previous program. The previous one didn't actually send mail, but this one does.

```php
<?php

$threshold = 320;    // minimum sensor value to trigger action.
```

▶▶ **Change this number to reflect the threshold of your own sensor.**

```php
// print the beginning of an HTML page:
echo "<html><head></head><body>\n";

// read all the parameters and assign them to local variables:
foreach ($_REQUEST as $key => $value)
    {
        if ($key == "sensorValue") {
            $sensorValue = $value;
        }
    }

if ($sensorValue > $threshold) {
    $messageString =
      " The cat is on the mat at http://www.example.com/catcam.";
    echo $messageString;
    send_mail("yourname@example.com", "the cat", $messageString);
} else {
    echo "<p> the cat is not on the mat.</p>\n";
}
// finish the HTML:
echo "</body></html>\n";

end;

// end of the main script. Anything after here won't get run
// unless it's called in the code above this line

//////////////////////////////////////////////////

function send_mail($to, $subject, $message) {
    $from = "cat@example.com";
    mail($to, $subject, $message, "From: $from");
}
?>
```

HTTP sender

Language: Processing

Uses the Processing net library to make an HTTP request.

```
import processing.net.*;        // gives you access to the net library

Client client;                 // a new net client
boolean requestInProgress;     // whether a net request is in progress
String responseString = "";    // string of text received by client
void setup()
{
  // Open a connection to the host:
  client = new Client(this, "example.com", 80);

  // Send the HTTP GET request:
  client.write(
    "GET /catcam/cat-script.php?sensorValue=321 HTTP/1.0\r\n");
  client.write("HOST: example.com\r\n\r\n");
  // note that you've got a request in progress:
  requestInProgress = true;
}


void draw()
{
  // available() returns how many bytes have been received by the client:
  if (client.available() > 0) {
    // read a byte, convert it to a character, and add it to the string:
    responseString +=char(client.read());

    // add to a line of |'s on the screen (crude progress bar):
    print("|");
  }
  // if there's no bytes available, either the response
  // hasn't started yet, or it's done:
  else {
  // if responseString is longer than 0 bytes, the response has started:
    if(responseString.length() > 0 )  {
      // you've got some bytes, but now there's no more to read. Stop:
      if(requestInProgress == true) {
        // print the response:
        println(responseString);
        // note that the request is over:
        requestInProgress = false;
        // reset the string  for future requests:
        responseString = "";
      }
    }
  }
}
```

Cat graphing and email program

Language: Processing

Reads in a string of characters until it gets a linefeed (ASCII 10). Then converts the string into a number. Then graphs it. If the number has changed significantly, and there hasn't been a big change in more than a minute, the program calls a PHP script to send an email message.

```
import processing.serial.*;
import processing.net.*;  // gives you access to the net library

int linefeed = 10;       // linefeed in ASCII
Serial myPort;           // The serial port
int sensorValue = 0;     // the value from the sensor
int graphPosition = 0;   // the horizontal position of the latest
                         // line to be drawn on the graph

int prevSensorValue = 0;    // the previous sensor reading
boolean catOnMat = false;   // whether or not the cat's on the mat
int threshold = 330;        // above this number, the cat is on the mat.

int timeThreshold = 1;   // minimum number of minutes between emails
int timeLastSent[] = {hour(), minute()}; // time last message was sent

// HTTP client variables:
Client client;                   // a new net client
boolean requestInProgress = false; // whether a net request is in progress
String responseString = "";      // string of text received by client

void setup() {
  size(400,300);
  // List all the available serial ports
  println(Serial.list());

  // I know that the first port in the serial list on my mac
  // is always my  Arduino, so I open Serial.list()[0].
  // Open whatever port is the one you're using.
  myPort = new Serial(this, Serial.list()[0], 9600);
  // read bytes into a buffer until you get a linefeed (ASCII 10):
  myPort.bufferUntil(linefeed);
  println(hour() + ":" + minute());
}


void draw() {
  if (sensorValue > threshold ) {
    // if the last reading was less than the threshold,
    // then the cat just got on the mat.
    if (prevSensorValue <= threshold) {
      delay(100);
      if (sensorValue > threshold) {
        catOnMat = true;
        sendMail();
      }
    }
  }
}
```

```
  else {
    // if the sensor value is less than the threshold,
    // and the previous value was greater, then the cat
    // just left the mat
    if (prevSensorValue >= threshold) {
      catOnMat = false;
    }
  }
  // save the sensor value as the previous value
  // so you can take new readings:
  prevSensorValue = sensorValue;

  if (requestInProgress == true) {
    checkNetClient();
  }
}

// serialEvent  method is run automatically by the Processing applet
// whenever the buffer reaches the  byte value set in the bufferUntil()
// method in the setup():

void serialEvent(Serial myPort) {
  // read the serial buffer:
  String myString = myPort.readStringUntil(linefeed);
  // if you got any bytes other than the linefeed:
  if (myString != null) {
    //trim off the carriage return and convert the string to an integer:
    sensorValue = int(trim(myString)) /2 -100;
    // print it:
    // println(sensorValue);
    drawGraph();
  }
}

void drawGraph() {
  int lineHeight = sensorValue /2;
  // draw the line:
  if (catOnMat) {
    // draw green:
    stroke(0,255,0);
  }
  else {
    // draw red:
    stroke(255,0,0);
  }
  line(graphPosition, height, graphPosition, height - lineHeight);
  // at the edge of the screen, go back to the beginning:
  if (graphPosition >= width) {
    graphPosition = 0;
    background(0);
  }
  else {
    graphPosition++;
  }
}
```

```
void sendMail() {
  // calculate the current time in minutes:
  int[] presentTime = { hour(), minute() };

  // print the current time and the last time you sent a message:
  print(sensorValue + "\t");
  print( presentTime[0] + ":" + presentTime[1] +"\t");
  println(timeLastSent[0] + ":" + timeLastSent[1]);

  // if you're still in the same hour as the last message,
  // then make sure at least the minimum number of minutes has passed:
  if (presentTime[0] == timeLastSent[0]) {
    if (presentTime[1] - timeLastSent[1] >= timeThreshold) {
      println("This is where you'd send a mail.");
      makeHTTPCall();
      // take note of the time this message was sent:
      timeLastSent[0] = hour();
      timeLastSent[1] = minute();
    }
  }

  // if the hour has changed since the last message,
  // then the difference in minutes is a bit more complex.
  // Use !+ rather than > to make sure the shift
  // from 23:59 to 0:00 is covered as well:
  if (presentTime[0] != timeLastSent[0]) {
    // calculate the difference in minutes:
    int minuteDifference = (60 - timeLastSent[1]) + presentTime[1];

    if (minuteDifference >= timeThreshold) {
      println("This is where you'd send a mail.");
      makeHTTPCall();
      // take note of the time this message was sent:
      timeLastSent[0] = hour();
      timeLastSent[1] = minute();
    }
  }
}

void makeHTTPCall() {
  if (requestInProgress == false) {
    // Open a connection to the host:
    client = new Client(this, "example.com", 80);

    // form the request string:
    String requestString = "/cat-script.php?sensorValue=" +
      sensorValue;
    println(requestString);
    // Send the HTTP GET request:
    client.write("GET  " + requestString + " HTTP/1.1\n");
    client.write("HOST: example.com\n\n");
    // note that you've got a request in progress:
    requestInProgress = true;
  }
}
```

```
void checkNetClient() {
  // available() returns how many bytes have been received by the client:
  if (client.available() > 0) {
    // read a byte, convert it to a character, and add it to the string:
    responseString +=char(client.read());

    // add to a line of |'s on the screen (crude progress bar):
    print("|");
  }
  // if there's no bytes available, either the response hasn't
  // started yet, or it's done:
  else {
    // if responseString is longer than 0 bytes, the response has started:
    if(responseString.length() > 0 ) {
      // you've got some bytes, but now there's no more to read. Stop:
      if(requestInProgress == true) {
        // print the response:
        println(responseString);
        // note that the request is over:
        requestInProgress = false;
        // reset the string  for future requests:
        responseString = "";
      }
    }
  }
}
```

Chapter 4

AIRNow Web Page Scraper
Language: PHP
Reads a web page and returns one line from it.

```php
<?php
    // url of the air quality index page for New York City:
    $url =
      'http://airnow.gov/index.cfm?action=airnow.showlocal&cityid=164';
    // open the file at the URL for reading:
    $filePath = fopen ($url, "r");

    // as long as you haven't reached the end of the file:
    while (!feof($filePath))
    {
        // read one line at a time, and strip all HTML and
        // PHP tags from the line:
        $line = fgetss($filePath, 4096);
        echo $line;
    }
    fclose($filePath); // close the file at the URL, you're done!
?>
```

Air Quality meter
Language: Wiring/Arduino (*pin numbers defined for Arduino*)
Microcontroller is connected to a Lantronix serial-to-ethernet device. This program connects to a HTTP server through the Lantronix module, makes a HTTP GET request for a PHP script, and parses the returned string. Lantronix device communicates at 9600-8-n-1 non-inverted (true) serial. Lantronix serial settings:

- Baudrate 9600, I/F Mode 4C, Flow 00
- Port 10001
- Remote IP Addr: --- none ---, Port 00000
- Connect Mode : D4
- Disconn Mode : 00
- Flush Mode : 00

```
// Defines for the  program's status (used for status variable):
#define disconnected 0
#define connecting 1
#define connected 2
#define requesting 3
#define reading 4
#define requestComplete 5

// Defines for I/O pins:
#define connectedLED 2    // indicates when there's a TCP connection
#define requestingLED 3   // indicates a HTTP request has been made
#define readingLED 4      // indicates device is reading HTTP results
```

```
#define requestCompleteLED 5   // indicates a successful read
#define programResetLED 6       // indicates reset of Arduino
#define deviceResetPin 7        // resets Lantronix Device
#define meterPin 11             // controls VU meter

// defines for voltmeter:
#define meterMax 130            // max value on the meter
#define meterScale 150          // my meter reads 0 - 150

// variables:
int inByte= -1;            // incoming byte from serial RX
char inString[32];         // string for incoming serial data
int stringPos = 0;         // string index counter
int status = 0;            // Lantronix device's connection status
long lastCompletionTime = 0; // counter for delay after last completion

void setup() {
  // set all status LED pins and Lantronix device reset pin:
  pinMode(connectedLED, OUTPUT);
  pinMode(requestingLED, OUTPUT);
  pinMode(requestCompleteLED, OUTPUT);
  pinMode(programResetLED, OUTPUT);
  pinMode(deviceResetPin, OUTPUT);
  pinMode(meterPin, OUTPUT);

  // start serial port, 9600 8-N-1:
  Serial.begin(9600);
  //reset Lantronix device:
  resetDevice();
  // blink reset LED:
  blink(3);
}

void loop() {
  stateCheck();
  setLEDs();
}

/*
  Check the status of the connection and take appropriate action:
*/
void stateCheck() {
  switch (status) {
  case disconnected:
    // attempt to connect to the server:
    deviceConnect();
    break;
  case connecting:
    // until you get a C, keep trying to connect:
    // read the serial port:
    if (Serial.available()) {
      inByte = Serial.read();
```

```
      if (inByte == 'C') {  // 'C' in ascii
        status = connected;
      } else {
        // if you got anything other than a C, try again:
        deviceConnect();
      }
    }
    break;
  case connected:
    // send HTTP GET request for CGI script:
    httpRequest();
    break;
  case requesting:
    lookForData();
    break;
  case reading:
    readData();
    break;
  case requestComplete:
    waitForNextRequest();
  }
}

/*
  Set the indicator LEDs according to the state of the program
*/
void setLEDs() {
  /*
  Except for the disconnected and connecting states,
  all the states of the program have corresponding LEDS.
  so you can use a for-next loop to set them  by
  turning them all off except for the one that has
  the same number as the current program state:
  */
  for (int thisLED = 2; thisLED <= 5; thisLED++) {
    if (thisLED == status) {
      digitalWrite(thisLED, HIGH);
    }
    else {
      digitalWrite(thisLED, LOW);
    }
  }
}

/*
  Command the Lantronix device to connect to the server
*/
void deviceConnect() {
  //   fill in your server's numerical address below:
  Serial.print("C82.165.199.35/80\n");
  status = connecting;
}
```

```
/*
  Send a HTTP GET request
*/
void httpRequest() {
  // make sure you've cleared the last byte
  // from the last request:
  inByte = -1;
  // reset the string position counter:
  stringPos = 0;
  // Make HTTP GET request. Fill in the path to your version
  // of the CGI script:
  Serial.print("GET /~myaccount/scraper.php HTTP/1.0\n");
  // Fill in your server's name:
  Serial.print("HOST:example.com\n\n");
  // update the state of the program:
  status = requesting;
}


/*
  Read the results sent by the server until you get a < character.
*/
void lookForData() {
  // wait for bytes from server:
  if (Serial.available()) {
    inByte = Serial.read();
    // If you get a "<", what follows is the air quality index.
    // You need to read what follows the <.
    if (inByte == '<') {
      stringPos = 0;
      status = reading;
    }
  }
}
/*
  read the number from the server into an array, terminating with a > character.
*/
void readData() {
  if (Serial.available()) {
    inByte = Serial.read();
    // Keep reading until you get a ">":
    if (inByte != '>') {
      // save only ASCII numeric characters (ASCII 0 - 9):
      if ((inByte >= '0') && (inByte <= '9')){
        inString[stringPos] = inByte;
        stringPos++;
      }
    }
    // if you get a ">", you've reached the end of the AQI reading:
    else {
      interpretResults();
    }
  }
}
```

```
/*
  convert the input string to an integer.
*/
void interpretResults() {
  // convert the string to a numeric value:
  int airQuality = atoi(inString);
  setMeter(airQuality); // set the meter appropriately.
  lastCompletionTime = millis();
  status = requestComplete;
}


/*
  scale the number from the request to the meter's range and set the meter.
*/
void setMeter(int desiredValue) {
  int airQualityValue = 0;
  // if the value won't peg the meter, convert it
  // to the meter scale and send it out:
  if (desiredValue <= meterScale) {
    airQualityValue = (desiredValue * meterMax /meterScale) ;
    analogWrite(meterPin, airQualityValue);
  }
}


/*
  Wait two minutes before initiating a new request.
*/
void waitForNextRequest() {
  if (millis() - lastCompletionTime >= 120000) {
    resetDevice(); // reset Lantronix device before next request.
    status = disconnected;
  }
}


/*
  Take the Lantronix device's reset pin low to reset it
*/
void resetDevice() {
  digitalWrite(deviceResetPin, LOW);
  delay(50);
  digitalWrite(deviceResetPin, HIGH);
  delay(2000); // pause to let Lantronix device boot up.
}
/*
  Blink the reset LED.
*/
void blink(int howManyTimes) {
  int i;
  for (i=0; i< howManyTimes; i++) {
    digitalWrite(programResetLED, HIGH);
    delay(200);
    digitalWrite(programResetLED, LOW);
    delay(200);
  }
}
```

SoftwareSerial example

Language: Wiring/Arduino

This program uses the SoftwareSerial library to send serial messages on pins 8 and 9.

```
// include the SoftwareSerial library so you can use its functions:
#include <SoftwareSerial.h>

#define rxPin 8
#define txPin 9

// set up a new serial port
SoftwareSerial mySerial =  SoftwareSerial(rxPin, txPin);

void setup()  {
  // define pin modes for tx, rx, led pins:
  pinMode(rxPin, INPUT);
  pinMode(txPin, OUTPUT);
  // set the data rate for the SoftwareSerial port
  mySerial.begin(9600);
}

void loop() {
  // print out a debugging message:
  mySerial.println("Hello from SoftwareSerial");
  delay(100);
}
```

SoftwareSerial example

Language: Wiring/Arduino

This program is a variation on the networked air quality meter. It uses the SoftwareSerial library to send serial messages on pins 8 and 9.

```
// include the SoftwareSerial library so you can use its functions:
#include <SoftwareSerial.h>

#define rxPin 8
#define txPin 9

// Defines go here

// variables go here

// set up a new serial port
SoftwareSerial mySerial =  SoftwareSerial(rxPin, txPin);

void setup() {
  // the rest of the setup() code goes here

  // define pin modes for SoftwareSerial tx, rx pins:
  pinMode(rxPin, INPUT);
  pinMode(txPin, OUTPUT);
```

```
  // set the data rate for the SoftwareSerial port
  mySerial.begin(9600);

  // print out a debugging message:
  mySerial.println("All set up");

}

void loop() {
  stateCheck();
  setLEDs();
}

void stateCheck() {

  // the rest of stateCheck() code goes here

}

void setLEDs() {
  // setLEDs() code goes here

}

void deviceConnect() {
  // print out a debugging message:
  mySerial.println("connect");

  //   the rest of deviceConnect() code goes here

}

void httpRequest() {
  // print out a debugging message:
  mySerial.println("request");

  // the rest of httpRequest() code goes here

}

void lookForData() {

  // wait for bytes from server:
  if (Serial.available()) {
    inByte = Serial.read();
    mySerial.print(inByte, BYTE);

    // the rest of lookForData() code goes here

}

void readData() {
  if (Serial.available()) {
    inByte = Serial.read();
    mySerial.print(inByte, BYTE);

    // the rest of readData() code goes here

}
```

```
void interpretResults() {
  // print out a debugging message:
  mySerial.println("interpret");

  // the rest of interpretResults() code goes here

  mySerial.println("wait"); // print out a debugging message.
}

void setMeter(int desiredValue) {
  mySerial.println("set"); // print out a debugging message.

  // the rest of setMeter() code goes here
}

void resetDevice() {
  mySerial.println("reset"); // print out a debugging message.

  // the rest of resetDevice() code goes here
}
/*
  Blink the reset LED.
*/
void blink(int howManyTimes) {
  int i;
  for (i=0; i< howManyTimes; i++) {
    digitalWrite(programResetLED, HIGH);
    delay(200);
    digitalWrite(programResetLED, LOW);
    delay(200);
  }
}
```

Lantronix serial-to-Ethernet HTTP request tester

Language: Processing

This program sends serial messages to a Lantronix
serial-to-Ethernet device to get it to connect to a remote
webserver and make an HTTP request. To use this
program, connect your PC to the Lantronix module's serial
port as you did when you were configuring the Lantronix
module earlier.

```
// include the serial library
import processing.serial.*;

Serial myPort;        // Serial object
int step = 0;         // which step in the process you're on
char linefeed = 10;   // ASCII linefeed character
```

```
void setup()
{
  // get the list of serial ports:
  println(Serial.list());
  // open the serial port appropriate to your computer:
  myPort = new Serial(this, Serial.list()[2], 9600);
  // configure the serial object to buffer text until it receives a
  // linefeed character:
  myPort.bufferUntil(linefeed);
}


void draw()
{
  //no action in the draw loop
}


void serialEvent(Serial myPort) {
  // print any string that comes in serially to the monitor pane
  print(myPort.readString());
}


void keyReleased() {
  // if any key is pressed, take the next step:
  switch (step) {
  case 0:
    // open a connection to the server in question:
    myPort.write("C208.201.239.37/80\r");
    // add one to step so that the next keystroke causes the next step:
    step++;
    break;
  case 1:
    // send a HTTP GET request
    myPort.write("GET /~igoe/index.html HTTP/1.0\n");
    myPort.write("HOST:example.com\n\n");
    step++;
    break;
  }
}
```

Test Server Program

Language: Processing

Creates a server that listens for clients and prints what they say. It also sends the last client anything that's typed on the keyboard.

```processing
// include the net library:
import processing.net.*;

int port = 8080;        // the port the server listens on
Server myServer;        // the server object
Client  thisClient;     // incoming client object

void setup()
{
  myServer = new Server(this, port); // Start the server
}

void draw()
{
  // get the next client that sends a message:
  Client speakingClient = myServer.available();

  // if the message is not null, display what it sent:
  if (speakingClient !=null) {
    String whatClientSaid = speakingClient.readString();
    // print who sent the message, and what they sent:
    println(speakingClient.ip() + "\t" + whatClientSaid);
  }
}

// ServerEvent message is generated when a new client
// connects to the server.
void serverEvent(Server myServer, Client someClient) {
  println("We have a new client: " + someClient.ip());
  thisClient = someClient;
}

void keyReleased() {
  // only send if there's a client to send to:
  if (thisClient != null) {
    // if return is pressed, send newline and carriage feed:
    if (key == '\n') {
      thisClient.write("\r\n");
    }
    // send any other key as is:
    else {
      thisClient.write(key);
    }
  }
}
```

Chapter 5

Pong client

Language: Wiring/Arduino

This program enables an Arduino to control one paddle in a networked Pong game. This listing uses the readSensors() method from the seesaw client in project #7.

```arduino
// Defines for the Lantronix device's status (used for staus variable):
#define disconnected 0
#define connected 1
#define connecting 2

// Defines for I/O pins:
#define connectButtonPin 2
#define rightLED 3
#define leftLED 4
#define connectionLED 5
#define connectButtonLED 6
#define deviceResetPin 7
// variables:
int inByte= -1;              // incoming byte from serial RX
int status = disconnected;   // Lantronix device's connection status

// variables for the sensors:
byte connectButton = 0;      // state of the exit button
byte lastConnectButton = 0;  // previous state of the exit button
/*
When the connect button is pressed, or the accelerometer
passes the left or right threshold, the client should send a message
to the server.  The next two variables get filled with a value
when either of those conditions is met.  Otherwise, these
variables are set to 0.
*/
byte paddleMessage = 0;      // message sent to make a paddle move
byte connectMessage = 0;     // message sent to connect or disconnect

void setup() {
  // set the modes of the various I/O pins:
  pinMode(connectButtonPin, INPUT);
  pinMode(rightLED, OUTPUT);
  pinMode(leftLED, OUTPUT);
  pinMode(connectionLED, OUTPUT);
  pinMode(connectButtonLED, OUTPUT);
  pinMode(deviceResetPin, OUTPUT);

  // start serial port, 9600 8-N-1:
  Serial.begin(9600);

  // reset the Lantronix device:
  resetDevice();
  // blink the exit button LED to signal that we're ready for action:
  blink(3);
}
```

```
void loop() {
  // read the inputs:
  readSensors();
  // set the indicator LEDS:
  setLeds();
  // check the state of the client and take appropriate action:
  stateCheck();
}
void readSensors() {
  // thresholds for the accelerometer values:
  int leftThreshold = 500;
  int rightThreshold = 420;

  // read the X axis of the accelerometer:
  int x = analogRead(0);
  // let the analog/digital converter settle:
  delay(10);

  // if the accelerometer has passed either threshold,
  // set paddleMessage to the appropriate message, so it can
  // be sent by the main loop:
  if (x > leftThreshold) {
    paddleMessage = 'l';
  } else if (x < rightThreshold) {
    paddleMessage = 'r';
  } else {
    paddleMessage = 0;
  }
// read the connectButton, look for a low-to-high change:
  connectButton = digitalRead(connectButtonPin);
  connectMessage = 0;
  if (connectButton == HIGH ) {
    if (connectButton != lastConnectButton) {
      // turn on the exit button LED to let the user
      // know that they hit the button:
      digitalWrite(connectButtonLED, HIGH);
      connectMessage = 'x';
    }
  }
  // save the state of the exit button for next time you check:
  lastConnectButton = connectButton;
}
void setLeds() {
  // this should happen no matter what state the client is in,
  // to give local feedback every time a sensor senses a change

  // set the L and R LEDs if the sensor passes the appropriate
threshold:
  switch (paddleMessage) {
  case 'l':
    digitalWrite(leftLED, HIGH);
    digitalWrite(rightLED, LOW);
    break;
```

```
  case 'r':
    digitalWrite(rightLED, HIGH);
    digitalWrite(leftLED, LOW);
    break;
  case 0:
    digitalWrite(rightLED, LOW);
    digitalWrite(leftLED, LOW);
  }

  // set the connect button LED based on the connectMessage:
  if (connectMessage !=0) {
    digitalWrite(connectButtonLED, HIGH);
  }
  else {
    digitalWrite(connectButtonLED, LOW);
  }

  // set the connection LED based on the client's status:
  if (status == connected) {
    // turn on the connection LED:
    digitalWrite(connectionLED, HIGH);
  }
  else {
    // turn off the connection LED:
    digitalWrite(connectionLED, LOW);
  }
}
void stateCheck() {
  // Everything in this method depends on the client's status:
  switch (status) {
  case connected:
    // if you're connected, listen for serial in:
    while (Serial.available() > 0) {
      // if you get a 'D', it's from the Lantronix device,
      // telling you that it lost the connection:
      if (Serial.read() == 'D') {
        status = disconnected;
      }
    }

    // if there's a paddle message to send, send it:
    if (paddleMessage != 0) {
      Serial.print(paddleMessage);
      // reset paddleMessage to 0 once you've sent the message:
      paddleMessage = 0;
    }
    // if there's a connect message to send, send it:
    if (connectMessage != 0) {
      // if you're connected, disconnect:
      Serial.print(connectMessage);
      // reset connectMessage to 0 once you've sent the message:
      connectMessage = 0;
    }
    break;
```

```
  case disconnected:
    // if there's a connect message, try to connect:
    if (connectMessage !=0 ) {
      deviceConnect();
      // reset connectMessage to 0 once you've sent the message:
      connectMessage = 0;
    }
    break;
    // if you sent a connect message but haven't connected yet,
    // keep trying:
  case connecting:
    // read the serial port:
    if (Serial.available()) {
      inByte = Serial.read();
      // if you get a 'C' from the Lantronix device,
      // then you're connected to the server:
      if (inByte == 'C') {
        status = connected;
      }
      else {
        // if you got anything other than a C, try again:
        deviceConnect();
      }
    }
    break;
  }
}
void deviceConnect() {
  /*
     send out the server address and
   wait for a "C" byte to come back.
   fill in your personal computer's numerical address below:
   */
  Serial.print("C192.168.1.20/8080\n\r");
  status = connecting;
}


// Take the Lantronix device's reset pin low to reset it:
void resetDevice() {
  digitalWrite(deviceResetPin, LOW);
  delay(50);
  digitalWrite(deviceResetPin, HIGH);
  // pause to let Lantronix device boot up:
  delay(2000);
}


// Blink the connect button LED:
void blink(int howManyTimes) {
  for (int i=0; i< howManyTimes; i++) {
    digitalWrite(connectButtonLED, HIGH);
    delay(200);
    digitalWrite(connectButtonLED, LOW);
    delay(200);
  }
}
```

Pong Server

Language: Processing

This program listens for TCP socket connections and uses the data from the incoming connections in a networked multiplayer version of pong.

```
// include the net library:
import processing.net.*;

// variables for keeping track of clients:
int port = 8080;                    // the port the server listens on
Server myServer;                    // the server object
ArrayList playerList = new ArrayList(); // list of clients

// Variables for keeping track of the game play and graphics:
int ballSize = 10;              // the size of the ball
int ballDirectionV = 2;         // the ball's horizontal direction.
                                // left is negative, right is positive
int ballDirectionH = 2;         // the ball's vertical direction.
                                // up is negative, down is positive
int ballPosV, ballPosH;         // the ball's vertical/horizontal
                                // and vertical positions
boolean ballInMotion = false;   // whether the ball should be moving

int topScore, bottomScore;      // scores for the top team and
                                // the bottom teams
int paddleHeight = 10;          // vertical dimension of the paddles
int paddleWidth = 80;           // horizontal dimension of the paddles
int nextTopPaddleV;             // paddle positions for the next player
                                // to be created
int nextBottomPaddleV;

boolean gameOver = false;       // whether a game is in progress
float delayCounter = millis();  // a counter for the delay after
                                // a game is over
long gameOverDelay = 4000;      // pause after each game
long pointDelay = 2000;         // pause after each point

void setup() {
  // set up all the pong details:
  pongSetup();
  // Start the server:
  myServer = new Server(this, port);
}

void pongSetup() {
  // set the window size:
  size(480, 640);
  // set the frame rate:
  frameRate(90);

  // create a font with the third font available to the system:
  PFont myFont = createFont(PFont.list()[2], 18);
  textFont(myFont);
```

```
    // set the default font settings:
    textFont(myFont, 18);
    textAlign(CENTER);

    // initalize paddle positions for the first player.
    // these will be incremented with each new player:
    nextTopPaddleV = 50;
    nextBottomPaddleV = height - 50;

    // initialize the ball in the center of the screen:
    ballPosV = height / 2;
    ballPosH = width / 2;

    // set no borders on drawn shapes:
    noStroke();
    // set the rectMode so that all rectangle dimensions
    // are from the center of the rectangle (see Processing reference):
    rectMode(CENTER);
}

void draw() {
    pongDraw();
    listenToClients();
}

// The ServerEvent message is generated when a new client
// connects to the server.
void serverEvent(Server someServer, Client someClient) {
    boolean isPlayer = false;

    if (someClient != null) {
        // iterate over the playerList:
        for (int p = 0; p < playerList.size(); p++) {
            // get the next object in the ArrayList and convert it
            // to a Player:
            Player thisPlayer = (Player)playerList.get(p);

            // if thisPlayer's client matches the one that generated
            // the serverEvent, then this client is already a player:
            if (thisPlayer.client == someClient) {
                // we already have this client
                isPlayer = true;
            }
        }

        // if the client isn't already a Player, then make a new Player
        // and add it to the playerList:
        if (!isPlayer) {
            makeNewPlayer(someClient);
        }
    }
}
```

```
void makeNewPlayer(Client thisClient) {
    // paddle position for the new Player:
    int h = width/2;
    int v = 0;

    /*
    Get the paddle position of the last player on the list.
    If it's on top, add the new player on the bottom, and vice versa.
    If there are  no other players, add the new player on the top.
    */
    // get the size of the list:
    int listSize = playerList.size() - 1;
    // if there are any other players:
    if  (listSize >= 0) {
        // get the last player on the list:
        Player lastPlayerAdded = (Player)playerList.get(listSize);
        // is the last player's on the top, add to the bottom:
        if (lastPlayerAdded.paddleV == nextTopPaddleV) {
            nextBottomPaddleV = nextBottomPaddleV - paddleHeight * 2;
            v = nextBottomPaddleV;
        }
        // is the last player's on the bottom, add to the top:
        else if (lastPlayerAdded.paddleV == nextBottomPaddleV) {
            nextTopPaddleV = nextTopPaddleV + paddleHeight * 2;
            v = nextTopPaddleV;
        }
    }
    // if there are no players, add to the top:
    else {
        v = nextTopPaddleV;
    }

    // make a new Player object with the position you just calculated
    // and using the Client that generated the serverEvent:
    Player newPlayer = new Player(h, v, thisClient);
    // add the new Player to the playerList:
    playerList.add(newPlayer);
    // Announce the new Player:
    print("We have a new player: ");
    println(newPlayer.client.ip());
    newPlayer.client.write("hi\r\n");
}

void listenToClients() {
    // get the next client that sends a message:
    Client speakingClient = myServer.available();
    Player speakingPlayer = null;

    // iterate over the playerList to figure out whose
    // client sent the message:
    for (int p = 0; p < playerList.size(); p++) {
        // get the next object in the ArrayList and convert it
        // to a Player:
        Player thisPlayer = (Player)playerList.get(p);
```

```
    // compare the client of thisPlayer to the client that sent a
    // message. If they're the same, then this is the Player we want:
    if (thisPlayer.client == speakingClient) {
      speakingPlayer = thisPlayer;
    }
  }

  // read what the client sent:
  if (speakingPlayer != null) {
    int whatClientSaid = speakingPlayer.client.read();
    /*
    There a number of things it might have said that we care about:
    x = exit
    l = move left
    r = move right
    */
    switch (whatClientSaid) {
      // If the client says "exit", disconnect it
      case 'x':
        // say goodbye to the client:
        speakingPlayer.client.write("bye\r\n");
        // disconnect the client from the server:
        println(speakingPlayer.client.ip() + "\t left");
        myServer.disconnect(speakingPlayer.client);
        // remove the client's Player from the playerList:
        playerList.remove(speakingPlayer);
        break;
      case 'l':
        // if the client sends an "l", move the paddle left
        speakingPlayer.movePaddle(-10);
        break;
      case 'r':
        // if the client sends a "r", move the paddle right
        speakingPlayer.movePaddle(10);
        break;
    }
  }
}

void pongDraw() {
  background(0);
  // draw all the paddles
  for (int p = 0; p < playerList.size(); p++) {
    Player thisPlayer = (Player)playerList.get(p);
    // show the paddle for this player:
    thisPlayer.showPaddle();
  }

  // calculate ball's position:
  if (ballInMotion) {
    moveBall();
  }
  // Draw the ball:
  rect(ballPosH, ballPosV, ballSize, ballSize);
```

```
  // show the score:
  showScore();

  // if the game is over, show the winner:
  if (gameOver) {
    textSize(24);
    gameOver = true;
    text("Game Over", width/2, height/2 - 30);
    if (topScore > bottomScore) {
      text("Top Team Wins!", width/2, height/2);
    }
    else {
      text("Bottom Team Wins!", width/2, height/2);
    }
  }
  // pause after each game:
  if (gameOver && (millis() > delayCounter + gameOverDelay)) {
    gameOver = false;
    newGame();
  }
  // pause after each point:
  if (!gameOver && !ballInMotion && (millis() >
    delayCounter + pointDelay)) {

    // make sure there are at least two players:
    if (playerList.size() >=2) {
      ballInMotion = true;
    }
    else {
      ballInMotion = false;
      textSize(24);
      text("Waiting for two players", width/2, height/2 - 30);
    }
  }
}

void moveBall() {
  // Check to see if the ball contacts any paddles:
  for (int p = 0; p < playerList.size(); p++) {
    // get the player to check:
    Player thisPlayer = (Player)playerList.get(p);

    // calculate the horizontal edges of the paddle:
    float paddleRight = thisPlayer.paddleH + paddleWidth/2;
    float paddleLeft = thisPlayer.paddleH - paddleWidth/2;
    // check whether the ball is in the horizontal range of the paddle:
    if ((ballPosH >= paddleLeft) && (ballPosH <= paddleRight)) {

      // calculate the vertical edges of the paddle:
      float paddleTop = thisPlayer.paddleV - paddleHeight/2;
      float paddleBottom = thisPlayer.paddleV + paddleHeight/2;
```

```
    // check to see if the ball is in the
    // horizontal range of the paddle:
    if ((ballPosV >= paddleTop) && (ballPosV <= paddleBottom)) {
      // reverse the ball vertical direction:
      ballDirectionV = -ballDirectionV;
    }
  }
}

// if the ball goes off the screen top:
if (ballPosV < 0) {
  bottomScore++;
  ballDirectionV = int(random(2) + 1) * -1;
  resetBall();
}
// if the ball goes off the screen bottom:
if (ballPosV > height) {
  topScore++;
  ballDirectionV = int(random(2) + 1);
  resetBall();
}

// if any team goes over 5 points, the other team loses:
if ((topScore > 5) || (bottomScore > 5)) {
  delayCounter = millis();
  gameOver = true;
}

// stop the ball going off the left or right of the screen:
if ((ballPosH - ballSize/2 <= 0) || (ballPosH +ballSize/2 >=width)) {
  // reverse the y direction of the ball:
  ballDirectionH = -ballDirectionH;
}
// update the ball position:
ballPosV = ballPosV + ballDirectionV;
ballPosH = ballPosH + ballDirectionH;
}

void newGame() {
  gameOver = false;
  topScore = 0;
  bottomScore = 0;
}

public void showScore() {
  textSize(24);
  text(topScore, 20, 40);
  text(bottomScore, 20, height - 20);
}
```

```
void resetBall() {
  // put the ball back in the center
  ballPosV = height/2;
  ballPosH = width/2;
  ballInMotion = false;
  delayCounter = millis();
}

public class Player {
  // declare variables that belong to the object:
  float paddleH, paddleV;
  Client  client;

  public Player (int hpos, int vpos, Client someClient) {
    // initialize the localinstance variables:
    paddleH = hpos;
    paddleV = vpos;
    client = someClient;
  }

  public void movePaddle(float howMuch) {
    float newPosition = paddleH + howMuch;
    // constrain the paddle's position to the width of the window:
    paddleH = constrain(newPosition, 0, width);
  }

  public void showPaddle() {
    rect(paddleH, paddleV, paddleWidth, paddleHeight);
    // display the address of this player near its paddle
    textSize(12);
    text(client.ip(), paddleH, paddleV - paddleWidth/8 );
  }
}
```

Chapter 6

IR transmit example
Language: Wiring/Arduino

This program reads an analog input on pin 0 and sends the result out as an ASCII-encoded string. The TX line of the microcontroller is connected to a Rentron TX-IRHS IR transmitter which can transmit at 19200 bps.

```
void setup(){
  //Open the serial port at 19200 bps.
  Serial.begin(19200);
}

void loop(){
  // Read the analog input:
  int analogValue = analogRead(0);
  // send the value out via the transmitter:
  Serial.println(analogValue, DEC);
  // delay 10ms to allow the analog-to-digital receiver to settle:
  delay(10);
}
```

RF Transmitter
Language: Wiring/Arduino

This program reads an analog input on pin 0 and sends the result out as an ASCII-encoded string. The TX line of the microcontroller is connected to an RF transmitter that is capable of reading at 2400 bps.

```
void setup(){
  // Open the serial port at 2400 bps:
  Serial.begin(2400);
}

void loop(){
  // Read the analog input:
  int analogValue = analogRead(0);
  // send the value out via the transmitter:
  Serial.println(analogValue, DEC);
  // delay 10ms to allow the analog-to-digital receiver to settle:
  delay(10);
}
```

RF Receive
Language: Processing

This program listens for data coming in through a serial port. It reads a string and throws out any strings that contain values other than ASCII numerals, linefeed, or carriage return, or that are longer than four digits. This program is designed to work with a Laipac RF serial receiver connected to the serial port, operating at 2400 bps.

```
import processing.serial.*;

Serial myPort;          // the serial port
int incomingValue = 0;  // the value received in the serial port

void setup() {
  // list all the available serial ports:
  println(Serial.list());

  // open the appropriate serial port.  On my computer, the RF
  // receiver is connected to a USB-to-serial adaptor connected to
  // the first port in the list. It may be on a different port on
  // your machine:
  myPort = new Serial(this, Serial.list()[0], 2400);
  // tell the serial port not to generate a serialEvent
  //until a linefeed is received:
  myPort.bufferUntil('\n');
}

void draw() {
  // set the background color according to the incoming value:
  background(incomingValue/4);
}

// serialEvent  method is run automatically by the Processing applet
// whenever the buffer reaches the  byte value set in the bufferUntil()
// method in the setup():
void serialEvent(Serial myPort) {
  boolean validString = true;  // whether the string you got is valid
  String errorReason = "";     // a string that tells what went wrong

  // read the serial buffer:
  String myString = myPort.readStringUntil('\n');

  // make sure you have a valid string:
  if (myString != null) {
    // trim off the whitespace (linefeed, carriage return) characters:
    myString = trim(myString);

    // check for garbage characters:
    for (int charNum = 0; charNum < myString.length(); charNum++) {
      if (myString.charAt(charNum) < '0' ||
          myString.charAt(charNum) > '9') {
```

```
      // you got a garbage byte; throw the whole string out
      validString = false;
      errorReason =
        "Received a byte that's not a valid ASCII numeral.";
    }
  }
  // check to see that the string length is appropriate:
  if (myString.length() > 4) {
    validString = false;
    errorReason = "Received more than 4 bytes.";
  }
  // if all's good, convert the string to an int:
  if (validString == true) {
    incomingValue = int(trim(myString));
    println("Good value: " + incomingValue);
  } else {
    // if the data is bad, say so:
    println("Error: Data is corrupted. " + errorReason);
  }
  }
}
```

XBee terminal

Language: Processing

This program is a basic serial terminal program. It replaces
newline characters from the keyboard with return characters.
You need it to talk to XBee radios with Linux/Unix/Mac OS
X because the XBees don't send newline characters back.

```
import processing.serial.*;

Serial myPort;          // the serial port you're using
String portnum;         // name of the serial port
String outString = "";  // the string being sent out the serial port
String inString = "";   // the string coming in from the serial port
int receivedLines = 0;  // how many lines have been received
int bufferedLines = 10; // number of incoming lines to keep

void setup() {

  size(400, 300);        // window size
  // create a font with the third font available to the system:
  PFont myFont = createFont(PFont.list()[2], 14);
  textFont(myFont);

  // list all the serial ports:
  println(Serial.list());
  // based on the list of serial ports printed from the
  // previous command, change the 0 to your port's number:
  portnum = Serial.list()[0];
  // initialize the serial port:
  myPort = new Serial(this, portnum, 9600);
}
```

```
void draw() {
  background(0); // clear the screen.
  // print the name of the serial port:
  text("Serial port: " + portnum, 10, 20);
  // Print out what you get:
  text("typed: " + outString, 10, 40);
  text("received:\n" + inString, 10, 80);
}


// This method responds to key presses when the
// program window is active:
void keyPressed() {
  switch (key) {
    // In Unix/Linux/OS X, if the user types return, a linefeed is
    // returned. But the XBee wants a carriage return:
    case '\n':
      myPort.write(outString + "\r");
      outString = "";
      break;
    case 8:    // backspace
      // delete the last character in the string:
      outString = outString.substring(0, outString.length() -1);
      break;
    case '+':  // we have to send the + signs even without a return:
      myPort.write(key);
      // add the key to the end of the string:
      outString += key;
      break;
    case 65535:  // If the user types the shift key, don't type anything:
      break;
    default:     // any other key typed, add it to outString:
      // add the key to the end of the string:
      outString += key;
      break;
  }
}


// this method runs when bytes show up in the serial port:
void serialEvent(Serial myPort) {
  // read the next byte from the serial port:
  int inByte = myPort.read();
  // add it to  inString:
  inString += char(inByte);
  if (inByte == '\r') {
    // if the byte is a carriage return, print
    // a newline and carriage return:
    inString += '\n';
    // count the number of newlines:
    receivedLines++;
    // if there are more than 10 lines, delete the first one:
    if (receivedLines > bufferedLines) {
      deleteFirstLine();
    }
  }
}
```

```
// deletes the top line of inString so that it all fits on the screen:
void deleteFirstLine() {
  // find the first newline:
  int firstChar = inString.indexOf('\n');
  // delete it:
  inString= inString.substring(firstChar+1);
}
```

XBee Analog Duplex sender
Language: Wiring/Arduino

This sketch configures an XBee radio via the serial port,
sends the value of an analog sensor out, and listens for
input from the radio, using it to set the value of a PWM
output. Thanks to Robert Faludi for the critique and
improvements.

```
#define sensorPin 0        // input sensor
#define txLed 2            // LED to indicate outgoing data
#define rxLed 3            // LED to indicate incoming data
#define analogLed 9        // LED that changes brightness with
                           // incoming value
#define threshold 10       // how much change you need to see on
                           // the sensor before sending
int lastSensorReading = 0; // previous state of the switch
int inByte= -1;            // incoming byte from serial RX
char inString[6];          // string for incoming serial data
int stringPos = 0;         // string index counter

void setup() {
  // configure serial communications:
  Serial.begin(9600);

  // configure output pins:
  pinMode(txLed, OUTPUT);
  pinMode(rxLed, OUTPUT);
  pinMode (analogLed, OUTPUT);

  // set XBee's destination address:
  setDestination();
  // blink the TX LED to indicate the main program's about to start:
  blink(3);
}
void setDestination() {
  // put the radio in command mode:
  Serial.print("+++");
  // wait for the radio to respond with "OK\r"
  char thisByte = 0;
  while (thisByte != '\r') {
    if (Serial.available() > 0) {
      thisByte = Serial.read();
    }
  }
```

```
  // set the destination address, using 16-bit addressing.
  // if you're using two radios, one radio's destination
  // should be the other radio's MY address, and vice versa:
  Serial.print("ATDH0, DL5678\r");
  // set my address using 16-bit addressing:
  Serial.print("ATMY1234\r");
  // set the PAN ID. If you're working in a place where many people
  // are using XBees, you should set your own PAN ID distinct
  // from other projects.
  Serial.print("ATID1111\r");
  // put the radio in data mode:
  Serial.print("ATCN\r");
}
// Blink the tx LED:
void blink(int howManyTimes) {
  for (int i=0; i< howManyTimes; i++) {
    digitalWrite(txLed, HIGH);
    delay(200);
    digitalWrite(txLed, LOW);
    delay(200);
  }
}

void loop() {
  // listen for incoming serial data:
  if (Serial.available() > 0) {
    // turn on the RX LED whenever you're reading data:
    digitalWrite(rxLed, HIGH);
    handleSerial();
  }
  else {
    // turn off the receive LED when there's no incoming data:
    digitalWrite(rxLed, LOW);
  }
  // listen to the potentiometer:
  char sensorValue = readSensor();

  // if there's something to send, send it:
  if (sensorValue > 0) {
    //light the tx LED to say you're sending:
    digitalWrite(txLed, HIGH);
    Serial.print(sensorValue, DEC );
    Serial.print("\r");

    // turn off the tx LED:
    digitalWrite(txLed, LOW);
  }
}
void handleSerial() {
  inByte = Serial.read();
  // save only ASCII numeric characters (ASCII 0 - 9):
  if ((inByte >= '0') && (inByte <= '9')){
    inString[stringPos] = inByte;
    stringPos++;
  }
```

```
// if you get an ASCII carriage return:
if (inByte == '\r') {
  // convert the string to a number:
  int brightness = atoi(inString);
  // set the analog output LED:
  analogWrite(analogLed, brightness);

  // put zeroes in the array
  for (int c = 0; c < stringPos; c++) {
    inString[c] = 0;
  }
  // reset the string pointer:
  stringPos = 0;
}
}


char readSensor() {
  char message = 0;
  // read the sensor:
  int sensorReading = analogRead(sensorPin);

  // look for a change from the last reading
  // that's greater than the threshold:
  if (abs(sensorReading - lastSensorReading) > threshold) {
    message = sensorReading/4;
    lastSensorReading = sensorReading;
  }
  return message;
}
```

BlueRadios Master Connection

Language: Wiring/Arduino

This program assumes that the microcontroller is connected to a BlueRadios bluetooth radio, and that the radio is in master mode. When the program starts, it releases the CTSpin pin of the radio, so the radio can send data to the microcontroller. Then it sends a connect message and listens. If more than 5 seconds passes, it attempts to connect again. If it receives a comma, which only appears in the CONNECT,<address> string, it assumes the radio is connected and starts sending data. If it receives an S, it assumes the radio is disconnected and stops sending.

```
#define sensorPin 0        // input sensor
#define txLed 2            // LED to indicate outgoing data
#define rxLed 3            // LED to indicate incoming data
#define CTSpin 4           // Clear-to-send pin
#define analogLed 9        // LED that will change brightness with
                           // incoming value
#define threshold 10       // how much change you need to see on the
                           // sensor before sending

byte lastSensorReading = 0;  // previous state of the pot
```

```
long lastConnectTry;           // milliseconds elapsed since the last
                               // connection attempt
long connectTimeout = 5000;    // milliseconds to wait between
                               // connection attempts
int inByte= -1;                // incoming byte from serial RX
char inString[6];              // string for incoming serial data
int stringPos = 0;             // string index counter

// address of the remote BT radio.
char remoteAddress[13] = "112233445566";
byte connected = false;        // whether you're connected or not
```

▶▶ **Replace with the address of your remote radio**

```
void setup() {
  // configure serial communications:
  Serial.begin(9600);

  // configure output pins:
  pinMode(txLed, OUTPUT);
  pinMode(rxLed, OUTPUT);
  pinMode (analogLed, OUTPUT);
  pinMode(CTSpin, OUTPUT);

  // set CTS low so BlueSMiRF can send you serial data:
  digitalWrite(CTSpin, LOW);

  // Attempt a connection:
  BTConnect();

  // blink the tx LED to say you're done with setup:
  blink(3);
}


void BTConnect() {
  Serial.print("+++\r");
  delay(250);
  Serial.print("ATDH\r");
  Serial.print("ATDM");
  Serial.print(remoteAddress);
  Serial.print(",1101\r");
}


int readSensor() {
  int message = 0;
  // read the sensor:
  int sensorReading = analogRead(sensorPin);

  // look for a change from the last reading
  // that's greater than the threshold:
  if (abs(sensorReading - lastSensorReading) > threshold) {
    message = sensorReading/4;
    lastSensorReading = sensorReading;
  }
  return message;
}
```

```
void blink(int howManyTimes) {
  for (int i=0; i< howManyTimes; i++) {
    digitalWrite(txLed, HIGH);
    delay(200);
    digitalWrite(txLed, LOW);
    delay(200);
  }
}


void loop() {
  if (Serial.available() > 0) {
    // signal that there's incoming data using the rx LED:
    digitalWrite(rxLed, HIGH);
    // do something with the incoming byte:
    handleSerial();
    // turn the rx LED off.
    digitalWrite(rxLed, LOW);
  }


  // if you're not connected and 5 seconds have passed in that state,
  // make an attempt to connect to the other radio:
  if (!connected && millis() - lastConnectTry > connectTimeout) {
    BTConnect();
    lastConnectTry = millis();
  }
}


void handleSerial() {
  inByte = Serial.read();
  delay(2);
  // comma comes only in the CONNECT,<address> message:
  if (inByte == ',') {
    // send an initial message:
    sendData();
    // update the connection status:
    connected = true;
  }


  //S comes only in the DISCONNECT message:
  if (inByte == 'S') {
    // turn off the analog LED:
    analogWrite(analogLed, 0);
    connected = false;
  }
  //R comes only in the NO CARRIER and NO ANSWER messages:
  if (inByte == 'R') {
    // turn off the analog LED:
    analogWrite(analogLed, 0);
    connected = false;
  }


  if (connected) {
    // save only ASCII numeric characters (ASCII 0 - 9):
    if ((inByte >= '0') && (inByte <= '9')){
      inString[stringPos] = inByte;
      stringPos++;
    }
    // if you get an asterisk, it's the end of a string:
    if (inByte == '*') {
      // convert the string to a number:
      int brightness = atoi(inString);
      // set the analog output LED:
      analogWrite(analogLed, brightness);

      // put zeroes in the array
      for (int c = 0; c < stringPos; c++) {
        inString[c] = 0;
      }
      // reset the string pointer:
      stringPos = 0;
      // Since this  byte (*) is the end of an incoming string,
      // send out your reading in response:
      sendData();
    }
  }
}


void sendData() {
  // indicate that we're sending using the tx LED:
  digitalWrite(txLed, HIGH);
  Serial.print(readSensor(), DEC);
  // string termination:
  Serial.print("*");
  // turn off the tx LED:
  digitalWrite(txLed, LOW);
}
```

Chapter 7

Lantronix UDP Device Query

Language: Processing

Sends out a UDP broadcast packet to query a subnet for Lantronix serial-to-ethernet devices. Lantronix devices are programmed to respond to UDP messages received on port 30718. If a Lantronix device receives the string 0x00 0x00 0x00 0xF6, it responds with a UDP packet containing the status message on port 30718. When the program starts, press any key on the keyboard and watch the message pane for responses. See the Lantronix integration guide from www.lantronix.com for the details. This program uses the Hypermedia UDP library available at hypermedia.loeil.org/processing/

```
// import UDP library
import hypermedia.net.*;


UDP udp;                    // define the UDP object
int queryPort = 30718;      // the port number for the device query


void setup() {
  // create a new connection to listen for
  // UDP datagrams on query port;
  udp = new UDP(this, queryPort);


  // listen for incoming packets:
  udp.listen( true );
}


void draw() {
  // twiddle your thumbs.  Everything is event-generated.
}


/*
  send the query message when any key is pressed:
  */
void keyPressed() {
  byte[] queryMsg = new byte[4];
  queryMsg[0] = 0x00;
  queryMsg[1] = 0x00;
  queryMsg[2] = 0x00;
  // because 0xF6 (decimal value 246) is greater than 128
  // you have to explicitly convert it to a byte:
  queryMsg[3] = byte(0xF6);


  // send the message
  udp.send( queryMsg, "255.255.255.255", queryPort );
  println("UDP Query sent");
}
```

```
/*
  listen for responses via UDP
 */
void receive( byte[] data, String ip, int port ) {
  String inString = new String(data);  // incoming data as a string
  int[] intData = int(data);           // data converted to ints
  int i = 0;                           // counter
  // print the result:
  println( "response from "+ip+" on port "+port );


  // parse the response for the appropriate data.
  // if the fourth byte is <F7>, we got a status reply:
  print("Received response: ");
  println(hex(intData[3],2));
  if (intData[3] == 0xF7) {
    // MAC address of the sender is bytes 24 to 30 (the end):
    print("MAC Addr: ");
    for (i=24; i < intData.length; i++) {
      print(" " + hex(intData[i], 2));
    }
  }
  // print 2 lines to separate messages from multiple responders:
  print("\n\n");
}
```

Toxic Report

Language: PHP

This program opens a socket connection to an Xport and reads bytes from the socket. It then sorts the bytes into packets, interprets the packets, reports the results, and saves them to a data log file.

```
<?php
// Global variables.
// These can be used by any of the script's functions:


global $ip, $port, $packetsToRead, $timeStamp, $messageString;


$ip = "192.168.1.236";  // IP address to connect to


$port = 10001;            // port number of IP.
$packetsToRead = 10;      // total number of packets to read
$totalAverage = 0;        // the summary of all sensor readings
$packetCounter = 0;       // counter for packets as you read them
$bytes = array();         // array for bytes when you're reading them
$packets = array();       // array to hold the arrays of bytes


// $messageString is used to return messages for printing in the HTML:
$messageString = "No Sensor Reading Taken";
```

▶▶ **Fill in the IP address of your Xport here**

```php
// Get the time and date:
$timeStamp = $date = date("m-d-Y H:i:s");

//if a filled textbox was submitted, get the values:
if ((isset($_POST["ip"])) && (isset($_POST["port"])) &&
    (isset($_POST["packetsToRead"]))) {
        $ip = $_POST["ip"];
        $port = $_POST["port"];
        $packetsToRead = $_POST["packetsToRead"];
}


// open a socket to the Xport:
$mySocket = fsockopen ($ip, $port, $errorno, $errorstr, 30);
if (!$mySocket) {
    //if the socket didn't open, return an error message
    return "Error $errorno: $errorstr<br>";
} else {
    // if the socket exists, read packets until you've reached
    // $packetsToRead:
    while ($packetCounter < $packetsToRead) {
        // read a character from the socket connection,
        // and convert it to a numeric value using ord(),
        $char = ord(fgetc($mySocket));

        // if you got a header byte, deal with the last array
        // of bytes first:
        if ($char == 0x7E) {
            // push the last byte array onto the end
            // of the packet array:
            array_push($packets, $bytes);
            $bytes = array(); // clear the byte array.
            // increment the packet counter:
            $packetCounter++;
        }
        // push the current byte onto the end of the byte array:
        array_push($bytes, $char);
    }
    // average the readings from all the packets to get a final
    // sensor reading:
    $totalAverage = averagePackets($packets);

    // update the message for the HTML:
    $messageString =
        "Sensor Reading at:". $timeStamp . ": " . $totalAverage;

    // if you got a good reading, write it to the datalog file:
    if ($totalAverage > 0) {
        writeToFile($totalAverage);
    }
    //close the socket:
    fclose ($mySocket);
}
```

```php
function averagePackets($whichArray) {
    $packetAverage = 0;       // average of all the sensor readings
    $validReadings = 0;       // number of valid readings
    $readingsTotal = 0;       // total of all readings, for averaging

    // iterate over the packet array:
    foreach ($whichArray as $thisPacket) {
        // parse each packet to get the average sensor reading:
        $thisSensorReading = parsePacket($thisPacket);

        if ($thisSensorReading > 0 && $thisSensorReading < 1023) {
            // if the sensor reading is valid, add it to the total:
            $readingsTotal = $readingsTotal + $thisSensorReading;
            // increment the total number of valid readings:
            $validReadings++;
        }
    }
    if ($validReadings > 0) {
        // round the packet average to 2 decimal points:
        $packetAverage = round($readingsTotal / $validReadings, 2);
        return $packetAverage;
    } else {
        return -1;
    }
}

function parsePacket($whichPacket) {
    $adcStart = 11;                 // ADC reading starts at 12th byte
    $numSamples = $whichPacket[8];  // number of samples in the packet
    $total = 0;                     // sum of ADC readings for averaging
    // if you got all the bytes, find the average ADC reading:
    if( count($whichPacket) == 22) {
        // read the address. It's a two-byte value, so you
        // add the two bytes as follows:
        $address = $whichPacket[5] + $whichPacket[4] * 256;

        // read $numSamples 10-bit analog values, two at a time
        // because each reading is two bytes long:
        for ($i = 0; $i < $numSamples * 2;  $i=$i+2) {
            // 10-bit value = high byte * 256 + low byte:
            $thisSample = ($whichPacket[$i + $adcStart] * 256) +
                $whichPacket[($i + 1) + $adcStart];
            // add the result to the total for averaging later:
            $total = $total + $thisSample;
        }
        // average the result:
        $average = $total / $numSamples;
        return $average;
    } else {
        return -1;
    }
}
```

```php
function writeToFile($whichReading) {
    global $timeStamp, $messageString;

    // combine the reading and the timestamp:
    $logData = "$timeStamp $whichReading\n";
    $myFile = "datalog.txt";    // name of the file to write to:

    // check to see that the file exists and is writable:
    if (is_writable($myFile)) {
        // try to write to the file:
        if (!($fh = fopen($myFile, "a"))) {
            $messageString = "Couldn't open file $myFile";
        } else {
            // if you could open the file but not write to it, say so:
            if (!fwrite($fh, $logData)) {
                $messageString = "Couldn't write to $myFile";
            }
        }
    } else {
        //if it's not writeable:
        $messageString = "The file $myFile is not writable";
    }
}

?>

    <html>
    <head>
    </head>

    <body>
        <h2>
        <?=$messageString?>
        </h2>
        <hr>

        <form name="message" method="post" action="toxic_report.php">
            IP Address: <input type="text" name="ip" value="<?=$ip?>"
                        size="15" maxlength="15">
            Port: <input type="text" name="port" value="<?=$port?>"
                size="5" maxlength="5">  <br>
            Number of readings to take: <input type="text"
              name="packetsToRead"
              value="<?=$packetsToRead?>" size="6">
            <input type="submit" value="Send It">
        </form>

    </body>
</html>
```

Lantronix UDP Tester

Language: Processing

Sends and receives UDP messages from Lantronix serial-to-ethernet devices. Sends a serial message to a Lantronix device connected to the serial port when you type "s". Sends a UDP message to the Lantronix device when you type "u". Listens for both UDP and serial messages and prints them out.

```processing
// import UDP library
import hypermedia.net.*;
// import serial library:
import processing.serial.*;

UDP udp;                      // define the UDP object
int queryPort = 10002;        // the port number for the device query
Serial myPort;
String xportIP = "192.168.1.20";  // fill in your Xport's IP here
int xportPort = 10001;            // the Xport's receive port
String inString = "";             // incoming serial string

void setup() {
  // create a new connection to listen for
  // UDP datagrams on query port;
  udp = new UDP(this, queryPort);
  // listen for incoming packets:
  udp.listen( true );

  println(Serial.list());
  // make sure the serial port chosen here is the one attached
  // to your Xport:
  myPort = new Serial(this, Serial.list()[0], 9600);
}

//process events
void draw() {
  background(0,0,255); // a nice blue background.
}

/*
 send messages when s or u key is pressed:
 */
void keyPressed() {
  switch (key) {
  case 'u':
    udp.send("Hello UDP!\r\n", xportIP, xportPort);
    break;
  case 's':
    String messageString = "Hello Serial!";
    for (int c = 0; c < messageString.length(); c++) {
      myPort.write(messageString.charAt(c));
    }
    break;
  }
}
```

```
/*
  listen for UDP responses
 */
void receive( byte[] data, String ip, int port ) {
  String inString = new String(data); // incoming data as a string
  println( "received "+inString +"  from "+ip+" on port "+port );

  // print a couple of blank lines to separate messages
  // from multiple responders:
  print("\n\n");
}


/*
  listen for serial responses
 */
void serialEvent(Serial myPort) {
  // read any incoming bytes from the serial port and print them:
  char inChar = char(myPort.read());

  // if you get a linefeed, the string is ended; print it:
  if (inChar == '\n') {
    println("received " + inString + "  in the serial port\r\n");
    // empty the string for the next message:
    inString = "";
  }
  else {
    inString += inChar; // add the latest byte to inString.
  }
}
```

XBee Packet Reader and Graphing Program

Language: Processing

Reads a packet from an XBee radio via UDP and parses it. Graphs the results over time. The packet should be 22 bytes long, made up of the following:

- byte 1: 0x7E, the start byte value
- byte 2-3: packet size, a 2-byte value (not used here)
- byte 4: API identifier value, a code that says what this response is (not used here)
- byte 5-6: Sender's address
- byte 7: RSSI, Received Signal Strength Indicator (not used here)
- byte 8: Broadcast options (not used here)
- byte 9: Number of samples to follow
- byte 10-11: Active channels indicator (not used here)
- byte 12-21: 5 10-bit values, each ADC samples from the sender

```
import hypermedia.net.*;

import processing.serial.*;
```

```
UDP udp;                        // define the UDP object
int queryPort = 10002;          // the port number for the device query
int hPos = 0;                   // horizontal position on the graph
int fontSize = 14;              // size of the text font

void setup() {
  // set the window size:
  size(400,300);
  // create a font with the second font available to the system:
  PFont myFont = createFont(PFont.list()[1], fontSize);
  textFont(myFont);

  // create a new connection to listen for
  // UDP datagrams on query port:
  udp = new UDP(this, queryPort);

  // listen for incoming packets:
  udp.listen( true );

  // show the initial time and date:
  background(0);
  eraseTime(hPos, 0);
  drawTime(hPos, 0);
}


void draw() {
  // nothing happens here.  It's all event-driven
  // by the receive() method.
}

/*
  listen for UDP responses
 */
void receive( byte[] data, String ip, int port ) {
  int[] inString = int(data); // incoming data converted to string
  parseData(inString);
}


/*
 Once you've got a packet, you need to extract the useful data.
 This method gets the address of the sender and the 5 ADC readings.
 It then averages the ADC readings and gives you the result.
 */
void parseData(int[] thisPacket) {
  int adcStart = 11;     // ADC reading starts at byte 12
  int numSamples = thisPacket[8];         // number of samples in packet
  int[] adcValues = new int[numSamples]; // array to hold
                                          // the 5 readings

  int total = 0;                // sum of all the ADC readings
  int rssi = 0;                 // the received signal strength

  // read the address. It's a two-byte value, so you
  // add the two bytes as follows:
  int address = thisPacket[5] + thisPacket[4] * 256;
```

```
  // read the received signal strength:
  rssi = thisPacket[6];

  // read <numSamples> 10-bit analog values, two at a time
  // because each reading is two bytes long:
  for (int i = 0; i < numSamples * 2;  i=i+2) {
    // 10-bit value = high byte * 256 + low byte:
    int thisSample = (thisPacket[i + adcStart] * 256) +
      thisPacket[(i + 1) + adcStart];
    // put the result in one of 5 bytes:
    adcValues[i/2] = thisSample;
    // add the result to the total for averaging later:
    total = total + thisSample;
  }
  // average the result:
  int average = total / numSamples;
  // draw a line on the graph:
  drawGraph(average/4);
  eraseTime (hPos - 1, fontSize * 2);
  drawTime(hPos, fontSize * 2);
}
/*
  update the graph
 */
void drawGraph(int graphValue) {
  // draw the line:
  stroke(0,255,0);
  line(hPos, height, hPos, height - graphValue);
  // at the edge of the screen, go back to the beginning:
  if (hPos >= width) {
    hPos = 0;
    //wipe the screen:
    background(0);
    // wipe the old date and time, and draw the new:
    eraseTime(hPos, 0);
    drawTime(hPos, 0);
  }
  else {
    // increment the horizontal position to draw the next line:
    hPos++;
  }
}
/*
  Draw a black block over the previous date and time strings
 */

void eraseTime(int xPos, int yPos) {
  // use a rect to block out the previous time, rather than
  // redrawing the whole screen, which would mess up the graph:
  noStroke();
  fill(0);
  rect(xPos,yPos, 120, 80);
```

```
  // change the fill color for the text:
  fill(0,255,0);
}

/*
  print the date and the time
 */
void drawTime(int xPos, int yPos) {
  // set up an array to get the names of the months
  // from their numeric values:
  String[] months = {
    "Jan", "Feb", "Mar", "Apr", "May", "Jun", "Jul", "Aug",
    "Sep", "Oct", "Nov", "Dec"              };

  String date = "";       // string to hold the date
  String time = "";       // string to hold the time

  // format the date string:
  date += day();
  date += " ";
  date += months[month() -1];
  date += " ";
  date += year();

  // format the time string:
  time += hour();
  time += ":";
  if (minute() < 10) {
    time += "0";
    time += minute();
  }
  else {
    time +=minute();
  }
  time += ":";
  if (second() < 10) {
    time += "0";
    time += second();
  }
  else {
    time +=second();
  }

  // print both strings:
  text(date, xPos, yPos + fontSize);
  text(time, xPos, yPos + (2 * fontSize));
}
```

Chapter 8

Sharp GP2D12 IR ranger reader
Language: Wiring/Arduino

Reads the value from a Sharp GP2D12 IR ranger and sends it out serially.

```
int sensorPin = 0;      // Analog input pin
int sensorValue = 0;    // value read from the pot

void setup() {
  // initialize serial communications at 9600 bps:
  Serial.begin(9600);
}

void loop() {
  sensorValue = analogRead(sensorPin); // read the pot value

  // the sensor actually gives results that aren't linear.
  // this formula converts the results to a linear range.
  int range = (6787 / (sensorValue - 3)) - 4;

  Serial.println(range, DEC);    // print the sensor value
  delay(10);  // wait 10 milliseconds before the next loop
}
```

SRF02 sensor reader
Language: Wiring/Arduino

Reads data from a Devantech SRF02 ultrasonic sensor. Should also work for the SRF08 and SRF10 sensors as well.
Sensor connections:
- SDA - Analog pin 4
- SCL - Analog pin 5

```
// include Wire library to read and write I2C commands:
#include <Wire.h>

// the commands needed for the SRF sensors:
#define sensorAddress 0x70
#define readInches 0x50
// use these as alternatives if you want centimeters or microseconds:
#define readCentimeters 0x51
#define readMicroseconds 0x52
// this is the memory register in the sensor that contains the result:
#define resultRegister 0x02

void setup()
{
  Wire.begin();  // start the I2C bus
  // open the serial port:
  Serial.begin(9600);
}
```

```
void loop()
{
  // send the command to read the result in inches:
  sendCommand(sensorAddress, readInches);
  // wait at least 70 milliseconds for a result:
  delay(70);
  // set the register that you want to read the result from:
  setRegister(sensorAddress, resultRegister);

  // read the result:
  int sensorReading = readData(sensorAddress, 2);
  // print it:
  Serial.print("distance: ");
  Serial.print(sensorReading);
  Serial.println(" inches");
  // wait before next reading:
  delay(70);
}
/*
  SendCommand() sends commands in the format that the SRF sensors expect
 */
void sendCommand (int address, int command) {
  // start I2C transmission:
  Wire.beginTransmission(address);
  // send command:
  Wire.send(0x00);
  Wire.send(command);
  // end I2C transmission:
  Wire.endTransmission();
}
/*
  setRegister() tells the SRF sensor to change the address
  pointer position
 */
void setRegister(int address, int thisRegister) {
  // start I2C transmission:
  Wire.beginTransmission(address);
  // send address to read from:
  Wire.send(thisRegister);
  // end I2C transmission:
  Wire.endTransmission();
}
/*
readData() returns a result from the SRF sensor
 */
int readData(int address, int numBytes) {
  int result = 0;        // the result is two bytes long

  // send I2C request for data:
  Wire.requestFrom(address, numBytes);
}
```

```
  // wait for two bytes to return:
  while (Wire.available() < 2 )   {
    // wait for result
  }
  // read the two bytes, and combine them into one int:
  result = Wire.receive() * 256;
  result = result + Wire.receive();
  // return the result:
  return result;
}
```

XBee Signal Strength Reader

Language: Processing

Reads a packet from an XBee radio and parses it. The
packet should be 22 bytes long. It should be made up of
the following:

- byte 1: 0x7E, the start byte value
- byte 2-3: packet size, a 2-byte value (not used here)
- byte 4: API identifier value, a code that says what this
  response is (not used here)
- byte 5-6: Sender's address
- byte 7: RSSI, Received Signal Strength Indicator
  (not used here)
- byte 8: Broadcast options (not used here)
- byte 9: Number of samples to follow
- byte 10-11: Active channels indicator (not used here)
- byte 12-21: 5 10-bit values, each ADC samples from
  the sender

```
import processing.serial.*;

Serial XBee ;                // input serial port from the XBee
Radio
int[] packet = new int[22];  // with 5 samples, the XBee packet is
                             // 22 bytes long
int byteCounter;             // keeps track of where you are in
                             // the packet

int rssi = 0;                // received signal strength
int address = 0;             // the sending XBee 's address
Serial myPort;               // The serial port
int fontSize = 18;           // size of the text on the screen
int lastReading = 0;         // value of the previous incoming byte

void setup () {
  size(400, 300);       // window size

  // create a font with the third font available to the system:
  PFont myFont = createFont(PFont.list()[2], fontSize);
  textFont(myFont);

  // get a list of the serial ports:
  println(Serial.list());
```

```
  // open the serial port attached to your XBee radio:
  XBee = new Serial(this, Serial.list()[0], 9600);
}

void draw() {
  // if you have new data and it's valid (>0), graph it:
  if ((rssi > 0 ) && (rssi != lastReading)) {
    // set the background:
    background(0);
    // set the bar height and width:
    int rectHeight = rssi;
    int rectWidth = 50;
    // draw the rect:
    stroke(23, 127, 255);
    fill (23, 127, 255);
    rect(width/2 - rectWidth, height-rectHeight, rectWidth, height);
    // write the number:
    text("XBee Radio Signal Strength test", 10, 20);
    text("From: " + hex(address), 10, 40);
    text ("RSSI: -" + rssi + " dBm", 10, 60);
    // save the current byte for next read:
    lastReading = rssi;
  }
}

void serialEvent(Serial XBee ) {
  // read a byte from the port:
  int thisByte = XBee .read();
  // if the byte is 0x7E, the value of a start byte, you have
  // a new packet:
  if (thisByte == 0x7E) {   // start byte
    // parse the previous packet if there's data:
    if (packet[2] > 0) {
      parseData(packet);
    }
    // reset the byte counter:
    byteCounter = 0;
  }
  // put the current byte into the packet at the current position:
  packet[byteCounter] = thisByte;
  //  increment the byte counter:
  byteCounter++;
}


/*
Once you've got a packet, you need to extract the useful data.
This method gets the address of the sender and RSSI.
*/
void parseData(int[] thisPacket) {
  // read the address. It's a two-byte value, so you
  // add the two bytes as follows:
  address = thisPacket[5] + thisPacket[4] * 256;
  // get RSSI:
  rssi = thisPacket[6];
}
```

GPS parser

Language: Processing

This program takes in NMEA 0183 serial data and parses out the date, time, latitude, and longitude using the GPRMC sentence.

```
// import the serial library:
import processing.serial.*;

Serial myPort;           // The serial port
float latitude = 0.0;    // the latitude reading in degrees
String northSouth;       // north or south?
float longitude = 0.0;   // the longitude reading in degrees
String eastWest;         // east or west?
float heading = 0.0;     // the heading in degrees

int hrs, mins, secs;        // time units
int thisDay, thisMonth, thisYear;

void setup() {
  size(300, 300);        // window size

  // create a font with the third font available to the system:
  PFont myFont = createFont(PFont.list()[2], 14);
  textFont(myFont);

  // settings for drawing arrow:
  noStroke();
  smooth();

  // List all the available serial ports
  println(Serial.list());

  // I know that the first port in the serial list on my mac
  // is always my  Keyspan adaptor, so I open Serial.list()[0].
  // Open whatever port is the one you're using.
  myPort = new Serial(this, Serial.list()[0], 4800);

  // read bytes into a buffer until you get a carriage
  // return (ASCII 13):
  myPort.bufferUntil('\r');
}

void draw() {
  background(0);
  // make the text white:
  fill(255);

  // print the date and time from the GPS sentence:
  text(thisMonth+ "/"+ thisDay+ "/"+ thisYear , 50, 30);
  text(hrs+ ":"+ mins+ ":"+ secs + " GMT  ", 50, 50);
  // print the position from the GPS sentence:
  text(latitude + " " + northSouth + ", " +longitude +" "+ eastWest,
     50, 70);
  text("heading " + heading + " degrees", 50,90);
```

```
  // draw an arrow using the heading:
  drawArrow(heading);
}


void serialEvent(Serial myPort) {
  // read the serial buffer:
  String myString = myPort.readStringUntil('\n');

  // if you got any bytes other than the linefeed, parse it:
  if (myString != null) {
    parseString(myString);
  }
}

void parseString (String serialString) {
  // split the string at the commas:
  String items[] = (split(serialString, ','));

  // if the first item in the sentence is the
  // identifier, parse the rest
  if (items[0].equals("$GPRMC")) {
    // get time, date, position, course, and speed
    getRMC(items);
  }
}


void getRMC(String[] data) {
  // move the items from the string into the variables:
  int time = int(data[1]);
  // first two digits of the time are hours:
  hrs = time/10000;
  // second two digits of the time are minutes:
  mins = (time%10000)/100;
  // last two digits of the time are seconds:
  secs = (time%100);

  // if you have a valid reading, parse the rest of it:
  if (data[2].equals("A")) {
    latitude = float(data[3])/100.0;
    northSouth = data[4];
    longitude = float(data[5])/100.0;
    eastWest = data[6];
    heading = float(data[8]);
    int date = int(data[9]);
    // last two digits of the date are year.  Add the century too:
    thisYear = date%100 + 2000;
    // second two digits of the date are month:
    thisMonth =  (date%10000)/100;
    // first two digits of the date are day:
    thisDay = date/10000;
  }
}
```

```
void drawArrow(float angle) {
  // move whatever you draw next so that (0,0) is centered
  // on the screen:
  translate(width/2, height/2);

  // draw a circle in light blue:
  fill(80,200,230);
  ellipse(0,0,50,50);
  // make the arrow black:
  fill(0);
  // rotate using the heading:
  rotate(radians(angle));

  // draw the arrow.  center of the arrow is at (0,0):
  triangle(-10, 0, 0, -20, 10, 0);
  rect(-2,0, 4,20);
}
```

CMPS03 compass reader

Language: Wiring/Arduino

Reads data from a Devantech CMPS03 compass sensor.

Sensor connections:
* SDA - Analog pin 4
* SCL - Analog pin 5

```
// include Wire library to read and write I2C commands:
#include <Wire.h>

// the commands needed for the SRF sensors:
#define sensorAddress 0x60
// this is the memory register in the sensor that contains the result:
#define resultRegister 0x02


void setup() {
  // start the I2C bus
  Wire.begin();
  // open the serial port:
  Serial.begin(9600);
}


void loop() {
  // send the command to read the result in inches:
  setRegister(sensorAddress, resultRegister);
  // read the result:
  int bearing = readData(sensorAddress, 2);
  // print it:
  Serial.print("bearing: ");
  Serial.print(bearing/10);
  Serial.println(" degrees");
  // wait before next reading:
  delay(70);
}
```

```
/*
  setRegister() tells the SRF sensor to change the address
  pointer position
*/
void setRegister(int address, int thisRegister) {
  // start I2C transmission:
  Wire.beginTransmission(address);
  // send address to read from:
  Wire.send(thisRegister);
  // end I2C transmission:
  Wire.endTransmission();
}
/*
  readData() returns a result from the SRF sensor
*/

int readData(int address, int numBytes) {
  int result = 0;        // the result is two bytes long

  // send I2C request for data:
  Wire.requestFrom(address, numBytes);
  // wait for two bytes to return:
  while (Wire.available() < 2 )  {
    // wait for result
  }
  // read the two bytes, and combine them into one int:
  result = Wire.receive() * 256;
  result = result + Wire.receive();
  // return the result:
  return result;
}
```

Accelerometer reader

Language: Wiring/Arduino

Reads 2 axes of an accelerometer and sends the values out the serial port

```
int accelerometer[2];     // variable to hold the accelerometer values

void setup() {
  // open serial port:
  Serial.begin(9600);
  // send out some initial data:
  Serial.println("0,0,");
}


void loop() {
  // read 2 channels of the accelerometer:
  for (int i = 0; i < 2; i++) {
    accelerometer[i] = analogRead(i);
    // delay to allow analog-to-digital converter to settle:
    delay(10);
  }
}
```

```
    // if there's serial data in, print sensor values out:
    if (Serial.available() > 0) {
      // read incoming data to clear serial input buffer:
      int inByte = Serial.read();
      for (int i = 0; i <  2; i++) {
        // values as ASCII strings:
        Serial.print(accelerometer[i], DEC);
        // print commas in between values:
        Serial.print(",");
      }
      // print \r and \n after values are sent:
      Serial.println();
    }
}
```

Accelerometer Tilt

Language: Processing

Takes the values in serially from an accelerometer attached to a microcontroller and uses them to set the attitude of a disk on the screen.

```
import processing.serial.*;     // import the serial lib

int graphPosition = 0;          // horizontal position of the graph
int[] vals = new int[2];        // raw values from the sensor
int[] maximum = new int[2];     // maximum value sensed
int[] minimum = new int[2];     // minimum value sensed
int[] range = new int[2];       // total range sensed
float[] attitude = new float[2]; // the tilt values
float position;                 // position to translate to
Serial myPort;                  // the serial port
boolean madeContact = false;    // whether there's been serial data in

void setup () {
  // draw the window:
  size(400, 400, P3D);
  // set the background color:
  background(0);
  // set the maximum and minimum values:
  for (int i = 0; i < 2; i++) {
    maximum[i] = 600;
    minimum[i] = 200;
    // calculate the total current range:
    range[i] = maximum[i] - minimum[i];
  }
  position = width/2; // calculate position.

  // create a font with the third font available to the system:
  PFont myFont = createFont(PFont.list()[2], 18);
  textFont(myFont);
  // List all the available serial ports
  println(Serial.list());
```

```
  // Open whatever port is the one you're using.
  myPort = new Serial(this, Serial.list()[0], 9600);
  // only generate a serial event when you get a return char:
  myPort.bufferUntil('\r');

  // set the fill color:
  fill(90,250,250);
}

void draw () {
  // clear the screen:
  background(0);

  // print the values:
  text(vals[0] + " " + vals[1], -30, 10);

  // if you've never gotten a string from the microcontroller,
  // keep sending carriage returns to prompt for one:
  if (madeContact == false) {
    myPort.write('\r');
  }

  // set the attitude:
  setAttitude();
  // draw the plane:
  tilt();
}
void setAttitude() {
  for (int i = 0; i < 2; i++) {
    // calculate the current attitude as a percentage of 2*PI,
    // based on the current range:
    attitude[i] = (2*PI) * float(vals[i] -
      minimum[i]) /float(range[i]);
  }
}

void tilt() {
  // translate from origin to center:
  translate(position, position, position);

  // X is front-to-back:
  rotateX(-attitude[1]);
  // Y is left-to-right:
  rotateY(-attitude[0] - PI/2);

  // set the fill color:
  fill(90,250,250);
  // draw the rect:
  ellipse(0, 0, width/4, width/4);
  // change the fill color:
  fill(0);
  // Draw some text so you can tell front from back:
  // print the values:
  text(vals[0] + " " + vals[1], -30, 10,1);
}
```

```
// serialEvent  method is run automatically by the Processing applet
// whenever the buffer reaches the  byte value set in the bufferUntil()
// method in the setup():
void serialEvent(Serial myPort) {
  // if serialEvent occurs at all, contact with the microcontroller
  // has been made:
  madeContact = true;
  // read the serial buffer:
  String myString = myPort.readStringUntil('\n');

  // if you got any bytes other than the linefeed:
  if (myString != null) {
    myString = trim(myString);
    // split the string at the commas
    //and convert the sections into integers:
    int sensors[] = int(split(myString, ','));
    // if you received all the sensor strings, use them:
    if (sensors.length >= 2) {
      vals[0] = sensors[0];
      vals[1] = sensors[1];

      // send out the serial port to ask for data:
      myPort.write('\r');
    }
  }
}
```

Chapter 9

Color Recognition Using a Webcam
Language: Processing
Reads an image from a camera and looks for a blob of a particular color. Click on a color in the image to choose the color to track.

```
import processing.serial.*;        // import the serial lib

int graphPosition = 0;            // horizontal position of the graph
int[] vals = new int[2];          // raw values from the sensor
int[] maximum = new int[2];       // maximum value sensed
int[] minimum = new int[2];       // minimum value sensed
int[] range = new int[2];         // total range sensed
float[] attitude = new float[2];  // the tilt values
float position;                   // position to translate to

Serial myPort;                    // the serial port
boolean madeContact = false;      // whether there's been serial data in

void setup () {
  // draw the window:
  size(400, 400, P3D);
  // set the background color:
  background(0);
  // set the maximum and minimum values:
  for (int i = 0; i < 2; i++) {
    maximum[i] = 600;
    minimum[i] = 200;
    // calculate the total current range:
    range[i] = maximum[i] - minimum[i];
  }
  // calculate position:
  position = width/2;

  // create a font with the third font available to the system:
  PFont myFont = createFont(PFont.list()[2], 18);
  textFont(myFont);

  // List all the available serial ports
  println(Serial.list());
  // Open whatever port is the one you're using.
  myPort = new Serial(this, Serial.list()[0], 9600);
  // only generate a serial event when you get a return char:
  myPort.bufferUntil('\r');

  fill(90,250,250); // set the fill color.
}

void draw () {
  // clear the screen:
  background(0);
```

```
// print the values:
text(vals[0] + " " + vals[1], -30, 10);


// if you've never gotten a string from the microcontroller,
// keep sending carriage returns to prompt for one:
if (madeContact == false) {
  myPort.write('\r');
}


// set the attitude:
setAttitude();
// draw the plane:
tilt();
}
void setAttitude() {
  for (int i = 0; i < 2; i++) {
    // calculate the current attitude as a percentage of 2*PI,
    // based on the current range:
    attitude[i] = (2*PI) * float(vals[i] -
      minimum[i]) /float(range[i]);
  }
}


void tilt() {
  // translate from origin to center:
  translate(position, position, position);

  // X is front-to-back:
  rotateX(-attitude[1]);
  // Y is left-to-right:
  rotateY(-attitude[0] - PI/2);

  // set the fill color:
  fill(90,250,250);
  // draw the rect:
  ellipse(0, 0, width/4, width/4);
  // change the fill color:
  fill(0);
  // Draw some text so you can tell front from back:
  // print the values:
  text(vals[0] + " " + vals[1], -30, 10,1);
}

// serialEvent  method is run automatically by the Processing applet
// whenever the buffer reaches the  byte value set in the bufferUntil()
// method in the setup():
void serialEvent(Serial myPort) {
  // if serialEvent occurs at all, contact with the microcontroller
  // has been made:
  madeContact = true;
  // read the serial buffer:
  String myString = myPort.readStringUntil('\n');
```

```
// if you got any bytes other than the linefeed:
if (myString != null) {
  myString = trim(myString);
  // split the string at the commas
  //and convert the sections into integers:
  int sensors[] = int(split(myString, ','));
  // if you received all the sensor strings, use them:
  if (sensors.length >= 2) {
    vals[0] = sensors[0];
    vals[1] = sensors[1];

    // send out the serial port to ask for data:
    myPort.write('\r');
  }
}
}
```

QRcode 2D Barcode Reader

Language: Processing

Uses the qrcode library from www.shiffman.net/p5/
pqrcode based on a Java library from qrcode.sourceforge.
jp. To use this, generate images from a QRcode generator
such as qrcode.kaywa.com and put them in this sketch's
data folder. Press spacebar to read from the camera,
generate an image, and scan for barcodes. Press f to read
from a file and scan. Press s for camera settings.
— *by Tom Igoe / Daniel Shiffman*

```
import processing.video.*;
import pqrcode.*;


Capture video;                          // Video capture object
String statusMsg = "Waiting for an image"; // a string for messages:


// Decoder object from pqrdecoder library
Decoder decoder;


// make sure to generate your own image here:
String testImageName = "qrcode.png";


void setup() {
  size(400, 320);
  video = new Capture(this, width, height-20, 30);
  // Create a decoder object
  decoder = new Decoder(this);


  // Create a font with a font available to the system:
  PFont myFont = createFont(PFont.list()[2], 14);
  textFont(myFont);
}
```

```
void draw() {
  background(0);

  // Display video
  image(video, 0, 0);
  // Display status
  text(statusMsg, 10, height-4);

  // If we are currently decoding
  if (decoder.decoding()) {
    // Display the image being decoded
    PImage show = decoder.getImage();
    image(show,0,0,show.width/4,show.height/4);
    statusMsg = "Decoding image";
    // fancy code for drawing dots as a progress bar:
    for (int i = 0; i < (frameCount/2) % 10; i++)
    {
      statusMsg += ".";
    }
  }
}

void captureEvent(Capture video) {
  video.read();
}

void keyReleased() {
  String code = "";
  // Depending on which key is hit, do different things:
  switch (key) {
  case ' ':         // Spacebar takes a picture and tests it:
    // copy it to the PImage savedFrame:
    PImage savedFrame = createImage(video.width,video.height,RGB);
    savedFrame.copy(video, 0,0,video.width,video.height,0,0,
      video.width,video.height);
    savedFrame.updatePixels();
    // Decode savedFrame
    decoder.decodeImage(savedFrame);
    break;
  case 'f':    // f runs a test on a file
    PImage preservedFrame = loadImage(testImageName);
    // Decode file
    decoder.decodeImage(preservedFrame);
    break;
  case 's':       // s opens the settings for this capture device:
    video.settings();
    break;
  }
}

// When the decoder object finishes
// this method will be invoked.
void decoderEvent(Decoder decoder) {
  statusMsg = decoder.getDecodedString();
}
```

Parallax RFID Reader
Language: Processing
Reads data serially from a Parallax RFID reader.

```
// import the serial library:
import processing.serial.*;

Serial myPort;       // the serial port you're using
String tagID = "";   // the string for the tag ID

void setup() {
  size(600,200);
  // list all the serial ports:
  println(Serial.list());

  // based on the list of serial ports printed from the
  // previous command, change the 0 to your port's number:
  String portnum = Serial.list()[0];
  // initialize the serial port:
  myPort = new Serial(this, portnum, 2400);
  // incoming string from reader will have 12 bytes:
  myPort.buffer(12);

  // create a font with the third font available to the system:
  PFont myFont = createFont(PFont.list()[2], 24);
  textFont(myFont);
}

void draw() {
  // clear the screen:
  background(0);
  // print the string to the screen:
  text(tagID, width/4, height/2 - 24);
}

/*
 this method reads bytes from the serial port
 and puts them into the tag string.
 It trims off the \r and \n
 */
void serialEvent(Serial myPort) {
  tagID = trim(myPort.readString());
}
```

ID Innovations RFID Reader
Language: Processing
Reads data serially from an ID Innovations ID12 RFID reader.

```
// import the serial library:
import processing.serial.*;

Serial myPort;       // the serial port you're using
```

```
String tagID = "";  // the string for the tag ID

void setup() {
  size(600,200);
  // list all the serial ports:
  println(Serial.list());

  // based on the list of serial ports printed from the
  // previous command, change the 0 to your port's number:
  String portnum = Serial.list()[0];
  // initialize the serial port:
  myPort = new Serial(this, portnum, 9600);
  // incoming string from reader will have 16 bytes:
  myPort.buffer(16);

  // create a font with the third font available to the system:
  PFont myFont = createFont(PFont.list()[2], 24);
  textFont(myFont);
}

void draw() {
  // clear the screen:
  background(0);
  // print the string to the screen:
  text(tagID, width/4, height/2 - 24);
}

/*
 this method reads bytes from the serial port
 and puts them into the tag string
 */
void serialEvent(Serial myPort) {
  // get the serial input buffer in a string:
  String inputString = myPort.readString();
  // filter out the tag ID from the string:
  tagID = parseString(inputString);
}

/*
  This method reads a string and looks for the 10-byte
  tag ID. It assumes it should get a STX byte (0x02)
  at the beginning and an ETX byte (0x03) at the end
  */
String parseString(String thisString) {
  String tagString = "";     // string to put the tag ID into

  // first character of the input:
  char firstChar = thisString.charAt(0);
  // last character of the input:
  char lastChar = thisString.charAt(thisString.length() -1);

  // if the first char is STX (0x02) and the last char
  // is ETX (0x03), then put the next ten bytes
  // into the tag string:
```

```
  if ((firstChar == 0x02) && (lastChar == 0x03)) {
    tagString = thisString.substring(1, 11);
  }
  return tagString;
}
```

ASPX RW-210 RFID Reader
Language: Processing
Reads data serially from an ASPX RW-210 RFID RFID reader.

```
// import the serial library:
import processing.serial.*;

Serial myPort;      // the serial port you're using
String tagID = "";  // the string for the tag ID

void setup() {
  size(600,200);
  // list all the serial ports:
  println(Serial.list());

  // based on the list of serial ports printed from the
  //previous command, change the 0 to your port's number:
  String portnum = Serial.list()[0];
  // initialize the serial port:
  myPort = new Serial(this, portnum, 19200);
  // incoming string from reader will have 12 bytes:
  myPort.buffer(12);

  // create a font with the third font available to the system:
  PFont myFont = createFont(PFont.list()[2], 24);
  textFont(myFont);

  // send the continual read command:
  myPort.write(0xFB);
}

void draw() {
  // clear the screen:
  background(0);
  // print the string to the screen:
  text(tagID, width/8, height/2 - 24);
}

/*
  this method reads bytes from the serial port
  and puts them into the tag string
  */
void serialEvent(Serial myPort) {
  int thisByte = 0;
  tagID = "";
  while(myPort.available() > 0) {
    int newByte = myPort.read();
```

```
      tagID += hex(newByte, 2);
      tagID += " ";
   }
}
```

Microcontroller RFID Reader
Language: Wiring/Arduino
Reads data serially from a Parallax or ID Innovations ID12
RFID reader.

```
#define tagLength 10    // each tag ID contains 10 bytes
#define startByte 0x0A  // for the ID Innovations reader, use 0x02
#define endByte 0x0D    // for the ID Innovations reader, use 0x03
#define dataRate 2400   // for the ID Innovations reader, use 9600


char tagID[tagLength];         // array to hold the tag you read
int tagIndex = 0;              // counter for number of bytes read
int tagComplete = false;       // whether the whole tag's been read

void setup() {
  // begin serial:
  Serial.begin(dataRate);
}

void loop() {
  // read in and parse serial data:
  if (Serial.available() > 0) {
    readByte();
  }
  if(tagComplete == true) {
    Serial.println(tagID);
  }
}


/*
  This method reads the bytes, and puts the
  appropriate ones in the tagID
*/
void readByte() {
  char thisChar = Serial.read();
Serial.print(thisChar, HEX);
  switch (thisChar) {
  case startByte:      // start character
    // reset the tag index counter
    tagIndex = 0;
    break;
  case endByte:      // end character
    tagComplete = true;  // you have the whole tag
    break;
```

```
  default: // any other character
    tagComplete = false;  // there are still more bytes to read
    // add the byte to the tagID
    if (tagIndex < tagLength) {
      tagID[tagIndex] = thisChar;
      // increment the tag byte counter
      tagIndex++;
    }
    break;
  }
}
```

X10 test
Language: Arduino
Sends out basic X10 messages from an Arduino module
using a PL513 ot TW523 X10 module.

```
// include the X10 library files:
#include <x10.h>
#include <x10constants.h>


#define zcPin 9        // the zero crossing detect pin
#define dataPin 8      // the X10 data out pin
#define repeatTimes 1  // how many times to repeat each X10 message
                       // in an electrically noisy environment, you
                       // can set this higher.


// set up a new x10  library instance:
x10 myHouse =  x10(zcPin, dataPin);


void setup() {
  // Turn off all lights:
  myHouse.write(A, ALL_UNITS_OFF,repeatTimes);
}


void loop() {
      // Turn on first module:
      myHouse.write(A, UNIT_1,repeatTimes);
      myHouse.write(A, ON,repeatTimes);
      myHouse.write(A, UNIT_2,repeatTimes);
      myHouse.write(A, OFF,repeatTimes);
      delay(500);
      // turn on second module:
      myHouse.write(A, UNIT_1,repeatTimes);
      myHouse.write(A, OFF,repeatTimes);
      myHouse.write(A, UNIT_2,repeatTimes);
      myHouse.write(A, ON,repeatTimes);
      delay(500);
}
```

RFID–to-X10 translator

Language: Arduino

Reads RFID tags and sends X10 messages in response to the tags.

```arduino
// include the X10 library files:
#include <x10.h>
#include <x10constants.h>

#define zcPin 9        // the zero crossing detect pin
#define dataPin 8      // the X10 data out pin
#define repeatTimes 1  // how many times to repeat each X10 message
                       // in an electrically noisy environment, you
                       // can set this higher.

#define tagLength 10   // each tag ID contains 10 bytes
#define startByte 0x0A // for the ID Innovations reader, use 0x02
#define endByte 0x0D   // for the ID Innovations reader, use 0x03
#define dataRate 2400  // for the ID Innovations reader, use 9600

// set up a new x10  library instance:
x10 myHouse =  x10(zcPin, dataPin);

char tagID[tagLength];        // array to hold the tag you read
int tagIndex = 0;             // counter for number of bytes read
int tagComplete = false;      // whether the whole tag's been read
char tagOne[] = "0415AB6FB7"; // put the values for your tags here
char tagTwo[] = "0415AB5DAF";
char lastTag = 0;             // value of the last tag read

void setup() {
  Serial.begin(dataRate); // begin serial.
  // Turn off all lights:
  myHouse.write(A, ALL_LIGHTS_OFF,repeatTimes);
}
void loop() {
  // read in and parse serial data:
  if (Serial.available() > 0) {
    readByte();
  }
  // if you've got a complete tag, compare your tag
  // to the existing values:
  if (tagComplete == true) {
    if (compareTags(tagID, tagOne) == true) {
      if (lastTag != 1) {
        // if the last tag wasn't this one,
        // send commands:
        myHouse.write(A, UNIT_1,repeatTimes);
        myHouse.write(A, ON,repeatTimes);
        myHouse.write(A, UNIT_2,repeatTimes);
        myHouse.write(A, OFF,repeatTimes);
        // note that this was the last tag read:
        lastTag = 1;
      }
    }
  }
  if (compareTags(tagID, tagTwo) == true) {
    if (lastTag != 2) {
      // if the last tag wasn't this one,
      // send commands:
      myHouse.write(A, UNIT_1,repeatTimes);
      myHouse.write(A, OFF,repeatTimes);
      myHouse.write(A, UNIT_2,repeatTimes);
      myHouse.write(A, ON,repeatTimes);
      // note that this was the last tag read:
      lastTag = 2;
    }
  }
}

/*
  This method compares two char arrays byte by byte:
 */
char compareTags(char* thisTag, char* thatTag) {
  char match = true;  // whether they're the same
    for (int i = 0; i < tagLength; i++) {
    // if any two bytes don't match, the whole thing fails:
    if (thisTag[i] != thatTag[i]) {
      match = false;
    }
  }
  return match;
}

/*
  This method reads the bytes, and puts the
  appropriate ones in the tagID
 */
void readByte() {
  char thisChar = Serial.read();

  switch (thisChar) {
  case startByte:     // start character
    // reset the tag index counter
    tagIndex = 0;
    break;
  case endByte:     // end character
    tagComplete = true;  // you have the whole tag
    break;
  default:     // any other character
    tagComplete = false;  // there are still more bytes to read
    // add the byte to the tagID
    if (tagIndex < tagLength) {
      tagID[tagIndex] = thisChar;
      // increment the tag byte counter
      tagIndex++;
    }
    break;
  }
}
```

HTTP Environment Variable Printer
Language: PHP

Prints out the HTTP environment variables.

```php
<?php
foreach ($_REQUEST as $key => $value)
  {
      echo "$key: $value<br>\n";
  }
  foreach ($_SERVER as $key => $value)
  {
      echo "$key: $value<br>\n";
  }
?>
```

IP geocoder
Language: PHP

Uses a client's IP address to get a latitude and longitude.
Uses the client's user agent to format the response.

```php
<?php
// initialize variables:
  $lat = 0;
  $long = 0;
  $ipAddress = "0.0.0.0";
  $country = "unknown";


  // Check to see what type of client this is:
  $userAgent  = getenv('HTTP_USER_AGENT');
  // Get the client's IP address:
  $ipAddress = getenv('REMOTE_ADDR');

  // use http://www.hostIP.info to get the latitude and longitude
  // from the IP address.  First, format the HTTP request string:
  $IpLocatorUrl =
     "http://api.hostip.info/get_html.php?&position=true&ip=";
  $IpLocatorUrl = $IpLocatorUrl.$ipAddress;

  // make the HTTP request:
  $filePath = fopen ($IpLocatorUrl, "r");

  // as long as you haven't reached the end of the incoming text:
  while (!feof($filePath)) {
      // read one line at a time, strip all HTML tags from the line:
      $line = fgetss($filePath, 4096);
      // break each line into fragments at the colon:
      $fragments = explode(":", $line);
```

```php
      switch ($fragments[0]) {
          // if the first fragment is "country", the second
          // is the country name:
          case "Country":
              // trim any whitespace:
              $country = trim($fragments[1]);
              break;
          // if the first fragment is "Latitude", the second
          // is the latitude:
          case "Latitude":
              // trim any whitespace:
              $lat = trim($fragments[1]);
              break;
          // if the first fragment is "Longitude", the second
          //is the longitude:
          case "Longitude":
              // trim any whitespace:
              $long = trim($fragments[1]);
              break;
      }
  }
  // close the connection:
  fclose($filePath);

  // decide on the output based on the client type:
  switch ($userAgent) {
      case "lantronix":
          // Lantronix device wants a nice short answer:
          echo "<$lat,$long,$country>\n";
          break;
      case "processing":
          // Processing does well with lines:
          echo "Latitude:$lat\nLongitude:$long\nCountry:$country\n\
n";

          break;
      default:
          // other clients can take a long answer:
          echo <<<END
<html>
<head></head>

<body>
   <h2>Where You Are:</h2>
      Your country: $country<br>
      Your IP: $ipAddress<br>
      Latitude: $lat<br>
      Longitude: $long<br>
</body>
</html>
END;
  }
?>
```

Mail Reader

Language: PHP

Reads email in PHP. Requires the **pwds.php** file listed below.

```php
<?php
include('POP3.php');

// keep your personal info in a separate file:
@include_once("pwds.php");

// New instance of the Net_POP3 class:
$pop3 =& new Net_POP3();

// Connect to the mail server:
$pop3->connect($host , $port);

// Send login info:
$pop3->login($user , $pass , 'APOP');

// Get a count of the number of new messages waiting:
$numMsgs = $pop3->numMsg();

echo "<pre>\n";
echo "Checking mail...\n";
echo "Number of messages: $numMsgs\n";

// Get the headers of the first message:
echo($pop3->getRawHeaders(1));
echo "\n\n\n";
echo "</pre>\n";

// disconnect:
$pop3->disconnect();
?>
```

pwds.php. This will contain your username and password info. You want to keep it separate from the main PHP file so you can protect it.

```php
<?php
$user='username';        // your mail login
$pass='password';        // exactly as you normally type it
$host='pop.example.com'; // usually pop.yourmailserver.com
$port="110";             // this won't work on gmail.com and
                         // other servers using SSL
?>
```

RFID mail reader

Language: PHP

Parses a POP email box for a specific message from an Xport. The message looks like this:

From: myAccountName@myMailhost.com
Subject: Notification: Tag one
Date: June 21, 2007 6:11:59 PM EDT
To: myAccountName@myMailhost.com

```php
<?php
include('POP3.php');

// keep your personal info in a separate file:
@include_once("pwds.php");

echo "Checking mail...";

// New instance of the Net_POP3 class:
$pop3 =& new Net_POP3();

// Connect to the mail server:
$pop3->connect($host , $port);

// Send login info:
$pop3->login($user , $pass , 'APOP');

// Get a count of the number of new messages waiting:
$numMsgs = $pop3->numMsg();

echo "<pre>\n";
echo "Number of messages: $numMsgs\n";

// iterate over the messages:
for ($thisMsg = 1; $thisMsg <= $numMsgs; $thisMsg++) {
    // parse the headers for each message into
    // an array called $header:
    $header = $pop3->getParsedHeaders($thisMsg);

    // print the subject header:
    $subject = $header["Subject"];
    // look for the word "Notification" before a colon
    // in the subject:
    $words = explode(":", $subject);

    // only do the rest if this mail message is a notification:
    if ($words[0] == "Notification"){
        // get the second half of the subject; that's the tag ID:
        $idTag = $words[1];
        // print it;
        echo "$idTag showed up at address\t";
```

```
        /*
            the IP address is buried in the "Received" header.
            That header is an array. The second element contains
            who it's from.  In that string, the IP is the first
            thing contained in square brackets. So:
        */

        // get the stuff in the right array element after the
        // opening square bracket:
        $receivedString = explode("[", $header["Received"][1]);
        // throw away the stuff after the closing bracket:
        $recdString2 = explode("]", $receivedString[1]);
        // what's left is the IP address:
        $ipAddress = $recdString2[0];

        // print the IP address:
        echo "$ipAddress at \t";

        // print the date header:
        $date = $header["Date"];
        echo "$date\t";
        echo "\n";
    }

}

echo "That's all folks";
echo "</pre>";

// disconnect:
$pop3->disconnect();
?>
```

Index

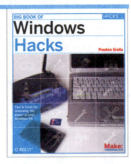